ISLAM
AND THE INTEGRATION
OF SOCIETY

ISLAM
AND THE INTEGRATION
OF SOCIETY

by

W. Montgomery Watt

NORTHWESTERN UNIVERSITY PRESS
1961

First published in the U.S.A. 1961
by Northwestern University Press
Evanston, Illinois

London :   *Routledge & Kegan Paul Ltd*

Copyright © *W. Montgomery Watt* 1961

*Printed in **Great** Britain*

CONTENTS

v

Contents

Contents

PREFACE

To try to write something which will be of interest to both orientalists and sociologists suggests the fool who rushes in. Yet that is what I have done. Perhaps this book, despite its imperfections, will bring home to sociologists the value of the material to which Islamists have access and will help Islamists to appreciate the importance of asking sociological questions.

Since the book is likely to be read by those who have not specialist knowledge of Islam, nothing has been assumed, but there are explanations of most matters and many repetitions. If to some readers the repetitions seem tedious, I would crave their indulgence and ask them to remember that not all have their specialist knowledge.

The sociologically-minded reader will find a good general account of Islam in Sir Hamilton Gibb's *Mohammedanism* (Home University Library), while Bernard Lewis's *The Arabs in History* is a convenient brief presentation of the historical background. The publication of this book is likely to be preceded by that of an abridgement of my two volumes on Muhammad, entitled *Muhammad, Prophet and Statesman*.

Arabic names have been transliterated according to one of the standard British systems. It proved impracticable to have diacritical marks in the text, but they are to be found in the index. One modification has been made in the system, namely, the use of an apostrophe between two consonants to indicate that they are not to be sounded together, e.g. Is'haq. Apart from this the pairs of consonants *dh, gh, kh, sh, th* represent each a single sound. The apostrophe elsewhere—between two vowels, or between a consonant and a vowel—stands for the glottal stop which the Arabs regard as a consonant.

Among the people to whom I am indebted are colleagues at Edinburgh, especially J. R. Walsh and Pierre Cachia, who have discussed various matters with me, and J. Spencer Trimingham, of Glasgow, who kindly commented on the first draft of the section on West Africa.

W. MONTGOMERY WATT

Edinburgh,
September, 1960.

ix

I

PROBLEMS AND PRESUPPOSITIONS

ONE of the distinctive marks of Islam, compared with the other great world-religions, is the variety of peoples and races who have embraced it,[1] and among whom there has grown up a strong feeling of brotherhood and a measure of harmony. There is nothing comparable until the nineteenth century expansion of Christianity, and that is generally held to have been less successful so far in producing a sense of brotherhood. In this 'one world', in which all races have been brought together physically, there is an obvious lack of brotherhood and harmony. Perhaps a study of the achievements of Islam may throw some light on how the integration of world society is likely to come about, and may even suggest ways in which man may consciously contribute to this process.[2]

It is frequently held that there is no real unity in Islamic society, and that we should rather take the view that there are several different societies, each with a religion which it traces back to the teaching of Muhammad. This is an over-statement of the diversity which is undoubtedly found among the adherents of Islam. For the purposes of the present study it is not necessary to deny that there is wide variety, but only to insist that in some important senses Islam is a unity and that Islamic society has achieved some measure of harmony and integration. The main aim of this book is to examine the positive achievements, and to try to discover the general laws and principles exemplified in them. The failures to achieve integration will only be considered where they throw light on the reasons for the successes.

An additional advantage in basing a study of this kind on Islamic material is that the Western scholar is able to approach it with

[1] Cf. Sir H. A. R. Gibb, *Mohammedanism*, London, 1949, 22; also al-Jahiz, *Tria Opuscula*, ed. Van Vloten, Leiden, 1903, 32: 'when we find the inhabitants of Sijistan, the Jazirah, the Yemen, the Maghrib and 'Uman (Oman) and the Azraqite, the Najdite, the Ibadite and the Sufrite, the *mawla* and the Arab, the Persian and the nomad, slaves and women, the weaver and the peasant, fighting on one side despite their difference of descent and habitation, we realize that it is religion which moulds them together'. (The diacritical marks which it has not been practicable to include in the text will be found in the index.)

[2] For religion as an integrative factor cf. J. Wach, *Sociology of Religion* London, 1947, 36ff.

1

relative detachment. Whether he is a Christian or not, he cannot study the place of religion in Western society without some sort of bias. His attitude towards religion in general may still affect his study of the place of religion in Islamic society; but the novelty of the material and the lesser emotional involvement reduce the distortion due to the initial bias.

The present study grows out of my previous work on the life of Muhammad and the origins of Islam. In particular *Muhammad at Mecca* emphasized the place of economic factors in the first appearance of Islam, and the relation to these of its fundamental ideas. Because of this emphasis the book was alleged to have a Marxist tendency by critics of both right-wing and left-wing sympathies.[1] It was certainly an elementary knowledge of Marxism which first suggested to me to look into the economic background of the rise of Islam, but the elaboration of the ideas was made without any conscious reference to Marxist thought. Quite apart from the spur of—admittedly very friendly—criticism, it was clear to me that the account of the origin of Islam raised profound questions about the relations of ideas to economic factors and, more generally, about the place of ideas in the life of society. I therefore decided to try to get some light on these questions by a careful examination of particular cases. Most of the cases are selected from the early formative centuries of Islam, though there are occasional excursions into later history. No attempt has been made to cover every facet of Islam, even in the early period.

At various parts of this study, and especially in chapter VIII, some use is made of the conception of 'ideology' which is prominent in Marx's teaching, though not invented by him. It is employed in the form in which it has been developed by Karl Mannheim in *Ideology and Utopia*[2], but it would be presumptuous to claim that he has been followed exactly.

Because so much attention is being paid here to ideas and idea-systems, it seems desirable to have an adjective corresponding to 'idea' in a neutral sense. 'Ideal' has other connotations, and 'ideological' is required for the technical sense. Clumsy as it is, 'ideational'

[1] G. H. Bousquet, 'Une explication marxiste de l'origine de l'Islam par un ecclésiastique episcopalien', *Hesperis*, xli (1954), 231-47. M. Rodinson, 'La vie de Mahomet et le problème sociologique des origines de l'Islam,' *Diogène*, xx (1957), 37-64; English version, *Diogenes*, xx. 28-51.

[2] London,1936 (originally Bonn, 1929); cf. esp. 85f., 173ff., 184f. Cf. pp. 254f. below. *The Sociology of Knowledge* by Werner Stark (London, 1958) appeared only after the manuscript of the present study was virtually complete, and it has not been possible to take into account the difference between Stark's view and Mannheim's.

seems to be most satisfactory; and if this is allowed, 'ideation' may occasionally be permitted, as a substitute for 'ideas' or 'idea-system'. A concern with ideology properly leads to questions about the truth and falsity of ideas, but these will not be fully discussed in this study. The sociological functioning of an idea-system does not presuppose its absolute truth. What is here assumed is that idea-systems (including religions) contain varying proportions of truth and error, but that all which are socially important contain a considerable measure of truth.

II

THE PLACE OF ECONOMIC
AND SOCIAL FACTORS

IT should be unnecessary at the present time to labour the point that economic factors have a profound influence on the course of history in general and of religious movements in particular. Some such view has become almost axiomatic with many historians and popular writers. Among the adherents of the various religions, however, there are many who are still not convinced. At the same time those who acknowledge the importance of economic factors are far from being agreed about the relation of these to the social and ideational factors.

This chapter is therefore devoted to a consideration of the precise nature and extent of the dependence of religious movements on economic matters. With regard to some of the main phases of Islam the question will be asked: Can we find in the background of this movement any important economic change to which it might conceivably be related? The examples discussed will, of course, be only specimens and will not exhaust the topic. Islam, like the other great religions, is a vast complex of phenomena, and a corresponding complexity might properly be expected in the economic basis. In particular there are several distinct phases in the development of Islam, and the economic factors present in each phase have to be considered separately.

Further, it is not enough to show that underlying a religious movement there is an economic change. Even if this could be done in every case, it might still be true that there was no connexion between the economic change and the religious movement, or at least that the latter was not dependent on the former. There are probably few tracts of history where some economic change is not to be found if one looks hard enough. This implies three things. Firstly, the economic change must be of a degree of importance commensurate with the importance of the religious movement. Secondly, an attempt must be made to show in detail how a particular economic change or set of changes leads to a particular religious movement. This involves trying to find a connexion between economic changes and social changes. There is also an ideational aspect, but that will not be

4

considered until the next chapter. Thirdly, the conclusions will be made more impressive if they can be linked up with a general account of the economic and social aspects of the life of the individual.

1. THE ORIGIN OF ISLAM

The religion of Islam originated in Mecca about 610 A.D. A native of Mecca, Muhammad, began to preach publicly, claiming that he had received revelations from God and that God had sent him to the Meccans to call them to worship Him and to warn them of the penalties which sooner or later fell upon the disobedient. A few of his fellow-citizens acknowledged him as prophet and performed special rites of worship along with him, but the majority of the Meccans, including the leading men of the city, rejected his message and made life difficult for Muhammad and his followers. In 622 a favourable opportunity presented itself for Muhammad to migrate to Medina, over two hundred miles to the north, along with seventy of his followers. He was here acknowledged as prophet by most of the inhabitants, and was also accepted as arbiter between warring factions whose strife had been making life in Medina unbearable. By his sagacity and statesmanship he built up his prestige and political power, so that by his death in 632 he was not merely undisputed ruler of Medina, Mecca and the surrounding territory, but was accepted as suzerain by many tribes throughout Arabia. Moreover, within ten years of his death the state which he created was able to meet in battle and defeat the armies of the two great empires of the Middle East, the Byzantine and Persian, and within a short time to overrun the latter completely. A hundred years after his death the empire of his successors extended from France to India.

It will be convenient at this stage to consider three phases of the origin of Islam, namely, the beginnings at Mecca, the development at Medina, and the extension to include most of Arabia.[1]

(a) Mecca

If it is asked whether any important economic change is to be found in the historical background of Muhammad's preaching at Mecca, one soon presents itself, namely, a change from nomadism to commerce. The Mecca of Muhammad's youth and early manhood

---

[1] For further details about the matters discussed in this section cf. W. Montgomery Watt, *Muhammad at Mecca*, *Muhammad at Medina*, Oxford, 1953, 1956.

—he was about forty in 610—was a prosperous commercial centre in which financial operations of some complexity were carried out. Mecca had come to control the rich caravan trade through western Arabia by which luxury goods from India and Abyssinia (conveyed to south Arabia by sea) were exchanged for the products of Syria and the Mediterranean. There seems to have been a great growth in this trade in the half-century before 610, perhaps because the wars between the Byzantine and Persian empires interfered with the route through 'Iraq. The Meccans certainly made the most of favourable circumstances. They eliminated rivals by wars and sharp practices; they organized caravans efficiently and made effective arrangements for their security all along the route; and as a result they established a virtual monopoly of the west Arabian caravan trade.

These merchants of Mecca, however, now making great fortunes from their trading enterprises, were not far removed from nomadic ancestors, whose livelihood had come from the pasturing of camels and other animals, with perhaps an occasional raid on agricultural lands and fees for guaranteeing the security of caravans and of settled communities. The scantiness of the source material does not enable us to say exactly when this change took place. Probably there was a period when the ancestors of the Meccans combined a little trading with nomadism. Mecca was built round a shrine which had long been a centre of pilgrimage. A certain area round the town was regarded as sacred, and the month or months of pilgrimage were also sacred; and at these places and times blood-feuds were in abeyance. Thus nomads from far and near could safely congregate here, and there would be many opportunities of trading, especially for the guardians of the shrine. The beginnings of a permanent settlement round the shrine are possibly to be attributed to Qusayy, the grandfather of Muhammad's great-grandfather. Unless this merely means that the camels of his tribe were never pastured more than a few days' journey away, it must imply a fair volume of trade, since no agriculture is possible at Mecca. It seems most likely, however, that the main expansion of trade, especially of the more lucrative types, took place in the decades before 610. Thus Muhammad's contemporaries may not have been more than one generation removed from at least a partial dependence on pastoralism; Muhammad's grandfather appears to have had extensive herds of camels. In Muhammad's time, however, many of the residents in Mecca must have gained a livelihood mainly from commercial operations. Thus in the course of a generation or two there had been a change from reliance on nomadic pastoralism to reliance on commerce.

Some of the social phenomena of Mecca in Muhammad's time

6

The Place of Economic and Social Factors

may be regarded as repercussions of this change in the economic basis of life. Foremost among these is a weakening of group solidarity, not only in the larger units which may be called tribes and clans but also in the smaller family units. For nomadic groups living in the desert a high degree of solidarity is necessary to survival. Custom prescribes various ways in which the members of a group must help one another and in which the chief of a group stands by those under him. Unquestioning loyalty to one's kin is reckoned a great virtue in all men, and likewise generosity to those in misfortune; the latter is especially a virtue of chiefs and other leading men. With the change from nomadism to commerce the leading men of the group begin to think of amassing personal fortunes. In the desert where the main form of wealth is camels no one can become very wealthy. Camels require men to tend them and to protect them against enemies, so that the size of a man's herd is limited by his ability to retain the allegiance of the men who look after them. Even if a man is strong enough to receive payment for guaranteeing security to weaker groups, some of this has to be shared with the followers whose arms make the guarantee effective, and most of the rest has to be consumed immediately since the nomad has no storehouses in which to keep goods indefinitely. The merchant living in a town, on the other hand, and dealing in luxury goods of small bulk, is able to increase his wealth almost without limit and to maintain a reserve against accidents. This seems to be what was happening at Mecca at the beginning of the seventh century.

While the rich merchants were increasing their personal wealth, they were also more and more disregarding their obligations towards the less fortunate members of their clan or family. The capital which had formed the basis of their earliest trading operations was probably the communal wealth of the group, of which they were only administrators; but the profits went into their own pockets, and before long there was no communal property left. Those in a socially weak position, notably widows and orphans, were shamelessly cheated and oppressed. It was probably only a handful of men in Mecca who were able to accumulate vast fortunes; but with the establishment of monopolies, their opportunities would be great, and they did not scruple to make full use of them. A large proportion of the inhabitants of Mecca might be involved in one of the great caravans (like that which led to the battle of Badr), but the lion's share of the profit would go to one or two entrepreneurs. Thus it would seem that the main social cleavage in Mecca in 610—the point at which 'class feeling' was most acute—was not between the rich and the poor, but between the very rich and the moderately prosperous. Moreover, while the very rich found a new security in their wealth, the rest of the Meccans were rather aware of their insecurity, through the loss of a sense of community and through the breakdown of the traditional customs.

Along with the matters mentioned there may have been a change from a matrilineal kinship system to a patrilineal one. The evidence is scanty, however, and not easy to interpret, and it cannot be categorically stated that such a change took place. What is certain is that in Muhammad's time matrilineal kinship was more prominent at Medina than at Mecca, but even at Medina, perhaps in part through his influence, was decreasing in importance. It may be that different tribes had followed different kinship systems from time immemorial. It would be in accordance, however, with what has been observed elsewhere of the growth of individualism that it should be accompanied by an increasing interest in patrilineal descent. It is only natural that the individualistic man should be more interested in his own sons than in his sister's sons. The Qur'an frequently accuses the rich men of Mecca of putting too much reliance on their wealth and their sons.

In contrast to this considerable, though by no means complete, break-down of group solidarity there was the appearance of new linkages through commercial interests. Quraysh, the tribe to which the majority of the Meccans belonged, was noted for its *hilm*, that is, its maturity, gravity or self-control. They were not carried away by anger to act rashly, but had an ability for composing their quarrels. It would seem that, in the best Mancunian fashion, they placed business before the indulgence of emotions. The *mala'* or senate of Mecca was usually able to reach decisions which won general acceptance, and there was certainly none of the bitter strife found at Medina.

This does not mean that there were no party divisions at Mecca. Among the clans or subdivisions of the tribe of Quraysh two main groups may be distinguished, while a number of clans adopted an attitude of neutrality and may be reckoned as a third group. Yet by Muhammad's time these clan groupings seem to have been deeply affected by mercantile interests. In Muhammad's youth his clan of Hashim was the leader of a group known as the Confederation of the Fudul[1] which came together in opposition to the attempt of another group (known as the Ahlaf or Confederates) to establish some kind of monopoly. Previously a group called the Mutayyabun or Perfumed, had been the opponents of the Ahlaf, probably disagreeing with them about the control of the arrangements for the

[1] Fudul could mean 'the virtuous', but there are other possibilities.

pilgrimage and the accompanying fair. The clans constituting the Confederation of the Fudul were nearly the same as those in the Mutayyabun, except that two clans which had prospered in trade did not enter the new Confederation but moved closer to the Ahlaf. Most of the monopolists belonged to these two clans or to the Ahlaf, while the clans in the Confederation of the Fudul were probably those unable to organize independent caravans and so shut out from the most profitable undertakings. While there is some uncertainty about the interpretation of details, it seems clear that the clan groupings in Muhammad's time were largely influenced by business interests.

It was in an environment characterized by these economic and social changes that Muhammad began to preach the religion of Islam. The ideational aspect of the new religion will be considered in the next chapter. Meanwhile something may be said about its attitude in respect of economic and social matters. The first thing to note is that the Qur'an fully accepts commerce and indeed 'big business'. There is no whisper of criticism of the mercantile economy of Mecca as such, only of particular points in the conduct and outlook of the merchants, such as their oppression of the weak and their undue reliance on wealth. On the contrary the Qur'an is deeply penetrated by mercantile terms, not merely in illustrative material but in the formulation of some of its main doctrines.[1]

There are also indications that Muhammad may have tried out some practical steps to break the hold of the monopolists. It is possible that one exploratory measure of this type was the sending of some of his followers to Abyssinia. This happened some years after he began to preach, perhaps about 615, and is usually said to be due to the growth of persecution in Mecca. This standard version, however, does not explain why some of this party of Muslims did not return from Abyssinia until 629, long after persecution had ceased. Since they presumably gained a livelihood by trade meantime, at least part of Muhammad's aim in sending them may have been to develop a trade route not under the control of the monopolists. A partial confirmation of this suggestion may be seen in the fact that all except two of the Muslims who went to Abyssinia belonged to the clans of the Confederation of the Fudul (with one slight modification which may be presumed to have occurred by this date).

Shortly after the migration to Abyssinia, perhaps in 616, another event happened which indicates that Muhammad had policies which met with the approval even of those who did not accept his religious teaching. This event was an agreement of all the clans of Mecca to

[1] Cf. C. C. Torrey, *The Commercial-Theological Terms of the Koran*, Leiden, 1892.

9

boycott Muhammad's clan of Hashim (together with the clan of al-Muttalib which was more or less merged in it) by having no business dealings nor intermarriage with them. This was ostensibly because Hashim, led by Muhammad's uncle Abu-Talib, refused to withdraw its protection from Muhammad or to make him abandon his preaching. It would of course have been dishonourable for the clan to cease protecting him simply because other clans threatened it, but had it seriously wanted to escape the boycott it could doubtless have found some reason for refusing him protection. That the clan defied the boycott for three years implies that the whole clan had some interest in the questions at issue. (Incidentally the boycott is an example of the methods used by the rich merchants to extend their monopolies, and it shows that Hashim must have been able to engage in some sort of trade, even if only on a small scale.) It would seem, then, that, somehow or other, the boycott was an incident not merely in the opposition to Muhammad's new religion but also in the struggle between the rich merchants and the lesser traders. The agreement to boycott Hashim was eventually broken by the leaders of some of the clans which were prospering in trade but were not members of the Ahlaf; this suggests the growth of a realization that the success of the boycott might give too much power to the rich merchants who had inaugurated it.

The remaining happenings of Muhammad's Meccan period show this intertwining of religion and business. About 619, soon after the end of the boycott, Abu-Talib died and was succeeded as chief of Hashim by another of Muhammad's uncles, Abu-Lahab. The latter was seduced from the traditional policy of Hashim by the offer of a share in the most lucrative enterprises. The deal was clinched by his marriage to the sister of Abu-Sufyan (of the clan of 'Abd-Shams or Umayyah), one of the two or three foremost merchants in Mecca. In return, when he became chief of the clan, he soon found an excuse for disowning Muhammad, and thus making it dangerous for Muhammad to remain in Mecca. Muhammad did in fact obtain the protection of the head of another clan, but doubtless only by accepting some restrictions on his freedom to preach. Under these circumstances Muhammad began to look for a field of activity elsewhere. He visited the neighbouring city of at-Ta'if, whose inhabitants had formerly been trade rivals of the Meccans but were now subject to them; he may have hoped that the bait of deliverance from the financial control of Mecca would be attractive, but, if so, he was disappointed and had to return to Mecca. Negotiations with the inhabitants of Medina were more satisfactory, and in 622 Muhammad and some seventy of his followers migrated to Medina.

The Place of Economic and Social Factors

This new phase will be considered for itself presently. Here it is to be noticed that in one respect it is a continuation of Muhammad's attempts to break the power of the monopolists. It is difficult to avoid the conclusion that before he went to Medina Muhammad planned to raid the northward caravans from Mecca—a procedure for which Medina was well situated—and perhaps also to organize independent caravans. His eventual overthrow of Meccan power was partly due to the stranglehold he obtained on their trade.

In respect of the social changes of the time the attitude of the new religion of Islam was that it accepted as something inevitable the movement away from tribal solidarity towards a large measure of individualism. The ethical prescriptions of the Qur'an are fundamentally individualistic, since the ultimate sanction for them is reward and punishment on the Day of Judgement, and it is as individuals that men are judged; the Qur'an frequently reminds those to whom it is addressed that on that day wealth and powerful kinsmen will avail them nothing. Although the acceptance of individualism is thus central in the Qur'an, the new religion was prepared to retain tribal solidarity where it still remained and had a useful social function to perform. In Mecca public security depended on the readiness of each clan to avenge injuries and wrongs suffered by its members; it was the continuing effectiveness of this system that enabled Muhammad to go on living and preaching in Mecca despite strong opposition. Similarly the kinship group had a part to play in the new Islamic state which Muhammad founded at Medina presently. At Mecca, on the other hand, the Muslims must have been more keenly aware than most of their fellow-citizens of the loss of a sense of community—on the basis of kinship, that is. Many of them were estranged from their clans because of their adherence to Islam. This was especially the case with near relatives of the rich merchants who were foremost in the opposition to Muhammad. With the growth of opposition, however, the Muslims must have been drawn closer together and have become conscious of their new relationship to one another in the religious community of Islam. To strengthen this feeling of belonging together and perhaps also to give something by way of compensation to those who were cut off from their clans, Muhammad arranged for the 'brothering' or pairing off of several of his followers; presumably there was a formal compact by which they agreed to treat one another as brothers. Whether such 'brothering' was previously practised or not, the pre-Islamic Arabs employed fictitious kinship in various ways.

Lists and biographical notices have been preserved of all Muhammad's earliest followers and of many of his later ones also.

Altogether we know the names of some ten or twenty thousand people who were in contact with Muhammad. Thus it is possible to form at least a rough estimate of the social position of his followers while he was still at Mecca. They appear to have come from three groups. Firstly, there were several men, mostly young, who were close relatives of the leading men of the most influential clans. These men were perhaps attracted to Muhammad and his anti-monopolistic policy because, though close to the richest monopolists, they were excluded from the most profitable enterprises. On the other hand, their dominant feeling may rather have been that the type of life in general and of personal relationships in particular which the new monopolistic economy tended to produce were unsatisfactory, and that from an individualistic standpoint (taking account of the limits and uncertainties of human life) the piling up of riches for oneself was meaningless. Whether it was for these reasons separately or in combination, or for some others, Muhammad certainly had the support of these young men from the richest families of Mecca.

Secondly, there were men from the other clans and families of Mecca, such as the clans in the Confederation of the Fudul. These men also were mostly young, but there were a few senior men from the weakest clans. In the case of this group it would seem that impoverishment, whether absolute or only relative, as a result of the monopolistic practices of the rich merchants, was the main reason for their attraction to Muhammad. The majority of the hundred or so Muslims of the Meccan period may be regarded as belonging to this group, though the boundary line between it and the previous group is not precise.

Thirdly, a comparatively small number of Muhammad's followers at Mecca are described as 'weak'. This probably means, not so much that they were poor (for some may even have been moderately prosperous), as that they had no effective clan protection. They were strangers in Mecca, not members of the tribe of Quraysh. They probably claimed to be attached to one of the Meccan clans either as confederates or as 'protected neighbours', but the clan in question for some reason or other repudiated their claims and was not prepared to defy the rich merchants on their behalf. Because of their 'weakness' in this sense this group suffered most from Muhammad's opponents, though some members of the first group also suffered, since no one could protect them against their own family. Thus the third group is frequently mentioned in the accounts of the 'persecution' of the Muslims, but it probably constituted less than a tenth of their total number. Its size and character give no justification for thinking that Muhammad was the leader of proletarians against

12

aristocrats. The families and clans in the second group had much the same origin as those in the first group. Some fifty years previously all had been more or less of the same social standing. In the interval, however, some families and clans had been more successful in their trading than others, and this had led to differences of wealth and influence.

Finally, it may be noted that the movement under Muhammad was not the only response to the social and economic changes at Mecca. Another possible response is suggested by an incident that took place shortly after 590. A man called 'Uthman ibn-al-Huwayrith entered into negotiations with the Byzantines to bring Mecca into their sphere of influence and to have himself installed as prince or phylarch. Little is known for certain about the incident, but it is not improbable that 'Uthman hoped for support from the groups which later supported Muhammad. The more lucrative branches of Mecca's trade presumably were only possible so long as Mecca remained neutral between the Byzantine and Persian empires; and thus a closer attachment to Byzantium would weaken the rich merchants and benefit the other members of the community, while the adoption of Christianity which 'Uthman envisaged would have supplied their spiritual needs. The scheme was in fact a fiasco because 'Uthman was denounced as aiming at kingship by a wealthy member of his own clan, so that 'Uthman lost both the protection of his clan and whatever popular support he had gained.

We also hear of responses to the malaise of the times along religious lines. One man, 'Uthman ibn-Maz'un, who was prominent among the early Muslims, had previously engaged in ascetic practices and been tending towards monotheism. There is also a well-known story of how four men agreed that they would abstain from the pagan sacrifices at Mecca and seek the pure religion of Abraham.[1] The story has clearly been moulded in the light of later Islamic ideas, but it may be true in showing that there was a quest for a religious solution of the problems of the times. Two of the four men became Christians: 'Uthman ibn-al-Huwayrith and another whose story is not told here. A third man became first a Muslim and then later, in Abyssinia, a Christian. The fourth died as a monotheist, but without attaching himself to any of the existing religions. This story of the four men thus raises the question why Arabia did not become Christian or Jewish rather than Muslim. The answer appears to be that both Christianity and Judaism would have led to political involvements which were distasteful to many influential Arabs.

[1] Ibn-Hisham, ed. F. Wüstenfeld, Göttingen, 1859-60, 143ff. (tr. by A. Guillaume, London, 1955, as *The Life of Muhammad*, 98ff.)

Christianity was primarily, from the standpoint of the Arabs, the religion of the Byzantine empire and Abyssinia, while Judaism had close associations with the Persian empire. It is noteworthy that the opposition to the Islamic state which appeared about the time of Muhammad's death had a religious basis, but that this religious basis—the so-called 'false prophets'—was independent of Judaism and Christianity, even though some of the tribes which rebelled against Medina were largely Christian.

(b) Medina

In Medina also, whither Muhammad migrated in 622, it is easy to find an economic change in the background. Medina was an oasis of some twenty square miles or more, whose inhabitants gained their livelihood by cultivating date-palms and cereals. There was also some commerce. The Jewish clan of Qaynuqa' were smiths and had a market. The people of Medina may have sent caravans to various places in the north, but their trade was probably only in foodstuffs and similar goods and not nearly so lucrative as the trade in luxury goods of which Mecca had the monopoly. Thus agriculture was the main support of Medina. The Arabs of Medina, however, like those of Mecca, had had nomads as ancestors in the not very distant past and had retained much of the social institutions of nomadism. There is, then, an important economic change in close proximity to the adoption of Islam at Medina, namely, the change from nomadism to a settled agricultural life.

There had also been social changes at Medina which had been linked up with the economic change, but the situation is more complex than at Mecca. Whereas at Mecca there had been the single tribe of Quraysh with its various sub-divisions or clans, at Medina there were the two Arab tribes of the Aws and the Khazraj, each divided into a number of clans, and also the three Jewish tribes or clans of Qurayzah, an-Nadir and Qaynuqa' besides a number of smaller Jewish groups. The Jews had been in the oasis longer than the Aws and the Khazraj, and apparently the clans of Qurayzah and an-Nadir still had the richest lands. The Arabs, however, or some of them, were now strongest, and dominated political relationships in Medina, but they were divided among themselves. Feuds between single clans had become linked up with one another, until, a year or two before 622, there had been a battle with much bloodshed at a place called Bu'ath. On one side at this battle had been most of the Aws, some of the Jews and one nomadic tribe from the neighbourhood, while on the other side had been most of the Khazraj, some of

14

the Jews and another nomadic tribe from the neighbourhood, while one section of the Khazraj had remained neutral. No peace settlement followed this battle, and the situation in 622 was still one of 'cold war'; indeed, anyone who went through the district of a hostile clan alone on a dark night was liable to be murdered.

One point to be noticed about this development is that the blood-feud as a method of providing a measure of security for life was breaking down. In the desert two tribes which had a blood-feud probably had few contacts with one another, and would seldom be within striking distance. In the relatively confined space of an oasis, however, hostile clans would always be within striking distance of one another and it would be difficult to avoid frequent contacts. At Medina, to increase security, there had grown up a system of forts or strongholds.[1] It has been suggested that these were not permanent residences but places of refuge in an emergency; but with the increasing insecurity after the battle of Bu'ath there may well have been a tendency for men to use the forts as residences. The larger and wealthier clans had many such forts. The people of Medina regarded the forts as impregnable, and once a man's opponents had reached their fort he gave up attacking them for the time being. The forts had perhaps originally been intended for protection from raiding nomads, and doubtless served that purpose well. Even with the forts, however, life in Medina in 622 was far from tolerable. Security demanded a single strong leader.

Another point to be noticed is the transformation of the tribal system. One aspect of this is the appearance of ever larger rival alliances or confederations which between them included most of the inhabitants of Medina. It was stated above that most of the tribe of the Aws was on one side and most of the tribe of the Khazraj on the other; and this might suggest that we were dealing with a restoration of bonds of kinship that had become weak. This was the traditional account, but there are grounds for suspecting it. The matter is a complex one, however, and the evidence slight. Not the least of the difficulties is that the geneaologies of the various clans whereby they are incorporated in the tribes of the Aws and the Khazraj are patrilineal, whereas until Muhammad's time matrilineal kinship had been prominent, perhaps predominant at Medina. In themselves, too, the patrilineal geneaologies of the Medinan clans inspire little confidence, since they contain many names that are otherwise unknown, and several of these are repeated many times. Yet, even if (as seems probable), the patrilineal geneaologies are a product of later Islamic times, there may have been a matrilineal

[1] Arabic *utum*.

15

basis for the two tribes. About this, however, it is impossible to be dogmatic. What may be said with some probability is that for a time the effective unit in Medinan society was the clan, and that when various clans felt the need of some closer association with other clans they based this association on kinship, conceivably fictitious, but more probably real though somewhat flimsy or shadowy.

A further aspect of the transformation of the tribal system is the appearance of groups whose principle of cohesion was locality and not kinship, whether fictitious or real. The chief example of this is a heterogeneous group of people known as 'the people of Ratij', Ratij being a locality of some sort, probably a fort. In order to defend a fort properly a certain minimum number of men was presumably necessary. If the membership of the group possessing a fort fell below this minimum, there would be good grounds for inviting some other small group to join them. Other cases where the real bond of cohesion is possibly local propinquity appear in the records as cases where one group are confederates of another, since according to Arab ideas local propinquity could never unite men. (Local propinquity was fundamental to the state Muhammad created at Medina, but the members of the state thought of their unity as resting on the act of confederacy involved in the Pledge of al-'Aqabah and in the Constitution of Medina). The reason for not being certain about the importance of local propinquity in these cases of confederacy is that the relationship of confederacy may have been introduced by the Islamic authors of the records to explain group cohesion on a matrilineal basis that was inexplicable on their own patrilineal principles. General considerations, however, and the example of the people of Ratij, show that locality had a share in transforming the tribal system.

The position of the Jewish clans in the community has also to be taken into account. They may have been in part of fairly pure Jewish descent, but there were also among them Arabs who had accepted the Jewish religion. There had also been intermarriage. A man called Ka'b ibn-al-Ashraf, prominent as a poet and an opponent of Muhammad, was the son of an Arab man (either pagan or, more probably, Christian) and a Jewish woman; but he was reckoned as belonging to his mother's clan of an-Nadir. Whatever the racial composition of the Jewish clans at Medina, they were very much arabized; indeed there was little to distinguish them from their Arab neighbours except their specific Jewish cult practices. The instance of Ka'b ibn-al-Ashraf suggests that they had adopted some Arab marriage practices (such as uxorilocal marriage) and a measure of matrilineal kinship. Their difference from the Arabs of Medina was

16

further lessened by a movement among the latter towards Jewish monotheism—a movement which facilitated the acceptance at Medina of the monotheism preached by Muhammad.

The Jewish clans participated in local politics in exactly the same way as the Arab clans. They did not form a bloc in opposition to the Arabs, but were allied with different Arab clans. Three or four of the smaller Arab clans, whose lands were interspersed among those of the two main Jewish agricultural clans, an-Nadir and Qurayzah, seem to have been satellites of the latter, for they did not at first accept Muhammad as prophet. The threat by one of the pre-Islamic Medinan leaders, 'Amr ibn-an-Nu'man, to expel an-Nadir and Qurayzah, was doubtless due to his desire for their rich lands rather then because of any hostility to Jews as such. Yet there may also have been some realization that the Jewish religion was liable to have political repercussions. In particular, the clan of Salimah, which was prominent in bringing Muhammad to Medina, was apparently hostile to the Jews, or at least opposed Muhammad's policy of assimilating his religious observances to those of the Jews. It is possible, however, that this attitude towards the Jews was mainly due to the alliance of an-Nadir and Qurayzah with Arab clans with which Salimah had a feud.

In this confused social situation at Medina there are traces of a trend towards the acceptance of a strong leader. The leader who has just been mentioned, 'Amr ibn-an-Nu'man, seems to have had the idea of extending his power in the oasis by military action, but his harshness lost him support, and at Bu'ath his party was defeated and he himself killed. A more promising policy was that of 'Abd-Allah ibn-Ubayy, of whom the biographers of Muhammad say that, but for the arrival of Muhammad, he would have become king of Medina. He was apparently reckoning on being supported by the Jews as well as by various Arab clans, but he did not completely commit himself to Judaism. This is probably because complete commitment would have given political power to the Jewish rabbis. Whether he could have retained Jewish support without becoming a Jew is another matter.

The coming to Medina of Muhammad and Islam led to further economic and social changes. The social changes are the more important, but the economic changes must also be noticed. There was, of course, to begin with no change in the economic basis of life; it remained the cultivation of palms and cereals. When the Jewish clan of Qaynuqa' was expelled in 624, this doubtless did not mean that their market ceased to function, but that it was transferred to some of the Emigrants (the Meccan Muslims who had followed

Muhammad to Medina). The Emigrants also tried to organize caravans to Damascus and elsewhere in the north. An entirely new factor was introduced, however, when Muhammad and the Emigrants engaged in expeditions which attacked Meccan caravans or conglomerations of hostile nomads and brought back booty to Medina. As Muhammad became more regularly successful and his prestige and power grew, this became an economic factor of some importance and men from nomadic tribes were attracted to Medina to take part in the expeditions and share in the spoils. Muhammad's increased power brought clans and whole tribes to seek his protection, and the payments which in one form or another he usually demanded of them helped to finance the state he had established. The economic position of Medina in the closing years of Muhammad's life was, of course, only a temporary one, since in the decade after his death Medina became the capital of an empire with all that that meant economically.

Such were the main economic consequences of Muhammad's migration to Medina and the acceptance of Islam there; but they were secondary. The social consequences were primary, or at least of greater importance, and the desire for these social consequences was at the bottom of the acceptance of Islam by the people of Medina, since Islam offered them the prospect of relief from their social troubles. The fundamental change was that the society of Medina was unified on a new basis, namely, religion, instead of the old basis of kinship, and that through this unification internal strife was stopped. This at least was the long-term result of the acceptance of Islam; but the actual course of events was complex.

It was probably in 620 that the first negotiations took place between Muhammad and six men of Medina, all of the tribe of the Khazraj. Further negotiations took place in which the Aws were represented as well as the Khazraj—doubtless because Muhammad insisted on a fully representative body, so that he could maintain neutrality and not be regarded as the ally of one of the warring factions. According to the traditional story (which is probably not far from the truth) a party of seventy-three men and two women went from Medina to Mecca for the pilgrimage of 622; they had already accepted the religion preached by Muhammad, and they now in addition pledged themselves to defend Muhammad as they would defend their own kin. This is known as the (second) Pledge of al-'Aqabah or the Pledge of War. Relying on this pledge, Muhammad's Meccan followers to the number of about seventy migrated to Medina; and some three months after the Pledge he himself joined these Emigrants (as they were called) at Medina.

The Place of Economic and Social Factors

In connection with these events there may also be considered a document purporting to be the Constitution of Medina.[1] This document is almost certainly genuine, but it seems to contain different strata and may not have taken its present form until some five years after the Hijrah or migration. Nevertheless it gives indications of how the new order in Medina was conceived by Muhammad and the leading men of Medina. The document begins as follows :

In the name of God, the Merciful, the Compassionate !
This a writing of Muhammad the prophet between the believers and Muslims of Quraysh and Yathrib (*sc.* Medina) and those who follow them and are attached to them and who crusade along with them.
They are a single community (*ummah*) distinct from (other) people.

Then there are nine articles stating that each of the nine main subdivisions of the community is to be responsible for blood-money and similar matters for its own members. The nine subdivisions are 'the Emigrants of Quraysh' and eight clans or rather clan-groups (since some include more than one clan) of the Aws and the Khazraj. After this there are nearly forty other articles dealing with the position of various Jewish groups, with certain mutual rights and duties of the believers (such as refraining from bloodshed), and with the avoidance of friendship with the pagan Meccans.

From what is known about the Pledge at al-'Aqabah, then, and from the Constitution of Medina, it is apparent that the new order in Medina could be regarded as a confederacy in accordance with traditional Arab ideas. It had been concluded between nine kinship groups, since even the Emigrants all belonged to the tribe of Quraysh, although in Mecca itself there might have been rivalry or hostility between their clans. At this level of thinking Muhammad is merely the chief of one of the nine kinship groups and not superior to the other eight. Further, however, the confederacy may be regarded as having in fact a local basis. The contracting parties are all residents in the oasis of Medina, and the other residents—presumably all of them—are also included, though as dependent for protection (according to old Arab ideas) on one or other of the contracting parties. In this way the relationship of confederacy is used to create a local community.

The religious element underlying the confederacy is also not far to seek. The confederacy is essentially one between Muslims, since all the nine contracting parties are groups of Muslims. The document is drawn up and promulgated by Muhammad as prophet, and his own

---

[1] An English translation will be found in *Muhammad at Medina*, 221-5; also in Ibn-Hisham, tr. Guillaume, 231-3.

group, the Emigrants, are given the honour of first mention Since.
the words 'Islam' and 'Muslim' were probably not used in the earliest
Medinan period, the original wording of the document was perhaps
'between the believers of Quraysh and Yathrib', and Muhammad,
who at first tried to achieve a reconciliation which would include
the Jews in his community, may have been prepared to rank the Jews
as 'believers' and as contracting parties provided they were ready to
make some acknowledgement of his prophethood. Whether this is
so or not, in the document as we have it the Jews appear nearly
always as attached to one of the Arab clan-groups—they are described as 'the Jews of the clan of Sa'idah' and so forth. Since the
Jewish clans of Qaynuqa', an-Nadir and Qurayzah are not mentioned
as such in the Constitution, and it is unlikely that in Muhammad's
first years at Medina they were dependent on Arab clans, this is a
weighty reason for thinking that the present form of the Constitution
dates to the period after the expulsion of the three main Jewish clans
(that is, after 627), and that the Jews mentioned in it are the small
groups which still remained. This somewhat conjectural matter,
however, does not affect the main point here about the religious
element underlying the confederacy.

This religious element affected the course of events at Medina
through the special position which it gave to Muhammad. To
become a Muslim involved acknowledging Muhammad as a prophet
who received revelations from God; and this presumably also
involved obeying the rules contained in any future revelations which
Muhammad might receive. A passage of the Qur'an[1] belonging
to Muhammad's Meccan period states that 'each community has a
messenger, and when their messenger comes, judgement is given
between them with justice, and they are not wronged'. This conception of a prophet as the arbiter of disputes within his community was
no doubt familiar to the Medinans and was the main thing that
attracted them to Muhammad. They do not at first, however, appear
to have formally conferred on him any special privileges. Article 23
of the Constitution runs: 'Wherever there is anything about which
you differ, it is to be referred to God and to Muhammad': and
article 42 is similar. Yet this does not necessarily mean more than the
acceptance of decisions based on the revelations which Muhammad
received. A verse of the Qur'an (42. 10/8) from which the phraseology
of Article 23 has perhaps been derived, prescribes only the referring
of disputes to God, that is, to a decision through revelation. This

---

[1] 10.47/48. (In the references to the Qur'an, where there are two verse-
numbers, the first is that of the standard Egyptian edition, the second of
Flügel's edition.)

would appear to be the position at the time of the Hijrah. Later, however, about the time of the battle of Uhud in 625, the Qur'an (4. 59/62) exhorts the believers to refer disputes 'to God and to the Messenger', and in numerous verses enjoins obedience to God and His Messenger. The existence of these verses at this period confirms the view that in the original agreement between Muhammad and the clans of Medina they did not undertake to obey him in his personal capacity. At first, apart from being prophet, he was only one of nine or so clan chiefs, and had sometimes to proceed with great tact. The acknowledgement of him as prophet, however, gave him an opportunity of building up a position of strength. He took full advantage of this opportunity, and by his skill as a statesman and his military successes had become by the time of his death in 632 unquestioned ruler of Medina and much of the surrounding part of Arabia.

It remains to say a word about the reasons for the acceptance of Islam at Medina. Before Muhammad arrived in Medina the leading men of most of the Arab clans—even those who were not present at al-'Aqabah—had apparently professed Islam and, together with their clans, entered into confederacy with him. Only four small clans, whose lands were interspersed among those of Jewish clans, kept out of the confederacy, though even they came in within a year or two. Some clans were more enthusiastic for Islam than others, perhaps those which were weaker economically or militarily and had most to lose from continued violence. Yet even 'Abd-Allah ibn-Ubayy—the man who looked like becoming king of Medina—entered the confederacy. It would seem that the people of Medina were so tired of their 'cold war' that they were ready to adopt any course which promised relief; and this popular feeling must have been so strong that men like 'Abd-Allah ibn-Ubayy could not go against it, however much it was contrary to their individual interests. In respect of dogma the ground had been prepared by the Jews, but the social implications of Muhammad's religion undoubtedly had a great attraction for the Medinans.

The establishment at Medina of a state ruled by Muhammad as the Messenger of God is the second stage in the development of Islam. In the background is the social malaise at Medina arising out of the transition from a nomadic to an agricultural economy. There is something accidental, moreover, about the way in which the dogmas of Islam met the needs of Medina. Islam, it must be emphasized, had not been developed with the needs of Medina in view, but with the very different needs of Mecca. One point in Islamic principles, however, the special authority of Muhammad as Messenger of God, was seen to be relevant to the needs of Medina and to give hope of a solution of Medinan troubles. This hope was in fact fulfilled.

(c) *The rest of Arabia*

The third stage in the development of Islam is its expansion from Medina until it was accepted throughout most of Arabia. This stage could be further subdivided; the acceptance of Islam by Muhammad's Meccan opponents, for instance, is different in various ways from the conversion of nomadic Arabs. There are differences also among the nomads, however, and on the whole it is most convenient to treat the expansion in Arabia as a single stage.

As a preliminary to this study it will be useful to give an outline of events between Muhammad's arrival at Medina and his death. A few months after the Hijrah small expeditions of Muslims—at first only Emigrants—went out to ambush Meccan caravans. There were many failures but some successes. The first notable success was the victory at Badr in 624. An expedition—large for this period—of over 300 men led by Muhammad himself tried to intercept a particularly rich Meccan caravan returning from Syria. The caravan and its guards escaped, but the Muslims ran into and defeated the relief force from Mecca and killed several of the leading merchants. In the following year a Meccan expedition to avenge this defeat had slightly the better of an encounter at Uhud on the outskirts of the Medinan oasis, but did not seriously incommode Muhammad or check the growth of his power. Two years later in 627 the Meccans raised the largest force they could not only of themselves and their dependents but also of various temporary allies. Their attempts to take Medina by storm were foiled by the trench or *khandaq* hastily contrived by Muhammad (which has given its name to the affair), and after a fortnight's siege the beleaguering alliance had broken up in mutual distrust. Though there was little fighting here, the failure of the Meccans to avenge themselves on Muhammad meant that he was now a power to be reckoned with in Arabian politics.

Now at least, if not before, Muhammad began to work not for the complete overthrow of the Meccans but for their acknowledgement of himself as prophet and thereby also as political leader. In 628 he went to Mecca with 1,600 men, ostensibly to make the pilgrimage. The Meccans refused to allow the Muslims to enter the sacred territory surrounding Mecca, but eventually signed a treaty with Muhammad in which the Muslims were given permission to make the pilgrimage in the following year and agreed to stop their attacks on caravans. This truce of al-Hudaybiyah lasted for over a year and a half, until an incident between dependents of the two parties caused Muhammad to march on Mecca with 10,000 men. He had already won over important Meccan leaders, and was able to enter Mecca practically without resistance (630).

In the years since the victory of Badr there had been numerous Muslim expeditions against hostile nomadic tribes in a wide region round Medina and even to some distant points on the route to Syria. In consequence many of the smaller tribes near Medina were now in alliance with Muhammad, and throughout west-central Arabia his prestige and power were considerable. Perhaps it was chiefly fear of his growing power that led a nomadic leader to gather together his allies and effect a concentration not far from Mecca. The nomads were hostile to the Meccans as well as to Muhammad, and even the Meccans who were still pagans went with Muhammad against this enemy. After coming within an inch of disaster Muhammad won a decisive victory at Hunayn. This made him unquestionably the strongest man in Arabia. For the remaining two years of his life there was no armed opposition to him except on a local scale. On the contrary, deputations flocked to Medina from all parts of Arabia asking for alliance with him. As conditions of alliance, the acceptance of Islam and acknowledgement of Muhammad as prophet were generally insisted on, together with certain payments to Medina, technically in the form of 'religious alms'. This does not mean that all the Arabs became Muslims. Often there would be two factions in a tribe and one—frequently the weaker—would seek Muhammad's alliance against its rival, while the latter kept aloof from Medina. Nevertheless many Arabs did become Muslims during Muhammad's lifetime, and, when the revolts against Medinan power after his death—the so-called wars of the Riddah or apostasy—had been quelled by the Muslim generals, the Islamization of Arabia was rapid.

When we ask whether behind this Islamization of Arabia any significant economic change is to be discerned, the answer at first appears to be a negative. It has been suggested that a gradual process of desiccation had been reducing the number of nomads for whom Arabia could provide a livelihood. This is mainly an inference from the expansion of the Arabs, however, and there is practically no direct evidence. While some measure of desiccation cannot be ruled out as a contributory cause of the situation about 630, it is not clear how desiccation would lead to the kind of social malaise which could be remedied by the acceptance of Islam. Desiccation might lead to increased fighting and bloodshed and to increased raiding of neighbouring settled lands; but this would presumably only bring about a reduction in numbers of some tribes and perhaps the complete elimination of others. If this happened gradually, however, there is no reason for supposing that the social system of the nomads would be disturbed as a system. The life of the nomad is always hard, or at least has its periods of hardship, and there is therefore always a tendency for the nomad, wherever he has a chance, to seize by force some of the luxuries of his settled neighbours. From the point of view of the present study, then, it seems best to neglect the possibility of desiccation.

If we conduct our search a little more widely, however, and look not merely for economic factors but also for political factors with an economic bearing, we may discover certain matters which enable us to give a positive answer to the question. The great political fact in the background is the struggle between the Byzantine and Persian empires, which had been going on since the second half of the sixth century. Both the empires had been interested in bringing Arabs to espouse their cause. The Persians controlled most of the settlements along the Persian Gulf and the south coast of Arabia through pro-Persian factions, and about 575 had conquered the Yemen and installed a Persian governor, expelling the Abyssinians who were allies of the Byzantines. The expansion of Nestorian Christianity among the Arabs of the desert was directed from al-Hirah in the south of 'Iraq, where the Christian kings were vassals of the Persians, and doubtless was accompanied by an increase of Persian influence. Similarly, the Monophysite Christianity spreading from Ghassan and other pro-Byzantine tribes to the south-east of the province of Syria probably indicated a growth of Byzantine influence. The Jews of Arabia were probably pro-Persian. In short, Arabia was becoming increasingly involved in the power politics of the day (though the policy of Mecca seems to have been to try to maintain neutrality as being best for business).

The corollary of this involvement was that the Arabs shared in the vicissitudes of the two great powers. While Muhammad was preaching at Mecca the tide of war turned swiftly in favour of the Persians. In 614 they took Jerusalem and by 619 had overrun Egypt and Asia Minor, while barbarian allies threatened some of the European provinces of the Byzantines. Nevertheless the Arabs had had an indication that the Persian empire was feeling the strain. At the battle of Dhu-Qar—of uncertain date, but perhaps about 611—a force of Arabs from the north-east of the peninsula had defeated Persian troops. Little is known about the battle, and it may not have been of great importance in itself, but it demonstrated to the Arabs that the Persians were not invincible. The Arabs may not have been altogether surprised, then, at the sudden debacle of the Persian empire. By 627 Heraclius had sufficiently reorganized the Byzantine empire to be able to mount an offensive against 'Iraq. Though he withdrew shortly afterwards, his victory over a Persian army may have hastened the internal decline. In February 628 the Persian emperor was assassinated, and the internal position was so perilous that the son who succeeded him had to seek peace, and by about March 628 it was clear that the Byzantines were victors in the long struggle. Negotiations lasted for some time, but in September 629 Heraclius made his triumphal entry into Constantinople and in the following March restored the Holy Rood to Jerusalem.

These events had repercussions in Arabia. The pro-Persian factions in the east and south seem almost without exception to have looked to Muhammad for support as soon as they realized that the Persians could do nothing more for them. The pro-Byzantine tribes in the north-west, on the other hand, while before 628 they may have been thinking of attaching themselves to Muhammad, after that date could not be detached from the Byzantines until Muhammad's successors at Medina had shown that they were able to defeat the Byzantine armies.

Here, then, are factors influencing events in Arabia which, though not economic, may be said to have economic repercussions, since they affect the subsidies received from outside and the persons in each locality entitled or able to levy tribute. Socially, the relationship of the Arabs to the two empires must in many cases have produced a feeling of insecurity, while the downfall of Persia would lead to an actual change in the balance of power within many small communities.

In addition to these potent influences from afar, there were economic effects from the growth of Muhammad's power at Medina. The chief of these was that the possibilities of raiding were reduced in certain directions and increased in certain other directions. In so far as tribes became allied to Muhammad it became difficult or even impossible for them to raid one another. Tribes hostile to Muhammad, on the other hand, soon became aware of his growing ability to take ample vengeance for any injuries suffered by his immediate followers or his confederates. In compensation for these restrictions on raiding there were, for those who joined the Muslim armies, ever increasing opportunities of participating in lucrative raids against the enemies of Muhammad and Islam. Even before the capture of Mecca and battle of Hunayn individuals and groups from the weaker tribes were attaching themselves to Muhammad and settling in Medina. After these events the number greatly increased. Moreover, with the growth of his power Muhammad realized the need for expansion beyond Arabia to provide an outlet for the energies of the Arabs, and sent several exploratory expeditions along the route to Syria, while entering into friendly relations with the tribes of north-east Arabia which were already raiding Persian outposts in 'Iraq.

The main economic basis of nomadic life was, of course, the breeding and pasturing of camels and other animals. Raiding, though a feature of desert life, can have contributed little from the economic standpoint, except when nomads raided agriculturalists or levied fees for protection from them. The gains and losses in raids between nomads must have roughly equalled one another. The development of the Islamic state at Medina, however, completely altered the picture, especially when the raids extended to settled districts of Syria and 'Iraq and when sovereignty was established over these provinces. Even from a comparatively early period, the proceeds of raids were an important part of the finances of the Islamic state, for a fifth of the value of any spoils taken had to be paid to Muhammad as administering the public treasury of the community. The proceeds of raiding expeditions must also have been important in many individual budgets. Here then is a new economic factor. During Muhammad's lifetime its importance, though considerable, was limited; but with the transformation of the Medinan state into an empire the proceeds of raiding, commuted into tribute and rents, were the economic basis of an Arab military aristocracy, and large numbers of Arabs found a comfortable and even luxurious livelihood in the work of fighting and administration.

The rise of the Islamic state during Muhammad's lifetime also meant the appearance of a new social factor in Arabia, namely, a large and closely-knit community. Arabia had known large federations in the past, but they had not been closely-knit. Often they had been held together by the strong man's personality, and had broken up on his death; and some contemporaries may well have thought that the same would happen to Muhammad's community as a political entity. Whatever the future might hold, however, it was soon clear that Muhammad could only be opposed by a social unit greater than the single tribe. Thus the Meccans, for their great effort which ended in the abortive siege of Medina, organized a large confederation; and it was another confederation which opposed Muhammad at Hunayn. The wars of the Riddah or apostasy at the time of Muhammad's death, where several of the leaders claimed prophetic gifts, might perhaps be taken as evidence that there was a realization that the old Arab idea of confederation could not produce a sufficiently closely-knit body to oppose the Muslims.

These, then, are the main economic and social factors underlying the acceptance of Islam by the majority of the inhabitants of Arabia either during Muhammad's lifetime or shortly afterwards. To many, especially after the battle of Hunayn, alliance with Muhammad promised greater security than was otherwise attainable. The security of the Pax Islamica was particularly appreciated by those whom the vicissitudes of the two great empires had made to feel insecure. Others may have looked rather to the economic advantages of alliance with Mecca. The acceptance of Islam as a political and economic system is, of course, not the same thing as the acceptance of Islamic beliefs and cult practices; but a consideration of the relation between the two acceptances will come more appropriately in the next chapter. Here it may be noted that there were probably few genuine conversions to Islam among the nomads so long as they remained in Arabia. Muhammad himself had a low opinion of the quality of their acceptance of Islam. Nevertheless, or perhaps just because of this, wherever he felt himself strong enough he insisted on formal profession of Islam by those who sought his alliance. In the case of weak tribes acceptance of Islam probably became necessary after the siege of Medina in 627, but in the case of strong tribes, such as those of north-east Arabia, which were probably Christian in the main, he seems to have been ready right up to the time of his death in 632 to enter into alliance without making them accept Islam or acknowledge himself as prophet. There was thus deliberate political pressure on many Arabs to accept Islam as a religion, and, though the details are often obscure, Muhammad's policy was certainly adhered to by his successors.

There were some special factors affecting the pagan Meccan opponents of Muhammad. The chief was his paralysing attacks on their trade. After the battle of Badr and until the peace of al-Hudaybiyah, that is, from 624 to 628, it seems to have been almost impossible to send caravans from Mecca to Syria. The Meccans tried roundabout routes to avoid going near Medina, but Muhammad received information about some of these attempts and intercepted the caravans. Thus Meccan trade, if not entirely at a standstill, must have become much less profitable. Caravans could still go to the Yemen without much difficulty, but the southern trade and the northern trade were presumably interdependent. While the Meccans were thus confronted by economic ruin, Muhammad after 627 showed himself prepared to ease the path of reconciliation. He doubtless foresaw that, if his state expanded as he hoped it might, there would be a great need for the administrative skill of the Meccans. Some of the Meccans, too, began to realize that their best

27

prospects of a career were in the Islamic state, and several important men had gone over to Muhammad before he occupied Mecca in 630. Once again the relation of political and economic motives to religious ones is not clear; but it may be noted that one of his bitterest opponents, 'Ikrimah ibn-Abi-Jahl (son of the Meccan commander killed at Badr), is reported to have become an enthusiastic Muslim.

In conclusion it may be said that, while there are economic and social factors underlying the Islamization of Arabia—both factors due to the growth of the Islamic state at Medina and other factors of a more general kind—these would hardly have produced a new religion. Islam only became possible as a religion for Arabia after it had established itself at Medina.

2. SOME LATER ISLAMIC DEVELOPMENTS

If the economic factors are in some sense fundamental, the presumption is that they underlie all the various aspects of the development of a religion—its expansion among other peoples than those among whom it began, its decline as a whole or in part, its division into sects and the appearance of heresies, and its varying theological emphases from age to age. Such a presumption must at least be a working basis for a study of the relations between economic, social and ideational factors. If economic factors are as important as the above survey suggests that they are, then it is likely that they will be operative everywhere, and we must look everywhere to see whether we can detect them. The one point at which economic factors might not be important is in the decline of religions, for a religion might decline chiefly because of some inner changes, such as a loss of psychical energy.[1]

It would be wearisome to multiply examples, and I therefore propose merely to indicate briefly the economic and social background of some of the later developments in Islam which will be studied more fully from other points of view in later chapters. This is enough to make out a *prima facie* case for some correlation between economic and social factors on the one hand and religious changes on the other. The more difficult task is to define exactly the nature of this correlation, and for that what is needed is not a multiplicity of examples but a consideration of the nature of man in general.

The incorporation of the Persians in the Islamic community is one of the great triumphs of Islam. At first sight there does not appear

[1] This point is dealt with in chapter VIII.

to be any basic change in the economic circumstances of the Persians between the Sasanian empire and the Umayyad caliphate; the chief difference was that taxes were paid to different rulers. Nevertheless an important change can be detected. Under the Sasanians there had been a steady process of urbanization, and this had meant the growth of commerce and the eastward spread of the ancient culture of 'Iraq. This process was continued and even accelerated under Islamic rule. The Islamic empire being larger, the possibilities of trade were greater. This economic change, and likewise the change of ruler, affected different groups differently; but there can be little doubt that these changes had an important bearing on the whole-hearted acceptance of Islam by the Persians (including the Perso-Aramaean inhabitants of 'Iraq).

During the period when the Persians were being integrated into the Islamic community, the latter was beginning to show signs of disintegration. The appearance of the two great sects or groups of sects, the Kharijites and the Shi'ites, may be dated about a quarter of a century after the death of Muhammad. These sects both appeared first among Arabs, though both later developed in many colourful ways. The economic change is not far to seek. In the quarter of a century the state founded by Muhammad had conquered an empire for itself. Great numbers of Arabs had given up their camel-herding and had joined the Muslim armies. The state gave them annual stipends and provided garrison-cities for them to live in. In this new way of life, however, there was to begin with a constant struggle for power and wealth between various groups. In this struggle it gradually became clear that certain old Meccan families were going to have the best of it, while certain groups of formerly nomadic Arabs were given inferior positions. Moreover, instead of tribal councils in which every man could say what he wanted, there was now a vast administrative system which rendered the former nomad impotent. He therefore turned, quite irrationally, against the existing system and engaged in revolutionary activities, but without any realistic conception of the new state and community he wanted.

Finally may be mentioned the fact that since the voyage to India of Vasco da Gama in 1498 and particularly since about 1800 the whole Islamic world has been deeply and increasingly penetrated by European and American commerce, industry and finance. This has led to many changes in the Islamic world—political reactions to imperialism and colonialism, a partial adoption of the European intellectual outlook, the birth of religious revival movements like that of Mirza Ghulam Ahmad in India, and even, as in Turkey, an apparently anti-Islamic revolution. Behind the purely religious

29

changes, such as the decline of belief among the Western-educated middle classes and the attempts to modernize theology, there can be discerned these economic factors.

Such, then, are a few brief indications of the way in which economic factors are present in the background of many of the later developments in Islam.

3. THE FUNDAMENTAL CHARACTER OF ECONOMIC CHANGE

A justification has now been given for assuming as a working hypothesis that there is some correlation between economic and religious changes. Before attempting to give a more exact account of the correlation, it is necessary to look at the precise nature of the economic changes.

(a) The economic changes underlying religious changes.

It is not possible to maintain that in every case the economic change connected with a religious change is a change in the means of production. Frequently the economic change is of this kind. This is especially so when the religious movement is in the main something new, and not merely a modification of an existing movement. A change in the means of production underlies the appearance of Islam at Mecca—men were gaining their livelihood by commerce instead of stock-breeding. The same is probably true of the beginnings of Hinduism and Buddhism.[1] If the era of the great prophets of the Old Testament is taken as the effective beginning of Judaism, then this may be regarded as the aftermath of the change from stock-breeding to agriculture.

As this last instance shows, however, it is often difficult to say what is a new movement and what is a modification of something older. All religious movements have an element of novelty and at the same time are founded on an existing tradition, and differ only in the relative importance of the two aspects. Thus Christianity ranks as a separate religion, but in its origins was only a modification of Judaism. In so far as Christianity is regarded as the modification of an existing movement (and contemporaries so regarded it for a

[1] Cf. Max Weber, *Gesammelte Aufsätze zur Religionssoziologie*, Tübingen, 1921, ii.252; Buddhism and Jainism are based on the 'Stadtadel und bürgerliche Patriziat', . . i.e. upon commerce and urban life. Hinduism seems to have grown out of the situation where nomads (the people of the Rigveda) became rulers in the agricultural economy of the earlier Indic civilization.

century at least), it confirms the assertion that changes in the means of production are usually correlated with new movements. The assertion must not be pressed too far, however, since Islam could be regarded as merely a modification of the Judaeo-Christian tradition. Perhaps one could say that important changes in the means of production were usually correlated with religious movements in which the element of novelty preponderated. In any case the point to be insisted on is that the economic changes connected with religious changes are not always changes in the means or methods of production.

Another important type of change that is found in the background of religious movements is a change of rulers or, more generally, what might be called a political change. One great example of this is the expansion of the Islamic religion within the framework of the Arab empire; but the outstanding example is the origin of Christianity. There is no suggestion that the fishermen who followed Jesus were the descendants of shepherds or peasants; but there is ample evidence in the New Testament of the social malaise resulting from the incorporation of Palestine in the Roman empire. Now political changes of this type have economic repercussions. There are changes in the division of the product of agriculture or commerce or whatever it may be. Some of the primary products of a country must be used to support the political administration, but a new administration may take a larger or a smaller share than the old administration, or may compute its share on a different basis. Moreover the incorporation of a country in an empire will open up fresh possibilities of trade for the merchants of that country, while perhaps closing some of the old channels of trade. Merchants from other parts of the empire will come to visit the country. In this way the whole pattern of its commerce will be altered.

There are certain economic changes which do not fall under either of the types mentioned. Improvements in the means of communication cannot be called changes in the means or methods of production; yet they are in a sense an economic technique and may lead, by enabling commerce to be expanded, to a better livelihood for many people. Sometimes the growth of commerce appears to follow on a more settled state of affairs throughout a country or region. This is in itself an economic change, but it appears to follow upon political and social changes.[1]

[1] Improvements in military technique may have important political repercussions; e.g. nuclear weapons. D. Ayalon, *Gunpowder and Firearms in the Mamluk Kingdom* (London, 1956), holds that the defeat of the Persian Safawis and the Egyptian Mamluks by the Ottomans was due to their superiority in firearms. The Mamluks knew about firearms, but did not realize their importance (cf. p.108f.)

There is thus great variety in the economic changes studied. Even if the application of the word 'economic' to all these cases is admitted questions are raised about the relation of the strictly economic factors to political and social factors, and to these questions it will be necessary to return.

(b) *The correlation of economic and religious changes*

This great variety among the relevant economic changes is not a good augury for our prospects of being able to find some simple correlation between these and the religious changes. There are also several other discouraging features.

A little reflection shows that closely similar economic changes do not always produce similar religious changes. Egypt and Persia were conquered by the Arabs about the same time, but the Islamization of Persia proceeded more rapidly than that of Egypt. European economic and political pressure was much the same on the Muslims and Hindus of the Indian sub-continent, but the response of the two groups was different, for the Hindus showed themselves readier to adopt European ways—an attitude which, if not exactly religious, has religious implications. Such differences of response must depend not on differences in the economic factor but on differences in the existing attitudes of the groups experiencing the economic changes. Thus religious change cannot depend solely on economic change. Besides the economic factor there must be at least one other factor, the factor of tradition.

This conclusion is reinforced by noticing that there is no simple correlation between the importance or extent of a religious change and of the corresponding economic change. The economic change in Mecca may be allowed to be comparable to the appearance of Islam there, but it is not comparable to the Islamization of the region from Morocco to Pakistan ; and there does not appear to be any single economic change underlying the process of Islamization throughout this area. Even if the expansion of the Arab empire could be regarded for this purpose as an economic change, it does not explain everything, since Islam has expanded beyond the sphere of Arab rule, even beyond the sphere of non-Arab Muslim rule.

With such differences in the extent of religious changes and the corresponding economic changes is linked the fact that the expansion of the great religions has in each case been a complex affair. The above discussions have illustrated this, and there will be further Islamic illustrations in chapter IV. The converts to the great religions come from very varied economic circumstances. In any country one social group or class will be specially attracted to the new religion, and will sooner or later bring over the rest of the community. In other words those who enter a religious movement, if it is at all widespread, do so for different reasons. Indeed one of the chief matters being studied in this book is precisely this integration of heterogeneous groups into some sort of a unity. The very heterogeneity of the adherents of the great religions makes it unlikely that the spread of a great religion is the outcome of a homogeneous economic change.

If it is further asked whether economic changes always lead to religious changes, a brief survey would suggest the following answer. Where the economic change is a change in the means or methods of production, then (as will be seen in the next section) this usually has social repercussions and these in turn lead to a religious change. On the other hand, where the economic change is a change of ruler, the effects seem to depend on whether the new ruler is of the same type as the old ruler or of a different type. Feudal overlords in medieval Europe would belong to the same type in this sense, and a change of overlord would not normally lead to a religious change. The Muslim conquerors of Persia, however, belonged to a different social system from its Persian rulers, and in course of time the conquest led to a religious change.

We conclude that there is no simple correlation between economic change and religious change. There is great complexity in the subject-matter, and tradition must also be recognized as an important factor beside the economic one. What might be said is that the situation in which a society has to live and act is constituted largely by these factors of economic technique and tradition. In this situation the economic factor has a basic position because it is concerned with the means of life; and neither men nor societies can attend to anything else until they have made satisfactory arrangements for keeping themselves alive. An economic technique—whether it be nomadism, commerce, agriculture or imperial administration (as in the case of the Arabs in the first century of the Islamic empire)—does not determine the whole life of a society, but it provides a relatively fixed framework for that life.

The statement that economic techniques constitute a framework for the life of a society implies that there is little choice about them. Theoretically the Arabs in the years immediately after Muhammad's death were free to go on living in the desert pasturing their camels; and a few of them actually did so. But vast numbers felt that life in raiding expeditions and conquering armies and occupation forces was not only more profitable but also more interesting and spiritually satisfying. These were free decisions, and yet, human nature being what it is, there was a certain inevitability about them. After the Arabs were committed to life as a military aristocracy ruling over a huge empire, it was still theoretically possible to contract out and go back to the desert, but practically more and more difficult. Similarly, it was theoretically possible for Persians, Berbers and other subject people to revolt against their Arab rulers; and of course there were some revolts. Yet on the whole the Arab political structure was a fixed and inevitable framework for the life of these peoples. Within this framework they had to try out social and religious adjustments.

This correlation of economic and religious changes, whereby religious movements take place within a relatively fixed economic framework, is a different phenomenon from that which is found where a religion has economic consequences. The prohibition of usury[1] was adopted in Islam in an attempt to make the Jews of Medina lend money freely to the Muslims ; but in the last century it has had the effect of retarding industrial development in Islamic countries, since it was interpreted as forbidding the formation of joint-stock companies. This is something which could not have been envisaged in the time of Muhammad himself. Such economic consequences of a religious movement are incidental; but in the production of the situation out of which the religious movement grows, the economic factor is of central importance.

4. THE DERIVATION OF SOCIAL FROM ECONOMIC CHANGES

Economic activity is a part or aspect of human activity in general. An economic technique is nothing apart from the whole way of life within which it is employed. This is normally the life of a group or society, not of a single individual. Even where the single family is capable of functioning as an independent economic unit, that is, satisfying all its need for food, clothing and shelter, it is usually found that there is also a wider social structure embracing many families.

An economic technique is usually found to be more effective in conjunction with some types of social system than with others. It does not follow that there is only one type of social system appropriate to a given economic technique. Conceivably two different social systems based on the same technique might both give tolerably good results; but it is difficult to be dogmatic on this point since, even when techniques are identical, geographical conditions may vary.

[1] Cf. *Muhammad at Medina*, 296f.

We find, in fact, that nomadism in Central Asia leads to a tribal structure not unlike that in Arabia.

The social system of the pre-Islamic Arabs of the desert may be described briefly to illustrate the relation between an economic technique and the social system in which it functions most effectively. The economic basis of nomadic life in Arabia was the breeding and pasturing of camels. Human beings could live for long periods entirely from the milk of the camels. The land was steppe, with sparse, irregular and localized rainfall. In order to find pasture for the camels it was necessary to roam over vast tracts of country. There were sandy regions with a lush vegetation after rainfall, and here the nomads could have an easy life so long as the vegetation lasted; incidentally it may be noted that such regions often had no wells, so that human beings had to obtain their requirements of liquid from the camels, who found sufficient in the vegetation. In other regions there were wells and perennial shrubs from which a bare subsistence could be gained in rainless seasons. Thus, while the nomads might remain in one camp for some weeks or even months, they had no fixed abode and their movements usually varied from year to year.

The units of nomadic society may be called 'tribes'. The tribes were kinship groups, perhaps mostly matrilineal. In the largest tribes —to judge from the reported numbers of Muhammad's opponents at the battle of Hunayn—there must have been several thousand men; but small tribes would have only a few hundreds. The tribe was, strictly speaking, a sovereign and independent body politic, but it might sometimes enter into alliance with other tribes, while there were certain usages and customs common to practically all who spoke Arabic, such as the observance of the sacredness of certain places and times. Within the tribe there was a series of divisions and subdivisions, for some of which it is convenient to use the word 'clan'. For these groups of kindred there are several words in Arabic, but there does not seem to have been any strict hierarchical order in the words in the earliest period. Moreover a group, whether it consisted of a dozen men or several thousands, could be referred to as 'the sons of N'. This makes it difficult to define a 'tribe' precisely. It is thought, too, by many Western scholars that common ancestors were sometimes invented to justify and strengthen an alliance between tribes. A further complication is that (as noted in the case of Medina) a change from matrilineal to patrilineal kinship seems to have begun before Muhammad's time and, to have been fostered by Islam. The tribal genealogies that have come down to us are almost entirely patrilineal, and are therefore somewhat suspect as the constructions of genealogists who lived a century or two after Muhammad.

The tribe, as the effective social unit, was a closely-knit kinship group. Its solidarity was manifested in protecting its camels, women and children against raiders from other tribes. Among the nomad's foremost obligations was to help his fellow-tribesman against a stranger. Ideally the help was given immediately, and no questions were asked about the rights or wrongs of the quarrel. Kin came before everything else. In such communities the blood-feud served to reduce irresponsible acts of violence. The tribe or clan had a duty to take vengeance for injuries inflicted on its members—an eye for an eye and a tooth for a tooth; but a man who acted recklessly and involved his tribe in needless blood-feuds could be repudiated and deprived of his privileges as a member of the tribe. Thus there was a check on wanton crime. In the wide spaces of the steppe where it was often difficult to know the whereabouts of an individual, a tribe usually had contacts sooner or later with any particular tribe. The system therefore worked tolerably well in nomadic conditions.

The extent of country needed by a tribe for pasture was so great that if a tribe prospered and increased in numbers, it usually divided into two tribes; and these would sometimes become bitter enemies. Such breaking up of a tribe is due to the loss of solidarity owing to the great distances involved. The dangers and hardships of desert life probably account for the restriction to adult males of the right to inherit (at least in patrilineal societies). The principle would be that only those who could share in the defence of the tribe were entitled to own camels. There was no right of primogeniture either in inheritance or in leadership. The chief of a tribe was usually succeeded by the best qualified male of the chiefly family. While the chief could, and often did, consult the members of the tribe, he had also responsibilities for making decisions on behalf of the tribe and for taking the initiative. It was thus sometimes a matter of life and death for the tribe to have a fully competent man as its chief.

The social system of which some of the main features have been described was well adapted to the Arabian environment and the economic technique of camel-breeding. With slight modifications it survived intact the disturbances at the beginning of the Islamic era and has continued to the present century when it is being seriously threatened by tanks, aeroplanes and oil companies. We may suppose that this social system developed by a series of modifications to a previous social system following upon the adoption of camel-breeding as the main or sole source of livelihood.[1] We may also

---

[1] It is now generally thought that nomadism follows a period of sedentary life, based perhaps partly on agriculture and partly on stock-breeding, but not restricted to camels. There are nomads on the edge of the steppe proper who have animals other than camels. Cf. A. J. Toynbee, *A Study of History*, London, 1951, iii. 7-22.

suppose that these modifications came about through a process of trial and error. Experiments would be made; if they were successful, the experimenting tribe would prosper and increase at the expense of its rivals; if the experiments were not successful, the experimenting tribe would either drop the experiment or dwindle away. This is in accordance with the principle of the survival of the fittest.

Apart from vague historical memories of how some tribes abandoned a sedentary life in south Arabia for a nomadic one, there is no direct evidence for these social changes. Since the economic changes at Mecca and Medina have been described in some detail, the social changes there may also be noticed. In a mercantile society there were disadvantages in adhering to the nomadic social structure with its attendant mores. Nomadism fostered co-operation with one's kin, whereas the merchant for certain purposes was most successful when he was co-operating with other merchants whose capital and administrative ability were comparable to his own. In order to facilitate such co-operation there were certain features of the old system which could be developed. A business associate from another tribe could become one's 'confederate' (*halif*) and thereby receive the protection of one's clan. Thus the Meccan clan of 'Abd-Shams or Umayyah had a number of confederates from the tribe of Sulaym; and this is doubtless the result of business interests in the mines in the territory of Sulaym. The head of the clan of Zuhrah was actually a confederate from the neighbouring (but politically subordinate) commercial town of at-Ta'if.[1] Business partnerships and the relationship of confederacy could be supported by intermarriage.

The idea of confederacy applied not only to individuals who became confederates of individual Meccans, and then had their status recognized by the Meccan clan. There were also confederacies or alliances between clans and tribes. The alliances between groups of Meccan clans in the later sixth century seem to have been based on common business interests, such as promoting or opposing monopolies in certain fields. The far-reaching ramifications of Meccan trade must have involved a number of agreements and understandings with tribes along the routes to north and south. There is little direct evidence for this; but at the siege of Medina in 627 we see the Meccans receiving military support from some of their allies.

The most extreme illustration of the break-down of the old system at Mecca is Muhammad's uncle, Abu-Lahab. When most of the

---

[1] The confederacy here, however, may be a later patrilineally-minded writer's attempt to explain a position which was in fact due to matrilineal descent. This would then be an instance of a business relationship sealed by marriage.

Meccan clans were banded together to boycott Muhammad's clan of Hashim, Abu-Lahab abandoned his own clan and associated with its opponents (though on what basis we do not know). He seems subsequently to have succeeded to the headship of the clan and, at the urging of his new business associates, to have denied Muhammad the protection of the clan (the ostensible grounds being that Muhammad had spoken disrespectfully of the ancestors of the clan by saying that as pagans they were in Hell). Abu-Lahab is thus an instance of business interests trampling on kinship rights and duties.

The nomadic social system was thus being modified in various ways in the commercial economy of Mecca. Those who adopted the modifications seem to have prospered, at least financially. They had also provoked social unrest, however, and, had Mecca been left to itself, there would doubtless have been several further stages of adjustment before equilibrium was reached. Social adjustment to the commercial economy, however, was interrupted when that economy was dislocated, first by Muhammad's attacks and then by Meccan participation in Arab expansion.

Similarly in Medina there were social changes taking place as a result of the change from nomadism to agriculture. The agri-culturalist needs to have peaceful relations with his neighbours, and for this some recognized method of removing causes of friction and settling disputes is essential. It was becoming clear that peace was unattainable so long as there was a system of independent clans following the principle of the blood-feud. As at Mecca the practice of confederacy was developed, but instead of business interests it was often neighbourhood in space which made clans join together. There is at least one instance of a small community which, though its members may have been confederates of one another, had for its real basis neighbourhood or locality, namely, common ownership of a fort or stronghold.[1] Of the parties at the battle of Bu'ath, the losers had lands contiguous to one another in a central position, while the lands of the victors stretched in a crescent round them; the lands of the neutrals were towards the edges of the settled area and away from the contested 'frontier'. Up to the time of Muhammad's arrival the system of alliances had not produced peace but only bloodier battles, even if they were at less frequent intervals (which is not certain). The arrival of Muhammad marks the introduction of an alternative system, whether this was deliberately intended or not. In this system when it had taken shape, there was a single recognised head of the community to whom disputes could be referred for peaceful solution; the student may claim that he is able to detect an

[1] Cf. p. 16 above.

advance of the new system at the expense of the old system of alliances, but the claim must not be pressed too far. There is some justification for it, but the feelings connected with the old alliances or factions had not completely disappeared. Before it is clear how social change was going to proceed in Medina, the quiet economy of the oasis was being transformed into that of the capital of an empire.

The events in Muhammad's closing years and in the following decade are an interesting example of the struggle for survival between two rival social adjustments to a new economic situation. The new economic situation is the opportunity for plundering 'Iraq as a result of the weakness of the Persian empire. Quite apart from Muhammad there were and would have been plundering raids into the settled lands. These were made by a single tribe or a group of tribes, and must generally have been very profitable. They were presumably organized in the usual nomadic fashion, the raiding parties returning to their normal haunts after the raid. On this basis it is unlikely that Persian weakness could ever have been exploited to the extent of a permanent occupation of 'Iraq. The alternative social basis for an exploitation of the situation was that provided by the Islamic state. This gave men a motive for raiding other than plunder, namely, fighting against the enemies of God; this was important for, however great the proportion of men attracted to Islam solely by the lust for plunder, there must have come a time when, but for some other motive, the desire for further plunder would have been less than the desire for respite from the hardships of campaigning. The Islamic state also provided an organization capable of maintaining security at the home base and of administering occupied lands effectively so as to permit further extension of the raids. To begin with, the Muslim forces and a tribe like Shayban may have engaged in raids jointly, more or less on an equal footing; but in course of time Shayban and similar tribes were engulfed by the superior social structure of the Islamic community.[1]

The above examples show the general relationship of social change to economic change. After an economic change has taken place the existing social structure is found to be inadequate in certain respects. These inadequacies may vary from slight maladjustments to serious dislocations. Individuals living in the new situation are aware of the inadequacies and try to remedy them. The remedies they try out are usually small modifications of the existing system, such as the development of the practice of confederacy at Mecca and Medina.

[1] Cf. *Muhammad at Medina*, 14 lf.; and al-Baladhuri, *Futuh al-Buldan*, Leiden, 1866, 241 (tr. by P. Hitti, New York, 1916, i.387).

Mostly, social change takes place slowly, because the proper functioning of a social system is dependent on a measure of stability in the attitudes and ideas of the members of the society. If modifications of the system are introduced which tend to destroy existing attitudes and ideas, then the disadvantages involved in the general disturbance of the society are greater than the advantages gained by the particular modification. In many, perhaps in most cases, social change is a gradual process, advancing step by step. The original economic change makes certain social modifications desirable. These in turn make other social modifications desirable, and so on. The social changes may result in economic changes, though these are normally of a minor kind and leave the basic economic situation unchanged. In this way the history of the world since the late eighteenth century may be regarded as a series of social adjustments to the industrial revolution and the subsequent developments in science and technology. Similarly the history of Europe from about 400 A.D. to the Reformation may be seen as a series of adjustments to the economic situation created by the barbarian invasions and the dissolution of the Roman empire; the course of events is complicated by the growth of commerce (a fresh economic factor) made possible by the earlier social adjustments.

In the course of these gradual social changes the men who make the particular decisions are not usually aware of the course of change as a whole or even of its general direction. They are only aware of a particular inadequacy or maladjustment and of the modification by which they are trying to remedy it. In various parts of the Middle East during the nineteenth century Arabs of the ancient Christian churches were much readier than Muslims to send their children to the schools being opened by missionaries. These Christian Arabs were doubtless thinking mainly of the material advantages a European education would confer on the children. Their action, however, meant that their children and grandchildren had superior qualifications for positions where education of a European type was needed —in commerce, for example, and (especially after 1918) in civil administration. It also meant that their descendants were more likely to make good as emigrants to the Americas. Thus a situation was eventually created in which the Christian Arabs in certain countries in the Middle East had a prominence in commerce and industry and in administration out of all proportion to their numbers, while many Christian Arab families were receiving substantial remittances from America. It cannot be maintained that this situation, with its potentialities of trouble, was intended or even foreseen by those who made the first decisions. In our own more self-conscious age it is

40

only a few of the intelligentsia who have any idea of the direction in which we are being carried forward by social forces.

A study of history soon makes it clear that there are times and places where the social maladjustment is so serious that it cannot be remedied by individual action. The modifications in the social structure that are regarded as desirable by some groups appear obnoxious to others. To overcome opposition those who want the structure modified have to combine with one another. In the modern world we have strike action by trade unions, which, it might be argued, is not political action; but, whatever the verdict on this point, in the Islamic world combined action by groups of individuals has nearly always been political, and has usually involved military operations. The chief exception would seem to be where rulers have deferred to the will of the populace of the metropolis as expressed in demonstrations. A notable example of a combined effort to effect a social change is that of the movement in the early Islamic empire which in 750 led to the replacement of the Umayyad dynasty by the 'Abbasid. This may be regarded as primarily a political movement, but it drew much of its support from the prominence it gave to a social aim, namely, ending the privileged status of the Arabs and establishing formal equality for all Muslims.[1]

This study of the relation of social change to economic change may be brought to a close by attempting to answer the following question. In cases where there are several social responses to a given economic situation, is the difference of response due to economic differences (of a minor kind, that is) or to something else, such as social tradition? There are empirical grounds for giving the answer, No. Many of the Christian Arabs who sent their children to missionary schools in the nineteenth century seem to have been in a similar economic position to many of the Muslim Arabs who did not do so. The different response was almost certainly due to the traditional Muslim suspicion of Christians on the one hand, and on the other hand to the tendency of the Christian Arabs to look upon Europeans as friends and protectors. Again, the varying responses within the socialist movement to the economic situation about the middle of the nineteenth century do not seem to be correlated with any essential economic differences. The rank and file came from the industrial proletariat, though there were variations in the economic position of the leaders. The very complexity of the subject, however, means that there is a loop-hole for questioning the interpretation of the empirical evidence—one may ask whether a particular economic difference is essential or not. The case for the negative answer to the

[1] Cf. p. 108 below.

opening question can therefore be strengthened by theoretical discussion.

Underlying the above account of the derivation of social from economic change is a certain view of human nature. Human nature is such that, in a given economic situation, certain social arrangements work more satisfactorily than others. This may be either human nature in general or human nature as moulded by a particular tradition. In both cases there is a certain fixity about human nature. We may not be able to say beforehand how a new social arrangement will turn out, but that is simply our ignorance. The outcome depends not on chance nor (except to a slight extent) on the will of those trying out the new social arrangement, but on this fixed, though unknown, human nature. Further, in many economic situations different social responses are possible, any of which would give a tolerably satisfactory result. The response selected by an individual or group depends on what occurs to it (that is, what is suggested by imagination and ingenuity) or on its rational and scientific analysis of the situation. Two persons or groups whose general motivation is identical may produce different rational analyses of a complex economic and social situation—as is constantly happening in the political field. One person may devise a more ingenious solution of a difficulty than another. The failures of experts to agree, however, and the occurrence of 'brain waves' are almost certainly due to a deficiency of intelligence and a creativity of imagination and not in any way to the economic background of the individuals.

Thus the conclusion is reached that, while economic change is a basic determinant of the situation in which social change occurs (another determinant being the existing social tradition), these economic and traditional factors do not completely determine the social response, since variations are possible through differences in intellectual and imaginative capacity.

III

THE ROLE OF IDEATION

THE last chapter considered in detail the view commonly held nowadays, that economic and social factors have an important influence on the course of events. The present chapter deals with the much more disputed question of the place and importance of the intellectual or ideational factor. Is the set of ideas held in any society entirely determined by economic and social factors? Is it merely an epiphenomenon? Or, on the other hand, does ideation have an important function—perhaps an indispensable one—in human activity? This last possibility seems to be the one which it is most useful to put in the forefront of this study. The taste of salt in one's mouth is determined by chemical action between a salt solution and certain cells of the tongue, but it is not a mere epiphenomenon; taste gives an organism a rough and ready guide to what is good to eat. Can we similarly indicate a role played by thinking or ideas in the life of human beings, both as individuals and as members of a society?

For the moment nothing will be said about the distorting influence of economic and social factors on a man's view of reality. Men have normally, of course, had some awareness of how economic and social interests prescribed ends for their actions, but they have normally assumed that their view of reality was objective and independent of group or personal interests. Plato hints at a different theory when he makes a cynical character suggest that justice is simply 'the interest of the stronger'; but it has been left to the nineteenth century to call attention to the ideological character of most human thinking. Nowadays it is widely recognized that, for example, in a society whose economy is based on agriculture and where political power is in the hands of the landlords, a view of reality will be current in which excessive importance is attached to property in land and excessive seriousness to a crime like trespassing. Such matters will be considered in the last chapter.

1. THE SOCIAL REFERENCE OF IDEATION: THE MECCAN WARNER

(a) The ideas in Muhammad's Meccan preaching

In the first part of the first section of the previous chapter something was said about the economic and social aspects of Muhammad's

43

Meccan period. Let us now turn to consider the ideational aspect of the new religious movement, that is, the ideas contained in the earliest passages of the Qur'an. It was on the basis of these ideas that Muhammad summoned men to adopt a new way of life. The ideas of the earliest passages of the Qur'an—if we may assume that the dating of modern European scholars is approximately correct—may be summarized under five heads.[1]

(1) God is the creator of everything in the world, including man; He controls all that happens in the world; and He is good.

(2) God raises men again after their deaths and brings them back to Himself on the Last Day to be judged; this judgement is based on their conduct during their lives.

(3) Man is summoned to acknowledge God's power and goodness and to worship Him, and not to rely solely on himself and his wealth.

(4) Man is summoned to act uprightly, and, in particular, to practise generosity and avoid niggardliness.

(5) Muhammad has been sent to his people by God as a 'warner', that is, to warn them about the judgement on the Last Day.

These are the main ideas in what are probably the earliest passages of the Qur'an. They are a positive message, and do not imply that Muhammad had already experienced any opposition. Opposition developed, however, and, as Muhammad deals with it, two other ideas appear in the Qur'anic message.

(6) God is one; idols can avail nothing against Him. At first the idols or pagan gods and goddesses are said to be inferior beings; at a later date they are said to be nothing at all.

(7) God vindicates His prophets, and those who follow them, against their opponents.

(b) The corresponding social programme

The ideas here enumerated led to certain forms of activity. Indeed some of the points were themselves calls to activity. In other cases the ideation led to the activity.

In the fourth point above the Meccans were summoned to certain forms of moral and social activity, in particular, to the practice of generosity. This was directed in the first instance to the merchant princes, and was a call to them to fulfil the obligations of the chief of a tribe or clan, by looking after the interests of the weaker members

[1] Cf. *Muhammad at Mecca*, 62-72. The word Allah is, of course, only the Arabic word for God, used by Christian Arabs as well as Muslims. Cf. 'The use of the word "Allah" in English', *The Muslim World*, xliii (1953) 245-47; Kenneth Cragg, *The Call of the Minaret*, New York, 1956, 35-37.

instead of oppressing them. Muhammad's followers during the Meccan period were not merchant princes, but some of them were moderately well off and (according to the Qur'an, 51.19) 'from their wealth was a share assigned to the beggar and the outcast'. To some extent, then, the early Qur'anic message included an attempt to remedy the evils arising from the unscrupulous money-making of the new mercantile individualism. It would be anachronistic, however, to regard this as similar to modern movements for the bettering of the conditions of the poor. The motivation is rather different. The great Arab *sayyid* of the desert did not look after the poor because he was concerned for the poor but because he was concerned for his own honour. Similarly the Qur'an mostly speaks about what generosity and niggardliness mean for the person who practices them. The call to be generous is a call to return to older attitudes, though in a new individualistic setting. In the practice of giving some of one's wealth there may even be a trace of the very ancient idea that by giving away some, one tended to ensure that one would enjoy what was left.[1] Yet, despite the strangeness to our modern way of thinking of some of the underlying attitudes, the appeal to men to be generous may be regarded as, in part at least, an attempt to deal with some of the social evils of the day.

On the whole, however, Muhammad and the Muslims seem to have been more interested in another form of activity, namely, the public worship and acknowledgement of God. The Muslims had adopted certain new beliefs, but their inward conviction was not yet deeply rooted and was in need of support by outward expression in a communal activity. This was not so distinct from the encouragement of generosity as might at first appear. The Qur'an regards the social troubles of the time as due to a wrong attitude, namely, reliance on wealth and political power and the belief that they control the course of events. Belief in God includes the belief that God controls the course of events and is thus directly opposed to the prevailing humanistic belief. The outward expression in worship of this belief in God will tend to give it and the corresponding attitude deeper roots in those who adopt it.

To begin with there seems to have been no special emphasis placed on the oneness of God, though it was presupposed. This was doubtless because the core of the ideational system that was causing the trouble was materialistic humanism and not the residual pagan religion. Men believed that in certain restricted ways they could obtain help from the pagan gods and goddesses; but the central determinant of their activity was materialistic humanism. In course

[1] Cf. *Muhammad at Mecca*, 168f.

45

of time, however, the pagan religion became involved in the opposition to Muhammad, and he began to attack idolatry and polytheism. It is not clear whether this came about because in the Jewish and Christian traditions belief in God had involved an attack on idolatry or because in the special circumstances of Arabia it proved impossible to attack humanism effectively without also attacking polytheism. When Islam became dominant in Arabia all pagan idols and shrines were destroyed; the Ka'bah and the surrounding area were regarded as a sanctuary of God. This opposition to paganism may be regarded as complementary to the activity of worshipping God.

The most distinctive activity connected with the new ideational system was the preaching implicit in the idea of Muhammad as a 'warner'. Muhammad publicly 'warned' the Meccans that they would be judged by God on the Last Day. At the same time those who believed in the ideas he was proclaiming joined with him in the worship of God. Gradually they came to form a separate association or community. To begin with they were perhaps not distinctly marked off from the rest of the Meccans, but, as opposition to Muhammad grew, his followers became more and more a community apart. They were encouraged to persist in their preaching and worship by the idea that in the past God had vindicated His prophets and their followers against their opponents.

The possibility was mentioned above[1] that the emigration of some of Muhammad's followers to Abyssinia may have been an attempt to break the monopolistic holds of the merchant princes. If so, it presumably aimed at establishing a new trading centre whose communal life would be in accordance with the ideas proclaimed by Muhammad. The whole matter is conjectural, however, and all that can be said is that the migration to Abyssinia could be interpreted as an activity in accordance with Muhammad's ideational system.

(c) *The rival assertions about reality*

Having seen something of the relation between the ideas Muhammad proclaimed and the activities engaged in by himself and his followers, let us proceed to analyse the ideas more deeply and to contrast them with the ideas of his opponents.

At this deeper level the central assertion of the Meccan preaching, contained in the second and fourth points above, may be formulated thus. Reality is such that the significance of a man's life is derived from uprightness in conduct, that is, from the practice of generosity and similar virtues, the avoidance of niggardliness and of oppression

[1] P. 9.

of the weak, and the absence of an undue reliance on human power. This is in strong contrast to the attitude of the merchant princes, whose central belief might be said to be that a man's life is significant when he is wealthy and powerful. The assertion of the Muslims is supported by allegedly historical instances of how God has vindicated the upright against their opponents and by the belief that God has an eternal reward in store for the upright, and eternal punishment for those who are not upright. The merchant princes, on the other hand, probably regarded their assertion as supported by their experience of the exercise of wealth and power. They would derive further support from their contention that death was a complete end; the Qur'an reports them as saying that 'there is nothing but this present life of ours'.[1]

The ideation of the Muslims included a second important assertion, namely, that it was in respect of the conduct of the individual, not of the family or clan, that significance could be given to human life. This was in contrast to the old outlook of the nomadic Arabs, according to which significance belonged essentially to the clan or tribe, and to the individual only as he exemplified the excellences of the clan or tribe. This idea was not prominent among the ideas of the merchant princes, at least as a guide to their activities. Yet it was involved in their thinking in so far as there were aspects of the old outlook of which they could take advantage. Some of the leading Meccan merchants seem also to have been chiefs of their clans and to have made use of the prestige and power which this gave them. Justice and public security in Mecca depended on clan solidarity, as elsewhere in Arabia. Because of this connexion the new religious movement had to oppose the central assertion of the old 'tribal humanism' as well as that of the mercantile individualism.

The conception of the 'warner' also implied an assertion of a fundamental character. This is the assertion that certain men have better knowledge than others of the total circumstances in which human activity takes place (such as the perspective of the Last Day). This knowledge comes to these men (prophets) from supernatural revelation. It follows that, in so far as ordinary activities come within the purview of the prophet, his knowledge of the total circumstances in which these ordinary activities take place is superior to that of other men (such as the merchant princes), and therefore he is able to give them the best advice about how to act. The merchant princes were doubtless aware of this implication of Muhammad's claim to be a 'warner', and rightly saw in it a threat to their control of events through wealth and power. The contrary assertion, presumably made

[1] 45.24/23.

by the merchant princes, would be that activity is most likely to be successful (in an absolute sense) when it is based on human planning.

(d) *The warping of ideation by social involvement*

We have now isolated some of the main features of the opposing ideational systems at Mecca in the years from 610 to 622, namely, those of the merchant princes on the one hand and those of the Muslims on the other hand. Are these ideational systems ideological? Have they been warped by the direction of the two social movements? Or is ideation (as an analysis of the situation) logically prior to the social movement and directive of it? Or is the truth somewhere between these two extremes? Let us consider first the opposition to Muhammad.

Muhammad's opponents cannot strictly speaking be called conservatives. They are not maintaining the state of affairs that had existed in Mecca for centuries. On the contrary, as a result of economic changes, especially the development of commerce along the west coast of Arabia and the gaining of control of this by Mecca, certain changes had taken place; and the opponents of Muhammad, the merchant princes, were taking advantage of these changes to develop monopolies and so to amass wealth and increase their own power. This was something that would have been impossible so long as the old nomadic economy and the corresponding ideational system remained intact. The difference between the merchant princes and the Muslims is thus not between conservatives and reformists or revolutionaries, but between those who were modifying the economic social and ideational system to benefit sectional interests and those who were doing so in the interests of the community as a whole. This is not to say that Muhammad and the Muslims were not moved by sectional interests. The opposite is almost certainly the case. Muhammad was an orphan, that is, relatively 'weak' since he had no father alive; and so he shared to some extent in the experience of the oppressed weak. Moreover his clan of Hashim seems to have been one of those which suffered from the growth of monopolistic practices; and there appears to have been a sense in which the new (primarily religious) movement was a continuation of the (primarily political) Confederation of the Fudul. Despite this, however, the activities of the Muslims did not promote merely their sectional interests but the welfare of the community as a whole in the long run, though of course they threatened the immediate welfare of the merchant princes as these regarded the matter.

The aim of the merchant princes was to retain and, if possible, increase their own wealth and power. This was in line with their assertion of the significance of the exercise of wealth and power, in virtue of which they may be called materialistic individualists. They were materialists since they regarded death as final. They were individualists in that they put their own private interest first, and disregarded tribal solidarity where it suited them; for example, they avoided the irksome duties of looking after the interests of widows and orphans and, instead of providing for them, oppressed them. On the other hand, they upheld tribal solidarity where it subserved their own interests. Each of them was glad to have the support of his clan and the prestige that accrued to him from his position in it. They probably criticized Muhammad because of his unimportance in this respect.[1] Again, one of the guiding principles of nomadic society was to keep to the 'beaten path' followed by earlier generations and not to make any innovations; and we find Muhammad's opponents implying that, while they followed in the steps of their fathers, he was innovating. Muhammad was discredited, too, by the allegation that he was dishonouring the ancestors of his clan (by holding that as pagans they were in hell); and it was this allegation together with the bribes of the merchant princes which towards the end of the Meccan period induced the chief of Muhammad's clan of Hashim, Abu-Lahab, to withdraw 'clan protection' from him. In such ways then, Muhammad's opponents made use of the older nomadic outlook, but their own actions were guided mainly by their materialistic individualism.

Now this materialistic individualism could not be a satisfying creed for a whole community, since all could not have an important degree of wealth and power. In so far as one accepted the beliefs of the merchant princes and was not oneself wealthy or powerful, all one could do to attain a significant life would be to try, by fair means or foul, to increase one's wealth and power. Many men, however, would not even be in a position to begin an attempt to increase their wealth and power. Many would not even have any hope of having a small share of power by becoming henchmen of a merchant prince. Thus materialistic individualism as found in Mecca deprived many Meccans of the chance of attaining a significant life. At the same time, because of the prominence of the merchant princes in the community, it was destroying the older views of what constitutes human significance which were bound up with the nomadic outlook.

There is a certain measure of truth in the views underlying the conduct of the merchant princes. As Meccan society was constituted about the year A.D. 610, wealth gave power, and the men with power

[1] Cf. *Muhammad at Mecca*, 129.

were performing certain functions of importance for the whole community—it must be remembered that the livelihood of Mecca depended entirely on its commerce. Those who have no power see that the wielder of power is free from many of the disadvantages and disabilities of which they are only too conscious in their own lives. They therefore regard wealth and power as highly desirable, and capable of giving man complete satisfaction. In the outlook of the merchant princes and their admirers, however, this truth became warped. They lived in an age of transition where the possibility of great increases of wealth and power had sometimes been realized. They therefore exaggerated the significance of wealth and power, and ascribed an absolute significance to what had only a relative importance. There is here at least a *prima facie* justification for holding that the warping is caused by the social involvement. The class of merchant princes (and those who followed and imitated them) may be regarded as using the assertion of the significance of wealth and power to defend their activity of pursuing them. This question, however, will require to be looked into later.

In a similar way the materialism of the merchant princes is an exaggeration of an obvious fact, namely, the fact that death is the end of man's life in this world. From the standpoint of the monotheistic religions the materialistic view is an exaggeration because—to put the point as abstractly as possible—human life despite its finiteness is capable of having a significance that transcends finitude.[1]

From this consideration of the opponents let us turn to examine the position of Muhammad himself. Muhammad's primary experience was an awareness of a disequilibrium and malaise in contemporary society. Correspondingly his aim at first must simply have been to remove this disequilibrium and malaise. This is essentially a negative aim without any positive content. That is to say, the end is not conceived in such a way as to indicate the means by which it is to be realized. Gradually, however, Muhammad became involved in a programme of activity. The beginning of this was the decision to proclaim publicly, at first to sympathetic friends and later to the whole community, the message he believed he had received from God. This activity of preaching, together with participation in certain new forms of worship, led in course of time to a distinction within Muhammad's tribe between those who accepted his messages and those who rejected them. So long as Muhammad remained at Mecca, the two parties continued in an uneasy 'coexistence'.

[1] In this question objectivity is impossible, since the personal views of the writer and reader are involved. For a statement and defence of the position adopted see Montgomery Watt, *The Reality of God*, London, 1957, 88-92.

The Role of Ideation

Underlying Muhammad's activity there were, as has been seen, three important ideas: the significance of uprightness in conduct (supported by the idea that God controls the historical process), the significance of the individual, and the existence of a transcendental source of knowledge. Can these ideas be said to have been warped by Muhammad's social involvement? The idea of the significance of upright conduct would certainly tend to promote the interests of the clan of Hashim and its allies. In so far, however, as we consider this idea in its application to the Arabia of Muhammad's time and do not think of Islam in its relations to a wider geographical context and to its rival religions of Judaism and Christianity, the idea appears to be true, even if the conception of upright conduct is somewhat narrow. Upright conduct, besides being (as we are taking for granted) of ultimate significance, was shown by Muhammad's success to be a suitable basis for a society from which disequilibrium and malaise had been removed. Thus in its immediate context the idea appears to be free from warping. It is not so easy, however, to hold the same of the complementary idea of the divine control of the historical process. There would seem to be some exaggeration here. It is not true that believers in God are always successful and unbelievers always failures. By holding an exaggerated view of God's control of events, Muhammad became involved in serious theological difficulties after his partial discomfiture at Uhud; and, had he not often been very lucky, the exaggerated character of the idea might have been even more obvious.

The idea of the significance of the individual also contains an element of exaggeration. This is doubtless only natural in a society which is just emerging from a high degree of communalism. In any case, Islam was not preaching individualism as a gospel, but was merely accepting the fact that individualism was growing, and on this basis providing a sanction for upright conduct (in the conception of the Last Day). The aim of Muhammad's preaching and later political activity was to prevent individualism going to excesses and producing oppression. The conception that the individual had the sole ultimate responsibility for his acts (and would be rewarded or punished on the Last Day) was an exaggeration as applied to Muhammad's own time since in many respects the kinship-group was still functioning; but it was an exaggeration that did not affect the relevance of the conception of the individual to the contemporary situation.

Similarly there is an exaggeration in the conception of a transcendent source of knowledge, yet the idea was fruitful and effective in its immediate application. It was necessary to have an authoritative

51

basis for the new ideational system that was to replace the existing one. It is difficult to see how anything other than revelation from God could have met this need. The idea contained an element of exaggeration, however, in that it claimed—or appeared to claim—that revelation gave knowledge which was also accessible by normal means (e.g. knowledge of historical events or of the desirability of political actions). During Muhammad's lifetime the claim to have revelational knowledge of historical events led to criticisms by the Jews which it was difficult to refute, and in the centuries since his death it has been a frequent cause of dispute. The conception of revelation also involved a merging of religion and politics since what were (on a Western view) properly political decisions were given a religious basis. Such decisions, however, came to an end on Muhammad's death, at least so far as regards the Sunnites, because the caliphs did not claim divine inspiration for their decisions.

The ideas, then, that are found in Muhammad's preaching contain exaggerations, and to that extent are not wholly true. Their exaggerations, however, do not affect their efficacy as bases for the transformation of Arabian society. They are genuinely 'utopian' (in Karl Mannheim's sense), and in this respect true. To put it in another way, they are the ideational complement of a social movement which led to a transformation of Arabian society; and we adopt the standpoint that this new organization of society was better than the old, and more harmonious and better adjusted to the environment. It is thus not appropriate in this case to say that social forces 'warped' the ideas. The question ought to be put somewhat differently, namely: Can these ideas be said to have been in any sense produced or determined by the social movement with which they are connected?

Muhammad's primary experience, it has been asserted above, must have been one of the malaise and disequilibrium and disharmony in Meccan society. This awareness of evil may be said to have determined an end for Muhammad's activity, namely, that of trying to remove the evil; (in a sense these are two aspects of the same thing). The acceptance of this end, however, does not prescribe any particular course of action. Various courses of action have to be considered, and it may be the case that of the courses of action which have suggested themselves to a man none is very satisfactory. In Muhammad's case the beginning of activity was the public proclamation of certain assertions. (Neither the fact that Muhammad believed this course of action to have been suggested to him by divine inspiration nor the possibility that the underlying ideas were derived from the human environment need be taken into account here, since the occurrence of the suggestion must have been followed by approval of it on his part and the decision to put into practice). For Muhammad to engage in such activity further presupposes that he had some general awareness of the ideas he was going to proclaim and approved of them. That is to say, there had been suggested to him the picture of a society based on these ideas instead of on the ideas on which contemporary Meccan society was based, and he had approved this picture of a transformed society. Perhaps one should also say that along with this approval of the picture and the ideational system there went a resolve to try to realize the picture; if that is so, there is no priority of ideation here, but ideation and activity (or at least the resolve to act) remain complementary. Can it be said that Muhammad's social involvement produced this ideational system in him?

It is possible to see vaguely in the abstract a mechanism by which a certain social situation could produce certain ideas. Awareness of evils in the situation in which one is involved might produce the idea of a state of society in which those evils were absent, and in some cases at least it might be possible to frame a positive picture of this state of society. In actual historical cases, however, the matter is seldom so simple, since many ideas are already present in the environment, so that the picture of a transformed society does not arise solely from the existing situation but owes something to the ideas already present and the earlier experiences which these enshrine. Thus Muhammad doubtless had some idea of the basis of society in the Byzantine empire. It would therefore seem that we must renounce the attempt to show that there is a simple causal connexion between a man's social situation and the ideas which occur to him. What we can say, however, is that once one or more ideas have been suggested to a man (however that has come about), his social involvement leads him to approve and act upon the set of ideas which promises to bring about the most satisfactory adjustment to the existing situation.

The relation of ideation to social change would thus in one respect be similar to the relation of social to economic change. When a social change has taken place and there is a situation of disequilibrium and disharmony, a new ideational system (with the corresponding activity) is not in any way mechanically dictated to the people in the situation; but the existing social situation does in a sense compel them to accept, probably out of several alternatives, that complex of ideation and activity which promises to do most to remedy the evils of which they are aware.

It may be objected here that Muhammad did not approve of the idea of the significance of upright conduct because he thought it would lead to a more satisfactory organization of society, but because he thought it was true. This is a difficult question to answer, and will have to be dealt with in the closing section of this chapter. The following remarks may serve as a preliminary approach to the difficulty. In dealing with matters which transcend sense-experience —for example, in assertions such as 'upright conduct is of ultimate significance', 'God controls the course of events so that those who believe in Him are vindicated in the end'—we simply 'see' the truth of assertions, or fail to 'see' it, or 'see' that something contradictory is true. We cannot justify such 'intuitions' or employ any objective criterion of their truth. (We have our subjective criteria, of course; for example, a man may believe an assertion because it is believed by persons whose judgement he trusts, or because it has psychological accompaniments which he believes in general to guarantee its truth). Further, study of people's 'intuitions' shows that in certain cases there is a constant correlation with external circumstances. For example, the exaggeration in Muhammad's belief that God vindicated prophets might be regarded as a compensation for his weakness and the apparent hopelessness of his cause during the later Meccan period; it has frequently been observed that where there was weakness there was a tendency to exaggerate a possible source of strength. Thus observation of people shows correlations between what they believe to be true and their material, social and psychological situation. We cannot explain this, but can merely note that this is so. It follows that, though a man believes something to be true because he 'sees' it to be so, that does not prevent us, as observers, from regarding his belief as, in some sense and to some extent, socially conditioned.

(e) *The function of the ideation of the Meccan period*

The above investigations suggest the view that there is a certain parallelism of activity and ideation, and this view will be defended in theoretical discussions at the close of the chapter. Meanwhile let it be noticed that from such a view it might be deduced that ideation is without any important function, and is comparable to the red light which goes on when an electrical device is in operation to indicate that this is so but which makes no contribution to the working of the electrical device. Are Muhammad's ideas thus mere otiose complements of his activities, or have they some function that makes them indispensable?

We remember that there are various situations when men act without thinking things out. There are two chief types of such situations: where basic personal relations are involved (including the relations of a man to his environment as a whole); and where simple physical situations have to be dealt with (as in volleying at tennis). We also remember that there are situations which cannot be dealt with except by thinking things out; for example, the phenomena considered in Einstein's theory of relativity. In the latter situations ideation, or the conscious thinking out of things, is necessary because the phenomena are complex and far removed from primitive human experience. This is not so, however, in the social situations with which Muhammad had to deal. What was the specific function of ideation there?

Before giving a direct answer to this question let us notice that Muhammad could not have inaugurated a reform so long as he continued to accept the ideational system of the merchant princes. (It may be, of course, that he never accepted it, but regarded it as a break away from the nomadic outlook; if so, the argument could be applied to the nomadic outlook instead). On the basis of the system of materialistic individualism all Muhammad could have done was to try to increase his wealth and power, and that of those who associated with him. Such a movement, if successful, would have led to a transfer of power, but not to any general reform of society which would have removed the malaise from which it was suffering. In other words, there is a close relation between a particular ideational system and a particular organization of society. The organization of society cannot be fundamentally changed on the basis of the corresponding ideational system. Hence, if to remedy certain evils a fundamental change in social organization is necessary, this must be based on or correlated with a new ideational system.

It also seems clear, however, that the change may be inaugurated before there is any explicit awareness of the new ideational system. Muhammad began to receive revelations and to communicate them to others without realizing all the implications of what he was doing.[1] The Qur'an bids him say he is 'only a warner', that is, the bearer of a religious message about the certainty of judgement, without any claim to special authority in political matters. No doubt this was genuinely how he felt ; yet in course of time it became clear that his transcendent source of knowledge was relevant also to the political sphere. From this it is seen that an explicit ideational system is not

---

[1] One distinct stage was probably when he realized that his revelations were identical in content with those of the Jews and the Christians. The identification is said to have been first made by a cousin of his wife's ; but, even if the story is not true, the belief in identity with the Judaeo-Christian tradition certainly was present from an early period.

necessary in order to make adequate responses to social situations, at least in so far as a single individual is concerned.

Social changes, however, imply many individuals. Here an ideational system is usually necessary. It is not absolutely impossible for there to be a social movement without ideation. Similar circumstances may lead many people to similar responses without any ideation held in common. This is unusual, however, and is not what is generally meant by a social movement. In the latter there is normally some conscious co-operation between individuals, and such co-operation is only possible where there is ideation. Thus ideation is necessary where men are to co-operate. Muhammad's bid to remedy the social evils of his time could not have succeeded unless he had brought other men to follow him, and this was impossible unless what he proclaimed was (or involved) an ideational system. From this we conclude that the function—or at least *a* function— of ideation is to make it possible for a large number of men to co-operate consciously.

Just as Muhammad himself began to respond to the circumstances of the time before he was fully aware of the ideas underlying his actions, so those who followed him on the basis of the ideational system he first proclaimed gradually (and mainly through the guidance of the Qur'an) became more explicitly aware of the ideas implicit in this response of theirs to the contemporary situation. Thus to begin with they appear to have been satisfied with a vague monotheism not sharply marked off from polytheism, but later they adopted a strict monotheism and opposed polytheistic practices. It should perhaps also be allowed that the later ideational system is not merely the earlier made more explicit and definite, but contains modifications of the earlier one which contradict it in matters of detail.[1]

One might also ask whether an ideational system could contribute to the life of an individual. When self-consciousness grows, a man wants to see the significance of the main activities of his life; and this significance becomes visible to him when he sees his life in a cosmic setting. In Muhammad's case the idea that his special work was to proclaim to the Arabs a message which other men, namely, prophets, had previously proclaimed to other nations may have given him a measure of self-confidence. In general one might say that a man is readier to carry out a course of action which suggests itself to him when he sees that it has adequate ideational support.

[1] The development of the ideational system will be further discussed later, especially in chapter vii.

The Role of Ideation

THE SOCIAL REFERENCE OF IDEATION: THE MEDINAN STATESMAN

(a) Ideational developments

Muhammad's move or Hijrah from Mecca to Medina in 622 led to a complete change in his social and political position. In Mecca he had been weak and persecuted, but in Medina he was one of the six or eight leading men in the community, and indeed had a primacy of honour over the others from the first, while in course of time he became unquestioned ruler of the Medinan state. Along with this change in Muhammad's position went certain developments in the ideational system he proclaimed.

The idea of 'warner' is developed into that of *rasul Allah*, 'the messenger or apostle of God'. (It should be noted that, though it is normal in European languages to refer to Muhammad as 'the prophet', for which the Arabic is *nabi*, this is not the standard way of referring to him by Muslims; it is at approximately the same level as 'warner'.) The *rasul* is someone who has been sent, in this case sent by God, either to convey a message or to carry out some commission. As messenger of God Muhammad was to be arbiter in disputes between the various kinship-groups in Medina.[1] He also stood in relation to the group of Emigrants in much the same relation as a clan-chief to his clan. Perhaps it was as chief of the Emigrants that Muhammad was recognized as leader in war of the Medinan Muslims; on the other hand the Medinans may have understood leadership in war as being involved in his position as messenger of God, since it was mainly war against the Meccans that they were thinking of at first, and the Meccans had persecuted Muhammad on account of his preaching. This position as arbiter and military leader was far from being that of an absolute autocrat. After Muhammad's military successes against the Meccans and various hostile nomadic tribes, however, he was gradually able to strengthen his position until at his death in 632 he was undisputed head of the Medinan state with its many dependent tribes throughout Arabia. Naturally the idea of 'the messenger of God' developed with the actual development of Muhammad's powers and responsibilities. The political relevance of his transcendent source of knowledge thus became realized in practice.

An idea which underlies many of the social and political developments of the Medinan period is that of the *ummah*, which may be translated 'religious community'. The idea appears in the Qur'an towards the close of the Meccan period, and is probably complementary to Muhammad's attempts, in view of his failure to make

[1] *Qur'an*, 10.47/48; cf. *Muhammad at Medina*, 229ff., and p.20 above.

further progress at Mecca, to find some other way of advancing the cause of reform. He had originally thought of a prophet as being sent to his 'people' or 'tribe,' in accordance with the older conception of tribal solidarity. The rejection of his message by the Meccans, however, made some revision of this idea necessary. So the *ummah* comes to be that section, out of the people to whom a messenger is sent, who accepts his message. An *ummah* is thus a community whose basis is not kinship but religion, namely, the common acceptance of a message and a messenger.

The conception of the *ummah* with its religious basis seems to involve a denial of the high significance attached to kinship in the ideational system associated with the nomadic economy. We commonly speak of those who made the Hijrah from Mecca to Medina with Muhammad as 'Emigrants' and so bring in a geographical connotation, but to the Arab the primary aspect of the Hijrah was probably that of separation from one's kinship-group. It was important, too, for the Meccan Emigrants in Medina in the years after 622 that the significance of kinship should be minimized, since they were engaged in a war against their kinsmen and sometimes, as at the battle of Badr in 624, had to meet them in battle. The importance of kinship, however, was too deeply rooted in the Arab outlook for it to be eradicated so easily. The document known as the Constitution of Medina says that all the Muslims in Medina from a single *ummah*, but this same document could be regarded as a treaty of alliance according to the old principles between nine main kinship-groups and a number of dependent groups, and the kinship-groups still have important functions to play in the maintenance of security.[1] Later in Muhammad's lifetime, after the capture of Mecca and the reconciliation of the Meccans, the need to minimize the importance of kinship ceased. Under the Umayyad dynasty (661-750) kinship regained some of its importance,[2] but with the 'Abbasids the religious basis of the political community was reaffirmed.

It may be noted here that the *ummah* was in some ways conceived as a tribe. In forming alliances with friendly tribes and in waging war against hostile tribes the *ummah* acts in much the same way as a tribe. As strong tribes gave protection to weaker groups (for a money payment or other consideration), so the *ummah* gives protection to non-Muslim groups, provided they are not pagan; and this principle is the basis of the toleration of non-Muslim minorities in Muslim states and the granting to them of internal autonomy. Similarly, just as the chief of a tribe received a quarter of the spoils taken by the

[1] Ib. 221-5, 247f. Cf. p. 19 above.
[2] Cf. p. 97 below.

tribe on raids, so Muhammad, and later the caliphs, received a fifth of the spoils captured by Muslim armies on official expeditions. That the *ummah* was thus conceived on the analogy of a tribe does not, of course, indicate a persistence of the principle of kinship; it merely means that there was no other type of political unit familiar to the Arabs, since they knew so little of the empires round them that they pictured these as administered in much the same way as large tribes.[1]

Besides the ideas of the messenger and the *ummah* a third idea seems to have been influential in the formation of the Islamic state, though it is not so clearly and explicitly present in the Qur'an and the other sources. This is the idea of the Arabs as a unity distinct from other peoples.[2] The basis of the unity is primarily language, but the groups whose native language was Arabic were also thought of as connected genealogically.[3] The idea of the geographical unit of the Arabian peninsula—the 'island of the Arabs' as it is called in Arabic —may also have been present in a subordinate role, especially after Muhammad's death, as, for example, when the caliph 'Umar (634-44) expelled all Jews from the Hijaz. Even before Muhammad's time, of course, Arabic-speaking tribes had spread far beyond the bounds of the Arabian peninsula, and many families had adopted a settled life, particularly in Syria. In some sense of the term 'Arabs', however, Muhammad seems to have come to think of himself as sent not merely to the Meccans or Medinans but to the Arabs as a whole.

(b) The new social and political programme

The first main task which confronted Muhammad when he went to Medina was the integration of Medinan society. This meant particularly the healing of the breach between the two main Arab tribes of the Aws and the Khazraj, but Muhammad also hoped at one time to include the Jewish groups. The effective factor in this integration was Muhammad's presence in Medina and his acceptance as prophet or messenger. The religious basis of his authority and prestige set him above the conflict of the rival kinship-groups and made him an acceptable arbiter in disputes, while his tact and statesmanship also contributed to the success of this policy. He was careful, too, to maintain his impartiality. His great-grandmother had belonged to

---

[1] Similarly the practice of 'brothering' sometimes employed by Muhammad and the Muslims (*Muhammad at Medina*, 249) is the application of a term indicating kinship to a practice where kinship is not involved.

[2] Cf. *Muhammad at Medina*, 143.

[3] In *two* vast families, not one.

the Medinan clan of an-Najjar, and he built his house in the area occupied by this clan; but he gave them no special privileges. He also avoided marrying any Medinan woman.

The idea of the significance of upright conduct was, of course, prominent in the details of administration. As an illustration of this one might cite the Qur'anic rules for inheritance.[1] Oppression was liable to occur in matters of inheritance when strong individuals appropriated for themselves what would normally have been used communally. The purpose of the Qur'anic rules is to ensure as far as possible that those who would have benefited from the deceased's estate under the old communal system received a fair share of what he left.

Another part of the programme at Medina was hostility towards Mecca. It is not clear whether this was planned before Muhammad left Mecca. It may well have been so, since otherwise it is difficult to see how his Meccan followers proposed to gain a livelihood. It is also possible, however, that they found after they had been a few months in Medina that they were being throttled by the Meccan grip on the trade of the Hijaz. Certainly Muhammad had not been long at Medina before he began to send out small expeditions to attack Meccan caravans and in general to provoke the Meccans to active operations against him. This was in accordance with the ideational basis of the Medinan state in the acknowledgement of Muhammad as messenger, since the Meccans had rejected his message and persecuted his followers. Muhammad may also have considered that his chances of restoring harmony to Medina were greater if the attention of the inhabitants was focussed on an external enemy. Hostility to enemies and opponents was always less important to Muhammad than the achievement of his positive aims, such as the building up of a community on the principles he preached. One of the most impressive features of his later years is the extent to which he succeeded in reconciling former opponents and even in some cases turning them into devoted Muslims. At least from the time of the raising of the siege of Medina in 627 he was thinking chiefly of how to win over the Meccans to his side, probably because he realized that their administrative skill would be required as the new Islamic body-politic grew.

A third aspect of the programme of Muhammad at Medina was the unification of Arabia. Again it is not clear how this idea came to Muhammad. Perhaps it was his failure at Mecca that made him look to a wider field. Certainly, while he was still at Mecca he is said to have approached nomadic tribes living some distance from Mecca;

[1] Cf. *Muhammad at Medina*, 289-93.

and this looks as if he now regarded his mission as being to the Arabs as a whole. If the idea did not come to him before the Hijrah, the favourable course of his struggle with the Meccans would show him that a large measure of unification was possible. Naturally this unification had to take place on Islamic principles. This was secured by insisting that those who adhered to the new state—or perhaps we should say 'federation'—should acknowledge Muhammad as messenger of God. In his early years at Medina this condition was probably sometimes omitted, and even in his last years it may have been omitted in the case of strong tribes whom he was anxious to have as allies. The corollary of this religious basis of the state or confederation was that its wars were regarded as holy wars. The idea of the *jihad* or holy war seems to have developed gradually during the Medinan period. *Jihad* properly means 'striving' or 'the exerting of effort', and is thus contrasted with the attitude of some of the Medinan Muslims in Muhammad's closing years, when they wanted to sit back and enjoy the fruits of victory.

(c) *Social involvement and ideation*

It remains to ask (as was done at greater length in the previous section) whether these ideas show any traces of having been exaggerated or otherwise warped as a result of Muhammad's social involvement.

The most likely example of warping in the Medinan period seems to be the idea of *jihad*. The raiding of other tribes was the normal practice, almost the sport, of the nomads. Muhammad must have realized that the tribes in alliance with him could not be kept at peace with one another unless he provided some outlet for the energies that would normally have been expended in mutual raiding. He therefore encouraged them to direct raids against tribes hostile to himself, or at least not in alliance with him. As the prospect of a federation embracing most of the tribes of Arabia came within the range of practical politics, Muhammad also realized that there would eventually be little scope for *jihad* within Arabia and that the Muslims must therefore think of breaking out towards Syria or 'Iraq. Apart from his hostilities with the Meccans the largest expeditions he sent out were those along the route to Syria, beginning with one of a thousand men in August 626 and culminating with the great expedition to Tabuk in the closing months of 630 which is said to have involved 30,000 men. There were thus reasons of a material nature for Muhammad's developing the idea of expeditions against non-members of his alliance in the surrounding lands. Moreover, such

The Role of Ideation

expeditions, especially after Muhammad was seen to be a successful leader, attracted men to him for the sake of the booty to be obtained.

Despite the existence of these strong social and political reasons for the adoption of the practice and conception of the *jihad*, that is not a complete account of the matter. Muhammad took over from the nomadic Arabs the practice of raiding expeditions, but he employed it in such a way that it contributed to the building up of a community on Qur'anic, that is, religious principles. Thus the raiding expeditions were for the sake of a religiously-based community against its enemies. who were presumably opponents of its religion, so that in an important sense these expeditions constituted a religious war. Further, Muhammad's expeditions were not a mere imitation of the nomadic expeditions owing to the fact that they were sub-servient to a far-reaching strategy such as was never found even when a strong leader of nomads built up a great confederacy. The difference appeared after the expeditions had been successful and the opponents sued for terms. Muhammad won men's support by leniency on the appropriate occasion, but he also insisted that he should be acknowledged as messenger of God and that the Islamic worship or prayers should be performed. In this way he created a community that included most of the Arabs and which eventually spread over a large part of the world.

So far as dating goes it appears that Muhammad adopted the practice of raiding expeditions long before he exhorted his followers to 'the expenditure of effort, *jihad*, in the way of God'. The activity of fighting has a clear priority over the idea. The idea is introduced in order to link up the practice with the basic ideational system of the Muslims, and so to strengthen their motives for participating in expeditions.[1] This presupposes that at least many of the Muslims genuinely accepted the ideational system. There are thus no grounds for holding that the social context has warped the idea of *jihad* and presented materialistic raiding activities under the guise of a holy war. The chief motives of many of the participants in the raids may indeed have been materialistic, but in the minds of those who directed them they belonged to a strategy aimed at building up a community on a religious basis, and the leaders and not a few of their followers accepted the ideational system associated with this strategy. Under these circumstances the idea of *jihad* in the way of God is not a piece of ideology, since it does not try to justify or make respectable a state of affairs that is socially bad and undesirable. In itself this idea is not even utopian, since it describes actual practices, but the ideational system with which it is connected has utopian elements. (The view

[1] See Additional Note, p.65ff.

that the idea of *jihad* is warped or ideological could only be justified on the supposition that the whole movement of Islamic expansion under Muhammad and later is the product of materialistic motives; it should not be necessary at this stage of the argument to show that such a supposition is untenable).

The ideas of the integration of the Medinan community (and the restoration of harmony) and of the unification of the Arabs went far beyond existing conditions, but they were genuinely utopian, and were to a considerable extent realized by Muhammad. It might be alleged that he exaggerated the religious basis of the new community, since in the early years he was ready to make alliances with pagans—a practice that was not in conformity with the ideational basis of the community. This allegation is not altogether fair. It seems to demand that Muhammad should have applied his ideas in a rigid doctrinaire way. He applied his ideas as a statesman dealing with real forces. He did not say: Those who accept what I preach are on my side, and all other men are enemies. His end as a statesman was the fostering of a religiously-based community, and alliances with friendly pagans were not contrary to this end. The point to be noticed here is the limitation of the function of ideation. An ideational system does not direct all the activity of an individual or society from the moment of its adoption, but only gradually extends its sway over the various aspects of that activity.

Muhammad's idea of including the Jews in the Medinan community was a sound idea in some ways. How different the world would have been had he managed to realize it! He failed to do so, however, largely because he did not understand the differences between the contents of the Qur'an and of the Jewish scriptures. He thought that his message was identical with that of Abraham and Moses (which is in a sense true), but was unaware of the particular ways in which theism had been developed in Judaism and of the associated social tradition of the Jews. Muhammad's failure is thus in part due to an inadequate knowledge of the relevant circumstances. It may also be asked, however, whether there was not something ideological in the refusal of the majority of the Medinan Jews to acknowledge a Gentile prophet. It looks as if a case could be made out for holding that they made use of religious ideas in order to maintain their worldly position; they had once dominated the Medinan oasis, and some probably hoped to recover that position of dominance.

The leader of the opposition to Muhammad at Medina during the first five years or so of the Islamic era was 'Abdallah ibn-Ubayy, the man who, but for the coming of Muhammad, might have become king of Medina. He became a Muslim, but acted patronizingly

63

towards Muhammad. Before the Hijrah he had shown less harshness and more statesmanship than some of the other Medinan leaders, and he had cultivated the friendship of some of the Jews; but he had no clear ideational system on which to base his reorganization of the Medinan community,[1] or at least, if he had one, our sources are too scanty to enable us to understand it. The same holds of various other groups of opponents at Medina.

(d) The necessity of ideational change

Let us now go on to ask whether the social changes effected by Muhammad could have been brought about without so far-reaching an ideational change, and let us consider first of all the restoration of harmony at Medina. On the basis of existing ideas it would have been difficult to produce real harmony at Medina. A strong man could presumably have attained supreme power, especially if he showed consideration for the interests of the weaker members of the community; but from his former opponents there would probably always have been some who were dissatisfied with his rule and hoping to supplant him. A measure of harmony could doubtless have been reached in this way, yet in the reaching of it there would have been certain ideational changes (for example, some recognition of locality as a basis of community), and there would have been further changes in the course of time. The disadvantages of such a form of integration were largely obviated by the ideational basis of Muhammad's activity. While 'Abd-Allah ibn-Ubayy was certainly jealous of Muhammad's success, the fact that Muhammad's authority was based on religion and not on kinship or wealth made it easier for him ultimately to overcome his jealousy. The idea of a community based on religion to which both belonged would also make it easier for the Aws and the Khazraj to forget their quarrel. The process was undoubtedly helped, of course, by Muhammad's military successes, which directed the attention of the Medinans outwards.

While for the restoration of harmony at Medina an ideational change may have been desirable but not absolutely necessary, for the unification of the Arabs and their subsequent expansion an ideational change was indispensable.[2] If the Arabs were to constitute a single

[1] The remark attributed to him by Ibn-Hisham, ed. Wüstenfeld, 726, that the Muslims are 'our rivals in power and number (or influence) in our land' perhaps shows that he saw that the community must be thought of as a *local* one; but this is at most only a facet of an ideational system.

[2] Cf. Montgomery Watt, 'Ideal Factors in the Origin of Islam', *Islamic Quarterly*, ii (1955/1375) 160-74, where the argument of this paragraph is stated in greater detail.

body politic, then according to traditional ideas this might be based on either kinship or alliance. Even if the genealogists, by going sufficiently far back, could have produced a common ancestor of all the Arabs, the bond thus created would have been very weak compared with men's loyalty to their tribes and families and would have snapped under any serious strain. Again, though before Islam there had been some great confederacies in Arabia, centred in a dominant personality, these also became more difficult to hold together the larger they became. Thus there are difficulties of a practical kind in conceiving Arab unity according to traditional ideas.

The crux of the difficulties is in the conception of the leader or ruler of the body politic. The head of a tribe was regarded merely as *primus inter pares*, expected to consult his fellow-tribesmen before important decisions, and with only limited powers of command. Such a conception of leadership would have been unworkable if applied to a union of all the Arabs. The position of the head of a confederacy was perhaps a little better, but not much; moreover, he had to contend with the jealousy of rivals who had once been more or less equal with him. The Arabs were also familiar with the idea of the king or prince who was above his subjects, and could give orders to them, but they hated this idea.

The unsuitability of these ideas as a basis for Arab unity was removed by the new Islamic ideation. Instead of the large kinship-group or the confederacy there was the *ummah*, the religiously-based community, which could be regarded as a confederacy, but which was able to evoke, at least in some of those who belonged to it, much deeper feelings of loyalty than could ever have been called out by any normal confederacy. Likewise the conception of 'the messenger of God' provided the *ummah* with a leader whose authority extended farther than that of the tribal chief and rested on a unique religious basis which placed him beyond the reach of any rival.[1] Without this ideational scheme the unification of Arabia and the expansion into the surrounding lands could not have come about.

Note on 'Jihad'

The verb *ja:hada* means to 'strive' or to 'expend effort', and its verbal noun *jiha:d* properly means 'striving' or 'the expending of effort'.[2] *Jiha:d* occurs four times in the Qur'an and other forms of the verb

---

[1] It is noteworthy in this connexion that those who attempted, shortly before and after Muhammad's death, to assert their independence of the Medinan government also claimed to be prophets.

[2] In this note colons are used to indicate long vowels.

thirty-one times, while there is one occurrence of *juhd* meaning 'effort'. There are two similar verses (29.8/7; 31.15/14) which tell a man not to obey his parents if they 'exert pressure on' (*ja:hada:*) him to worship idols. Otherwise all the usages of the words are with reference to taking part in razzias or expeditions. Sometimes 'strive' is used without qualification, but frequently the phrase is 'striving in the way of God' or 'striving with goods and person' or a combination of the two. The word was apparently applied first of all to the activities of the Emigrants. Two verses (8.72/73, 74/75) distinguish the Emigrants from the Medinan Muslims, referring to the former as 'those who believed and emigrated and strove with goods and person in the way of God' and to the latter as 'those who gave shelter and help'; another verse (16.110/111) speaks of 'those who emigrated after being persecuted and strove and bore (hardships) patiently' (*ja:hadu: wa-sabaru:*). This is in accordance with the traditional view that the expedition to Badr was the first in which the Medinan Muslims took part.[1] The command, 'O believers, fear God . . . and strive in His way' (5.35/39), which Richard Bell thinks is early Medinan, may be intended to encourage the Medinans to join the Emigrants on their expeditions. Many of the usages of the word belong to the closing periods of Muhammad's life when he insisted that *jiha:d* was a duty for all able-bodied male Muslims, although some considered that their victories should have allowed them to take things easily.

The use of *ja:hada* without qualification, especially in 16.110/111, seems to make it clear that the practice of raiding (or whatever it may have been) was established before it was thought of as being 'in the way of God'. It must be borne in mind, too, that, if the hypothesis of revisions of the text by Muhammad is accepted, the words 'in the way of God' could have been added in his later years to some of the passages where they now stand. Where striving is not 'in the way of God', it is presumably on a level with other activities such as emigrating and enduring hardship. On the other hand, if 5.35/39, apparently addressed to all believers, is intended to encourage the Medinans to join the expeditions, it is appropriate that the words 'in the way of God' should be added, to reinforce their secular motives with a religious one.

Finally, attention may be called to two passages which speak of 'striving in (respect of) God', where the reference is not necessarily to fighting or going on expeditions, though the Muslim commentators take it in this way. One (29.69) follows a verse which speaks of men inventing falsehood about God and denying His revelations, and

[1] Cf. *Muhammad at Medina*, 3.

so could conceivably mean 'insist on the truth of God's revelations' and could be Meccan. The other (22.78/77) which commands the believers to 'strive in (respect of) God worthily of Him,' is very general and need not refer to campaigning; but it is probably close in time and meaning to 5.35/39, and may have the same implications.

Apparently, then, the Emigrants started going on expeditions without any revealed command to do so, and this was referred to as 'striving' or 'expending effort'; when it seemed desirable that the Medinan Muslims should join them, the activity was brought into connexion with religious ideation by being called 'striving in the way of God'.

3. THE SOCIAL REFERENCE OF IDEATION: THE ASSASSINS

The points at present being considered may be further illustrated by an instance of a rather different kind from a later period of Islamic history, namely the development of the Nizari branch of the Isma'ili movement in 'Iraq and Persia from about 1050 to 1250. This is the religious and political community usually known as 'the Assassins'. There is much in its history that is still obscure, but the increasing agreement among scholars about the broad outlines should suffice as a basis for the present discussion.[1] Certain theological materials enable us to give a tolerably full account of the ideas of the community during the main phases.

The Isma'ili movement is itself a branch of the Shi'ah or Shi'ites (about whom more will be said in the next chapter). About 909 some adherents of this movement established a small state in Tunisia, of which the rulers came to be known as the Fatimid dynasty. The small state prospered until in 969 it conquered Egypt. Shortly afterward it founded Cairo and transferred its capital thither. Unlike most previous Muslim dynasties hostile to the orthodox caliphate the Fatimids claimed the caliphate for themselves, that is, a certain headship and primacy among all Muslims. This claim, as the Fatimids understood it, was in fact a claim to sovereignty over all Muslims. In support of this claim the Fatimids sent agents to carry on underground propaganda throughout the Islamic world and particularly in the areas which still acknowledged the 'Abbasid caliphate of Baghdad.[2] In the latter areas a large underground revolutionary

[1] The most important works used for this section are Bernard Lewis, *The Origins of Isma'ilism*, Cambridge, 1940 and M.G.S. Hodgson, *The Order of Assassins: the Struggle of the early Nizari Isma'ilis against the Islamic World*, 's-Gravenhage, 1955.

[2] E.g. Ibn al-Athir, *Kamil*, under 436 A.H. (*Al-Kamil fi't-Ta'rikh*, Cairo, n.d., viii. 39f.): this corresponds to 1044/5.

movement appears to have been built up. Three phases of this movement will be specially considered here, namely (*a*) the establishment of a state by Hasan ibn-as-Sabbah about 1090, (*b*) the era of the Qiyamah, 1164-1210, and (*c*) the reconciliation with the Sunnites, from 1210 until about 1250.

(a) *The work of Hasan ibn-as-Sabbah*

Hasan ibn-as-Sabbah comes to the fore as leader of the Isma'ili movement in Iran with the seizure of the fortress of Alamut in 1090. For a decade or two before this he had apparently been prominent in the movement but in subordinate positions. With the change over from underground organization to open revolution he seems to have come to the supreme direction of affairs. The revolt prospered to the extent of seizing and holding a line of fortresses in mountainous territory, but it failed to overthrow the rule of the Seljuq sultans (at this time the dominant power in the 'Abbasid caliphate). Nevertheless an independent regime was set up which maintained itself in being until the capture of Alamut by the Mongols in 1256.

The adoption of this new policy of open revolt by the Iranian Isma'ilis seems to be related to the contemporary situation. Fatimid propaganda had appealed to various depressed and discontented groups.[1] It presumably promised them redress of their grievances by the victory of the Fatimids over their actual rulers. This was a message of hope so long as there was a reasonable chance of the Fatimids expanding eastwards from Syria (which was also part of their dominions). They actually occupied Baghdad for a few months in 1056-7. By about 1078, however, when al-Hasan is said to have visited Egypt, it must have been clear to shrewd observers that Fatimid power was declining and that there was now no likelihood of their extending their frontiers eastward. At the same time the Seljuq sultans were consolidating their power in 'Iraq and Iran, especially during the viziership of Nizam-al-Mulk from 1065 to 1092, and their general policy was to favour Sunnites at the expense of Shi'ites. In these circumstances al-Hasan and his friends may well have thought that it was a case of 'now or never'. If they did not act publicly in the near future, the Isma'ili movement, which had been growing up for a century and was now of a considerable size, would begin to wither away. Al-Hasan therefore spent the years between 1078 and 1090 in travelling about the region and preparing for revolt.

The period from the seizure of Alamut in 1090 until about 1105

[1] Lewis, *Origins of Isma'ilism*, 92f.

may be regarded as a period of Isma'ili successes, while from 1106 until 1118 their fortunes were declining.[1] When one considers the whole area of the 'Abbasid caliphate, however, the extent of their success is not impressive. They held a number of castles in mountainous country and these served as bases, but they did not manage to gain any important town.[2] This is strange in view of the numerous adherents of the Isma'ili movement in the towns. It seems to mean that the armed revolt was the work of mountaineers or of bands of rough adventurers of a similar type, though al-Hasan himself was an intellectual. Moreover the Isma'ilis do not seem to have attempted to put a large army in the field to meet the Seljuq armies. Apart from their guerrilla tactics they employed the method of political assassination (giving their name to it).[3] Many young Isma'ilis seem to have been willing to lose their lives in order to destroy prominent opponents at the command of the Grand Master.

The ideational basis of the Iranian Isma'ili movement at this period is known from a summary of its teaching, apparently by Hasan ibn-as-Sabbah, preserved by ash-Shahrastani,[4] and from the criticisms of it by al-Ghazali.[5] From the long account by al-Baghdadi (d.1037)[6] it is seen that the main lines of Isma'ili teaching had not changed from his time, except that certain points were presented with greater logical force.

The fundamental point insisted on by al-Hasan and earlier Isma'ilis was that knowledge, especially knowledge of God and of the conduct He prescribed for men, could only be gained from an authoritative and infallible teacher. The teacher *par excellence* was the imam of the Isma'ilis, that is (until the schism of 1094) the Fatimid caliph in Cairo, but authoritative teaching could of course also be given by those who had been 'taught' by an imam or his accredited emissary. There was indeed a hierarchy of such 'teachers'. Complementary to this doctrine of the imam was the doctrine of

[1] Hodgson, *Assassins*, 72-98.

[2] For a time an Isma'ili governed the town of Takrit on the Tigris, but it is not clear that he was acting on the instructions of al-Hasan ibn as-Sabbah, or even in concert with him; cf. Hodgson, 80.

[3] The English word 'assassin' is derived from an Arabic word meaning 'users of the drug *hashish*', but it is not clear why the word was applied to the Isma'ilis.

[4] *Al-Milal wa-'n-Nihal*, Cairo, 1948, i. 339-45 ; Eng. tr. by Hodgson, *Assassins*, 325-8.

[5] E.g. in *Al-Munqidh min ad-Dalal*; Eng. tr. by Montgomery Watt in *The Faith and Practice of al-Ghazali*, London, 1953, esp. 43-54. Cf. I. Goldziher, *Die Streitschrift des Gazali gegen die Batinijja-Sekte*, Leiden, 1916.

[6] *Al-Farq bayn al-Firaq*, Cairo (1910)/1328, 265-99; Eng. tr. A. S. Halkin, Tel-Aviv, 1935 ('Moslem Schisms and Sects'), 107-57.

esoteric interpretation. The revealed scriptures of Islam were held to have both an exoteric and an esoteric meaning.[1] The exoteric meaning was the obvious, commonsense meaning attached to the words by ordinary men, but it was not the true meaning. The true meaning was the esoteric meaning, and this could only be learnt from the infallible imam. In practice the esoteric interpretations of the Isma'ilis were based on an elaborate philosophical system akin to Neoplatonism. A group of philosophers and scientific writers known as Ikhwan-as-Safa', 'the brethren of purity', which flourished in Basrah about the end of the tenth century, supported the Isma'ili movement; and al-Baghdadi, rightly or wrongly, accuses the movement of making capital out of the erudition of such scholars by claiming that the factual knowledge in their books was derived from the imam, whereas it mostly came from Greek philosophy or Arab wisdom.[2]

These two concepts or doctrines of the infallible imam and esoteric interpretation have special implications which must now be considered. Firstly, there may be noted the attack on the intellectual leadership of the Sunnite Muslims, that is, on the ulema or scholar-jurists. Reason, thinking and scholarship were belittled as an avenue to truth, and the results attained by them were alleged to belong at best to the inferior realm of the exoteric. The superior esoteric truth was to be learnt only from the imam. That is to say, the Sunnite scholar-jurists were to be replaced by the Isma'ili *da'is* or propagandists. Moreover, the *da'is* were in theory completely dependent on the imam, who was also the political leader, whereas the scholar-jurists though dependent on the political ruler in so far as they were appointed by him, were theoretically independent in matters of scholarship, that is, in the formulation of legal principles and in the application of these to particular cases.

Secondly, along with this attack on the scholar-jurists there was an attack on some aspects of Islamic law. It is difficult to know, however, just how far this attack went. Al-Baghdadi, for example, sees in the esoteric interpretation of legal prescriptions an attempt to restore certain pre-Islamic Persian practices, notably, the drinking of wine and the marriage of sisters and daughters (which had not been considered incestuous).[3] As modern scholars have pointed out,

[1] *Zahir, batin*; from the latter comes the name Batiniyyah, often applied to the sect. Similarly from their emphasis on 'authoritative teaching' (*ta'lim*) they are known as Ta'limiyyah.

[2] *Farq*, 294f.; cf. al-Ghazali, *Munqidh*, Damascus, 1939/1358, 120 (= *Faith and Practice of al-Ghazali*, 53).

[3] *Farq*, 270; for a criticism see Lewis, *Origins of Isma'ilism*, 90ff.

however, the Isma'ili movement as a whole cannot be understood as the manifestation of Magian revivalism or Persian nationalism, since it contains many other aspects. At most, then, al-Baghdadi's view could only mean that in certain areas the adherents of the movement were encouraged to expect the restoration of these Persian practices. When the Shari'ah or revealed law was publicly abrogated at Alamut in 1164, wine may have been drunk openly with official approval, but there is no mention of a change in the law of incest. The chief innovations seem to have been in respect of ritual prescriptions of the Shari'ah; the five daily 'prayers' or acts of formal worship were discontinued, and a festival was instituted in the middle of the Sunnite fast of Ramadan.

It seems clear, then, that, while the Isma'ilis might criticize the Shari'ah, they had no positive alternative to it except in the sphere of worship. One might go farther and say that the Iranian Isma'ilis had no real understanding of what was involved in administering a state of the size of the Seljuq dominions. They had an elaborate philosophy, but there was little in it which could serve as a basis for social and political action apart from its argument for the replacement of existing rulers by an Isma'ili imam. There was no programme to guide the imam once he came to power, and there could not be any such programme, since the imam himself was the fount of all wisdom, political and otherwise. In effect the imam was an irresponsible autocrat surrounded by a religious halo. Because of the bankruptcy of political thought among the Iranian Isma'ilis, it is not surprising that their success was so limited. Even the Fatimids, despite the fact that they ruled Egypt for about two hundred years, had no distinctive tradition of political thought. They provided an alternative set of rulers to the 'Abbasids but not an alternative system.[1] They were thus unable to provide their Iranian associates with a programme.

While the Fatimids had prospered through military strength, the Iranian Isma'ilis, as already noted, do not appear to have tried to raise an army, but turned instead to assassination. From the sociological standpoint this is in keeping with the absence of a political programme. Though assassinations of the Isma'ili type might seriously weaken the existing regime, especially where that depended on one or two outstanding personalities, they were essentially a negative protest without any positive complement. Everything goes to suggest that the Isma'ili revolt in Persia and Syria at the end of the eleventh century was not a serious attempt to replace the Seljuqs

[1] Cf. Gaudefroy-Demombynes et Platonov, *Le Monde Musulman et Byzantin jusqu' aux Croisades*, Paris, 1931, 438.

and 'Abbasids but a manifestation of the discontent of people who were largely impotent to better their position.[1]

With the death of the Fatimid caliph al-Mustansir in 1094 two things happened to the Iranian Isma'ilis: politically, they became independent of Egypt, while ideationally they acknowledged the succession of al-Mustansir's son Nizar to the imamate (and so may now be properly called Nizaris). Here again there is unfortunately much that is obscure. Probably what happened was that at one time al-Mustansir had designated Nizar as his successor but that on his death in 1094 the vizier (who was the effective ruler of Egypt) had Nizar supplanted by another son, al-Musta'li, who would be less likely to curb his (the vizier's) authority. Nizar and some supporters resisted, but their resistance was soon crushed and Nizar probably murdered in prison. In Egypt there is no trace of any continuing movement in the immediately following years. In Persia and Syria, on the other hand, Nizar continued to be acknowledged and al-Musta'li disavowed. The political action of renouncing allegiance to the *de facto* rulers of Egypt and the ideational action of maintaining the claims of Nizar against those of al-Musta'li are thus closely related. Can it be said that one is cause and the other effect? Before trying to answer this question let us consider various aspects of the matter.

From the time of his visit to Egypt in 1078 al-Hasan ibn-as-Sabbah probably realized that the Fatimid government was too weak to interfere in the east. It is conceivable that the Fatimid caliph (or the vizier) encouraged al-Hasan to prepare a revolt; it might distract some of their enemies. It seems more probable, however, that the Fatimids had nothing to do with the preparations for revolt, but that this new policy represents the reactions of al-Hasan and other Iranian leaders to his reading of the situation in Egypt in the light of the growing Seljuq power. Al-Hasan probably also realized that the caliph had less power than the vizier, and this may have made him readier to adopt the new policy. The dependence of the caliph on the vizier must have made things difficult for any Isma'ili who believed in the infallibility of his imam.

On the assumption that al-Mustansir had designated Nizar to succeed him and that the Iranians had accepted this, it would be natural for them in 1094, after the coup which made al-Musta'li caliph, to continue to recognize Nizar. This was the easier course

---

[1] One wonders how far the failure of the revolt in the towns, despite numerous adherents there, was due to repression by the Seljuqs, and how far the town-dwelling Isma'ilis came to realize that the extension of the rule of al-Hasan ibn-as-Sabbah would give them not Paradise but less desirable governors than those they already had.

doctrinally, though there was also some doctrinal justification for not recognizing Nizar. The supporters of al-Musta'li claimed that the latter had been designated by al-Mustansir on his death-bed, though their evidence was not convincing. From the political viewpoint the Iranians, now acting on their own with some success, had little to lose by rejecting the claims of al-Musta'li; they were presumably receiving no material help from Egypt.

The critical point must have been the moment when al-Hasan became convinced that Nizar had disappeared. As noted above Nizar is said to have been murdered, but in the circumstances of the time it would be difficult to know for certain whether Nizar was dead or merely in hiding. What al-Hasan must have known, however, was that he had lost all contact with Nizar and with any faction in Egypt actively supporting him. By continuing to acknowledge Nizar, al-Hasan would become in effect head of the Iranian movement without any superior, though he doubtless claimed that he was merely the representative of Nizar until he or his successor once again became manifest.[1] It might therefore seem that the continued recognition of Nizar was dictated by material advantage. In making this judgement, however, we are in part moved by our disbelief in the doctrinal system and also by the presumed disbelief of the Egyptian viziers in it (since Nizar could hardly have been opposed by one who believed in his infallibility). It should not be assumed, however, that al-Hasan disbelieved in the doctrines. He may well have been fully convinced of their truth and may have regarded the disappearance of the imam as a misfortune which thrust upon himself a heavy and unwelcome responsibility. He may have regarded the new rulers of Egypt as traitors to the Isma'ili cause, who ought to be vigorously opposed.[2] It is thus possible that al-Hasan was not moved even unconsciously by consideration of his own temporal interests, but acted for the good of the Isma'ili movement as he understood it.

(b) The proclamation of the Resurrection

The second phase of the movement to be considered here is that which was inaugurated at Alamut on the 8th of August, 1164 by the proclamation of the Resurrection. Al-Hasan ibn-as-Sabbah had been

---

[1] Al-Hasan appears to have been known as the *hujjah* or 'proof' of the imam; the title was familiar to the Isma'ilis—cf. Hodgson, 67 and n., and W. Ivanow, *A Creed of the Fatimids*, Bombay, 1936, §38.

[2] There is some evidence of a struggle between the two parties for the adherence of the Syrian Isma'ilis; cf. Hodgson, 70f. Eventually they all became Nizaris.

succeeded by a colleague and he by a son and then (presumably) by a grandson. The latter is called al-Hasan II by some Western scholars, but was apparently referred to by his followers as al-Hasan Peace-at-his-mention (*'ala dhikri-hi 's-salam*) or simply Peace-at-his-mention. He became leader of the community in 1162, and two years later summoned all his followers to an assembly in the prayer grounds beneath the fortress of Alamut. Here he announced that an envoy had come to him from the imam bearing a letter, and the letter was then read with great pomp. Ten weeks later there was a second assembly and a second letter was read. In these letters three important changes were made: (*a*) the imam removed from his people 'the burden of the obligation of the Shari'ah'; (*b*) he 'brought them to the Resurrection'; (*c*) al-Hasan was declared to be God's caliph or representative on earth.[1]

The point of these ideational changes will be better understood if something is said about the general historical background. In the three-quarters of a century since the outbreak of the revolt in Persia little had been achieved. Since about 1105 the fortunes of the movement had been stationary or declining. The Nizaris were indeed maintaining themselves in their hill-strongholds and were in control of a little of the surrounding territory; but they had had no successes in urban districts. The Seljuq regime had persecuted them in the towns, and it is possible that most of their adherents there had now been lost. Many perished in the persecutions, while of the others the more eager would go to the strongholds and the rest would cease to profess Nizari doctrines. The net effect was thus that the Nizari community was cut off from the main body of the Muslims. This separation of the Nizaris was made more definite by their 'excommunication' by the Sunnite jurists. They were declared to be not heretical Muslims but infidels or non-Muslims, and this had the consequence, since they had once been Muslims, that they were now apostates and as such liable to death.[2]

Now that the Nizaris were thus cut off from the Sunnites, it was only natural that they should abandon the Shari'ah (that is, presumably, not the legal or ethical part of it, but only such ritual observances as daily worship and fasting). They had been in the habit of observing the Shari'ah merely to avoid trouble with the Sunnite majority among whom they lived. According to their doctrines the ritual observances of the Sunnites were mere external forms and were unnecessary for those who had been initiated into

---

[1] Cf. Hodgson, *Assassins*, 148-51.
[2] Cf. Goldziher, *Streitschrift*, 67-72.

Isma'ilism. Moreover their doctrines also permitted and encouraged the practice of *taqiyyah*, the dissimulation of one's real religious allegiance in order to avoid persecution. Since the Nizaris in their own little enclaves were now in fact no longer intermingled with Sunnites, there was no point in continuing to observe the external Sunnite forms in order to gain Sunnite approval.

The second of the changes mentioned, the declaration that the Resurrection had taken place, is less easy to understand. The Isma'ilis were in the habit of interpreting external and material happenings in an inward and spiritual sense. They may have thought of the Resurrection as bringing 'a higher quality of life', perhaps one characterized by certain mystical experiences. They seem to have held that there was a Resurrection at the end of each of the cycles into which they supposed world history to be divided. From our standpoint as detached observers it seems probable that the proclamation of the Resurrection marks a turning of the community from the political sphere, where their efforts had ended in failure, to the sphere of the inner life.[1]

The third change was an enhancement of the leader's position. The details are not clear, probably because as time went on higher claims were made. One might have thought that when al-Hasan was first given the title of 'caliph' (or representative) he would have been caliph of the imam, but he is spoken of as 'caliph of God' and in the same position as al-Mustansir (Fatimid caliph and imam, 1035-94). Later he himself seems to have claimed the imamate, probably as a spiritual descendant of previous imams. After his death the official view of the community became that he was the son of a son of Nizar who had been taken secretly to Alamut at the time of his father's imprisonment. Whatever the details, however, the general tenor of the change is clear. The leader was given a position of greater prestige within the community, which doubtless made it easier for him to carry out readjustments to the new situation. The renewed contact with the imam (by the alleged receipt of letters from him) would infuse fresh zeal into flagging spirits. The recognition of Nizar had been advantageous to the Persian Isma'ilis in that it enabled them to assert their independence of Egypt; but in the course of time it had the disadvantage that the community felt themselves to be without an imam (and perhaps attributed their misfortunes to this fact). The main body of the Shi'ites were content with an imam who was completely 'hidden', but the Isma'ilis insisted that the imam must in

---

[1] In a sense there may also have been a decision to abandon missionary work and leave the rest of the world to its fate. There is a mention of a conversion, however, in *Haft Bab-i-Baba Sayyid-na* (tr. Hodgson, *Assassins*, 282).

some way remain in touch with his community.[1] The heightening of the rank of the leader, culminating in the assertion of his imamate, must have heartened the community, since they could feel that they were once more being guided by divine wisdom.

This examination of the changes associated with the proclamation of the Resurrection shows the place of ideation in the life of the Nizari community, the 'order of the Assassins'. On the whole the community accepted the ideational changes. At the time of the proclamation of the Resurrection those who disapproved were permitted to leave the territories of the Nizaris. Though al-Hasan was murdered in 1166, probably because of opposition to his policy, his opponents were too weak to overthrow the dispensation of the Resurrection, despite the fact that his son and successor, Muhammad was only nineteen years old. It is difficult to say to what extent al-Hasan Peace-at-his-mention was himself sincere. He no doubt made political calculations, but, since sheer worldliness was probably rare in his time, the likelihood is that he believed most of his new teaching. He must have known, of course, that he had not received any letter from the imam in the physical sense, but the Isma'ilis belittled what was external and material, and he may well have believed that he had received a spiritual communication from the imam, perhaps through a dream.

(c) *The reconciliation with the Sunnites.*

The dispensation of the Resurrection remained in force until the end of Muhammad's reign in 1210. Meanwhile the historical scene had been changing. The Seljuqs had declined, and the leading dynasty was now that of the Khwarizmshahs. The Nizaris had apparently grown in strength during the last half century of retrenchment, and felt themselves able to take part in the politics of the day. In particular it suited them to become allies of the 'Abbasid caliphs against the Khwarizmshahs. It was perhaps not altogether surprising, then, that al-Hasan III, Muhammad's son, shortly after he succeeded to his father, proclaimed that the Shari'ah was once more obligatory. Moreover, the Shari'ah was not now practised in a Shi'ite form as it had been before 1164, but in one of the four recognized Sunnite forms, probably the Shafi'ite.[2] The purpose of

---

[1] Cf. Ivanow, *Creed of Fatimids*, §37: 'There is no *ghaybah*, i.e. time when the Imam entirely disappears from the world, and does not control it. The Imam cannot disappear completely, but even if he is not manifest to the masses he is in touch with the chosen ones, and his whereabouts are known to them.

[2] Hodgson, *Assassins*, 217.

this change is clear. The new imam of the Nizaris wanted his little state to live no longer in isolation, but as one of a fellowship of Muslim states. To make this possible there had to be at least a measure of outward conformity. Since the Sunnites were now in the ascendant, the adoption of Sunnite forms was clearly desirable.

The ideational justification of this change was perhaps not so difficult as might at first sight appear. The Isma'ilis had always had a tendency to regard history as cyclic. Hence the Resurrection was not necessarily for them a unique occurrence, but might come at the end of every cycle. The return to the Shari'ah would in their eyes only be concerned with externals and would not imply the abandonment of Isma'ili for Sunnite doctrines. It would in fact be a return to *taqiyah*, that is, outward conformity and dissimulation of one's real beliefs. This view came to be more and more prominent after the death of al-Hasan III.

For the Isma'ilis, too, the imam was an absolute autocrat, whose decrees had to be accepted. However strange his new decision might seem, a loyal follower could not question it, since he was bound to regard the imam as knowing better than himself. In fact the community seems to have followed al-Hasan III without hesitation. He himself may genuinely have believed that he was acting in the best interests of the community. Perhaps he hoped that after some successes in the political field there would be further conversions; but if so, his hopes were not realized. Possibly during the dispensation of the Resurrection, when it was withdrawn into itself, the community lost the missionary fervour it had had in the previous century. Certainly the renewed contacts with the main body of Islam brought about no further expansion, and the Nizaris settled down to be one small community of Muslims among many others.

This phase in the life of the Nizari community came to an end with the Mongol invasion. In 1256 Alamut surrendered and was destroyed, and in the following year the imam met his death (probably murdered) and there was a widespread massacre of the Nizaris. It may be further mentioned that, despite this catastrophe and the fact that it has never since had a territory of its own, the community was not exterminated and the line of imams was maintained unbroken. During the last century there has even been a revival, dating from the flight from Persia to India in 1840 of the 46th imam, the grandfather of the recently-deceased imam, H. H. the Agha Khan. To the Indian Nizaris or Khojas have been united groups in Persia, Syria and elsewhere, and the whole now forms a closely-knit, wealthy and important community.[1] The sufi or mystical strand in Isma'ilism has been developed, and emphasis placed on personal piety.[2]

4. IDEATION AND SOCIETY: CONCLUSIONS

The argument so far has shown a certain parallelism between ideation and activity, that is, when we consider the ideation which is, or includes, the awareness of ends. Both ideation and activity proceed from the movement of life or psyche, and with regard to both there is usually a process of exploration. Both are present together in the life of the individual or society where there is a high degree of integration, and seem to fulfil complementary functions. Indeed both ideation and bare or analysed activity may be said to be derived by analysis (or should we say, by an increase of self-consciousness?) from naive or unanalysed activity. Because of this close connexion it seems proper to speak of the ideational complement of activity and of the actional complement of ideation. From this position let us go on to consider in further detail how ideation functions in social change.

It was seen in the previous chapter that social change normally follows upon some inescapable material change. This may be economic or political, or it may be the primary adjustment to an economic or political change. In Mecca, for instance, after the economic change (the growth of commerce) there was a primary social adjustment, namely, the development of monopolistic practices with its ideational complement of materialistic individualism. By the time Muhammad began to preach, this social adjustment had gone so far that it can be regarded as part of the inescapable material conditions with which he had to deal, and his preaching may therefore be regarded as inaugurating a secondary social adjustment. These social changes have ideational systems associated with them, and the problem now before us is to try to make some more precise statements about the relations between the ideation and the social change.

First it has to be noticed that the ideational system of a society places certain limits to its responses to a novel situation. Thus the ideational tradition of the nomadic Arabs defined their general end as the preservation of the life of the tribe and the maintenance of

[1] E.I. (*Encyclopedia of Islam*) (1), arts. 'Isma'iliya', 'Khodja'; *E.I.* (2), art. 'Agha Khan'.

[2] Cf. Shihab ad-Din Shah (a son of the 47th imam), *Risala dar Haqiqat-i Din*, ed. and tr. W. Ivanow, Bombay, 1933.

its honour; and consequently any course of action to be adopted would have to be conducive to the realization of this end. Their ideational tradition also fostered certain attitudes and rules of conduct; for example, it was normally held that a man and a tribe should keep to the 'beaten path' of the ancestors and should not make innovations. Hence any response to a situation which appeared to be an innovation was likely to be rejected in favour of a response that was in accordance with traditional practice. Perhaps it was because of this dislike of innovation that Muhammad claimed that his message was identical with that of previous prophets. Again, the ideational tradition of a society conditions its analysis of a novel situation and also the ideational complement of any movement of social reform. The early Islamic analysis of the situation of the Meccans as one of impending punishment because of their rejection of God's message was conditioned by the monotheistic tradition of the environment; while the ideational complement of the third phase of the Assassin movement (as described above), namely, the reconciliation with the Sunnites, had to take account of the fact that the immediately preceding period had been based on the idea that the Resurrection had been realized. In general, then, the ideation associated with a social adjustment must be a modification of the previous ideational system.

The extent of the modification that is required varies considerably. It depends in part on the closeness of the connexion between the ideational system and the social order and on the extent of the social change required. Sometimes there has to be a very fundamental change. Such would be Muhammad's attempted reform at Mecca, where the old religious beliefs had to be replaced by Islam, and Mustafa Kemal Atatürk's reform in Turkey which was based on a rejection of Islamic institutions. On other occasions there is only a very slight ideational change; examples of this would be the proclamation of the Resurrection by the head of the Assassins and the ending of the era of the Resurrection. Sometimes accidental concatenations seem to have an important share in moulding events. Muhammad's adoption of the prophetic office was with a view to the Meccan situation, and it was fortuitous that the office of the prophet or messenger of God met the very different needs of Medina. It is arguable (though improbable) that reform could have been carried out in Turkey without abandoning Islam, and that the anti-religious character of the reform movement was due to the accident of Atatürk's personal views.

The influence of an ideational tradition on the response to a novel situation has often something of this accidental character. The

The Role of Ideation

prohibition of usury in Islam, as already noted, was directed in the first place against the Jewish allies of the Muslims in Medina, since Muhammad thought they ought to regard the Muslims as their brothers and lend to them without interest.[1] There was therefore something accidental in the effect of this prohibition in hindering the development of large-scale industry in Islamic countries in modern times.

After these general remarks let us look more in detail about the relation between ideation and social change in some of the examples discussed above. The materialistic individualism of the merchant princes of Mecca was ideological, and in a sense conservative; but their social conduct was not simply a continuation of what had always been done in Mecca. It is rather to be regarded as the first social adjustment to a novel economic situation. Their unscrupulous pursuit of their own interests and their disregard for the welfare of their kinsmen were something new, though they had developed gradually and imperceptibly out of existing attitudes and practices. The creation of monopolies probably came about through a process of 'exploration'. In the case of these merchant princes the activity, that is, the new social conduct, was almost certainly prior to the ideation. The latter, which was ideological and was a modification of the ideation associated with the nomadic tribal system, doubtless appeared in order to defend and justify the activity. The ideation thus arose out of satisfaction with existing conditions (after the first adjustment) and the desire to maintain them.

The movement begun by Muhammad, on the other hand, arose out of awareness of the malaise of the times, that is, out of dissatisfaction with existing conditions. Ideation was present from the first, but neither ideation nor activity was adequate to effect a satisfying secondary adjustment to the situation. The activity of preaching was a piece of exploration which led to a dead end. The visit to at-Ta'if, the approaches to the nomadic tribes and the negotiations with Medina were all exploratory, but only the last discovered a road worth following.

The Isma'ili movement, some centuries after Muhammad, also arose out of dissatisfaction with existing conditions, and in it also ideation seems to have been present from the beginning. Indeed, by the time of al-Hasan ibn-as-Sabbah there was an elaborate ideational system associated with the movement. The rising, of which the capture of Alamut formed part, was a piece of exploration with a view to a wider extension of the realization of the movement in actual life; but little came of it. The reason was that, while the ideational

[1] *Muhammad at Medina*, 296-8, cf. p.34 above.

80

complement was sufficient for the early stages of a movement of social reform, it gave no help in subsequent stages. The ideational system pointed to a new leader and to the need for absolute allegiance to him, and this was useful when one was trying to overthrow the regime in power but was bankrupt when it came to a reorganization of society. The failure of the Isma'ili movement to reform the social system may thus be attributed mainly to its ideational weakness.[1]

Here then are three types of adjustment to a novel situation. In Mannheim's terminology, the first is ideological and the others utopian, but one of the utopian systems is successful and the other a failure.[2] The ideology arises from satisfaction with existing conditions and the desire to maintain them, the utopias from dissatisfaction with existing conditions and the desire to change them. So far as the function of ideation goes, however, this difference is not important, nor is the fact that activity preceded ideation in the case of the merchant princes but not in the other two cases. Those who make the first steps in a reform of society do not see clearly where these steps are leading them; at nearly every stage of the journey there has to be some exploration, and a fresh decision to proceed in a particular way or to make definite what has hitherto been indefinite. In this way a movement of reform (if it is successfully meeting the challenges which come to it) becomes more integrated and its ideation and activity more closely linked. No religious or social movement reaches maturity without passing through many stages, each of which is marked by fresh difficulties to surmount. At each stage the questions arise : can the ideational system be modified to meet the new situation, and can activity be devised adequate to the new situation? In the preliminary stages of a movement there may be naive activity (doubtless of an exploratory character) without any corresponding ideation, or, less frequently, ideation may be unduly developed beyond activity. When a movement is mature, however, it would seem that there must always be a marriage of ideation and activity.

The successive stages may be seen in the case of Muhammad. His original message was accompanied by the activity of preaching. The later form of the Meccan message corresponds to the period when he had to organize his followers to resist various kinds of pressure. At Medina his activities had become those of the head of a political

---

[1] Max Weber spoke of a political party without ideals as an 'organization of jobhunters' (*From Max Weber: Essays in Sociology*, ed. H. H. Gerth and C. W. Mills, London, 1947, 108.

[2] Cf. p.254 below.

community. And the developments in doctrine in the century after his death are parallel to the expansion of his small state into an empire. The Isma'ili movement, on the other hand, though it was successful up to a point, showed its bankruptcy as soon as it came to power. The Fatimid branch of the movement after its conquest of Egypt merely continued the Sunnite form of social structure, while the Iranian revolutionaries under al-Hasan ibn-as-Sabbah, were still farther from having a positive programme. The movement, indeed, was saddled with an ideation which was difficult to develop; at least it did not manage to develop it.

At first sight the ideological ideation of the Meccan merchants does not offer the same possibilities of development. They were not trying to reform society, but to preserve their ill-gotten gains. Ideology, indeed, seems to be always the ideation of a minority making a social adjustment in its own interests. Nevertheless, it is conceivable that this ideology could have been developed to make a viable, if not entirely ideal, basis for the growth of a community with a measure of harmony. It would have been difficult for this to come about, since the ideology supported a sectional interest; but what is not impossible is that this sectional interest might have been linked up with a general interest that would have been sufficient to gain a measure of support for the policy in other sections of the community. In fact, the ideation of the Meccan merchants was not developed. This way of looking at the matter, however, shows that it is not essentially different in its social function from the utopian ideation of the Isma'ilis. Both explore a line of activity and ideation in order to achieve social adjustment to a novel situation; and neither leads to a satisfactory result. Both therefore give way before a completely different system of ideation and activity.

Again, the difference between the exponents of ideologies and utopias in respect of their awareness of the need for the disintegration of the existing social tradition is not an absolute difference. The minority which holds an ideology is largely unaware both of the ends which its activities are tending to promote and of the fact that these activities are contributing to the disintegration of society. Nevertheless (both in general and at Mecca in particular) because of the changes which have already taken place the society cannot be improved without further disintegration, that is, without a loosening of the tie between activity and the traditional ideation. The ideologically minded minority is not aware of this process of disintegration, and to that extent its activity is still naive. If the ideology is to be developed into the ideational complement of an even moderately successful process of social adjustment, there must be an awareness of this need for disintegration and also of the need for a positive foundation for the rebuilding. In the case of a utopian ideation, on the other hand, since it is a protest against the existing order, there is some awareness of the need for disintegration from an early period, though not necessarily from the beginning. Muhammad, for example, was probably aware of the need for the break-up of the existing order of Meccan society from about the middle of his period as a 'warner' there. This difference, then, between ideologies and utopias seems to be merely in the order in which certain aspects of integration take place, and not to affect the essential function of ideation in making integration possible.

After this long discussion it is possible to state briefly the two chief functions of ideation in social life. The primary function is to clarify and express and make manifest for the members of a society the ends which it is pursuing, and to place the various ends in an order of subordination and super-ordination. This involves also a statement of the view about the nature of reality on which the society bases its pursuit of its ends. In the case of social changes ideation and activity are normally parallel in a mature society, in that before a course of action is adopted it has to be seen to be in accordance with (that is, integrated into) the tradition of the society, both of ideation and of action. A mature society hesitates about a novel course of action until it finds a satisfactory ideational link between the action and its ideational tradition. The appearance of this ideational link thus tends to be followed 'automatically' by the decision to act; and the ideation and the activity are in this sense parallel. This is the main function of ideation in society.

The secondary function is that, once an ideational system has been adopted by a society, it tends to guide and direct subsequent activities. As noted above, this often happens in an apparently accidental way. On the other hand, in so far as the ideational system corresponds to general features of all social systems, the guidance it give will be appropriate to novel situations because of the system's essential soundness, and will not be fortuitous.

There remain three difficulties to be considered. One is that men accept ideation because they hold it to be true, and not because it leads to a satisfactory order of society. This difficulty arises from the fact that we are dealing with two levels of ideational phenomena, which may be called the experiential and the observational. The phenomena of the experiential level are those which belong to the experience of the actors in the historical process; those of the observational level are those which belong to the experience of an observer, such as a modern sociologist. At the experiential level one must always ask in respect of ideation: Is this true? Even the sociologist must do this when he is taking part as an actor in the historical events of his own day. His beliefs as a sociologist may be relevant to the practical decisions he has to make, for there are correlations between the experiential and observational levels. There is no strict logical passage, however, from the latter to the former. The observational ideation of sociology never gives a man or a society a complete answer to the question whether the ideas on which it is proposed to base activity are true. When a man has gone as far as he can by applying the criteria proper to sociology, he must turn to the criteria—or, more generally, the ways of deciding about truth—proper to the experiential level. Thus we have the curious position that, while the ideation and ideational procedures of the experiential level are part of the subject matter of sociology, they preserve their autonomy over against sociology.

The second difficulty is with regard to the social determination of ideation. What exactly does it mean to say that ideation is socially determined, and to what extent is it true? Let us consider two points. Muhammad wanted to bring about a change in the conduct of the Meccan merchants in certain respects, and supported his appeal to them by the assertion that they would be raised from the dead and judged. The merchants opposed Muhammad, since they desired to continue as they were, and asserted that death was the end and that there was no resurrection or judgement. To say that these beliefs or assertions are socially determined means that the sociologist sees a correlation between them and other phenomena (at the observational level) such that he has to postulate a causal relationship. This cannot mean, however, that the assertion that death is the end is *produced* by the merchants' desire to continue their present conduct —it is in part at least a response to Muhammad's assertion. Likewise, Muhammad's assertion that there is resurrection and judgement is not *produced* by his desire to remedy the evils caused by the conduct of the merchants; the idea existed long before Muhammad. The most that can be said is that social factors (the interest in their personal welfare shown both by the merchants and also by Muhammad along with those in a similar position) cause men to regard as true those ideas which best support the course of action to which their interests lead them.

This is possible because in many cases there is no universally acknowledged way of ascertaining truth. In many cases, of course, the opposite holds. Every sane person believes that two and two make four, and so it is never suggested that social factors could make one believe that two and two make five. Where, however, a matter is not clear and there are grounds for holding both of two opposing views, then it is not merely possible but probable that social factors will make a man or society incline to accept the truth of the view which best supports the course of action indicated by these social factors. (It may be noted in passing how this links up with what was said in the previous paragraph. Men hold a certain view because they think the arguments in favour of it are true, or at least stronger than the arguments against; this is at the experiential level. There is also, however, it would seem, a certain weighing of argument against argument which goes on below the level of consciousness. This at least is postulated at the observational level by the sociologist, and it is at this point, he maintains, that social factors have influence. Because of social factors a man comes to see that an idea is true, or at least truer than the alternative.)

In the case of the Meccan merchants the activity appeared first, and only afterwards, when it was criticized, the justificatory ideation. The activity—the forms of conduct to which Muhammad objected —thus appears to be the primary expression of the social factors or interests, and the ideation something secondary. In other cases, however, especially where the ideation is utopian, ideation appears to be temporarily prior to activity. This question of temporal priority is relevant to that of determination by social factors. If activity is taken to be the primary expression of the social factors, then, where ideation precedes activity, social factors cannot determine ideation. The solution of the problem appears to be to hold that ideation and activity are essentially parallel, and that both proceed from the psyche or the movement of life. The psyche responds to the situations in which it finds itself, and these are always social situations. Thus the activity which proceeds from the psyche is always in an important sense social activity, and the ideation social ideation. What must be borne in mind here is that the psyche seeks integration, that is, both the ordering of the activities of the individual to form a harmonious whole, and the ordering of the activities of many individuals to make the life of their society harmonious. Such integration is impossible, as has been maintained above, without an ideational basis. Sometimes the response of the psyche to a situation consists in naive activity, or activity without an ideational basis integrating it into the life of the individual or society. Most frequently, however—and this seems to be normal in mature individuals and societies—an activity is accompanied by integrative ideation.

Now, if by 'social factors' are meant tendencies in the psyche to act in certain ways, then to say that social factors influence ideation is in accordance with what has just been said about the psyche. It must be remembered, however, that these tendencies are not discrete entities but at the most aspects of the psyche, and that the activities to which they are tendencies are not naive activities but ideationally-based activities. Thus, while for various reasons naive activities sometimes proceed from the psyche, it would be wrong to regard the naive activities as the primary expression of the psyche and ideation as additional or secondary. Both ideation and activity are required for the full expression of the psyche, and in this full expression they are complementary.

The third difficulty is that there appears to be a close connexion between the views which are apparently about matters of fact (for example, whether death is or is not the end) and certain features of society. Why, if Muhammad and the Meccan merchants disagreed about the conduct of the latter, should they spend time in disputing whether death is the end of everything? After the previous discussions the answer is fairly obvious. Human activity tends to be an integrated whole, based on a coherent view of the particular situations and of the universe in general. This view is, of course, accepted as true by those who act upon it. Where men differ (as Muhammad and his adversaries did) about courses of action, one way of influencing the activities of one's opponents is to show that they are mistaken about some point in their view of the universe or ideational system. It is normally impossible to apply to the whole of an ideational system objective criteria of truth (that is, criteria accepted by both the opposing parties.) Consequently each side tries to find some point at which the opponents are constrained, by a criterion which they accept, to admit that there is a mistake in their ideational system. The merchants insisted that death is the end because they thought it was obviously true and because it contradicted an important point in the ideational basis of Muhammad's attack on their conduct. This search for a mutually acceptable criterion may lead men by a process of argument and counter-argument to the most recondite matters, since there is practically nothing that may not become relevant to the conflicts between opposing social groups. The abstruse discussions about the Christian doctrine of the Trinity, like the almost equally abstruse Muslim discussions about the attributes of God, were closely linked with social conflicts. Thus matters of fact (and everything that purports to be an assertion about the nature of reality) are relevant to social structures and activities because these are based on an ideational system which is ultimately a view of the nature of all reality. Conflicts between societies or groups involve disputes about matters of fact (in the widest sense) because these offer attackable points in the ideational system of one's opponents.

IV

THE WILL TO UNITY AND DISUNITY

THE previous two chapters have dealt with the place of economic, social and ideational factors in the life of a society. The society has been treated for the most part as a homogeneous unit; that is to say, no attention has been paid specifically to the existence of different groups within the society. In most societies, however, there are important differences of economic status, of class and even of race. It is one of the noteworthy achievements of Islam that it has united in a great society men of different races and social traditions. In the present chapter, therefore, we turn to consider how a measure of integration is attained in this society consisting of heterogeneous groups. Since the following chapters will be devoted to the integration of political life, social life and intellectual life, the present chapter will study the matter only in a general way. Besides looking at the material and other factors in cases where unity has been attained, it is also desirable to look at examples of disintegration or the break-up of an existing unity, so that any positive conclusions we may reach may be supported by the corresponding negative results. The phrases 'the will to unity' and 'the will to disunity' are not to be taken in any technical sense, but only as indicating that there is in a society or group a general trend towards or away from unity.

1. THE UNIFICATION OF THE ARABS

The early history of Islam has already been discussed several times from different viewpoints, and it would be wearisome to go over it again in any detail. Since the first notably integrative achievement of Islam, however, was the unification of the Arabs, a brief consideration of this topic seems to be unavoidable.

(a) The various groups of Arabs.

Several different types of men or groups were included in the unity of the Arabs achieved by Muhammad and his immediate successors. The main ones are: (1) the early Meccan converts, most of whom became Emigrants at Medina; (2) the Medinan Muslims or Ansar; (3) the Meccan opponents of Muhammad who subsequently accepted Islam and served under him; (4) the nomadic tribes, which were very numerous, and whose circumstances varied from tribe to tribe; (5) the groups in the Yemen and on the Persian Gulf which had been supported by the Persians.

When one asks what material factors underlie the union of these groups in the Islamic state, one finds that after an initial diversity there is a certain similarity. The early converts were responding to the social malaise of Mecca, which can be traced to the growth of monopolistic practices among the great merchants. The men of Medina saw in the recognition of Muhammad as 'messenger of God' a way of gaining relief from the social insecurity which resulted from attempting to run an agricultural community on a basis of nomadic ideation. As Muhammad's prestige and power increased, there were attempts to get rid of him, but the majority of Medinans supported him because they still dreaded a return to the previous state of insecurity. When Muhammad died, the Medinans accepted as his successor in political matters a Meccan Emigrant, Abu-Bakr, partly because of the possibility of insecurity, but mainly because they realized that their material interests were best served by the continuance of the political institution established by Muhammad and that, for this, Meccan leadership was essential.

This last factor, the satisfactory character of the new body-politic, came more and more to be the chief material factor underlying fresh accessions to it. It was a case of 'nothing succeeds like success' and everyone jostling to get on the band-waggon. After the failure of the siege of Medina in 627 the Meccan merchants began to realize that their commercial empire was irretrievably lost and that the future lay with the community Muhammad was building at Medina. Some of the younger men were the first to go over. Abu-Sufyan, the leader and inspirer of Meccan military efforts from 624 to 627, became a Muslim before the fall of Mecca in 630, and helped to bring that about peacefully. Most of the more intransigent Meccans were later reconciled to Muhammad and some even became enthusiastic Muslims. All this presumably came about because they realized that as opponents of Muhammad they had no opportunities for profitable commerce, whereas as members of his community there were good prospects both for commerce and, more particularly, for the exercise of their administrative gifts and experience in positions where they would have a satisfactory personal status.

For the nomadic tribes the attraction was analogous. At first individuals and small, weak tribes joined him because they would have more hope of plunder in his expeditions than in their own razzias, and because he was in a better position to guarantee security to his followers than any other leader in that part of Arabia and maintained a high degree of justice and fair-play between the various sections of his community. As Muhammad's strength grew, these reasons became even weightier, until latterly large and important tribes were ready to seek his alliance even though it meant some loss of self-determination. In much the same way the pro-Persian groups in the Yemen, 'Uman (Oman), and other places, when they saw the break-up of the Persian empire on which they had been relying, turned to Muhammad as the strong leader able to provide security and a measure of prosperity.

Thus, if one had studied the relevant material factors at the time when Muhammad began preaching, one would have found great diversity. There are certain fundamental needs, however, common to all men; all require a measure of security of life and property and desire a standard of living comparable to that of their neighbours. The material factors which led to the establishing of the Islamic state were diverse in their specific natures; but once it was established, it satisfied these fundamental needs to a pre-eminent degree compared with any other body-politic in the region.

(b) *Muhammad's concern for unity*

In this consideration of the material factors leading to Arab unity, nothing has been said about the ideational factors, although in the previous chapter it was maintained that there was a parallelism between activity and ideation. In the case of the first two groups, the early Meccan converts and the Medinans, the activity in response to the material situation and the acceptance of Islamic ideation may be said to be parallel. With the other groups, however, this was not so. The primary attraction of the Islamic community for them appears to have been material and not ideational. Indeed, in the early years of the Medinan state, and later too in the case of important (probably Christian) tribes, Muhammad was ready to receive non-Muslims as allies. It required a certain pressure to make them accept Islamic ideation. This pressure was of two kinds.

Muhammad insisted on a measure of ideational unity. When he went to Medina he was intent on bringing harmony to its people. The chief means for doing this was that all should acknowledge him as 'messenger of God' and should perform the Islamic worship or prayers. This involved acceptance of at least the main doctrines of Islam. Thus from its inception at the Hijrah there was this measure

89

of ideational unity in the Islamic state. The unity was carefully preserved and fostered by later regulations. In Muhammad's closing years most of those who wanted to become his allies had to acknowledge him as 'messenger' and perform the worship (besides making an annual payment); the leaders of a tribe might be given instruction in Islamic ritual and doctrine at Medina, or else instructors might be sent to the tribe. This policy was also reinforced by practical measures. The pilgrimage to Mecca in its Islamic form must have given the participants a strong sense of belonging together, while the prohibition of apostasy and the insistence that all should take part in the great expeditions prevented divisions. Such threats of division as appeared were sternly dealt with. On one occasion three men who absented themselves from an expedition without valid excuse were 'sent to Coventry' for several weeks. Another incident was when some Medinans built what came to be known as 'the mosque of dissension', ostensibly for the performance of the Muslim worship. Muhammad was asked to be at an opening ceremony, but first of all postponed his visit, then sent some of his closest followers by night to destroy the mosque; presumably he had information that it was to be used for hatching plots.

The concern for the unity of the Islamic state was continued by the caliphs, who were the successors to the political powers of Muhammad. Indeed the caliphate remained as a symbol of religious and social unity after political unity had been lost. The 'wars of the apostasy' (or Riddah) at the time of Muhammad's death were the attempt of various tribes to secede from the Islamic state and build up rival political alliances;[1] and the defeat of the 'apostates' by the Muslims under Abu-Bakr led to a greater degree of political unification in Arabia than ever before. This also meant greater ideational unification, since paganism was no longer tolerated among the Arabs. There were still some Jews and Christians in Arabia proper, but these were transferred elsewhere during the caliphate of 'Umar I (634-44). This was primarily a military move, since Arabia was the Muslims' base and the fighting men came to be increasingly absent from it, but it also made for greater ideational unity in Arabia. The largely successful attempt under the next caliph 'Uthman (644-56) to establish a standard text of the Qur'an also shows a concern for unity in this respect.

These definite measures by Muhammad and his successors to preserve and extend the political and ideational unity of the Islamic state placed considerable pressure on the pagan Arabs, and even on

[1] Caetani and others have maintained that the Riddah was purely political and not at all religious; cf. *Muhammad at Medina*, 79f., 146-8.

90

the Christian Arabs and the Arabic-speaking Jews. Material interests made alliance with Muhammad desirable, but this was not be be had except by accepting Islam.[1] The pressure on the Arabs to accept Islam, however, was not merely of this material kind. There was also a pressure that was felt at deeper levels. As the Arabs regarded the achievements of Muhammad the thought will have occurred to some that there must be much truth in the faith that could bring into being this strong new state. The success of Islam in creating an obviously desirable type of life was probably connected in their minds (to the increase of its influence) with their previous admiration for the civilizations of the Byzantine and Persian empires. The Byzantine empire, in Arab eyes and as a result of their most frequent type of contact, was associated with the monophysite form of Christianity, and the Persian empire with Judaism and the Nestorian form of Christianity; with Orthodoxy and Zoroastrianism they had presumably had less contact. Muhammad's claim that his message was essentially the same as that of Christianity and Judaism, but in an Arab dress, doubtless brought about a transfer to Islam of some of the respect and admiration formerly given to these great empires with their associated religions.

While noticing this second type of pressure as a basis for the acceptance of Islam from real conviction, we should also remember that the Arabs were probably more hesitant than modern Europeans about making public profession of beliefs they did not hold. The European often thinks that religious beliefs do not matter one way or the other, and out of indifference is ready to perform public acts without real conviction. We can understand the Arab outlook better from political analogies. We would say that it is inconceivable that on election day a staunch conservative should wear a red rosette and a convinced socialist a blue one (where red and blue are the colours of socialists and conservatives respectively). In much the same way a sense of honour would generally keep an Arab from professing Islam where his attitude was one of sheer disbelief.[2] In any case what would trouble him would be not intellectual qualms but superstitious fears. If he became a Muslim outwardly and suffered no harm from the offended pagan deities, that would greatly strengthen a genuine conviction of the truth of Islamic teaching.

[1] For a time some Christian Arab tribesmen seem to have been able to join in the Muslim campaigns outside Arabia, but eventually they had either to become Muslims or to accept the status of 'protected persons' (*dhimmis*) which excluded military service.

[1] The Hypocrites (*munafiqun*) who professed Islam without full conviction, were few in number, and were essentially political opponents.

(c) Arab national feeling

It remains to say a word about what—if the anachronism and inexactitude is permitted—may be called Arab nationalism. The first point to note is that there was, prior to Islam, little awareness among the Arabs of their belonging together. They were probably more conscious of the differences between tribe and tribe. At most they seem to have been aware that there was a wide circle of people who were mutually intelligible (and who acknowledged a number of desert customs, such as recognizing sacred places and times), and that beyond this circle there were many people who were not intelligible to them. The sense of Arab unity may thus be said to have been present, but only in an embryonic or potential form. It presumably came more into consciousness as the Arabs were in more frequent contact with non-Arabs after their conquests. Nevertheless there seems also to have been present among them (perhaps especially among the Meccans whose commercial operations brought them into contact with non-Arabs) a dislike of foreigners and a fear of being dominated by them.

This sense of Arab unity cannot be said to have been a positive factor in Muhammad's political achievements. At no time was it part of his professed aim to create a pan-Arab union. On the contrary, there are passages in the Qur'an which seem to mean that Islam is intended for all mankind;[1] and there were non-Arabs in Islam from an early period (though they were persons who, like the Abyssinian freedman Bilal, had been incorporated into Arab society). Even the dominance of the Arabs in the Islamic state under the Umayyad dynasty (661-750) seems to have come about accidentally. The state was thought of as a confederation of bodies in alliance with Muhammad (or the caliph) or protected by him. It happened, how-ever, that all the allied bodies were Arab tribes; the non-Arab bodies who made treaties with Muhammad or the caliph consisted of Jews, Christians or Zoroastrians, and, since they did not become Muslims, they had the status of 'protected persons' (*dhimmis*). If a member of one of these subsequently became a Muslim, he had to be attached to one of the allied bodies; and in practice this meant that he had to become a client of an Arab tribe, with a suggestion of inferiority. Thus Arab unity was never a guiding concept for the Islamic state.

What can be said, however, is that awareness of the difference between Arab and non-Arab, and fear of foreign domination, contributed to Muhammad's success. There seems to have been a certain movement towards monotheism in Arabia before

[1] 34.28/27; 36.70; 61.9; etc.

92

Muhammad's time, but many who were more or less monotheists in belief held back from attachment to either Judaism or Christianity because of the political implications of such a step. The Jews, apart from any purely Jewish political ambitions, had connexions with Persia, while the Christians tended to be dependent on the Byzantine or Abyssinian empire. Such unattached monotheists consequently welcomed a form of monotheism which did not involve any submission to foreign political control. In this way the sense of 'being Arabs' made a negative contribution to the growth of the Islamic state. It is worth noting in this regard that the movements of revolt against the Islamic state about the time of Muhammad's death took not merely a religious form but, despite the fact that many of the tribes participating were partly Christian, a specifically *Arab* religious form under independent 'prophets'.

It is also clear that Muhammad deliberately moulded the new religion to make it more Arabian. For a time after he went to Medina he hoped that the Jews there would accept him as a prophet, and emphasized the common features of his teaching and theirs. At the end of some months, however, he realized that there was no chance of gaining Jewish recognition, and (not unlike Paul turning to the Gentiles[1]) began to introduce distinctively Arab elements, apparently in accordance with the desires of at least a section of the Medinan Muslims.[2] Previously he had told his followers to face Jerusalem when they performed the worship. Now, according to the traditional story, while he was conducting the worship in the prayer-place of one of the Medinan clans, he received a revelation to face Mecca instead, and he and all the congregation turned round and completed the worship facing Mecca. Ever since then Mecca has been for Muslims all over the world the *qiblah* or direction to be faced in worship. In this way was dramatized the 'break with the Jews'. There had already been Arab elements in Islam—the revelation had been 'an Arabic *qur'an*', that is, a religious lection for Arabic-speakers,[3] and the Ka'bah had been acknowledged as a house of God. Now Mecca and the Ka'bah were linked up with Abraham,[4] and at the first opportunity Muhammad himself attempted to perform the pilgrimage to Mecca and circumambulation of the Ka'bah, thereby islamizing several old Arabian rites.[5]

Despite this admission of many Arabian features in Islam, it has

---

[1] *Acts*, 13.46.
[2] Cf. *Muhammad at Medina*, 202.
[3] Ibid. 143.
[4] Ibid. 204f.
[5] Ibid. 309-15.

to be concluded that neither the material factor of the existence of a sphere of mutual intelligibility (where Arabic was spoken) nor the ideational factor of the conception of Arab unity played much part in the growth of Islam. What had some effect, however, was the desire to be free from political control by non-Arabs.

2. THE BEGINNINGS OF DISUNITY—KHARIJITES AND SHI'ITES

In order to understand how Islam came to integrate various hetero- geneous groups it is useful also to look at its failures to integrate, and in particular to look at cases where, after a measure of integration, there appeared an opposite trend towards disintegration. The obvious examples here are the Kharijite and Shi'ite movements, both of which began less than half a century after Muhammad's death, and both of which continue still, though only the Shi'ite movement remains of importance.

It is worth remarking here, by way of preface to the study of these two movements, that not every sectional and factional interest leads to a divisive and disintegrative movement. There were different factions in the Islamic state from the first. There were probably even factions in the embryonic religious movement before it became a state at Medina. The traces of such factions have been largely covered up, however, except in the accounts of intrigues between different groups of Muhammad's wives. In a somewhat similar fashion there were rival groups within the Kharijite and Shi'ite movements, and some of these are reckoned distinct sub-sects in the books of the heresiographers, though others disappeared as easily as they appeared. All this means that the problem to be considered is not simply to show how divisions come into being but to explain why some, but only some, sectional interests harden into permanent sects and thereby impair the unity of the society.

(a) The early Kharijite movement[1]

The Kharijites (or Khawarij) are generally stated to have their origin in a movement of disapproval against the caliph 'Ali at the time of the

[1] The following discussion of the Kharijites and Shi'ites is based on an investigation of the relations between the material given by the historians and that given by the heresiographers. Cf. my articles, 'Shi'ism under the Umayyads', *Journal of the Royal Asiatic Society*, 1960, and 'The Kharijites in the Umayyad period', *Der Islam*, 1960. The former or historical material by itself was fully studied by Julius Wellhausen in *Die religiös-politischen Oppositionsparteien im alten Islam*, Göttingen, 1901.

battle of Siffin (in 657). The Kharijites themselves, however, claimed to be the successors of the revolutionary party responsible for the assassination of the caliph 'Uthman (644-56). It is therefore necessary first of all to try to understand what underlay the widespread movement of dissatisfaction with 'Uthman.

In the spring of 656 bands of malcontents marched to Medina from Egypt, Basrah and Kufah[1]. Each of these bands seems to have represented only certain sections of the local garrison of Arabs, but there does not seem to have been any essential economic or social difference between those who were dissatisfied with 'Uthman and those who were prepared to tolerate him. The most that can be said is that old tribal rivalries may have played a part in deciding whether a given group would support 'Uthman or take an active part in the movement against him. Certainly among the Quraysh of Mecca members of clans formerly in alliance with 'Uthman's clan tended to support him and members of clans of the rival group tended to oppose him. The group which had fared worst economically, or at least had the most genuine economic grievance, was the Ansar, the old inhabitants of Medina, for, despite their support of Muhammad in the difficult years immediately after the Hijrah, they were no better off than the Meccans who had fought against him during these same years. Nevertheless their grievances did not make them join with the provincials in the insurrection against 'Uthman. At one point they are said to have made an attack on 'Uthman themselves; but mostly they stood aloof, and neither assisted the insurrectionaries nor opposed them[2].

A preliminary survey, then, suggests that there are no sectional economic grievances sufficient to account for the divisive movements within the Islamic community. At the same time there had been a fundamental change in the economic basis of life for most of the Muslims. Formerly they had been nomads and had gained their livelihood from breeding and pasturing animals, from raiding and from making levies on agricultural populations. Now they had become the standing army of an empire, with their leaders as its corps of administrators. They received annual stipends from the central or local administration (which was essentially a military one). After their campaigns they no longer returned home to their pasture-grounds in the steppe, but only to camp-cities in 'Iraq and Egypt (and apparently to a lesser extent in Syria).

[1] At-Tabari, *Annales*, ed. M. J. de Goeje, Leiden, 1879-1901, i 2954f.; incidental references, ibid., 2908, 2917, 2920, 2928, 2943f., 2986, 2991, 3017-21, 3034, etc.

[2] Meccan and Medinan opponents of 'Uthman are mentioned by at-Tabari, i 2943, 2961, 2980f., 3004f., 3029f., 3048.

When one takes into account the extent of the adjustment which was thus necessary, it must be admitted that the system adopted by the caliphs was as fair a one as could be devised. There are several variations in the recorded details of the stipend-roll, and this doubtless indicates that the stipends actually allocated varied from time to time. One version says that 5000 dirhams annually were given to the men of Badr, 4000 to early converts, to the emigrants to Abyssinia and to the men of Uhud, 3000 to other emigrants up to the conquest of Mecca (and presumably to men of Medina not at Uhud), 2000 to converts at the conquest of Mecca and the sons of emigrants, and sums of from 2000 to 300 dirhams to former nomads in the armies of Syria and 'Iraq[1]. Such a stipend-roll leaves room for complaints about details, and there seems to have been a tendency to raise the amounts given to the lower grades; but there does not appear to have been any serious criticism of the general principles on which it was based, namely, that the captured lands should belong to the Muslims as a body, only the taxes on them being divided, and that in the division of the common income higher shares should be given to those who became Muslims earliest. This, then, was the economic basis of the life of the Muslims, and, after some initial protests at the non-distribution of captured lands, it seems to have been accepted as fair.

Two matters which seem to be of rather a secondary character are mentioned as grievances against 'Uthman. One was that he began to give certain persons grants of land in 'Iraq. To the ordinary Muslim this must have appeared a breach of the agreement not to divide up captured lands, though technically it was not so. The grants were made from certain special classes of land which from the first had belonged to the caliph and not to the Muslims in general.[2] The appearance of unfairness, however, was certainly present, even though the grants may have been made in the hope of increasing stability and security[3]—a matter which was in the interests of the

---

[1] Al-Baladhuri, *Futuh al-Buldan*, 450f. The version in at-Tabari, i 2411-14, includes more men in the second and later grades. One presumably early version puts the Medinans at Badr in a lower grade than the Emigrants; al-Mawardi, *Al-Ahkam as-Sultaniyah*, ed. M. Enger, Bonn, 1853, 346-8 (tr. by E. Fagnan, Algiers, 1915, 433-5); cf. al-Baladhuri, 453. Other accounts in Ibn al-Athir, *Al-Kamil*, Cairo (1929)/1348, ii 350f.; Abu Yusuf, *K. al-Kharaj*, Bulaq (1885)/ 1302, 24-26 (tr. E. Fagnan, Paris, 1921, 66-69); cf. also L. Caetani, *Annali dell' Islam*, Milan, 1905 etc., A.H. 20, §247-353.

[2] Al-Baladhuri, 272-4, cf. 351; Abu Yusuf, 32.

[3] Cf. the settlement of men in Syria near ports to constitute a garrison; D.C. Dennett, *Conversion and the Poll-Tax in Early Islam*, Cambridge, U.S.A., 1950, 60, with references to al-Baladhuri.

Muslims as a whole. The other grievance was that he gave some of the most important (and most lucrative) governorships to men of his own clan[1]. In this, too, there is an appearance of unfairness, even though there is considerable justification for 'Uthman. If he appointed relatives, it was because they combined administrative efficiency with reliability. He refused the importunate requests of inefficient relatives. Yet, even if it is allowed that there were more skilled administrators among his relatives than anywhere else in Arabia (though this is not clearly so), this policy, while understandable, was unwise.

Despite the presence of these economic factors, however, at the end of 'Uthman's caliphate, they do not account for the violence of the insurrection against him. As a tentative hypothesis to explain the insurrection the following might be suggested. The bitter hostility of certain groups towards 'Uthman arose from a sense of insecurity within the new social structure in which they found themselves, and 'Uthman was, as it were, the representative of this social structure. In their nomadic tribes they had had a large measure of freedom and a certain say in the affairs of the tribe; but now they were overwhelmed in a vast bureaucratic organization. Perhaps there was also a feeling that the 'super-tribe' of Islam to which they now belonged had become too much engrossed by stipends and other worldly affairs and had abandoned its former moral standards, so that they could no longer glory in it or boast of its virtues as they had once gloried or boasted about their tribe. Let us examine whether subsequent events support this hypothesis.

After the death of 'Uthman (in June 656) the Muslims present in Medina elected 'Ali caliph. His election, however, was not universally recognized. The governor of Syria, 'Uthman's kinsman Mu'awiyah, refused to take the oath of allegiance to 'Ali; and some members of the group of lesser Meccan clans from which the first two caliphs, Abu-Bakr and 'Umar, had come took up arms against 'Ali, but were defeated by him near Basrah in December 656 (they appear to have been moved by no more than individual desires for wealth and power). About the middle of 657 'Ali marched from 'Iraq against Mu'awiyah, and a battle took place at a place called Siffin. After several days of indecisive fighting, the Syrian army is said to have placed a copy of the Qur'an on a lance, and this was taken to be an appeal to the opposing army, their fellow-Muslims, to accept the judgement of the Qur'an. A strong group within 'Ali's army forced him, not merely to stop fighting and agree to an

---

[1] Cf. the list of governors, at-Tabari, i 3057f.

arbitration, but to appoint as his representative on the board of arbiters a man who was not whole-heartedly his supporter[1].

So many versions of this arbitration were given by later Muslim historians that it is difficult to know the truth of the matter. It is likely, however, that the first matter to be settled by the two arbiters was not, as is usually stated, who was to be caliph, but whether 'Uthman had been justly or unjustly killed. It seems likely also that the arbiters, at a first meeting, decided that 'Uthman had been unjustly killed. When this decision was accepted by 'Ali, many of those who had forced him to agree to the arbitration 'went out' or seceded from him (and so gained the name of Kharijites or Khawarij, 'those who go out'). They adopted as their slogan the phrase 'the decision is God's alone'[2]. By this they meant that the question of the justness of killing 'Uthman should never have been submitted to human decision, since (as they held) the divine law made it clear that he was guilty (through not inflicting a divinely-prescribed punishment on a provincial governor, and similar matters) and that his killing was therefore just. Some time after their first decision was announced the arbiters held a second session to consider who was to be caliph. They found against 'Ali, but he protested against their finding on the grounds that it was not in accordance with the Qur'an and the tradition of the Prophet. As a result nothing came of the arbitration.

'Ali managed to reconcile the first party of Kharijites by giving provincial governorships to their leaders. A second secession, however, did not completely yield to either threats or blandishments, and when 'Ali had recourse to military force, his vastly superior army massacred the handful of Kharijites who stood firm. Even this severity did not stamp out the Kharijite movement. In the remaining year or two of 'Ali's rule five Kharijite risings are mentioned by the historians, each involving about 200 men;[3] while during the caliphate of Mu'awiyah (661-680) some fifteen risings are recorded, the number of participants varying from thirty to 500[4]. About most of these risings we know very little, but there are no grounds for rejecting the statement of the historians that they were Kharijite

---

[1] For the events of 656 and the following years cf. J. Wellhausen, *The Arab Kingdom and its Fall*, Calcutta, 1927, 75-104; L. Veccia Vaglieri, art. ' 'Ali b. Abi Talib' in EI1 (2), also 'Il conflitto 'Ali-Mu'awia e la secessione Kharigita..', *Annali dell'Instituto Universitario Orientale di Napoli*, iv (1952). 1-94.

[2] *La hukm illa li-llah;* cf. Qur'an, 6.57; 12. 40, 67.

[3] Ibn-al-Athir, *Kamil*, iii. 187f., 200f. (A.H. 38, 41).

[4] At-Tabari, i. 3310, 3339, 3380; ii. 10, 15f., 20f., 27, 29, 35f., 40-59, 61, 64, 67, 76, 83, 90f., 181-7; Ibn-al-Athir, iii. 205-7, 209-17, 225f., 229, 244, 254-6; etc.

risings. One small group is said to have shouted their slogan of 'The decision is God's alone' in the mosque at Kufah, and the others doubtless justified their rising by this slogan and pointed to some violation of the divine law by the local authorities. Unfortunately the historians make no mention of special grievances.

With regard to these Kharijite revolts two points are worthy of note. The first is that the Kharijites were just as much opposed to 'Ali as to 'Uthman and the Umayyads, and this tends to support the hypothesis that their dissatisfaction was with the whole social structure and not simply with a particular man or family. It is true that 'Ali came from another section of the Meccan aristocracy, and in this respect was no improvement on 'Uthman from the standpoint of former nomads. It is also true that 'Ali had supporters whose attitude (at least as it was later developed) was diametrically opposite to that of the Kharijites. Nevertheless, the Kharijite hostility to 'Ali remains to some extent evidence for their dissatisfaction with the system. The second point to be noted is that in these revolts of small bands of men the Kharijites were recreating something like the tribal or clan units with which they had been familiar in their lives as nomads. This may have come about unconsciously, but it cannot have been a purely accidental development, since—as we shall see presently—it was elaborated in practice and given a measure of theoretical justification by the Azraqites.

So far as our information goes, those involved in the risings up to 681 made practically no contributions to the development of Kharijite doctrine.[1] After that date, however, and especially among the Kharijites of Basrah, there were a number of interesting modifications of the original theological position of the movement. These modifications took place along two lines, one extremist or radical, the other moderate.

The main exponents of the extremist interpretation of Kharijite doctrine are the Azraqites or Azariqah, the followers of Nafi'-ibn-al-Azraq. These left Basrah about 684, going eastwards into certain mountainous regions of Persia, and, despite the death of Nafi' in 685, maintained themselves there as a strong military body until 698. The severity of some of their measures made their name a synonym for terrorism, and for a time they were a serious threat to the security

---

[1] The chief sources for Kharijite doctrine are: al-Ash'ari, *Maqalat al-Islamiyin*, ed. H. Ritter (2 vols.), Istanbul 1929-30, i. 86-131; al-Baghdadi, *Al-Farq bayn al-Firaq*, Cairo, 1910, 54-92; ash-Shahrastani, *K. al-Milal wa-'n-Nihal*, Cairo (3 vols.), 1948, i, 170-222; also ed. E. Cureton, London, 1846, 85-103. Cf. also A. S. Tritton, *Muslim Theology*, London, 1947, 35-42; E. A. Salem, *Political Theory and Institutions of the Khawarij*, Baltimore, 1956.

of Basrah itself. From the first the militant Kharijites had engaged in the practice of *isti'rad*, that is, the killing of those, even Muslims, who did not accept all their views. Their justification for this was that such persons, although professing Islam, were not really Muslims; the only true Muslims were their fellow-sectaries. The Azraqites, however, now went a step further. To be a true Muslim, in their eyes, it was necessary not merely to hold the beliefs they held but also to go out to their camp in the mountains. To 'sit still' at home was a mark of unbelief. Moreover, since the 'unbelievers' thus defined were the enemies of the 'Muslims', the Azraqites considered it lawful to kill them and to enslave their women and children.

A point of interest in this development is that the Azraqites were in fact forming a social unit not unlike the old desert tribes. It was comparable in size and structure, and it presumably lived mainly by raiding and levying tolls. It is also noteworthy that some of the leaders of the Azraqites were among the greatest Arab poets of the age. All this goes to confirm the hypothesis that the Kharijite movement is in part a revival of Arab nomadism. There is the important difference, however, that its basis is not kinship but religion. In this respect the Azraqite sect is parallel to the original Islamic community formed by Muhammad at Medina. The leaders were aware of this parallelism, and spoke, for example, about making the *hijrah* to their camp (just as one had made the *hijrah* to Medina); and this doubtless connoted not merely the physical migration, but also the breaking of one's former ties of kinship. Where the Islamic community had had a living source of revelations, however, the Azraqites were tied to the fixed rules of the Qur'an, and it is not surprising that they did not repeat the success of the Medinan state.

Most of the other Kharijite sects described by the heresiographers exemplify in varying degrees the moderate interpretation of the original position. Closest to the Azraqites were the Najdites or Najadat, the followers of Najdah ibn-'Amir. About the time the Azraqites went eastwards the Najdites went southwards to the district of the Yamamah in the centre of Arabia. At the height of their power they ruled a large part of Arabia, but as an organized body there they were destroyed by an Umayyad army in 693. The less radical attitude of the Najdites is doubtless due to their responsibility for governing a wide region. They came to realize that expulsion from the community is too severe a penalty for every instance of sins like theft, and also that circumstances often arise where the Qur'an does not state explicitly what conduct is right and what wrong. This led to a moderation in their attitude that was not present in that of the Azraqites.

The Will to Unity and Disunity

In the end, however, it was not experience of responsibility that produced the development of Kharijite doctrine in a moderate direction, but the willingness of certain Kharijite groups in Basrah to live under the rule of non-Kharijite Muslims. From at least about 660 there had been moderate Kharijites in Basrah who disapproved of the practice of killing non-Kharijites and lived devout lives. The chief exponents of this tendency were the sects of the Ibadiyyah and Sufriyyah, each of which had several subdivisions. They justified their attitude by saying that the 'sphere' in which they found themselves was not 'the sphere of Islam' (*dar-al-Islam*) or 'the sphere of openness' (*'alaniyah*), that is, the 'sphere' where Kharijite principles were in force, but 'the sphere of prudent fear' (*taqiyyah*), where it was permissible for a Kharijite to dissemble his true beliefs, or, at least, where it was not his duty to demand that the authorities should enforce them. A state based on Kharijite principles still remained their ideal, but in the meantime they were prepared to tolerate something else; and in this intermediate period conduct was permissible which would not be allowed in the true Kharijite state.

In the half century or so after 680 there must have been many discussions in Basrah about the working out of this moderate Kharijite position. Echoes of these discussions are preserved by the heresiographers. One such discussion was about the selling of 'believing' (Kharijite) slave-girls to 'unbelievers' (non-Kharijite Muslims). Islam in general, of course, forbids the marriage of Muslim women to non-Muslims; so the point at issue (since slave-girls would normally have marital relations with their masters) is whether non-Kharijite Muslims are to be regarded as standing closer to the Kharijites than men who do not profess Islam in any form. The majority of moderate Kharijites, in accordance with their acceptance of non-Kharijite rule, were prepared to regard the non-Kharijite Muslims as in some sense constituting one community with themselves. Some went to the length of saying that they were in 'the sphere of monotheism' (*taw'hid*), and, while continuing to insist that other Muslims were not 'believers' (*mu'minun*), of allowing that they were 'monotheists' (*muwahhidun*).

While the belief and practice of the social group as a whole was a prominent concern of most moderate Kharijites, so that they might be said to think in communal terms, there were also some whose outlook was individualistic. This found expression in their attitude to children, especially the children of their opponents. The more usual view was that the children of 'unbelievers' and 'polytheists' were 'unbelievers' and 'polytheists', and were to be treated as such. The individualists, on the other hand, contended that no one was an

101

'unbeliever' until he had come of age, had been summoned to embrace Islam and had refused. Some extreme individualists even thought that they ought to have no dealings with their own children until they had come of age and had accepted Islam for themselves. This strain of individualism, however, though it prepared the way for the important sect of the Mu'tazilites, never became dominant among the Kharijites.

Despite the communalism of most Kharijite thinking, they have no special name for the social unit which they formed. They spoke of themselves as 'the believers' or 'the people of Paradise'. Non-Kharijite Muslims were 'unbelievers' (*kafirun*) and 'polytheists' or 'idolaters' (until some of the moderates pointed out that the latter term should properly imply some ignorance or denial of monotheism); they were also 'the people of Hell'. The use of these terms, especially 'the people of Paradise' and 'the people of Hell', shows that the Kharijites in general thought of membership of the social unit as conferring salvation and non-membership of it as leading to damnation. This communal way of thinking explains the Kharijite concern about 'associating' with 'the people of Paradise' and 'dissociating' from 'the people of Hell'. It must have been difficult not to feel that a social group which contained wrongdoers could not be 'the people of Paradise'. Hence the insistence of the early and the more extreme Kharijites, and even of many of the moderates, that wrongdoers had ceased to be members of the social unit.

The communalism of Kharijite thinking is further shown in the interpretation given to the doctrine of the Last Day. The modern Western reader of the Qur'an would take that doctrine as stated there to be essentially an individualistic one; a man is rewarded or punished for his own good or bad deeds, and his kinsmen—that is, the community to which he belongs—cannot help him in any way. The Kharijites, however, as they came to realize that it is impracticable to exclude men from the community for every sin, introduced a new interpretation of the rewards and punishments of the Last Day. Najdah, for example, distinguished between what was fundamental in religion and what was not, and held with regard to sins in non-fundamentals that God's punishment for them would not be in Hell and would not be eternal; that is, a man who committed a single act of theft did not thereby become one of 'the people of Hell'. All this implies that membership of the social unit or community of the believers led to salvation, provided a man showed a modicum of diligence in observing the rules of the community (so as not to be expelled from it).

It cannot be accidental that there is a close parallel between such

102

ways of thinking about the Islamic community and the way in which the pre-Islamic Arabs thought about the tribe. We know something about the latter from the poetry which has been preserved. For the pre-Islamic Arabs a man's life was meaningful or significant in so far as it exemplified the virtues they admired, which are summed up in their ideal of *muruwwah* or 'manliness'. Manly qualities, however, were thought of as belonging primarily to the tribe, and only secondarily to the individual because of his membership of the tribe. If a man showed outstanding courage, it was because he came of courageous stock. While it was possible for the individual in actual life to fail to live up to the virtues of his tribe, any virtue seen in a man's conduct redounded to the credit of his stock. Moreover, the tribe followed its own fixed custom, sometimes called the 'beaten path' or *sunnah*. Not to follow this custom was a serious fault, and grave breaches or persistence in lesser ones led to expulsion from the tribe. Life for the Muslim became meaningful through the attainment of Paradise, and this, according to the communalistic strain of thought, happened through membership of the Islamic community and the following of its 'beaten path', the precepts of the Qur'an. (It would be anachronistic at this period to emphasize the *sunnah* or practice of Muhammad, since it was probably only towards the year 800 that it assumed the importance it now has, though the phrase 'the Sunnah of the Prophet', had been used from an early time.)[1]

The results, then, of this study of the early Kharijite movement are as follows. The movement was not a movement to obtain redress of economic grievances. There had indeed been a vast change in the economic basis of life for most of the full members of the Islamic state, and in the course of this change a few men had done very well for themselves; but on the whole the principles on which the wealth of the state was distributed were regarded as fair. The social repercussions of the economic change did much more to create a feeling of malaise. Those who had been accustomed to tribal society missed the security, essentially in a religious or spiritual sense, provided by the old system; nothing in the new system quite replaced it. The Kharijite movement is first and foremost an attempt to mould the Islamic community in such a way that membership in it gave to the life of the individual something of the significance formerly given to it by membership of the tribe. That meant, as they saw it, that the Islamic community had to become a virtuous community according to the new Islamic ideal of virtue. What was set out as a tentative

---

[1] The phrase '*sunnah* of the Prophet' was used by al-Mukhtar in 685, according to at-Tabari, ii 569f.

hypothesis a few pages back has been well supported by further examination.

(b) *the early Shi'ite movement*

The Shi'ah is etymologically just 'the party'. It is specially applied, however, to 'the party of 'Ali', though not all the supporters of 'Ali can be reckoned as belonging to the Shi'ah or being Shi'ites, but only those specially characterized by party-spirit or partisanship. Up to the time of the battle of Siffin 'Ali had the support of some who later became Kharijites, and there was presumably also a middle group of men who were neither Kharijites nor Shi'ites. The beginning of the Shi'ite movement (if the report may be accepted) was on a day in 658 when a group of 'Ali's followers swore that they would be 'friends of those whom he befriended and enemies of those to whom he was hostile'.[1] That is to say, on a great many matters they were prepared to accept 'Ali's judgement absolutely. It was doubtless because they were partisans in this sense that the Shi'ites became 'the party' *par excellence*. It was a matter of principle with them that the ruler ruled by a kind of divine right and not as the nominee of the people. The difference between the Kharijites and the Shi'ites may be described by saying that the Kharijites wanted an impersonal law to control the state, while the Shi'ites wanted the supreme control to be given to a charismatic leader. It is not surprising that the two movements were bitterly opposed to one another.

In the lists of men who showed Kharijite or Shi'ite tendencies in the earliest period, many tribes are represented on both sides. What is significant, however, is that an unexpectedly high number of men from South Arabian tribes are found among the Shi'ites, while those Kharijites responsible for the theological advance of the movement are mainly from a few northern tribes, notably Tamim, Hanifah and Shayban.

It is important to try to account for this difference of attitude. If one looks for economic differences, there are some to be found. The northern tribes had been raiding the nearest settled lands of 'Iraq while the latter were still part of the Persian empire and before Muslim expansion had begun to move in this direction; and these northern tribes may therefore have been wealthier and have had higher stipends than the tribes from the south who joined in the raids only after the Muslims began to organize them. This point cannot be pressed very far, however. Jarir ibn-'Abd-Allah of the southern tribe of Bajilah had a part in the early raids comparable to

[1] At-Tabari, i 3350f.

104

that of the northern tribes; and Bajilah was Shi'ite on the whole. Further there are no records of complaints by the southern tribes against the northern. It seems unlikely, then, that the different attitudes were due to economic differences.

It should also be considered whether the division into Kharijite and Shi'ite tribes corresponded roughly to earlier political alliances. This is unfortunately a very obscure subject. The alliances which are found in the later Umayyad period were probably only coming into being in the caliphates of 'Ali (656-61) and Mu'awiyah (661-80). Yet, even if (as is likely) political factors determined the attitude of some tribes or parts of tribes, the problem still remains. Why did one group of tribes in alliance adopt one attitude and another group of tribes in alliance another attitude?

Another possible reason for the difference is the religious affiliation of the various tribes. It could be argued that in South Arabia there had been much monophysite Christian influence from Abyssinia, whereas the northern tribes had been rather under Nestorian influence from al-Hirah. This argument could be further supported by the fact that there is a certain correspondence between Shi'ite and monophysite views and between Kharijite and Nestorian views. The monophysites placed emphasis on the 'theandric (or super-human) activity' of Christ as a divine leader, while the Nestorians insisted on the need for fulfilment of the moral law. Unfortunately for this argument, it seems to be the case that most of the Christians of South Arabia in Muhammad's time were Nestorians, while the northern tribe of Shayban was monophysite. Such facts make it impossible to explain the adoption of a Kharijite or Shi'ite attitude by a tribe's previous religious (Christian) affiliation. The correspondences mentioned, however, demand some explanation; and, if we had fuller knowledge of the penetration of the various tribes by Christianity, it might be possible to see some connexion between their Christian affiliation and their later Muslim attitudes.

More significant than the economic and political differences between the tribes which showed Kharijite and Shi'ite tendencies respectively is the fact that the South Arabian tribes came from a region where for about twenty centuries there had been a tradition of large political units with a high degree of civilization. Latterly the civilization had been in decline. The Himyarite kingdom came to an end in 525, and thereafter Abyssinian and Persian invaders governed the region (to some extent) for half a century each, until it was incorporated in the Islamic state. Nevertheless something of the tradition still remained. In the South Arabian kingdoms the king had been regarded as a charismatic leader (a superhuman being);[1] and something of the aura of kingship seems to have clung to the kinglets or princes of South Arabia who still maintained themselves as local rulers especially of the settled population — nomads and agriculturalists were intermingled in most parts of the region.

With such a background it is not surprising that, in the malaise caused by the transition from the pre-Islamic to the Islamic social structure, many of these people from South Arabia turned towards the conception of a superhuman or semi-divine leader. Perhaps they had been originally attracted to Islam because they unconsciously found in Muhammad a leader of this sort. The underlying idea would be that salvation or significance was to be found in membership of a community with a semi-divine leader. Some of 'Ali's early followers retorted to Kharijite critics that 'Ali had 'truth and guidance', and the latter word particularly has a religious connotation; it is 'guidance' in the way of God, the way to Paradise. Thus, while the Kharijites revived in an Islamic form the tradition of the nomadic tribe, the Shi'ites, to begin with at least, were giving an Islamic form to the old South Arabian tradition of a kingdom with a semi-divine king. This difference in background and tradition is the chief reason why some former nomads became Kharijites and some Shi'ites.

In the subsequent development of the Shi'ite movement there is not the same proliferation of petty risings by handfuls of men as among the Kharijites. Shi'ite risings are mostly serious attempts to gain control of the caliphate as a whole or of some sizeable part of it. Such attempts must be carefully prepared, and so a feature of the Shi'ite movement is 'underground' planning. Kufah was the chief centre. There was a Shi'ite revolt there against the Umayyads in 671, there was the ineffectual attempt of al-Husayn to seize the caliphate in 680, encouraged but in the end not supported by the men of Kufah; in Kufah was organized in 684 the unsuccessful rising of the so-called Penitents (who, be it noted, had four thousand men);[2] from the remnants of this rising and from other sources al-Mukhtar in 685 collected an army which enabled him to control Kufah and the surrounding region for over a year. After this there were no more Shi'ite risings for over fifty years, and by that time it was probably obvious that the disintegration of the Umayyad caliphate was

[1] Cf. J. Ryckmans, *L'institution monarchique en Arabie méridionale avant l'Islam*, Louvain, 1951. For a brief summary of our present knowledge of South Arabia, cf. M. Rodinson, in R. Grousset and E. G. Léonard, *Histoire Universelle*, ii (Encyclopédie de la Pléiade, vol. iv), Paris, 1957, 13-20.

[2] Lists of participants in the above three risings are found in At-Tabari, ii. 136; 386; 497, etc.

imminent. We hear of two Shi'ite sectarian leaders being executed in 737 and one in 742;[1] but they were still at the stage of plotting and planning. The first actual revolt was that of Zayd ibn-'Ali (a grandson of al-Husayn) in 740 which came to nothing.[2] Another, led by a great-grandson of Ja'far ibn-Abi-Talib in 744, fared better for a time but also in the end came to nothing.[3] Finally, the insurrection of Abu-Muslim which was successful in bringing the 'Abbasid dynasty to the throne was in some respects a Shi'ite movement.

The first point to notice about this phase of the Shi'ite movement is that several actual leaders (notably al-Mukhtar), who did not themselves belong to the Meccan clan of Hashim, the clan of Muhammad and his kinsmen, adopted the device of the absent leader. They claimed that a member of the clan of Hashim, that is, a charismatic leader, had appointed them to lead the revolt in its preliminary stages. In many cases there was no truth in the claim, but in the circumstances of the time it could not be refuted, and it was useful in that it enabled men with gifts for leadership to mobilize a following of Shi'ites. Up to the end of the Umayyad caliphate, and even later in the official 'Abbasid view, the charismata were regarded as belonging to the whole clan of Hashim and not merely to the descendants of Muhammad through his daughter Fatimah.

From this conception of the absent leader it was not difficult to pass to messianic ideas. In several cases where the charismatic leader died it was claimed that he had not really died, but was living on in concealment and would one day return as the Mahdi ('the guided one', a being similar to the Messiah in some Jewish thought) and would establish justice and righteousness on the earth. It is worth noting that the Shi'ite idea of the hidden imam or leader had a similar function to the Kharijite idea of 'the sphere of prudent fear'. It justified the Shi'ites in accepting the existing social and political structure without forcing them to admit that it was perfect. It is interesting that Zayd, the leader of the revolt of 740 and a great-great-grandson of Muhammad, denounced the idea of the hidden imam and insisted that any true imam must be active and come forward publicly. Such an attitude was perhaps justified at a time when the Umayyad caliphate was disintegrating; but part of the reason for Zayd's failure was that he made concessions to the main body of non-Shi'ite Muslim opinion which alienated the extreme

[1] Ibid. ii. 1619f.; an-Nawbakhti, *Firaq ash-Shi'ah*, ed. M. Ritter, Istanbul, 1931, 34; etc.

[2] An-Nawbakhti, 50f.; etc.

[3] Cf. ibid. 29, 31; and I. Friedlaender, in *Journal of the American Oriental Society*, xxix, 124ff.

Shi'ites. Dissatisfaction with an imam who was merely hidden is to be seen in the attempts of some groups to regard as superhuman their actual successful leaders (like Abu-Muslim) or the actual caliph (like al-Mansur in 758).[1]

The movement in favour of the 'Abbasids as directed by Abu-Muslim brought together several strands of the Shi'ite movement and its ideas. The idea of the representative of the absent imam was prominent. Abu-Muslim, though in fact appointed by the head of the family of al-'Abbas, claimed to be acting on behalf of an imam of the clan of Hashim who had not yet been chosen or designated. In this way he gained the support of many who would not have been ready to support him had they known that the imam from the clan of Hashim would in fact be from the family of al-'Abbas. For the groups which had been involved in the rising of al-Mukhtar and had then turned to messianic ideas he claimed (presumably only after the first 'Abbasid had been publicly named as imam and caliph) that the son of al-Mukhtar's imam had bequeathed the imamate on his death (about 716) to the head at that time of the family of al-'Abbas.[2] For those who had followed Zayd in 740 and subsequently his son Yahya he claimed that he was seeking vengeance for their blood. All in all the idea of the charismatic leader or imam played an important part in 'Abbasid propaganda. The continuing importance of this idea is shown by the fact that the 'Abbasid caliphs after the first are known not by their name but by a title which implicitly or explicitly contains the name of God and means that the caliph is divinely aided and supported. Thus the second caliph is known as al-Mansur, and this title means 'the one rendered victorious (by God)'; similarly Harun ar-Rashid is Harun (or Aaron) 'the one rightly guided (by God)'.

Another important feature of the 'Abbasid movement and indeed of the Shi'ite movement in general was that more and more the rank and file (and some of the leaders) came to be not Arabs but non-Arab Muslims. Up to the end of the Umayyad period the Islamic community or *ummah* seems to have been thought of as a federation of Arab tribes to which a number of non-Arab (and non-Muslim) groups were attached as dependents. If a man who was not an Arab made a profession of Islam, he was attached to an Arab tribe as a 'client' (*mawla*, plural *mawali*); apparently this was the only way in which he could exercise his rights as a full citizen of the Islamic state, and draw his stipend (when he had one). Since the *mawali* or clients

[1] Cf. an-Nawbakhti, 46f.; also Tritton, *Muslim Theology*, 23-28; Watt, 'Shi'ism under the Umayyads', *Journal of the Royal Asiatic Society*, 1960.

[2] Cf. S. Moscati, art. 'Abu Hashim' in *Encyclopedia of Islam*, second edition.

also included slaves who had been set free, a certain inferiority was felt to attach to the status, and the non-Arab Muslims came more and more to resent this. The rising of al-Mukhtar in 685 was supported at first by both Arabs and *mawali;* but some of the Arabs were annoyed when al-Mukhtar accorded equal treatment to the *mawali*, and he latterly came to rely more and more on the *mawali*. Protection of 'the weak' (that is, the *mawali*) was a prominent item in the programme of Zayd in 740 and also in that of Abu-Muslim. The latter being himself a Persian *mawla* gained the support of many other Persians, and this was probably the decisive factor in the success of the 'Abbasids.

It is necessary here to try to explain why the Shi'ite ideas came to have so much attraction for the *mawali*. Unfortunately the matter is obscure, for Arab writers usually consider it sufficient to say that a man is a *mawla* and give no further indication of his racial origin. Only occasionally are there statements or hints about it, and these have not yet been thoroughly studied by Western scholars. In the closing stages of Abu-Muslim's rising there were certainly many Persian *mawali*, but it seems probable that many of the *mawali* of Kufah who became Shi'ites under al-Mukhtar were descended from the old Aramaic-speaking inhabitants of 'Iraq. Since these were the majority of the population there this is what might be expected; and the presumption is supported by a number of little pieces of information (while other such pieces show that there was even a number of *mawali* of Arab descent).

The question of the identity of the *mawali* is not of primary importance in the present study, since in any case 'Iraq had seen a considerable fusion of Persian and Aramaean elements in the previous century or two. If it may be assumed, however, that there was a large number of Aramaean *mawali*, this makes it possible to explain how Shi'ism passed from the Arabs to the *mawali* and especially to the Persians. The Arabs adopted Shi'ism because they felt that life was given significance by belonging to a community with a charismatic leader. The Aramaeans of 'Iraq, however, were also the heirs of a tradition, even older than that of South Arabia, in which large populations had looked for salvation to the activity of a divinely appointed king on their behalf.[1] A more recent allegiance to monophysite Christianity perhaps formed a bridge between some of the South Arabian Arabs and the Aramaeans of 'Iraq. This would explain how Aramaeans came to join Shi'ite Arabs, while the intermingling of Aramaean and Persian traditions in 'Iraq would ease the incorporation of Persians also.

[1] Cf. H. Frankfort, *Kingship and the Gods*, Chicago, 1948.

109

It has to be noticed, however, that *mawali* were attracted to Kharijite as well as to Shi'ite doctrines. There is the report of a Kharijite (whose date is unfortunately not given) who proclaimed the coming of a Persian prophet; and this doubtless indicates that he himself was of Persian stock.[1] Among the minor figures of the earlier Kharijite movement some *mawali* are mentioned; and in North Africa many Berbers adopted Kharijite doctrines. It was not surprising that many *mawali* should become Kharijites, for it was a Kharijite principle that the position of imam or caliph was open to all good Muslims and was not restricted to Arabs, still less to the tribe of Quraysh. Despite this theoretical insistence of the Kharijites on the equality of all Muslims, it is possible that it was more difficult among the Kharijites for a non-Arab to attain real power, at least in the eastern provinces of the Islamic empire. Because of the prominence of communal ideas among the Kharijites, the Arabs with their strong tradition of tribal solidarity and their belief in their superiority would tend to receive the leading positions. (The case was different in the western provinces where the Berbers also had a strong tribal tradition.) Among the Shi'ites, on the other hand, though for the majority the imam had always to be an Arab of the clan of Hashim, he might be hidden or absent, and the actual leadership, as the instance of Abu-Muslim shows, might be in the hands of a non-Arab.

From this study of the early Shi'ite movement, then, we conclude that it was a way in which spiritual needs were met for those belonging to a tradition in which an important part was played by the charismatic leader. The economic position of those who became Shi'ites was much the same as that of those who became Kharijites. Some had specific economic grievances, but the movement as a whole was an attempt to remedy the social malaise resulting in the change from nomadism to being the military caste of an empire (or, in the case of the *mawali*, from the breakdown of the Persian empire).

(c) *The will to separation*

Individuals and groups of men are constantly quarreling with one another about all sorts of matters. Conflicts of economic interests or of personal ambitions are frequent reasons for such quarrels. The accounts which have been preserved of the sects just studied, the Kharijites and Shi'ites, show that, even within the sub-sects of each, splits were constantly occurring. Not all such splits and quarrels, however, are relevant to the study of the disintegration of a society,

[1] Al-Ash'ari, *Maqalat*, i. 103.

110

but only those which attain a degree of permanence. Many quarrels soon die out and are forgotten. The phrases 'will to disunity' and 'will to separation' are here used only where a quarrel or split has become more than temporary. The problem before us, then, is why some little quarrels quickly fade away while others spread until they produce century-long major divisions of a great community.

By way of preliminary it may be noted that, where the will to separation appears among a whole collection of people or of groups of people, that implies that there is in the collection a measure of integration or unification. Moreover, what integrates or unifies a sect of Kharijites or Shi'ites is presumably the same kind of thing as integrates the Islamic community as a whole. This process of integration in its general aspects is the main subject of study in the present chapter, and further discussion of it must wait until the concluding section. Meanwhile what has to be considered is how within an integrated whole there can be a focus of partial integration leading to a division of the whole.

It should perhaps also be emphasized that the phenomenon here being considered is that of division within a unity. When one reflects upon it, the strength of the will to unity within the Islamic community is seen to be remarkable. In certain regions, such as Transoxiana and North Africa, there was vigorous resistance to incorporation within the Islamic state, but once people had been incorporated they hardly, ever tried to become independent again. The Islamic state, of course was immensely powerful, and it would have been a costly business for any group of independence-lovers to assert their independence. Even so, it is surprising that we hear practically nothing of movements for absolute autonomy, but only of movements for autonomy within an Islamic framework, like those of some Kharijite sects. In general the Arabs, who might have had a large measure of autonomy by retiring to the steppes of Arabia, were firmly in favour not merely of the Islamic state (which is not surprising in view of the material advantages it conferred) but also of the Islamic religion. There is no mention of any desire to return to Arab paganism. In view of the contrast between the Islamic outlook and that of pre-Islamic Arabia this is remarkable. The wide acceptance of the new social and political structure we can understand; it is like the general acceptance in India of the outward aspects of Western culture, despite the efforts of Gandhi with his spinning-wheel to avoid becoming dependent on Western technology. The acceptance at the same time, however, of the Islamic religion seems to require for its explanation the admission that the Arabs were unable even to *think* of their new political structure except in Islamic terms. They might say that the Islamic state was like the Byzantine and Persian empires; but, if they went on to say how it differed, they had to use religious terms. It was ruled by a caliph, who was not one of a line of emperors, but the successor to the temporal powers of a prophet; the caliph's powers were limited by the sacred law revealed in a sacred book, and the stipends they received for soldierly activities were for taking part in a holy war against unbelievers. This strong will to unity on an Islamic basis, then, underlies the separative movements of at least the first century and a half of Islam (apart from the wars of the Riddah at the time of Muhammad's death).

In so far as a sect of Kharijites or Shi'ites acted as a unity, what was it that brought them together? The above studies show that it was not common material interests (though these may sometimes have given the first impulse to common action). What we found was a common reaction to an economic and social situation; but the common reaction was primarily due to a common religious tradition. These points are confirmed by looking at the directions in which the most vigorous efforts were made. Though (as is allowed) the Kharijite and Shi'ite movements were responses to an economic and social situation, their chief efforts were not directed towards altering the existing system, except in so far as the 'Abbasid movement aimed at ending the inferiority of the *mawali*. What the Kharijites wanted above all was the fuller application of the revealed law, while the Shi'ites gave great prominence to the need for a charismatic leader. There is further confirmation of the above contentions in the criticisms which the Kharijites and Shi'ites made of one another. The former argued against the latter that the community might fall into sin if it promised to obey all the commands of a leader, since the leader might give a wrong command; and the latter urged against the former that an imam who was merely elected by his followers (and so had no charisma) was liable to lead his community astray.

Thus the insistence of the Shi'ites on the elevation of the imam above the law was felt by the Kharijites to endanger the salvation (or significance) of the community and its members as they (the Kharijites) understood the matter. The Shi'ites in their turn felt that the salvation of the community was threatened by the Kharijite lack of concern for a charismatic imam. Each of the two sects regarded the other as its bitterest enemies, but each was also opposed to the body of non-Kharijite and non-Shi'ite Muslims because of their neglect of the points which each sect considered necessary for salvation. Here is the secret of the will to separation. It becomes deep and enduring when quarrels occasioned by other matters come to be linked up with the question of salvation or, in less religious terms, of

112

the significance and meaningfulness of the lives of individuals and communities. If you feel that continued association with someone is liable, because of the way he thinks or acts, to deprive your life of its significance, then you are strongly moved to have nothing to do with him and to exclude him from the community of which up till now you have both been members. You probably go on to exaggerate the factors making for significance in your own community and those making against it among the people from whom you are separating. The line of division between you and your opponents becomes more definite and more rigid. Certain simple tests are used to decide on which side of the line a man stands; and so the will to separation becomes something settled.

This curious phenomenon of a separative process occurring *within* an integrative process without completely cancelling it out—for example, though the Shi'ites separate themselves from the Sunnites or orthodox, they continue to be Muslims, accepting the Qur'an, and so on—may be explained by the conception of the 'dynamic image'. By 'dynamic image' I mean an image capable of generating or releasing psychical energy. This is much the same as what is sometimes called an 'archetype' (notably by C. G. Jung) or a 'primordial image', but is intended in a metaphysically neutral sense, that is, without the metaphysical connotations sometimes attached to these other phrases. I shall use the term 'dynamic image', then, mainly at the phenomenal level to indicate the fact that in an ideational system such as that belonging to a religion, where there is a wide context of imagery, a certain image (or a small number of images) which is embedded in this system and context is specially effective in generating or releasing psychical energy. Observation further shows that there is some connexion between the power of a dynamic image and the strength of the tradition behind it; and this point has been implicit in some statements made above.

The application of this conception to the will to separation is as follows. Islam as preached in the century after Muhammad is an example of an ideational system (even though it was not theologically systematized). In accepting Islam men were accepting this ideational system and the images embedded in it. Most men probably accepted the system as a whole without being clearly aware of the importance they attached to the various aspects. Yet almost certainly they were moved by certain images or parts of the system more than by others; and different men would be moved by different images. Those groups which became Shi'ite were doubtless from the first attracted and moved by the dynamic image of the charismatic leader which was present in the figure of Muhammad, the Messenger sent by God;

while for those who became Kharijites the attraction would be the image of the holy or charismatic community which had received and was based on the Word of God. In the social malaise which became acute about the year 650 their thoughts began to be more occupied with the dynamic images that had first moved them, and they became more explicitly aware of them and saw the need for greater emphasis on them in the ideational system of Islam. It is because an ideational system such as that of Islam contains a number of dynamic images and because some men are chiefly moved by one and some by another that it is possible to have separative processes within a wider integrative process.

3. THE INCORPORATION OF THE PERSIANS

So far this study has been mostly concerned with the Arabs, though in the last section there were references to Persians. One of the outstanding achievements of Islam has been its incorporation of Arabs and non-Arabs into a community with a large measure of unity and integration. Among the non-Arab races thus incorporated a distinction may be drawn between those of the heartlands, like the Persians, the Berbers, and the Turks, who came within the Islamic empire at an early period of its existence, and those of the periphery, like the peoples of East and West Africa, Malaya and Indonesia. The Persians cannot be said to be typical of the non-Arab peoples of the heartlands, for in their relations to Islam there are many differences between them and the Turks and the Berbers, for example. Yet it is inevitable that something should be said about the Persians because of their important place in Islamic civilization; and what is said about the Persians may indicate in a general way the kind of factors which led to the incorporation of other non-Arab people of the heartlands into the Islamic community.

The position of the Persians in the Islamic community is a subject of great fascination for the sociologist. Here is a people (or group of peoples) with a long cultural tradition of their own, who become merged in a civilization whose central ideas are not theirs, and yet who within this foreign civilization attain to a rich flowering of their own special gifts. Then, after a time, they become separated from the main body of the Muslims and form a special sub-community of their own (from the beginning of the sixteenth century). While the fascination for the student of this whole course of development is clear, it soon becomes equally clear, when he tries to answer some of the obvious questions, that it is a subject of very great difficulty,

114

and that a great deal of research on small points has to be done before anything like adequate answers can be given to some of the main questions.

One of the first points that becomes clear is that the Persians of the seventh and eighth centuries cannot be treated as a unity. The chiefs of semi-settled tribes with their followers, and the *dihqans* (a kind of local gentry or squires) with the villagers under them, were in a vastly different position from the town-dwellers of 'Iraq. Many of the references to Persians in the first three centuries of Islam, especially in contexts dealing with literature, are to the latter group, who were probably persianized Aramaeans rather than pure Persians. Despite the differences, however, all the groups who are in any sense Persian had come to some extent under the influence of the Iranian cultural tradition. Apart from everything else they had been for four centuries under the rule of the Sasanid dynasty which supported the Zoroastrian religious institution and was supported by it, and which in this way was spreading Iranian culture. Thus there was both unity and variety among the Persians, but it is difficult to say how much there was of each.

This study of the incorporation of the Persians in the Islamic community is thus a study which at present consists more in asking questions than in answering them. If tentative answers are given here, it is mainly in order to stimulate other scholars to discover better answers.

(a) Economic factors

The first question to be asked is whether there were any economic factors which facilitated or encouraged the islamization of the Persians. At first sight it might seem that there were no important economic factors. The Sasanian empire had been conquered by the Arabs, but that led to no radical change in the economic basis of the lives of the inhabitants. Even the detailed administration was little altered at first. The main change was that the ultimate recipient of the taxes was the Arab ruling institution and not the Sasanian. It was also the case that some remission of taxation followed upon conversion to Islam, and this motive undoubtedly led to many conversions. Nevertheless it seems unlikely that such a selfish and material motive could have produced that deep acceptance of Islam which must be presupposed as a basis for the flowering of Persian culture within Islam.

The economic situation, however, was more complex than the above description suggests. A gradual economic change had been taking place under the Sasanian empire, and this change continued, still gradually, under the Islamic. It has been described by Barthold as a process of urbanization,[1] and it came about naturally through the presence in the Sasanian empire of the land of 'Iraq with its high culture and its deep tradition of settled life. Indian influences, connected with the expansion of Buddhism into Sogdia and the upper Oxus valley, may also have contributed to the process of urbanization, but they can only have been of secondary importance, and may be neglected here.[2] Basically, urbanization was one aspect of the growth of commerce and hand-industry. At the same time, however, it meant the spread of the higher cultures, especially the 'Iraqian, and the assimilation to these of the indigenous Iranian culture. The situation was not unlike that in the modern world, where Asia and Africa are busily taking over the technology and industry of the West and at the same time are being influenced willy-nilly by some of the ideas present in Western culture.

The Arab conquest, though it did not greatly change the economic basis of life throughout the former Sasanian empire, continued and developed the process of urbanization. New cities grew up, sometimes out of Arab military camps, like Basrah and Kufah. The Arabs who administered the empire mostly came from the former Meccan merchant class, and their system of administration might be expected not to discourage trade, perhaps actively to encourage it. Moreover the Islamic caliphate was much larger than the Sasanian empire, by the inclusion of rich provinces like Syria and Egypt, and the possibilities of trade were therefore greater. If most Persians had found it desirable to share in the material culture of the Sasanian empire, they had even more reason to want to share in that of the caliphate.

(b) Social factors

In attempting to discover the social repercussions of this economic change we must again go back to the Sasanians. In early Sasanian times there are said to have been four classes, namely, the Zoroastrian clergy, the soldiers, the bureaucracy or secretaries, and the people; the latter could be further subdivided into peasants, artisans and traders[3]. Within the military aristocracy there were distinctions

[1] W. Barthold, 'Die persische Su'ubija und die moderne Wissenschaft', *Zeitschrift fur Assyriologie*, xxvi (1912), 250.

[2] B. Spuler, *Iran in fruhislamischer Zeit*, Wiesbaden, 1952, 217-20, with further references.

[3] A. Christensen, *L'Iran sous les Sassanides*, second edition, Copenhagen, 1944, 97-113.

between the heads of the great families, the provincial governors (along with vassal princes), and the squires or village-lords (*dihqans*); and the relative importance of these groups varied from time to time. The important change, however, was the growth in the power of the secretary-class at the expense of the clergy and the soldiers. The more civilized the empire became, the more heavily the ruler had to lean on the bureaucracy. Naturally, too, the bureaucracy was drawn largely from the most civilized part of the population, the persianized-Aramaean town-dwellers of 'Iraq. Unfortunately we do not know much about these people. Were all the secretaries Aramaeans, or were some pure Persians? What was their religious outlook? How far was their education in their own hands, and how far was it controlled by the Zoroastrian clergy?

The Zoroastrian clergy certainly played an important role throughout the Sasanian period. Zoroastrianism was the official religion, and provided the ideational framework for the state. The clergy thus had considerable influence. They controlled the judiciary and the higher education. Opposition to the official religion was curbed by persecution, the motives for this being mainly political. Nevertheless the masses of the people seem to have felt as time went on that the clergy were chiefly interested in maintaining their own power, and that to do this they supported the interests of the ruling institution against those of the people. The Mazdakite movement in the early sixth century was an expression of popular discontent. In 'Iraq many turned to Manichaeanism—perhaps members of the secretary class[1]—quite apart from the large numbers who became Christians. Thus, despite the great power of the Zoroastrian clergy in the Sasanian empire, the foundations of that power were gradually eaten away, and, when the ruling institution of the empire broke up in the face of the Arab invasion, the religious institution also collapsed. For a time a nominal head of the Zoroastrians was recognized by the Muslims,[2] but apart from that the hierarchy disappeared. Groups of people here and there in the Islamic empire remained faithful to their religion for centuries, but others decided it was better to emigrate to places like Gujarat in India. The great majority, however, became Muslims.

Along with the Zoroastrian clergy much of the Sasanian administrative machine was swept away by the Arab conquest. The Arabs, however, were anxious to retain as much as possible, since they were in no position to create a whole administration *ex*

[1] Cf. Barthold, op. cit., 259—a chief secretary called Aprahim.

[2] Cf. Spuler, *Iran*, 186. The local clergy retained some power; e.g. a *herbadh* at Darabjird (al-Baladhuri, 388).

117

nihilo. The higher officials disappeared, therefore, but the local administrators and the secretaries were retained. These local administrators were primarily the class of squires (*dihqans*). In 'Iraq and Persia, while a few towns and villages had come to terms with the Arabs before being attacked and had thus secured treaties which guaranteed local autonomy and restricted the tribute payable to a fixed amount, most of the country had been ' taken by force' and could be disposed of by the caliph as he pleased. Even where there was no treaty, however, the caliphs found it advisable to confirm the position of the squire in each village and make him responsible for collecting the taxes and administering justice. After the Arab conquest the class of squires and local magnates thus retained their position in the social structure.

This social security meant that it was not in any way urgent for the squires to become Muslims. Some had actually adopted Islam, however, and made treaties with the Arabs at an early stage in the conquests before the final pattern of Arab administration had become clear. Others felt a certain degradation in the fact that as non-Muslims under Muslim rule they had to pay a poll-tax, since under the Sasanians only the lower classes had paid such a tax; and this is explicitly mentioned as a motive for the conversion of some squires near Isfahan.[1] Whether the squires of 'Iraq felt in the same way on this matter is a point on which we cannot be certain, but it seems clear that sooner or later they all accepted Islam.

The position seems to have been a little different in the east, especially in Sogdia, the region beyond the Oxus round Bukhara and Samarqand. Here commerce had long flourished, and next to 'Iraq this was the most civilized part of the Sasanian empire. There was strong Buddhist influence. The local leaders, some of whom were more important than squires, had much independence of spirit. They accepted the Islamic state, but tried to maintain a distinctive position within it and did not at first become Muslims. This independent attitude is no doubt connected with the strength of the commerce-based regional economy. In course of time, however, they presumably came to see that if they were to maintain their commerce they must be full members in the Islamic empire. Similarly in Khurasan, where there had been considerable Arab settlement, the leaders must have realized that in order to share in the commerce and culture of the empire they must be Muslims.[2] Thus the attraction of 'Iraqian

[1] Al-Baladhuri, *Futuh al-Buldan*, 314; the evidence on which this paragraph and the previous one is based is clearly summarized in D.C. Dennett, *Conversion and the Poll Tax in Early Islam*, Cambridge (U.S.A.), 1950, 14-42, esp. 28-33.

[2] Cf. Dennett, 116-28; H. A. R. Gibb, *The Arab Conquests in Central Asia*, London, 1923.

culture for the other inhabitants of the Sasanian empire continued under the Muslims, and was an important factor in bringing many Persians to accept Islam.

The secretaries were in a somewhat different position, since they were, themselves, at least to a large extent, the bearers of the old 'Iraqian culture. For a time they were in no danger of losing their positions, since their work was almost identical with what it had been under the Sasanians, and there was no one else who could perform it. Offices passed from father to son.[1] About 702, however, al-Hajjaj, the governor of 'Iraq, is said to have decided to stop using Persian as the language for official business and to use Arabic instead. This was made possible by the fact that he had a Muslim available who knew both Persian and Arabic. Since this Muslim was a client of the tribe of Tamim, there is some justification for supposing that he was a persianized Aramaean and a recent convert; he had served in junior positions under the former Persian-speaking head of the bureau (who had just been killed). The latter's son, who probably expected to succeed, was sceptical of the possibility of conducting the business in Arabic[2]. Despite this opposition from 'vested interests', however, the change was carried through, and it probably did more than anything else to make the secretary-class of 'Iraq adopt Islam. They presumably did not feel strongly on religious matters in any case, and thus, if non-conversion was to mean loss of their livelihood and position in society, or even relegation to inferior posts, they were ready to become Muslims at least outwardly.

(c) *Ideational aspects*

With the scanty information in our posssion it is difficult to assess the influence of Zoroastrianism on the thinking of those who, until the Arab conquest, had been its adherents in name if not in fact. One might conjecture that there was a definite Zoroastrian outlook among most of the inhabitants of what is now Persia, since it was there, in certain limited circles, that a revival and purification of Zoroastrianism took place. On the other hand, there was probably little genuine Zoroastrianism in 'Iraq, where the people if they had dualistic leanings, turned to Manichaeanism of some similar sect.

The precise status of the Manichaeans in 'Iraq is obscure. It would seem that there was an organized community, since a number

[1] Cf. the case of Zadan Farrukh (below) who had succeeded his father, and whose son hoped to succeed him.

[2] Al-Baladhuri, 300f.

I   119

of the names of leaders in it have been preserved[1]. The Manichaeanism, however, of which much is heard in the early 'Abbasid period (from 750), appears to extend beyond the bounds of this organized community. Indeed it is first and foremost a trend of thought found among certain groups of Muslims or nominal Muslims. The word *zindiq* came to be used loosely for any theological deviation in the direction of dualism, but in many cases it indicates some acceptance of Manichean doctrines.[2] An early exponent of such doctrines was the secretary Ibn-al-Muqaffa' (d. 757), who made an important contribution to the development of Arabic prose style. He appears to have been of Persian rather than of Aramaean extraction, and is said to have been converted from Zoroastrianism. When there was a persecution of *zindiqs* from about 779 to 786, several of those mentioned were sons of prominent administrators under the 'Abbasids; such men were not members by birth of any Manichaean community, but must have adopted Manichaean views out of conviction and because these met some inner need.

In trying to understand this phenomenon it must be remembered that there was still much fluidity in Islamic doctrine. Consequently it would not be at once apparent that the views held by Ibn-al-Muqaffa' were inconsistent with a sincere acceptance of the outward forms of Islam, or even with profession that there is no god but God and that Muhammad is His messenger. Since a great many of these Muslims with Manichaean sympathies belonged to the secretary class, it would appear that this trend in theology is to be linked up with some interest of the secretaries as a class.[3] It was noted above that once some members of the secretary class became Muslims, there would be a likelihood of the best jobs going to Muslims, and therefore some pressure on all secretaries to become Muslims. On the other hand, since the caliph and his chief advisers realized that they could not do without a vast bureaucratic machine, it is unlikely that they took any notice of the theological deviations among nominally Muslim secretaries until these had some political implications. Can we detect any class-interest of the secretaries which would explain the attraction of Manichaean views?

It must be kept in mind that the secretaries had been the chief

---

[1] Ibn an-Nadim, *Fihrist*, Cairo (1929)/1348, 472f. Ash-Shahrastani, *Milal*, ii, 82 (a man who flourished in 884). Cf. G. Vajda, 'Les zindîqs en pays d'Islam au début de la période abbaside', *Rivista degli Studi Orientali*, xvii (1937). 173-229.

[2] G. Vajda, op. cit.

[3] Cf. H. A. R. Gibb, 'The Social Significance of the Shu'ubiya', *Studia Orientalia Ioanni Pedersen . . dicata*, Copenhagen, 1953, 105-114.

The Will to Unity and Disunity

bearers of the Perso-'Iraqian culture of the later Sasanian period. Most of them were probably only nominally Zoroastrian, and not a few of them may have had definite leanings to Manichaeanism. On the whole, however, there was probably little connexion between their religion and their culture, and the culture was therefore largely secular. This meant that they had little difficulty in accepting Arab rule and the Arabic language. They still, however, remained the bearers of the Perso-'Iraqian cultural tradition, and much of the work of Ibn-al-Muqaffa' was the continuance of this tradition in Arabic by means of translations. The leading secretaries must have considered themselves much superior in culture to the Arab governors and generals whom they served. Throughout the Umayyad period they presumably felt that their position was secure, since they had no serious rivals in the cultural sphere. By the beginning of the 'Abbasid period, however, what has been called the 'religious institution' of Islam[1] was taking shape. The ancient schools where legal and other religious matters were discussed were given a measure of recognition by the ruling institution. Subsidiary studies, such as Arabic grammar and lexicography, began to be cultivated. Thus the secretaries, the bearers of the Perso-'Iraqian culture, saw their position threatened by another group of men with another culture. In the eyes of the secretaries this culture was inferior, but its bearers were gaining an important place in the structure of the empire, and one not unlike that held by those former rivals of the secretaries, the Zoroastrian clergy.

In their attempts to hinder the advance of this rival class the secretaries found Manichaeanism useful. On the one hand it was a philosophical or near-philosophical presentation of some of the fundamental ideas of the old 'Iraqian culture, and in this way gave them positive satisfaction. On the other hand it gave them a basis from which to criticize the Muslims.[2] Apart from pointing to difficulties in the Muslim view of the origin of evil, they attacked the Qur'an and tried to find inconsistencies in it. They alleged that its style was poor, and produced imitations which they held to be superior. This was much more, of course, than a quarrel about literary appreciation. Had the secretaries been able to maintain their viewpoint against their adversaries, they would not merely have destroyed the nascent Islamic religious institution, but would have cut away the whole religious foundation of the Islamic empire.

The interest of the secretaries in Manichaeanism was somewhat

[1] E.g., H. A. R. Gibb, in *The Muslim World*, xlv (1955). 12.
[2] Cf. M. Guidi, *La Lotta tra l'Islam e il Manicheismo*, Rome, 1927 (a book of Ibn-al-Muqaffa, criticizing the Qur'an, refuted by al-Qasim b. Ibrahim).

121

The Will to Unity and Disunity

checked, in its strictly theological aspect, by the persecution of 779-786. What must be reckoned as part of the same movement, however, though it was confined to non-theological material, was the Shu'ubiyyah. The Shu'ubiyyah was not so much a definite sect or group of persons as a trend of thought. It included depreciation of the Arabs and their contributions to culture, and praise of the non-Arab peoples of the empire. Prominent in the thought of the Shu'ubiyyah was criticism of the Qur'an and of Arab literary style in general, and it was on such matters that critics of the Shu'ubiyyah like al-Jahiz (d.869) and Ibn-Qutaybah (d.889) argued with them.[1] As Goldziher showed, these anti-Arab sentiments not merely found expression in poetry, but affected the study of geneaology and linguistics.[2] Nevertheless, as what has been said above should make clear, it would be a mistake to regard the Shu'ubiyyah as a purely literary movement. At its core was the secretary class, even if some of the ideas found acceptance in wider circles; and the secretaries, as representatives of Perso-'Iraqian culture, were hostile to the bearers of the new religious culture based on the 'Arabic humanities'.[3]

When the matter is looked at in this way, there is little to be said for the view that the Shu'ubiyyah were moved by 'national feeling', Persian or otherwise. There may well have been some low degree of awareness of sharing in a common Persian tradition, but this cannot have been strong enough to affect men's conduct deeply. The different dialects in the various parts of the country, and the variations in cultural level, hindered the growth of a feeling of unity among the Persians. Zoroastrianism had too little popular support in some regions to be an effective integrating factor. Thus men's loyalty was given to something much smaller than the (hypothetical) 'Persian nation' as a whole. Moreover the Shu'ubiyyah were drawn almost solely from the inhabitants of 'Iraq, whose outlook was far removed from that of the men of Khurasan and Sogdia. The chief aim of the Shu'ubiyyah was to oppose Arab culture; in so far as they had a positive aim it was to assert not Persian culture in general but that particular form of it which we have called Perso-'Iraqian culture.

Reflection on these matters shows why this whole movement of *zindiqs* and Shu'ubiyyah failed. The attitude of the secretaries had two aspects. On the one hand, they accepted the Islamic state and the Arabic language; Ibn-al-Muqaffa', the fountain-head of the anti-Arab movement, nevertheless took a prominent place in early Arabic literature. On the other hand, the movement was vigorous in criticizing

[1] Cf. al-Jahiz, *Al-Bayan wa-'t-Tabyin*, Cairo, 1927/1345, iii. 1-71.

[2] *Muhammedanische Studien*, Halle, 1888, i. 147-216.

[3] Cf. Gibb, 'Social Significance', 105.

122

things Arab. This criticism, however, was not at the deepest level. They did not put forward any radical criticism of the Islamic state or any alternative system of government for the empire. At most they wanted slight adjustments within the system—in particular such adjustments as would maintain their position and prevent the religious institution from becoming stronger than themselves. This was a limited view, supporting their own interests and little else. It did not take into account the close connexion between the Islamic empire and the religious ideation of Islam. Thus the secretaries were involved in contradiction. They wanted the Islamic empire, but they did not want the necessary condition of that empire, namely, the religious ideation in which a special place was given to a divine revelation *in Arabic*. It was not surprising that nothing much came of their movement.

The beginnings of a distinct consciousness of a common Persian tradition are due above all to the work of the epic poet Firdawsi (d.c.1020).[1] The milieu out of which he came, and for which in the first place he was writing, was Sogdia and Khurasan. Sogdia had had a comparatively high culture based in part on its lucrative commerce, and had been the centre of the Samanid state (874-999). Under the Samanids Persians had asserted a measure of political independence over against the caliph in Baghdad, and to support their political position had fostered memories of Persian achievements in pre-Arab days. This distinctive outlook, Persian and yet also Islamic, was inherited by the Ghaznavid state (at its height, 1000-1050) from the Samanid despite the Turkish origin of the Ghaznavid dynasty. In these regions a perennial feature had been the struggle against wandering tribes from the Central Asian steppes, and this was little altered by the coming of the Arabs. For a time (until the early eighth century) the Sogdians hoped to maintain their independence against the Arabs, and their final acceptance of Islam was long in coming. By the Samanid period, however, the Islamic empire had been accepted, and the Sogdians and Khurasanians had shared in the advance to the Jaxartes and beyond. Once more these Persian peoples found themselves in their historic role of defenders of civilization against the less civilized tribes from the steppes.

It was to this situation that the ideas of the *Shahnamah* were adapted. It contained no suggestion of a return from the Islamic empire to a Sasanian one; there was no attack on Islam, and no mention of Zoroastrianism. The chief theme was the age-old Persian

[1] Cf. E. G. Browne, *A Literary History of Persia*, ii, (London, 1906), 129-46; G. E. von Grunebaum, *Islam: Essays in the Nature and Growth of a Cultural Tradition* (Menasha, 1955), 168-77.

one of the struggle of light with darkness, and these were represented in particular by Iran and Turan, the Persians and the Turks. Though there was something essentially Persian in this conception, it was not inconsistent with Islamic thought, for in this also there was a struggle of good and evil in the opposition of God and Iblis. The fact that the 'villain' of the *Shahnamah* is given an Arabic name[1] does not seem to indicate a vehement attack on the Arabs, though it may spring from resentment of Arab success. It is more important, however, to notice that the idea of Iran's opposition to Turan is compatible with Persian membership of the Islamic empire, and brought out the significance of what Persian Muslims were in fact doing. In other words, the ideas of the *Shahnamah* may be held within a framework of Islamic ideation. Nevertheless they are not in complete harmony with that ideation, and the nationalistic conceptions of Firdawsi's epic helped to make possible the separation of the Persians from the rest of Islam in the early sixteenth century when the Shah of Persia officially adopted Imamite Shi'ism.

(d) The reasons for conversion

By the time that the claims of Islam thrust themselves upon the attention of the Persians the Arab empire was already in existence (even if it was not certain where its eastern frontier was going to be); and the fundamental reason for their acceptance of Islam was that they wanted to belong to this empire. For this desire to belong there were various material motives.[2] In so far as the Islamic empire was a continuation of the Sasanian, the Perso-'Iraqian secretary-class wanted to retain its position and function, and Persians from less advanced regions wanted to share in that higher culture which had already been attracting them under the Sasanians. For the merchants of Sogdia the issue was not immediately clear, but in the long run they seem to have taken the view that the advantages of full membership of the empire as Muslims outweighed the disadvantages.

These economic and social factors underlying the desire to belong to the empire were probably reinforced, at least in some cases, by an awareness of the empire as a holy or charismatic community. It is noteworthy that of the two most prominent opponents of the Shu'ubiyyah one, al-Jahiz (d.669), though client of an Arab tribe, had probably African ancestry,[3] while the other, Ibn-Qutaybah

[1] Dahhak instead of the Persian Dahak; cf. Browne, op. cit., i. 114f.

[2] Cf. B. Spuler, 'Iran and Islam', in G. E. von Grunebaum (ed.), *Studies in Islamic Cultural History*, 47-56.

[3] Pellat, *Le Milieu Basrien et la Formation de Gahiz*, Paris, 1953, 51-58.

(d.889), is said to have been of Persian descent. Another man who wrote against the Shu'ubiyyah, al-Baladhuri the historian (d.892), belonged to the Perso-'Iraqian secretary-class and was able to translate from Persian into Arabic, but may have been of Christian Aramaean stock in view of the fact that his great-grandfather's name was Dawud[1]. All these belonged to the circles of traditionists who constituted a large part of the religious institution at this time, and thus were involved in the working out through the Shari'ah (or revealed law) of the idea of the charismatic community[2]. It is also worth mentioning that the dynasties based on the more civilized populations, such as the Tahirids, the Samanids and the Ghaznavids,[3] supported the Sunnite form of Islam in which the idea of the charismatic community had an important place, whereas those dynasties, like the Buwayhids, which were based on less civilized, but perhaps militarily stronger, populations, favoured Shi'ite views. This matter is a complex one, however, and various interpretations are possible.

The desire to be members of the Islamic empire is the basis of the growth of a will to unity. This will to unity was present in the Perso-'Iraqian secretaries and the Sogdian and Khurasanian merchants, princelings and squires; and neither the class-interest of the one nor the 'nationalism' of the other was sufficient to change this will to unity into a will to separation. They did not altogether like the Islamic empire, but they were unable to imagine any feasible alternative. In the end, therefore, they decided to be members of the empire and not to struggle against it.

Thus the attraction of the Islamic empire for the Persians was not simply economic and social. Even if they were not all explicitly aware of the fact, the majority of the Persians were fascinated by this divinely-constituted community. Moreover it was for them the fulfilment of longings that had been stirring in them during the Sasanian period and that probably went much further back[4]. This helps to make intelligible the flowering of Persian culture under Islam. If the views expressed have some truth in them, that flowering was no accident and no *tour de force*, but came about because Islam met a deep need of the Persian soul.

[1] Al-Mas'udi, *Muruj*, iii. 109, refutation of Shu'ubiyyah. Yaqut, *Irshad*, ii. no. 78, grandfather secretary to a governor of Egypt. For an instance of a secretary who became a Christian (early sixth century) cf. J. Labourt, *Le Christianisme dans l'Empire Perse*, Paris, 1904, 163f.

[2] See below, pp.199-204.

[3] Cf. Spuler, *Iran*, 160f., but contrast 173.

[4] Sir Hamilton Gibb speaks of ' the millennial concept of the "Universal Empire" and the *Pan-basileus*' (*Studia Islamica*, iv. 16).

4. THE ISLAMIZATION OF WEST AFRICA

An adequate study of Islam as an integrating factor would have to survey all the main areas where Muslims are now found. In the present context, however, it will be sufficient to consider a single example of a peripheral area; and for this purpose West Africa seems to be as suitable an example as any other. There are indeed differences between it and other peripheral areas like the Indian sub-continent and Indonesia and East Africa. Despite these differences, however, it has much in common with these other areas. None of them (with the exception of parts of north-west India) ever belonged to the Umayyad or 'Abbasid caliphate; their populations did not become solidly Muslim until long after the populations of the heartlands of Islam, and indeed for the most part cannot yet be said to be thoroughly islamized; they are at the frontiers of Islam where it has come up against societies which resist conversion. The aim of this study of West African Islam will thus be to try to discover the kind of reasons which have induced these Muslims of the periphery to abandon their previous religions, and to estimate the extent to which they have been integrated into the Islamic community.[1]

(a) The first phase of islamization

Two main phases may be distinguished in the islamization of West Africa, the first of them lasting until about 1600, and the second beginning about then but not becoming important until after 1800. The form taken by Islam as a religious and social phenomenon is different in these two phases; but the differences are related to the economic circumstances of West Africa in the two periods. The economic factors may therefore be considered first.

For present purposes West Africa is the region between the Saharan desert and steppe and the Gulf of Guinea, extending from the Atlantic ocean in the west to beyond Lake Chad in the east. West Africa as thus defined is roughly rectangular in shape, rather less than a thousand miles broad and three thousand miles long. In

[1] The study is based on the following works: T. W. Arnold, *The Preaching of Islam*, London, 1935; E. W. Bovill, *Caravans of the Old Sahara*, London, 1953; J. D. Fage, *An Introduction to the History of West Africa*, London, 1955; A. Gouilly, *L'Islam dans l'Afrique Occidentale Française*, Paris, 1952; J. S. Trimingham, *Islam in West Africa*, Oxford, 1959; J. N. D. Anderson, *Islamic Law in Africa*, London 1955.

the south along the coast of the Gulf of Guinea is a belt of equatorial forest, usually a hundred miles or more broad. North of this runs a belt of woodland from four to five hundred miles broad, which merges gradually into what may be called a belt of grassland of a hundred to two hundred miles. The latter in its turn merges into poor steppe and desert where cultivation is seldom possible and life can be maintained only by pasturing animals. It is with the belts of grassland and woodland that we shall be chiefly concerned, since, apart from a few cases in recent times, Islam has had little success with the tribes of the equatorial forest, while the black races of the grasslands and woodlands have shown slight inclination to enter the desert.

These belts of grassland and woodland, which may also be referred to as the western and central Sudan, are able to support a large population on the basis of agriculture. In the early centuries of the Christian era only a limited number of food plants seem to have been known, and domesticated animals seem to have been restricted to goats, pigs and hens. A change came over the economy of West Africa, however, as a result of the introduction of the camel to North Africa during the period of Roman domination. The camel not only made it possible for men to live in parts of the Sahara which consisted of poor steppe rather than desert, but it enabled men to cross the Sahara much more easily. This new possibility of communication led in due course to the development of trade between North Africa and West Africa, and this trade became of considerable importance. The north wanted the gold and the slaves which were easily obtainable in the Sudan, while the Sudan, lacking salt, was ready to pay almost its weight in gold for this commodity, of which there were deposits in the south of Morocco[1]. The trans-Saharan trade was in the hands of white races from North Africa, at first Berbers or possibly Jews; and it not merely enriched the participants but stimulated the development of trade within the Sudan. Trade presupposes a certain measure of security, and that in turn presupposes some degree of political organization; but the development of trade also encourages the formation of still larger and better organized political units. The period up to 1600 is characterized by attempts with varying success to form large political units in the Sudan, and these attempts are linked with the development of trans-Saharan and internal trade.

Such political units tended to form in six areas. Indeed until the European occupation at the end of the nineteenth century there has nearly always been a state in each of these areas; and these states,

[1] At Taghaza; other deposits further south were discovered in the Islamic period.

however much they might extend their own influence, have seldom been able to dominate the heart of any of the neighbouring areas. (1) From early times there has been a state with its centre on or near the lower course of the Senegal, but never extending more than three hundred miles inland from the Atlantic. From about the ninth century this was the state of Takrur, which extended some distance north of the river and was in touch with Mauritania. From about the seventeenth century, the area was dominated by the later state of Futa Toro with its centre south of the river. (2) The higher land to the north and north-west of the Upper Niger (above Timbuktu), together with the valley of the river, seems to be propitious for the growth of a large state. Here developed Ghana, the first of the 'empires'[1]. It was apparently difficult to maintain unity in the area, for sometimes there were three sizeable states in it. (3) There has usually been one or more states in the basin of the upper Volta, and these have managed to remain independent of the states on the upper or middle Niger. (4) The middle Niger, from Gao downstream for some four hundred miles, and particularly the region of Dendi at the south of this area, gave birth to the state out of which was formed the Songhay 'empire'. (5) To the west of Lake Chad was the state of Bornu, perhaps the most stable of all the West African states, since it lasted from the tenth century until the beginning of the twentieth. To the east of Lake Chad was Waday. (6) To the west of Bornu were the Hausa states, not of much political importance before their conquest by 'Uthman dan-Fodio in the early nineteenth century, but with a cultural influence that was extending south-westwards and southwards towards the Niger.

The first 'empire' to develop was that of Ghana, in the area to the north and northwest of the upper Niger. The political organization out of which it grew appears to have been begun about the fourth century by white trans-Saharan traders, and to have grown steadily. In 770 a black Soninke dynasty seized control and maintained the 'empire' in a prosperous condition until the second half of the eleventh century when it was broken up by a series of expeditions from the north, directed against the Sudan by the Almoravids (Muslim rulers of North Africa and Spain). The latter were unable themselves to control the area where Ghana had been paramount, and for a time it was divided between several smaller states.

In the first half of the thirteenth century these states were swallowed up in a short space of time by the Mandingo 'empire' of Mali, which was at its height in the first half of the fourteenth

[1] The modern state of Ghana has taken the name of this old 'empire', but there is no historical or geographical connexion.

century and then declined gradually until by about 1500 it was once more a small state. At its most powerful Mali had a much wider influence than Ghana. It controlled the whole valley of the upper Niger from Gao, and the gold-bearing area of Wangara on the upper Senegal; none of this had been under Ghana. Its influence also extended further into the desert.

The third and last important state in the period up to 1600 was the Songhay 'empire' of Gao (or Kawkaw). Once again the beginnings of its organization seem to be due to 'white' settlers from the north, perhaps associated with a community of Niger fishermen. It gradually spread several hundred miles upstream until by the eleventh century it included Gao, doubtless coming in this direction because of its interest in the desert routes. It was now a moderately large state and continued so till after the middle of the fifteenth century when under Sonni 'Ali and Askia Muhammad it expanded rapidly into an 'empire'. At its greatest extent it controlled the valley of the middle Niger for a third of the way from Timbuktu to the sources. Beyond that the now small state of Mali maintained itself. The Songhay 'empire', however, also controlled a belt of grasslands from the area north of the upper Senegal in the west to the territory of the Hausa states in the east, and from this it was able to dominate a large tract of desert and poor steppe. This 'empire' was kept in being for about a century, being destroyed in 1591 by an expedition from Morocco carrying firearms.

In these three 'empires' and in several of the smaller states the pattern of Islamic advance was similar. The first Muslims everywhere were traders. To begin with these seem to have been 'white' nomads (usually Berbers) from the Sahara, who extended their operations into the cultivated lands. But in course of time, through intermarriage with local populations, they came to be to all intents and purposes another Sudanese tribe, or perhaps tribes. The Fulbe or Fulani, who played an important part in recent times in spreading Islam, are thought to have had such an origin. In so far, however, as the traders moved from place to place, most forms of animism became unsatisfactory, since they presupposed the attachment of a kinship-group to a particular piece of land. After Islam had spread to the Saharan tribes it became more and more common for traders to be Muslims; indeed it became the normal state of affairs. Presumably the traders felt that Islamic brotherhood and the Islamic community gave them a satisfactory substitute for relations within the tribe on the basis of animism.

The various states, however, were not usually founded by the trader or merchant class alone, but in concert with a ruling dynasty or aristocracy. The more intelligent rulers must have seen that co-operation with the traders would lead to greater wealth and power. Just how Islam came to be formally accepted in the state varied according to local circumstances. Frequently a ruler found that the trading community, which was Muslim, was becoming so strong that he must co-operate with it or lose his power; and co-operation involved a formal profession of Islam. Such a profession of Islam by the king and trading community, however, did not mean that the state became gradually an Islamic state similar to those in the Middle East. Sudanese culture accepted the presence of Islam as the religion of a segment of society, and thus effectively insulated it from influencing the rest of society. The agriculturalists, who were the bulk of the population, retained their animism. Despite the fact that the king was formally a Muslim, the official conception of his place in the society was derived from animism. Animism provided the cement of religious forms which held the political structure together. In none of the states prior to 1600 does anything of the conception of the community seem to have come from Islam. Our knowledge of such matters is certainly slight and has many gaps; but it seems clear that each of the political structures had been developed out of more primitive forms of political organization found in the Sudan, and in particular in the tribe or tribes which created the state. (This is a matter in which further study would lead to interesting results; in the present state of our knowledge nothing further can usefully be said here).

The first phase of islamization in the Sudan thus leads to the curious result that, though in many states the ruling families and the trading class are Muslims, the states are not Islamic states. The nearest to being such was the latest in time, the Songhay 'empire'. Here there were judges who applied Islamic law to the Muslims in the towns, while at Timbuktu Muslim scholarship was encouraged. The wars of the 'empire' were formally regarded as a *jihad* or 'holy war' of Muslims against infidels. The Songhay 'empire' thus resembles the Islamic or 'theocratic' states of the nineteenth century. Yet even in it the basis of the king's position was entirely animistic, and it must therefore be classed with the states and 'empires' of the first phase.

(b) The second phase of islamization

The second phase of islamization may be said to begin about 1600 and to last until the present time. Perhaps future generations will be able to see that 1957, with the transformation of the Gold Coast into

130

the independent state of Ghana (with the name but not the site of the old 'empire'), marks the end of the second phase and the beginning of a third. The second phase is characterized by the appearance of a novel economic situation, with all its repercussions, and also by a change in the nature and extent of islamization. In both respects it is very different from the first.

The new economic situation has two facets. The one is the decline of trans-Saharan trade, the other the growth of trade with Europeans through ports on the coast. With regard to conditions in the Sahara there is much that is obscure. One of the factors determining these conditions was the migration to North Africa of large numbers of Arab nomads from Upper Egypt. This began in 1052, and in the course of the next few centuries the Arabs spread over large areas of the Sahara. Of the nomadic Berbers already there, some became arabized, while others withdrew before the Arab advance. This movement of turbulent nomads tended to weaken the influence of the larger political units on the north and west of the Sahara and to increase the pressure from the desert on the settled lands of West Africa. Under such circumstances trade, though probably never at a standstill, became more difficult. The Christian reconquest of Spain, culminating in the fall of Granada in 1492, probably also discouraged trans-Saharan trade by closing some of the European markets for which it catered. At the same time the European development of sea communications meant that European markets were increasingly losing interest in the goods transported across the Sahara. The expedition of 1591 from Morocco which broke up the Songhay 'empire' is a focus of the destructive influences from the desert which were now affecting West Africa. This expedition was not strong enough to create any alternative large-scale organization in West Africa, which consequently was reduced to a number of small communities fighting with one another. The expedition, in that it introduced firearms may also be said to exemplify European influences reaching West Africa across the Sahara.

The Portuguese had discovered the whole of the Guinea coast by 1475, and from this date West Africa has had commercial relations with the Europeans through the ports there. As the name of the Gold Coast indicates, gold was one of the things for which the Europeans traded here. In the course of time, however, the trade in slaves became predominant. At first these went to Europe, but soon the chief markets for them came to be in the Americas. The extent of the trade may be judged from the following figures:[1]

[1] Fage, *Introduction to the History of West Africa*, 83.

16th century (from 1530)   900,000 = 13,000 a year
17th century   2,750,000 = 27,500 a year
18th century   7,000,000 = 70,000 a year
19th century (to 1880)   4,000,000 = (125,000 in 1830)

The slave trade and its ramifications added greatly to the unsettled condition of West Africa. The stronger political units raided the weaker ones for slaves. Even within a single body politic the ruling faction might sell dissidents into slavery. All this increased feelings of insecurity throughout the region. In addition it was necessary to adjust the economy of the region to the new circumstances in which trade through the Guinea ports was more important than trade across the Sahara. One aspect of this adjustment was the growth in the eighteenth century of states on or near the Guinea coast such as Dahomey and the Yoruba state of Oyo.

In the religious history of West Africa in recent centuries a notable feature is the growth of Muslim religious orders, especially the Tijaniyyah and Qadiriyyah; and this is doubtless due in large part to the disturbed circumstances and general feeling of insecurity. A new expansion of Islam through the work of the orders seems to have begun about the closing decades of the eighteenth century. Where Islam had previously been professed for external reasons—because it linked traders together in a loose brotherhood—it now came to be associated with inner religious experience. In West Africa, as elsewhere, the religious orders met the spiritual needs of ordinary men in a way in which the formal worship of Islam and the brotherhood of all Muslims did not. This new basis of genuine Islamic conviction underlies the growth of the 'theocratic' states about to be described, in the sense that these states could not have arisen had there not been this widespread acceptance of the Islamic faith and attachment to the community of Islam. Genuine Islamic conviction, however, was independent of the 'theocratic' states, and went on developing after the states had shown themselves failures.

The 'theocratic' states were states whose rulers held their positions because they were Muslims. They might themselves be religious leaders with charismatic gifts, or they might be soldiers and administrators who acted as 'defenders of the faith'. In neither case was their rule based on animistic ideas of the divine king (though it might be held that these ideas, completely transformed, contributed to the power of the idea of the Islamic leader). On the contrary, their authority as rulers presupposed the acceptance of Islam by many of their more influential followers. It is the position of the ruler rather than the extent to which the states were subject to

The Will to Unity and Disunity

Islamic law which justifies the description of 'theocratic'. The limited application of Islamic law by West African Muslims in the twentieth century makes it certain that it must have been more limited in its application in the seventeenth century.

The first great theocratic leader was 'Uthman (or Usuman) dan-Fodio (1754-1817). Earlier there had been at least two minor leaders of the same type, who had been partly successful in founding small 'theocratic' states at Futa Jalon (about 1725) and Futa Toro (1776). These men claimed to rule as Muslims, they applied the Shari'ah, and they declared the *jihad* on neighbouring animists. Their states continued in existence until the French conquest, but remained small and suffered from internal dissensions. 'Uthman dan-Fodio, whose later activities were partly inspired by these small states in the west, was first and foremost a religious leader, disgusted at the accommodation of Islam to paganism in his country (one of the northerly Hausa states), and filled with zeal for the expansion of Islam. From 1786 to 1804 he was an itinerant preacher. His call to a purer Islam led him in 1804 into conflict with the local rulers, who as members of the Hausa ruling class were in any case unfriendly to the Torodbe or Tokolor (?) clerical class to which 'Uthman dan-Fodio belonged. He now therefore formally claimed to be 'commander of the faithful' (*amir al-mu'minin*), and proclaimed a *jihad*. He was supported by the nomadic Fulbe or Fulani. By 1808 most of the Hausa rulers had been defeated and their states annexed, and in 1809 he founded his new capital of Sokoto. The state of Sokoto became one of the largest ever created in West Africa. By the time Northern Nigeria came under British control, this state had split into separate emirates, but the emirs continued to acknowledge the religious authority of the Sultan of Sokoto.

Other examples of 'theocratic' states may be dealt with briefly. Shaykh Hamad, after being influenced by the preaching and example of 'Uthman dan-Fodio, about 1810 set up the small 'theocratic' state of Masina in the district of Jenne on the Upper Niger. Al-Hajj 'Umar (c.1797-1864), of the clerical class of Futa Toro, spent several years in making the pilgrimage to Mecca. In the course of it he was initiated into the Tijaniyyah order, and his authority rested largely on his position as a dignitary of that order. About 1837, after visits to Sokoto and Masina, he began teaching and initiating in Futa Toro and round about. Later he consolidated his organization and built up an army of Tokolor. In 1853 he declared a *jihad* and established a state which grew rapidly. Ultimately it extended from just east of the upper Senegal to Timbuktu. The state might have been larger, but defeat by the French in the west left only the possibility of eastward expansion. His son was driven farther eastwards by the French and eventually took refuge in Sokoto. About the time of al-Hajj 'Umar's death in 1864 another Islamic state was established to the south of his state by Samori (c.1833-1900), based not on Fulani but Mandinka. Samori, however, seems not to have been a devout Muslim but a politician—the leader of a forlorn attempt to resist the French advance—who made use of Islam to buttress his cause.

Even when genuine Islamic motives were present, they were not necessarily the sole determinants of action, though the actors themselves may have been unaware of these other determinants. There was certainly a racial factor present. Most of the 'theocratic' states were created by a union of clerical Torodbe and nomadic Fulani against their rivals in each locality, while the movement led by Samori was essentially one of Mandinka. There were also economic factors. These states depended on something like a regular army provided with firearms. To maintain this army money was required and also a supply of arms and ammunition. The chief source of both money and weapons was the sale of slaves to the Europeans. In this connexion the conception of the *jihad* against pagans was useful as a justification for the enslavement of one's enemies.

Despite this dependence on the Europeans, another factor contributing to the formation of at least the later 'theocratic' states was anti-European feeling. Al-Hajj 'Umar, for example, tried to boycott European goods. The association of anti-European feeling with Islam was in some respects accidental. When Africans became aware of how they were being threatened by European penetration, the chief political units capable of organizing resistance had an Islamic basis, while much of the penetration was being done by the French who, after their experiences in Algeria, regarded Islam with considerable hostility. It was not altogether accidental, however, that Islam became the focus of anti-European sentiments, for since the earliest days of Islam Muslims had been a little afraid of Christians and very suspicious of them. Whether accidental or not, the association of Islam with anti-Europeanism is clear. Some of the pagan groups in the Senegal basin who opposed al-Hajj 'Umar and clung to animism, regarding a French protectorate preferable to Muslim domination, in course of time reacted against European influence and became fervent Muslims (the breakdown of animism through European contacts doubtless contributing to their conversion).

It must be emphasized that the 'theocratic' states, though properly called Islamic states (since the authority of the ruler was based not on animism but on his qualifications, charismatic or otherwise, as a Muslim), owed little in their organization to Islam. The sultanate of Sokoto is described as retaining the Hausa political structure with a veneer of Islam, and something similar is true of the others[1]. Yet one feature of these states fitted in well with Islamic tradition. The military power of each rested on an army which gave most of its time, if necessary, to fighting; and the men in this army were in a position very similar to that of the Arabs in the decades after the death of Muhammad. They, as Muslims, were the essential citizen body of the state. Such a basis for political life might have been tolerable had it been treated in accordance with Islamic tradition. Unfortunately there were many abuses. Muslims with whom one disagreed about trivial matters might be declared infidels, so that they became objects for the *jihad* and so for enslavement. Justice was not always administered fairly, so that the weaker members of the community felt insecure. In short, the acceptance of Islam did not involve the acceptance of any political system which could at once be put into operation in West Africa.

The continuation, after the failure of the idea of the 'theocratic' state, of the religious movement connected with the Islamic orders is illustrated by two sets of phenomena associated chiefly with the west of French West Africa though having repercussions elsewhere. Senegal was the region which was first affected on a large scale by European occupation, and the location of the centres of these new movements is doubtless due to this fact. One is the appearance of a new branch of Qadiriyyah order, known as the Muridiyyah; the other is a movement of reform within the Tijaniyyah, known as the Hamalliyyah.

The Muridiyyah were founded by Amadu (or Ahmad) Bamba, who was born in Futa Toro about 1860 of Wolof stock, and became an initiate of the Qadiriyyah order. The French occupation, which after 1880 began to extend rapidly eastwards from the Senegal basin, made it impossible for him to play any prominent political role (though at one time he seems to have hoped for this), and instead he became the leader of a religious movement and eventually founded the Muridiyyah order. This order may be described as an africanized form of the Qadiriyyah, and was instrumental in completing the movement of the great majority of the Wolof into Islam. Amadu Bamba died in 1927, and his memory is held in high respect. The order has also been fortunate in those who succeeded him in the

[1] In a private communication J. Spencer Trimingham writes that 'the organization of some of the other theocratic states, in particular that of Masina, was more solidly based on an Islamic state structure.'

leadership, and it has consequently achieved for the time being a creative adjustment to the new circumstances. Two features may be emphasized. One is the adaptation of the practices and structure of an Islamic religious order to the 'African soul', and in particular to the 'soul of the Wolof'. To this something of its success is doubtless due. Whether as a result it will cease to be genuinely Islamic is a question that can hardly be answered yet; it does not seem to have aroused the same opposition as the Hamalliyyah. The other notable feature is the way in which French political control was accepted and the members of the order encouraged to make the best of the new situation. In particular they were encouraged to engage in manual work (which had hitherto been performed mostly by slaves) both in agriculture in the villages and in various urban occupations. In this way the order has managed not only to fill the coffers of its Grand Master, but also to produce many useful citizens, though the French authorities have sometimes regarded it as politically suspect.

The Hamalliyyah may also be said to have arisen out of the social chaos following the French occupation and the ending of slavery, but, in contrast to the Muridiyyah, they cannot yet be said to have achieved a creative adjustment to the situation. On the contrary the movement seems to be becoming so African that it has ceased to be Islamic, even turning in worship towards the West African shrine of Nyoro instead of towards Mecca. Though those responsible for founding it were genuine mystics it has tended to emphasize mystical experience at the expense of good conduct in social relationships, and the result has been that it has become mixed up with tribal feuds and other unsavoury practices of animistic days. Like the Muridiyyah it has spread far beyond the area in which it was founded, but unlike that order it has no organization and no leader.

Such is the present stage in the development of Islam in West Africa, and these are the two most significant movements of the present century.

(c) Conclusions

We are considering to what extent West Africans have been integrated into the Islamic community, and to what extent disintegrative tendencies are present; and we must now glance back over the outstanding points in West African Islamic history with these questions in mind.

Throughout the centuries West Africans seem to have been attracted to Islam chiefly because it was a great brotherhood including countless races and states. This attracted the traders in the earlier days and has also been behind the latest 'mass movements' into Islam. The situation in West Africa indeed resembled that in Arabia in Muhammad's time. For various reasons the old kinship-groups were breaking down. In Islam both Arabs and West Africans found something that was like a clan or tribe, only much bigger, and not liable to be disturbed by the earthquakes which had overthrown the older kinship structure. Islam is essentially a religion for individuals who have been uprooted from their community or whose communities have vanished from under their feet. In the early days Islam widened the restricted horizons of the Sudanese animists in their little communities, and conversions gave a man the entree to a world society. It was not surprising that the pilgrimage to Mecca was popular despite its ardours. In recent times Islam has also appeared as a world society hostile to the hated Europeans and to some extent capable of holding its own against them. Thus throughout the centuries acceptance of Islam by West Africans has implied a will to unity, a will to be incorporated into this great society.

Acceptance of Islam, however, did not imply acceptance of the distinctive Islamic social behaviour codified in the Shari'ah. The motive for becoming Muslims cannot have been the desire to adopt Muslim ways (as these exist in the Middle East). The slight extent to which the Shari'ah has prevailed in West Africa shows that the attraction was elsewhere. It was because men wanted to be Muslims, and to be good Muslims, proper Muslims, that they tried to carry out the Shari'ah. Consciousness of their differences from other Muslims made them all the more eager to be proper Muslims. Mansa Musa of Mali (*regnabat* 1312-37), passing through Cairo on his way to Mecca, is said to have heard for the first time of the restriction of wives to four in Islam, and to have decided without hesitation that on his return home he would get rid of his superfluous wives. The adoption of the strictest legal rite, the Malikite, is mainly due to its position in North Africa (which served as model to West Africa), but its strictness would in no way come amiss to the West African who wanted to be a proper Muslim. Despite this zeal for conformity, however, the influence of the Shari'ah on African Muslims has been slight. The old customs of animistic times have largely been retained, usually in a modified form, but sometimes hardly even that. Changes have been most drastic in the sphere of worship, for the ancestral cults have been replaced by Islamic forms. The success of Islam here, however, is not necessarily due to its own attraction, but is probably the result of the disappearance as effective social units of the groups with which the old cults were associated. The Shari'ah is certainly capable of prescribing suitable conduct for a mass of detribalized persons, such as some of the late nineteenth century armies were, but for any great change to take place there must be a strong desire in such persons to be regarded as good Muslims. On the whole, then, it may be said that there has been little integration of the conduct of West African Muslims with standard Islamic practice.

Still less has there been any integration in the intellectual sphere. There has been Muslim scholarship in West Africa, sometimes of high standard in restricted fields; but the deep need for conformity has ruled out any attempt by competent scholars to rethink Islam in the light of the West African situation. There can be no attempt to adapt the Shari'ah to West African needs and to express its essential values in a form suited to existing West African ideas of conduct. Similarly there can be no attempt to restate Islamic doctrine in terms of West African categories of thought. In the present phase of development such things would make orthodox scholars feel that they had ceased to be proper Muslims. They therefore uphold the Shari'ah as an ideal, and in practice follow custom to a great extent. Undoubtedly orthodox scholarship is failing to meet the needs of the moment, and unorthodox Muslims, like the founders of the Muridiyyah and the Hamalliyyah, are trying to meet the need in ways of which the orthodox cannot approve[1].

It does not follow that the situation is hopeless. The orthodox scholars of the heartland of Islam are not precluded like those on the frontiers from attempting to meet the intellectual and practical needs of the times. If they find a way of doing this, it may help West African Islam. Moreover there is a steady pressure towards conformity which in the course of centuries would probably lead to a much greater degree of moral and intellectual integration. Unfortunately the issue is no longer one merely between Islam and animism, since Western culture has also entered the field. Imbued with the inherited suspicion of Islam for Christendom, West African Islam has delayed the reception of Western culture by its adherents, and thereby also their adjustment to the impact of the West. Animistic and Christian West Africans are thus ahead of Muslims in the long process of coming to terms with the intrusive culture (just as Hindus went ahead of Muslims in the Indian subcontinent). This retardation may be only temporary, however. We have now arrived indeed at the present situation, and, though we may discern many of the factors, we cannot say what will happen. We can only

[1] Trimingham notes that the communities established during the present century are ready to come to terms with the contemporary world, but that the old-established communities tend to be conservative.

ask questions. Will the Arabs or Turks or Pakistanis achieve an adjustment to the West that will be of help to the West Africans in meeting their problems of adjustment ? Will they achieve it in time ? May political factors create in West Africa a will to separation from the rest of Islam, or will they strengthen its will to unity ? Only in the future can these and similar questions be answered. All that seems clear at the moment is that, while West African Islam is genuinely a part of Islam, it is not yet fully integrated, and in its present stage of incomplete integration must look to the heartlands for help and have little to contribute to them.

5. THE WILL TO UNITY

After looking in detail at some of the heterogeneous groups which were included in Islamic society, we must try to answer the general question: What makes such groups want to be one?

(a) The need for definite decision

An important preliminary point is that, in matters such as those being studied, it is often impossible to avoid making a definite decision. These are matters of actual living in the world of men, and academic aloofness is impossible. A man usually has to decide whether to belong to a society or to oppose it, whether to work with a certain group of men or to oppose them.

Neutrality is indeed sometimes possible. Absolute neutrality is hardly possible, since in order to exist a man must be a member of some society. Within a great society, however, such as the Islamic empire, there are smaller societies, and membership of one of these does not necessarily involve opposition to others. Membership of the more moderate Kharijite sects was compatible with some sharing of a common life with non-Kharijite Muslims. In such a case membership of one society (the Kharijite sect) may be accompanied by an attitude to other societies within the great society which is roughly one of neutrality (or at least of postponement of the decision to oppose actively). Common membership of the great society limits the opposition to other societies. Neutrality of this sort, however, is not an argument against the need for belonging both to the great society and to one of the smaller societies within it.

There appear to be cases where a partial acceptance of a society is possible. Many members of the Sasanian secretary class in 'Iraq were ready to serve as secretaries in the Islamic empire, but did not become Muslims; that is, they accepted the new society in its political aspect, but not in its religious aspect. Again, many West African Muslims, both as individuals and as constituting Muslim states, accept some of the religious precepts of Islam but not others. It would seem, however, that this partial acceptance of the Islamic society is a temporary stage. Once some of the secretaries in 'Iraq become Muslims, it was necessary for all to become Muslims, at least in name, or else to cease being secretaries, since a Muslim vizier or governor would normally prefer a Muslim to a non-Muslim. Thus circumstances forced on the secretaries a decision about full acceptance of the Islamic society. In West Africa and other peripheral areas the time comes when somone says, 'If you want to be good Muslims, you must give up such and such customs, for they are pagan'. The partially islamized individual or group is then faced with a decision whether to go forward to a fuller acceptance of Islam or to enter on a course which will presumably lead them right out of the Islamic community.

Thus on examination it turns out that the apparent exceptions are not real exceptions. A non-committal attitude towards a society or community is usually impossible. A man must either belong to it or belong to some other rival and opposed society.

(b) The place of economic and social factors

The studies in this book so far have shown cases where common economic interests helped to create a unified religious movement. This was often because common economic interests led to common social interests. On the other hand, the phenomena of the class struggle in Europe in the last century and a half make it clear that economic and social interests alone are just as likely to produce disunity as unity. The most that can be said is that in favourable conditions economic and social factors produce conditions which favour a growth towards unity.

It must be added, however, that it is only in the early stages of religious movements that the economic factors can be treated in isolation. It is not too difficult to study the influence of economic factors on Islam during Muhammad's life-time and during the period of the early conquests, but it is much more difficult in the maturity of Islam, for instance in the early 'Abbasid period (from 750 onwards). By this time the Islamic society is a 'going concern', and as such is itself an economic and social factor. Membership of the Islamic society has economic and social advantages, and non-membership has corresponding disadvantages. The advantages and disadvantages connected with membership of the society frequently become more important for individuals and groups than any other economic and social factors; that is to say, they are more and more forced to decide whether to belong or not to belong. If they are on the frontiers between two great societies, they will normally have to decide whether to belong to one or the other. If there is only one great society in their neighbourhood, they have to decide whether to become members of it or to try to maintain themselves in independence as a small society on its borders.

The last point may be illustrated by recent world history. The outstanding feature of the last few centuries has been the expansion of the European or more generally the Western society. Although the Western society had not complete political unity, it had a measure of unity, exemplified by common diplomatic practices. The political subdivisions of Western society—the states or nations—recognized one another. Especially after the great advances in science and technology in Western society, membership of this society had great economic advantages. Colonialism and imperialism, whatever their faults, made non-Westerners aware of these economic advantages. All the countries of the world now want to belong to this Western society, and, moreover, to be accepted as members of the Western family of states. Within this Western society now embracing the whole world there are two great subsocieties or blocs, the Communist powers and their dependents and the Atlantic powers and their dependents, while a number of nations, of which India is the largest, try to remain independent. At the present moment (in 1960) both blocs have a certain residual momentum from their democratic and Communist political faiths respectively, and it is not clear what their future relations will be. It does seem clear, however, that the neutrals will not be able to maintain their neutrality indefinitely unless they find some positive faith with a distinctive ideal for the ordering of the world community. If the Atlantic powers, the Communist powers or the neutrals can find a satisfactory ideal of this kind, and on the basis of it can constitute an expanding subsociety, the rest of the world will sooner or later be faced with the decision whether to belong to this subsociety or not to belong.

(c) The ideational factor

The previous discussions have shown the place of ideas in the development of a great society like the Islamic empire. Economic and social factors alone cannot attract men to such a society and hold it together; there must also be ideational, that is, religious, factors.

141

Above all, men must be able to see that membership of the society gives significance to their lives as individuals, and that involves them seeing that the life of the society has a significant place in the world as a whole.

In the system of ideas proper to a religion certain ideas or images have a greater power to attract men to the religion. These dynamic images are the real foundation stones of the religion. The ideational systems of the great religions would appear to include many dynamic images, and to attack different people through different sets of dynamic images. A very important image of this kind is that of the charismatic or supernatural leader, which occurs in several forms. In Islam attraction to this image was specially characteristic of the Shi'ites though it is precisely the history of the Shi'ites which shows that this dynamic image does not by itself produce unity, but rather leads to disunity, since there are so many people who may be regarded as charismatic leaders. Yet the unity of Islam, so far as it has achieved unity, appears to be due first and foremost to a dynamic image, the image or idea of what has here been called the charismatic community. It is not impossible, of course, for different communities to be regarded as the charismatic community, for instance, rival Kharijite sects. But once the main body of the Islamic religious movement put forward a reasoned claim to be the charismatic community founded by Muhammad it was more or less impossible to make a successful claim for any other body. The measure of integration attained in Islam was primarily the work of those who were attracted to this dynamic image and received psychical energy from it. The importance of this image or idea of the charismatic community will be further seen in the following chapters.

V

THE INTEGRATION OF POLITICAL LIFE

I N this and the two following chapters three aspects of the life of the Islamic world are considered in greater detail. The present chapter considers the political aspect. The religious movement which we call the growth of Islam had its political repercussions, and what we are now to study is the manner and extent of the control by religion of the political affairs of the Muslims. In particular we must see how the ideas of Islam influenced political thinking.

1. GENERAL CONSIDERATIONS

The phrase 'integration of political life' may have two meanings, either the political unification of the Muslims, or the control of political life by Islamic ideation. It is chiefly the latter with which we are here concerned. There was political unity in Islam during Muhammad's lifetime, and this may be said to have continued until the fall of the Umayyads in 750, though it was frequently threatened by insurrection and civil war. By 750 the rule of Muslims extended so far that, with the slow communications of the time, it was not really possible for any man or even group of men to maintain effective rule over the whole area. The political unity of the Islamic world continued to be a distant ideal, but there were even a few theoretical writers who considered that this ideal unity was not impaired by the existence of two imams at widely separated centres[1]. As a result of the improvement of communications through European technology, the political unity of all Muslims, or at least of all predominantly Muslim lands, has ceased to be such a remote possibility; and from the middle of the nineteenth century to the present time there have been politicians who in one form or another have advocated the attempt to realize some such unity. Despite the interest of this trend to political unity, however, it is here left aside.

Before considering the influence of the Islamic religion on political

---

[1] Cf. al-Baghdadi, *Usul ad-Din*, Istanbul, 1928/1346, 274, and contrast al-Ash'ari, *Maqalat*, 462f. Cf. also H. Laoust, *Essai sur . . . Ibn Taimiya*, Paris, 1939, 282.

institutions by way of creating new institutions or modifying old ones, it is worth noting that political institutions have a certain autonomy. Where a political institution or practice has proved effective in one society, there will be a tendency for other societies to adopt it, even if their world-view is different, provided it is not incompatible with some institution they already possess and prize. Many countries have abandoned hereditary monarchy, and have decided instead to have an elected president, considering this the best way to reduce internal tensions. On the other hand, there have been several cases where, when a new country was established, it was felt that a hereditary monarchy was most likely to give it stability. Now both these institutions, the hereditary monarch and the elected president are found in a great variety of different countries. There have been Jewish, Christian, Muslim, Hindu and Buddhist kings. We may therefore argue that, because hereditary monarchy has proved politically effective in societies dominated by many different religions, it is an institution that for the most part functions independently of its religious milieu, and is in this sense autonomous.

This autonomy of political institutions is not unlike the autonomy of the economic side of life which was noted above (in chapter II). Where a new economic technique is greatly superior to existing techniques, societies tend to adopt it, whatever their general world-view. The autonomy of economic institutions is not absolute, however, since cases occur where the ideas held by a society or some of its social attitudes and practices, make it difficult for it to adopt a particular technique. The autonomy of political institutions is even more restricted than that of economic ones, since political institutions are more closely related to men's ideas. Yet, even in the political field, the basic elements in institutions are largely autonomous, and the intellectual environment influences not so much the institution itself as the way in which men conceive it, and the precise function which it performs. The Umayyad and 'Abbasid caliphs were in many respects hereditary monarchs, yet they were not thought of in this way. Again, in the decades before the revolution of 1952 Egypt had parliamentary institutions not dissimilar to those of Great Britain, yet the place of the Egyptian parliament in the life of the country was very different from that of the British.

These considerations show the points on which attention must be focussed—the modification of existing political institutions by Islam, and the subordination of political institutions to the properly religious ends of the Muslim community.

The chief end of the life of the individual is the attainment of Paradise; the Qur'an (4.13/17; 85.11; etc.) calls this 'the great success'.

This is therefore the proper end of the society of Muslims. The caliph's function was sometimes regarded as being to look after the welfare of the Muslims, spiritual and temporal, by defending them from internal and external enemies and by seeing that the revealed laws were observed;[1] but some writers went deeper and saw that the ultimate aim of the Islamic community (and therefore of its head) was to make the world a place in which God was perfectly served and worshipped by all men[2]. The second point on which attention is to be focussed is therefore the extent to which actual political institutions in the Islamic world subserve this end.

2. THE COMMUNITY

(a) The community in Muhammad's lifetime

The only political structure known to the majority of pre-Islamic Arabs was the tribe. A few of them must have had some acquaintance with the Byzantine and Persian empires and with the smaller Abyssinian kingdom, but the stories that were current about these states shows that the popular mind conceived of them simply as very large tribes. Thus for the new political structure erected by the Muslims at Medina the only feasible model was the tribe or the confederation of tribes.

The Arab tribe was in Muhammad's time—and still is—a kinship group. The core of the tribe was a body of men descended from a common ancestor. In Muslim times descent has always been reckoned patrilineally, but previously in some cases it may have been reckoned matrilineally. However reckoned, this common descent was the basis of the tribe. It was also possible, however, for a person not related by blood to be attached to the tribe; this might be as a confederate or ally (*halif*), a 'protected neighbour' (*jar*) or a client (*mawla*), but the details are not of any importance here. The sources suggest that in Muhammad's time a tribe usually had attached to it a large number of persons not descended from the common ancestor. Some might reside with it only for a time, but others would do so permanently. Both groups, but particularly those living permanently with the tribe, would tend to intermarry, and thus they would become kinsmen of the full members of the tribe either in the male or female line. The element of genealogical

---

[1] Al-Mawardi (d.1058), *Al-Ahkam as-Sultaniyyah*, Bonn, 1853, 23f.; L. Gardet, *La Cité Musulmane*, Paris, 1954, 155f.

[2] Laoust, *Essai*, 297f.

confusion introduced in this way would enable the groups of protected persons to claim eventually that they were members of the tribe by blood. There are grounds for regarding as fictitious some of the tribal genealogies of the pre-Islamic period; they seem to be constructions to explain or justify later social relationships[1]. It also seems to have been customary in certain circumstances (though we cannot say precisely which circumstances) for a man to be called the son of someone who was not really his father and was known not to be; the Arabic word for such a person, *da'i*, is usually translated 'adopted son', but it probably did not imply anything comparable to modern legal adoption[2].

The Arab tribe of Muhammad's time was thus by no means a simple kinship group, but had a complex structure. This structure, however, was *thought of* in terms of kinship, and where there was no actual kinship a fictitious kinship was sometimes asserted. The large and powerful tribe was a sovereign body politic, owing no obedience to anyone, and maintaining itself and giving security to its members by its own military strength. A large tribe was divided into parts and these again into other parts and so on; the subdivisions, which were also based on kinship in the same way as the main tribe, may be spoken of as sub-tribes, clans and families. If a tribe fared badly and its numbers dwindled, so that it could not defend itself adequately, it might seek the protection of a strong tribe; it would then become dependent on the strong tribe and have an inferior standing, and it might eventually be assimilated. A number of tribes might also band themselves together in a confederacy or alliance, either temporarily or permanently. This tribal system was the foundation of such security as there was for life and property, since the tribe tried to prevent violence between its members and by its vigour in retaliation discouraged violence from members of other tribes.

When Muhammad went to Medina in 622 with some seventy of the Meccan Muslims, he was at once presented with the problem of security for himself and these Emigrants, as they were called. By their *hijrah* or 'emigration' they had cut themselves off from the protection of their clans in Mecca, and therefore required something in place of that. The matter had probably been settled before Muhammad decided to go to Medina. The settlement may be presumed to have been along the lines indicated in the document known as the Constitution of Medina, even if the extant form of that

[1] Cf. Nallino, *Raccolta di Scritti*, iii. 72-79.

[2] The Qur'an (33.4) protests (§2) against the practice; cf. *Muhammad at Medina*, 282. Ibn al-Athir, iii. 303 (61 A.H.), mentions 'Abbad ibn-al-Akhdar, who was called after his mother's husband, though his real father was known.

document is to be dated about 628.[1] According to the Constitution of Medina the Emigrants function as a kinship group in respect of security (e.g. through the common responsibility for the payment of blood-money). The Emigrants were indeed akin, since they all belonged to the tribe of Quraysh, though to different clans of it. Further, the Emigrants, as one clan, were in alliance with eight Medinan clans. The nine groups were to join in protecting one another from violence, especially at the hands of the pagan Meccans. Thus the new body politic which was formed when Muhammad went to Medina could be regarded as constituted on traditional Arabian lines; it was an alliance of clans for mutual support and defence. Indeed some use was even made of fictitious kinship, since Muhammad declared some of his Medinan followers to be 'brothers' of the various Emigrants, and this 'brothering' was apparently treated as effective for purposes of inheritance.

There was also a sense, however, in which this new body politic, sometimes known as the *ummah* or 'community', was based not on kinship and alliance, but on religion. To judge from the extant document membership of the alliance which formed the community was open only to those who accepted Muhammad as the Messenger of God. The various clans in the alliance could be in league with bodies not in the alliance. The Medinan clans had close relationships with the various Jewish groups in Medina, and with some of the nomadic tribes in the neighbourhood; and some of the earlier treaties between Muhammad and the surrounding nomadic clans may not have required them to become Muslims. Such relationships, however, though recognized and honoured by the Medinan community, did not make the tribes and clans in question full members of that community. Thus the alliance constituting the Medinan community though in accordance with Arab tradition, was a special kind of alliance. The community produced was one in which every one acknowledged Muhammad as Messenger of God. Old forms had been observed, but the community was essentially founded on this common acknowledgement. Its basis was not kinship and alliance but religion.

The creation of the Community at Medina already shows an extensive modification of an existing political institution. When Muhammad first preached at Mecca he would have been content had men turned to worship God, while political structures remained as they were. The pagan opposition, however, probably with a clearer realization than Muhammad had of the political implications

---

[1] *Muhammad at Medina*, 221-8; pp. 238-49 give further evidence for some of the statements in this section.

of his preaching, would not accept his message in any form of which he could approve. This seems to have forced upon Muhammad the choice between abandoning his preaching and becoming involved in politics. He had begun by holding that a prophet or messenger was sent by God to his own people or tribe; but it was difficult to go on holding this when the majority of his tribe was against him. The Qur'an therefore tends to cease speaking of the prophet's tribe or people (*qawm*), and to speak instead of his 'community' (*ummah*). A community in this sense is essentially a religious body; the Jews were one such community and the Christians another. Similarly the 'believers', that is, those Meccans and Medinans who followed Muhammad, were another community. The old Arab idea of the tribe or kinship group was thus gradually modified, until it had been replaced by the community based on religion. The new body politic at Medina could perhaps have been set up simply as an alliance according to the traditional conception, but the subsequent development of that alliance and especially Muhammad's attainment of a position of leadership in it would not have been possible without the new conception.

The little Muslim community of Medina prospered. It won battles. Its successes in raids were more numerous than its failures. Individuals and groups began to attach themselves to it. After the capture of Mecca and victory of Hunayn in 630 there was a constant stream to Medina of deputations from tribes and parts of tribes who wanted to become allies of Muhammad. To these deputations the regular answer was that in order to become allies they must promise to obey God and His Messenger and to pay the impost of the *zakat* (or legal alms). In this way the special position of Muhammad as Messenger of God came to have great political importance. In the first months at Medina this special position conferred on him little more than prestige, but in the closing years of his life his authority was absolute.

A number of treaties and other legal documents from Muhammad's last years have been preserved, and most appear to be genuine. They never speak of the community as *ummah*, but use other terms—for instance, *jama'ah*—which suggest a federation of tribes. Later developments make it almost certain that this is how the Islamic state was conceived at the time. What is not clear is whether the wider alliance of the closing years was regarded as being the same as the alliance described in the Constitution of Medina, or whether the *ummah* continued as a more closely knit body within the wider alliance. Whichever alternative is nearer the truth, the Islamic state remains a federation of tribes, though with a religious basis. It is

148

also not certain whether a man could be an active Muslim—and so
a member of this state—without being a member of a tribe which had
an alliance with Muhammad. Muhammad undoubtedly accepted
individual conversions. Converts from the Meccan tribe of Quraysh
could simply be added to the 'clan' of Emigrants at Medina. Individuals and groups of other tribes who came to settle in Medina (unless
they were sufficiently important to have a treaty of their own) were
perhaps added to the Emigrants as confederates, 'protected neighbours', or clients. On the other hand, there were instances of men
claiming to be Muslims and yet being killed by Muslim troops ; but
this may simply be due to the fact that the implications of the new
conception of the state had not been properly grasped by the average
man. Eventually it is probable that all Muhammad's chief lieutenants
were authorized to receive converts.

While the Islamic state could thus be looked on as a federation of
tribes (with a religious basis), it was also in some ways regarded as
a tribe. The Muslims were brothers of one another[1], and therefore
inviolate, like the members of a tribe. At the same time, because of
the religious basis, all non-Muslims, except those who had a treaty-
relationship with Muhammad, were enemies or potential enemies and
to be treated as such. In the political sphere this was a set of ideas
capable of uniting the Arabs and directing their raiding propensities
outwards. First they raided Arab tribes not members of the alliance
until all became Muslims; then they moved further and further afield
against the surrounding lands and their inhabitants. Islam thus
modified the traditional Arab institution of the tribe and federation,
and used it in its modified form to bring about the conversion of the
Arabs and to create a new kind of empire.

The Arab conception of the tribe also gave a neat solution of what
is nowadays called the problem of minorities. It had been normal
practice for a strong tribe to take weaker tribes and other small
groups under its protection. Where Muhammad was faced with
groups which for one reason or another did not want to become
Muslims, he had recourse to this practice. At first he may have had
relations of this sort with pagan tribes, allowing them to remain
pagan; but as his power grew he tended to demand the conversion
of pagans and to restrict this status of 'dependent tribe' to groups of
Christians and Jews. When Islam spread outside Arabia, many
Christian groups made treaties with the Muslim invaders and
acquired this status. It meant that they retained internal autonomy,
that they paid certain sums of money to the Islamic state, and that in
return for this payment the Islamic state guaranteed protection.

[1] Cf. Qur'an 3. 103/98; 49.10.

Just as it was a matter of honour for the nomadic tribe to give effective protection to those it had undertaken to protect, so the Islamic state in general felt itself bound to respect the guaranteed rights of its 'protected groups' (*ahl-adh-dhimmah;* the individual was a *dhimmi*). This has meant that on the whole Islam has had an excellent record for the treatment of religious minorities. Those who did not respond to the first summons to surrender to the Arabs, but fought against them and were defeated and had to surrender unconditionally, had at first a different status from those who came to terms voluntarily; but eventually their status was assimilated to that of those with treaties. At first, too, such protection was confined to 'the people of the Book', that is, monotheists with a written scripture, and in particular Jews and Christians; but when the Muslims came into contact with populations of Zoroastrians, Buddhists, Hindus and others, who would have resisted conversion, these were all reckoned as 'people of the Book' and given the status of 'protected groups'.

(b) Tribalism and equality

The old Arab tribe had a complex structure. Between the chief and the full members of the tribe there was not much inequality, but the various dependents of the tribe were looked upon as inferior. This inequality within the tribe was perpetuated in Islam and even increased, since it was the normal practice, when non-Arabs became Muslims, for them to be registered as 'clients' (*mawali*) of Arab tribes. Why this should have been so is never explained, but it must somehow or other have been due to the all-pervasive character of the conception of the tribe. Perhaps it was due to the connexion of tribalism with security. In so far as the Muslims were all brothers, the injuries of one of them should have been the concern of the whole body. Yet the Constitution of Medina shows that the various clans there had a part to play in the system of public security. In the old system the tribe had not acted as a monolithic body, but its subdivisions, the clan and the family, had had special responsibilities in respect of security; and it was only natural that there should be something similar in the new body politic. As has been noticed above, when individuals or small groups came to Medina and professed Islam, they probably became clients or confederates of Muhammad and his 'clan' of Emigrants. It was probably difficult or even impossible for those brought up in a tribal system to conceive of an individual Muslim who was a member of the Islamic community but not a member of smaller groups within it. It is not surprising that, as the community grew, the older kinship units regained something of their importance.

To attach non-Arab Muslims to Arab tribes as clients was thus, when the practice began, a very reasonable thing to do. The Christian of Syria or 'Iraq who became a Muslim was by his conversion being detached from the 'protected group' to which he belonged. It was unthinkable for him to remain as an isolated individual. The obvious course was to make him a client of the general or other official before whom he professed Islam or of the leader under whom he wanted to serve as a soldier (since in the early days most converts would want to do this and to share in the stipends paid to all campaigning Muslims). Administrative convenience in the payment of stipends may also have prompted the authorities to attach non-Arabs to Arab tribes. It is doubtful whether the caliph or the provincial governors kept a list of all the individual Muslims entitled to receive stipends. More probably they only had lists of the heads of the smallest units (of perhaps from fifty to two hundred men, all of one clan); each of these heads would be given the total stipend for his unit and would have to divide it out. In order to receive a stipend the non-Arab Muslim would have to belong to such a unit, which would be a part of a clan and tribe respectively. Even if a whole unit consisted of non-Arabs, they would be a part of a wider group which would normally be a clan or tribe.

These suggestions about the way in which the practice came about seem reasonable, but, whether they are right or wrong, there is no doubt about the practice. Even a Muslim of long-standing like the Abyssinian freedman, Bilal, who was Muhammad's muezzin, was attached to an Arab tribe, the tribe of Khath'am. (There are also cases where, for reasons not known to us, Arabs were attached as clients to tribes other than their own)[1].

Since the client of the nomadic tribe had been regarded as inferior to the full members of the tribe, the non-Arab Muslims came to be reckoned as inferior to Arab Muslims. There are grounds for thinking that the Arabs often treated them in ways which made them conscious of their social inferiority; for instance, they are said to have used a less respectful mode of address than they used to other Arabs[2]. As the non-Arab Muslims grew more numerous and came to have a much larger share in the activities of the Islamic state, they became

[1] Cf. Ibn-Sa'd, Tabaqat, v. 208f., 220, 228.

[2] They used *ism* or *laqab* and not *kunyah;* cf. Goldziher, *Muhammedanische Studien*, i. 26 and R. Levy, *The Social Structure of Islam*, Cambridge, 1957, 59. To Goldziher's examples of clients with a *kunyah* may be added many from Ibn Sa'd, v, vi, vii.

more and more dissatisfied with this social inferiority. This dissatisfaction was one factor in the movement which substituted the 'Abbasid dynasty for the Umayyad, and it also contributed to the movement of the Shu'ubiyyah which maintained that Persians and others were superior to the Arabs. Yet social inferiority was not the only reason for the discontent of the non-Arabs. There were also more material reasons.

The system of paying stipends to the Muslims in return for their services as soldiers or in other capacities created some fresh inequalities. The Muslims were divided into five main groups with some subdivisions. The first group received very high stipends, the following groups less, and the last just sufficient to keep a man alive.[1] The groups were formed according to the extent of a man's services to Islam, measured by the 'priority' of his conversion. This principle worked fairly on the whole, since the earlier converts had not merely served Islam well in the past, but were mostly continuing to serve it well in important administrative positions in the army or in civil government. It was rather unfair, however, to the clients who had become Muslims some time after the first conquests, especially when these were taking a full share in fighting. Generals realized this and tried to see that the non-Arabs received a fair share of the money distributed after a successful campaign. The Arab soldiers and their leaders, however, objected to Arabs and non-Arabs being treated alike; indeed during the rising of al-Mukhtar the Arabs supporting him objected to the non-Arabs receiving any share at all of the spoils[2]. This inferiority in pecuniary reward would strongly reinforce the discontent arising from social attitudes.

The non-Arab Muslims played a prominent part in the military rising which brought about the fall of the Umayyads, and under the succeeding 'Abbasid dynasty they had a share in ruling the state commensurate with their part in its life. In some way or other (though we do not know exactly how) it ceased to be the case that all non-Arab Muslims were automatically clients of an Arab tribe. Public security was sufficiently provided for to make the tribal system unnecessary; and the stipend-roll had disappeared and presumably been replaced by a system of payment for actual service on campaign (and also by other devices, such as the granting of fiefs to those prepared to fight regularly). The rivalry between Arabs and other races still remained, but it found its chief expression in literature (in the Shu'ubite movement). So far as the Islamic state was concerned Muslims of all races were essentially equal. Little was left even of the social inequalities which had existed under the Umayyads,

[1] Cf. p. 96 above; al-Mawardi, 354 (tr. 442).   [2] At-Tabari, ii. 634, 649.

whether due to the stipend-roll's principle of 'service to Islam' or to old Arab ideas of nobility. As the stipend-roll faded out, the Islamic nobility it had established was perhaps maintained by grants of land in the conquered countries. The 'Abbasids, however, used the elaborate court ceremonial to create a new social hierarchy in which all the positions were in their own gift. This might be called a principle of 'present service' rather than of 'past service' (like the stipend-roll). Such social changes are not precisely the effect of Islamic ideas, yet they are not out of place in a movement which was largely inspired by the idea of the equality of all Muslims.

In general the disappearance of inferior status for non-Arab Muslims may be claimed as a triumph for Islam over the racial pride of the Arabs despite the reinforcement of that by their great military successes. Early passages of the Qur'an had insisted that wealth and family—the things that conferred a high social position—were of no avail to a man when he came before God to be judged; and that implies the equality of all Muslims in the sight of God. It is possible, however, that this specifically Islamic idea was supported by tribal conceptions or attitudes applied to the Islamic community as a whole. The full members of a tribe were usually held to be essentially equal in honour; consequently, in so far as the Islamic community was regarded as a tribe, the full members of it (who could be of any race) ought to have been regarded as equal.

It is seen to be remarkable, when one reflects a little, that the principles and attitudes underlying Muhammad's little state at Medina should, with only slight modification, have been capable of sustaining a vast empire. To begin with, of course, there was no great difficulty. Though the Arabs had conquered great stretches of territory, they had made no changes in local administration. Local units had been incorporated into the Islamic state as 'protected groups', retaining their internal autonomy; and this was the status of nearly all the inhabitants of the empire. The only change was that the higher levels of administration had passed into the hands of the Muslims, and they also constituted the armies for garrison purposes and frontier defence. Though the empire was enormous, it was only this small military aristocracy of Muslims (at first almost exclusively Arabs) who were full members of the Islamic state and governed according to its principles. In the course of a century, however, a great transformation took place, perhaps occasioned mainly by the need of greater man-power for the armies than the Arabs could supply (especially when some of them began to find soldiering irksome). Soldiers had to be Muslims, and so full members of the state. Besides, a state based on a missionary religion like Islam

153

could not turn away would-be converts, even if some governors tried to restrict the political rights of non-Arab Muslims. The consequence of the movement of conversion was that when the 'Abbasid dynasty came to power in 750 the full members of the state were not a mere handful of Arabs but a considerable proportion of every race; and under the 'Abbasids the proportion of Muslims steadily increased.

Despite this transformation from a relatively homogeneous city-state into a large multi-racial empire it was possible to retain as a basis, with only slight modifications, the same principles and attitudes. The detailed course of the transformation and the nature of the modifications required (such as the abolition of an inferior status for all non-Arab Muslims) are worthy of study, but that cannot be undertaken here in full.

It is interesting also to note the persistence in the modern world of the Islamic conception of the community. The European and American conception of a democratic state requires that all inhabitants of a given territory should have equal political rights. Modern Islamic states which claim to be democracies of the Western type have therefore to give equal political rights to Muslims and non-Muslims. Even when this is done on paper, it remains in conflict with the deep-seated Islamic attitude which restricts full citizenship to Muslims, and therefore is difficult to make effective in practice. The Islamic conception, though it tends to perpetuate the distinctive character of minorities and prevent their assimilation, has much to be said for it; and Western democracies are beginning to realize that they cannot function unless a basic ideational system is held by all citizens alike.

(c) Collectivism and disruptive tendencies

For the nomadic tribe of pre-Islamic times the honour or nobility of the tribe was of supreme importance. This was shown by the way in which the members of the tribe exhibited in their lives the moral excellences admired by the Arabs, such as manliness, endurance of hardships and generosity. All members of the tribe, and especially the leading men, were expected to attain certain standards of conduct. These standards were concretely thought of as the 'beaten path' (*sunnah*) of the fathers. These, then, were the mores of the tribe and constituted its honour. In this honour all the members of the tribe shared. If a man performed a noble deed, its performance was mainly due to the noble blood of the tribe in his veins and redounded to the honour of the tribe. At the same time, dishonourable conduct by one member disgraced the tribe; and it was possible and

154

customary in certain circumstances to expel an individual from his tribe. The attitudes implicit in all this did much to mould Islam in its formative period.

✓ An urgent need of the new community at an early stage was a new 'custom' to serve as guide in situations where previous customs were no longer applicable or had been abused or where different tribes had had different customs. This need was met in part by the fact that the Qur'an contained certain rules of conduct. Muhammad must also have given decisions about cases which were not covered by Qur'anic rules. An example of such decisions in a formal document are the provisions about the blood-wit in the Constitution of Medina; but he no doubt also settled other matters informally as well as giving general instructions to the agents he sent to represent him in various parts of Arabia. Thus by the time of Muhammad's death a new set of customary usages was being developed for the 'tribe' of Muslims.

Apart from this tendency of the nomadic Arab to rely on following the 'beaten path' it is difficult to account for the appearance in the Islamic state of a law which is essentially customary law. In Syria the invading Arabs would learn something of the working of Roman law, but this knowledge could not have been effective in the earliest days. There was no comparable system of law in the Persian empire. More likely to have influenced the Arabs was the knowledge of the laws which the Jews had in their scriptures; indeed there was a certain parallelism between the Qur'an and the Pentateuch in that both contained rules of conduct. Yet this influence must not be exaggerated. It probably made itself felt chiefly at two points. Firstly, in facilitating the acceptance by the Muslims of revelations containing rules of conduct, and perhaps also in causing Muhammad to expect such revelations. Secondly, at a much later date, after the formative period had been succeeded by one of consolidation, the Jewish example probably suggested to some Muslim scholars that the customary law of Islam could only be stabilized and unified by linking it up with the Qur'anic prescriptions, and indeed making them its core. In the formative period itself, however, customary law grew through responses to particular situations. There was little conscious attempt at systematization, but the development took place under constant pressure from the Arabs' inner need for a 'beaten path' to follow.

The detailed contents of the customary law and the processes by which it was systematized are two topics which will receive some consideration at a later stage. At the moment the point to be emphasized is that Islam found the Arabs with a deep-seated attitude which may be described as that of following the 'beaten path', and that it used this attitude to bring about a wide acceptance throughout its multi-racial community of a set of usages which were a satisfactory basis for the life of an advanced culture. With all due allowance for local divergences, the similarity of mores throughout the Islamic world is still remarkable. The nature of the process was partly recognised by those theorists who made 'consensus' (*ijma'*) one of the roots of law.

Since the 'beaten path' of the community was also the command of God, deviance was a serious matter, for it implied disobedience to God's command and that was punishable by Hell. This series of implications is relevant to the Kharijite movement (described in the last chapter). In a sense it is a recrudescence of pre-Islamic tribalism, yet it takes place entirely within Islam; there is not the slightest attempt to go back from Islam to the previous paganism. The little groups of insurrectionaries are strangely similar to tribes or clans, and their fighting to tribal razzias. More important, their expulsion from their community of the person guilty of deviance resembles the expulsion of a deviant tribesman. They divided mankind into 'the people of Paradise' and 'the people of Hell'; the former group comprised the true Muslims, however restricted in number these might be, while the latter had all the others. Just as the disgrace incurred by one member of the tribe affected the whole tribe, so conduct worthy of Hell by one member of the community seems to have been felt to imperil the salvation of the whole community. The man who had disobeyed God's command was therefore expelled from 'the people of Paradise'. Moreover, just as expulsion from a tribe meant that protection by the tribe came to an end, so did expulsion from the community of true believers; indeed, the expelled person was now one of 'the people of Hell' whom it was a duty for the true believers to kill. In this way the Kharijites justified the assassination of 'Uthman, alleging he had disobeyed divine commands, and also the later practice of murdering those who did not accept their theological views.

The practice of excluding the deviant from the community worked in the small desert communities, but it was not feasible in a large state. The extreme Kharijites, despite their reckless courage, could build no enduring political structure. Groups of non-militant Kharijites found a *modus vivendi*, consonant with their principles, in the caliphate as it actually was. Other theologians—notably the Murji'ites and then the Sunnite orthodoxy—learning from the Kharijites and also reacting against them, worked out a theological basis for the Islamic state that satisfied the deep demand to belong to 'the people of Paradise' and at the same led to a practical way of dealing with deviance. The deviant, according to the nature of his deviance, was either to be punished by the caliph or his subordinates or else left to God to punish after death; in the latter case it was usually held that the punishment might or might not be in Hell, but that, if it was in Hell, it would not be eternal and the person so punished would eventually be admitted to Paradise. The Islamic community thus remained 'the people of Paradise' and membership of it made a man's life of ultimate significance.

It is somewhat surprising that this development should have taken place. When Muhammad began to preach, Mecca was suffering from a malaise which was largely due to a movement from communalism or collectivism to individualism; and the Qur'an, in its doctrine of the Last Day, provides a sanction for an individualistic ethics. Here, however, the pendulum has swung back towards collectivism. One part of the old Arab attitude to the tribe—deriving the meaning of life from membership of it—has reasserted itself. Islam has managed to find a place for this attitude within itself and so has grown in strength and removed a possible source of disintegration. Yet the price was high—a radical change of the Qur'anic conception of God's judgement on the Last Day as purely individual and as an either-or matter.

Creative changes, or attempts to effect readjustment where something has become maladjusted, begin as deviance. Because of the religious basis of the Islamic community the ideational complement of such deviance tends to be theological. The obvious examples are the early Kharijite and Shi'ite movements. Even the subdivisions within them are theologically justified. The Fatimid propaganda against the Seljuqs in the latter part of the eleventh century was theological. This cannot be taken as an absolute rule, however. One exception seems to be the introduction of Persian practices into the central administration by the early 'Abbasid caliphs (though the process had begun under the Umayyads); but it may be that, since such matters were beyond the ken of ordinary Muslims, and since the central administration was not closely dependent on religious ideas, no justification of the change was necessary. Apart from such exceptions, however, there was a need for theological justification of political and administrative changes, and this normally took the form of showing that they were in accordance with genuine Islamic principles. This was the form taken in the Islamic world by the resistance to change of an established cultural tradition.

(d) Relations to non-Muslims

✓The Islamic community consisted of those who acknowledged Muhammad as the Messenger of God and who thereby committed themselves to living according to the precepts contained in the Qur'an and the other practices developed in the community during Muhammad's lifetime and later. Those who refused to worship God and acknowledge Muhammad were behaving in a way insulting to God and must therefore be regarded as enemies by the Muslims. Between the pagans or atheists and the Muslims stood the Jews and the Christians (and the other communities given the same status). Towards these the Muslim attitude was not altogether consistent. In Muslim eyes they had received genuine revelations from God, and they were therefore at least partly justified in continuing to worship God according to the revelations they had received. From the Muslim point of view, however, they were not justified in denying (as they usually did) that Muhammad was the Messenger at least to the Arabs. Despite this obstinacy, as it appeared to them, the Muslims were prepared to tolerate Jews and Christians as 'protected groups' within the Islamic state and to admit that their presence did not conflict absolutely with its religious basis.

For the paganism of the old Arab religion, on the other hand, there was no toleration. The Arab pagans were 'the people of Hell' and between them and 'the people of Paradise' there could be no lasting friendship. There may indeed have been treaties with pagan tribes in the first few years after the Hijrah when Muhammad was still weak, but, as his strength grew, he was able to make acceptance of Islam a condition of alliance with himself. Towards the end of his life Muhammad's state was in the position of an Arab tribe which had declared all other tribes not in alliance with itself to be enemies or potential enemies. It is conceivable that a nomadic tribe might have done this had it felt strong enough. For Muhammad such a conception had the advantage that it directed the energies of his followers outwards against tribes not members of his alliance. At the same time the religious basis of the alliance made it easy, for tribes which found Muslim pressure too much for them, to join the alliance and take part in the outward movement. Thus the conception of the 'holy war' (*jihad*) against the pagans was of the utmost importance in giving direction to the first phase of Arab expansion; and it continued to have some importance throughout the Umayyad caliphate.

By the time the Islamic state had become an empire, however, it is doubtful whether the idea of the holy war was more advantageous than disadvantageous. While it may be possible for a desert tribe to regard all its neighbours as enemies, it is not easy for a large and complex state to behave in this way. There is, of course, a sense in which every state is the enemy, or at least the rival, of every other. A case could perhaps be made for the adoption by an empire of the principle of the holy war, but this principle would have to be modified to allow an alliance or an armistice with rival states where military or political considerations demanded it. In a sense the idea of the holy war is too simple for the complexities of an empire's foreign policy. It is military and political considerations which determine it in detail. This, at any rate, is what seems to have happened in the Islamic state. During the Umayyad caliphate much energy was expended in campaigns against the Byzantines, although, so far as the principle of the holy war is concerned, one might have expected that the Muslims would have been prepared to tolerate the Byzantines as Christians.[1]

Along with the fading out of the idea of the holy war as a directive of foreign policy went its fading out as the basis of the organization of the army. In Muhammad's closing years it had been obligatory for every able-bodied Muslim to take part in the campaigns unless excused. In this way the Islamic state had a large army which made possible the enormous conquests in the years up to 650. Most Muslims seem to have been content to remain liable to military service throughout their lives; they had the privilege of living as part of a ruling aristocracy. When the expansion slowed down, however, and the fighting became harder and the booty less plentiful, many were unwilling to leave the camp-cities for arduous expeditions on the distant frontiers. Special promises of rewards had to be made in order to attract men. Other devices were also employed, such as the granting of lands in return for military services. Eventually Muslim leaders are found employing mercenaries, who might not even be Muslims.

Thus the idea of the holy war ceased to have much real importance. Among ascetics and mystics there was a tendency to transfer it to the warfare against the evil in oneself, but the original idea did not disappear. Zeal for the conversion of non-Muslims did not flag. Except in the early days and in the case of Arab pagans, conversion had not been closely associated with the holy war. Outside Arabia there seem at first to have been no deliberate efforts to make converts. In later centuries the extension of the faith has been a specific

[1] The presumption is that raids on Constantinople were continued because the prize was a rich one, while raids in France were discontinued because the possible booty was not worth the dangers incurred; cf. p. 171 below, n. 2.

aim of some of the religious orders. Yet through all the centuries the idea of the holy war against the infidels has persisted and has continued to have a hold on masses of ordinary Muslims. Political leaders with little belief themselves in the idea have used it to raise the morale of their forces. They have sometimes unscrupulously branded other Muslims as heretics so as to be able to claim that they were fighting a holy war against them. The Ottoman Sultan in 1914 declared a holy war against the 'infidel' British (though he was in alliance with the equally 'infidel' Germans and Austrians); but the Muslims of the British empire paid no attention to him. So the idea continues, for the most part outdated, yet retaining certain grains of truth, and, where not misused, capable of fostering worthy attitudes.

This is perhaps the weakest part of the conception of the Islamic community as it has been developed out of the old Arab idea of the tribe. In general the conception has shown itself capable of providing the basis for a unified empire. If Islam has failed to remain a political unity, that is mainly due to its inability to discover a suitable ruling institution—a matter to which we now pass.

3. THE RULING INSTITUTION

(a) The rule of the Messenger of God

The traditional Arab ruling institution was the chief of the tribe or clan. His authority was not very extensive, unless he himself was a man of commanding personality. In general his decisions had to be approved by an assembly of all the full members of the tribe, and he had no power to coerce recalcitrant members to carry out his decisions. If his decisions were reasonable, of course, tribal solidarity would make it difficult for members not to carry them out. Relations with other tribes were normally handled by the chief. A strong chief would insist that he alone had the right to give hospitality to strangers, and this provided contacts and information which facilitated the conduct of 'foreign relations'. The chief was not necessarily the leader in war, but it was one of his privileges to receive a quarter of any booty taken in razzias. This privilege helped him to discharge the obligation of looking after poor members of the tribe and of arranging for the payment of ransoms and blood-wits. Disputes within a tribe or clan would often be referred to the chief, but might also be referred to arbiters. If two tribes were involved, there were arbiters in various parts of Arabia—men with a reputation for wisdom and impartiality—to whom the matter could be taken. Sometimes recourse was had to male or female diviners.

The Integration of Political Life

The position of Muhammad as it is seen in the Constitution of Medina closely resembles that of a clan chief. The Emigrants are treated like one of the Medinan clans, and Muhammad is their chief. Only in two points does the Constitution give him a special place. One is that it is stated (§23, §42) that, where there are disputes in the community, they are to be referred 'to God and to Muhammad'; the other is that razzias against the enemies of the community are not to be undertaken without Muhammad's permission. The reference of disputes to Muhammad could be taken as a development of the conception of the community as a tribe and Muhammad as its chief, or as an acceptable arbiter. It may also, however, be influenced by the practice of taking questions to persons with a religious charisma. A Meccan passage of the Qur'an says that it is one of the functions of a Messenger of God to judge justly between the members of the community to which he is sent[1]. Probably one of the things which led the Medinans to call Muhammad into their city was that he would be able to settle their disputes as an impartial arbiter. Yet it can hardly have been compulsory for them to do so. At least the repeated commands in the Qur'an to do so imply that it was not always in fact done[2].

The requirement of Muhammad's permission for razzias is in accordance with the control of external relations by the chief of a tribe. In fact Muhammad seems to have organized all the razzias of the Medinan community, and either to have led them in person or to have appointed a leader. It may be, however, that they were regarded primarily as expeditions of the Emigrants which the Medinans were invited to join. It was early decided that Muhammad was to receive a fifth of the booty taken on raids; and the Qur'an prescribed certain communal purposes for which it was to be used. This was closely parallel to the tribal chief's quarter of booty, and to his traditional obligations, such as looking after the poor.

The comparative weakness of Muhammad's position in the early years at Medina is shown by the way in which he had to handle the so-called 'affair of the lie'. This happened as late as 627, just before the siege of Medina by the Meccans and their allies. Muhammad had been accompanied on a razzia by his young wife 'A'ishah, travelling in a litter on camel-back. At the last halt before they returned to Medina she was left behind while looking for a necklace, and, as her litter was closed, no one noticed her absence. A few hours later

---

[1] 10.47/48; the points here being made are discussed more fully in *Muhammad at Medina*, 228-38. For this section in general, cf. T. W. Arnold, *The Caliphate*, Oxford, 1924.

[2] E.g. 42.10/8.

161

she returned attended by a handsome young man. The malicious gossip of Muhammad's enemies in Medina accused 'A'ishah of infidelity, and the incident was used to discredit Muhammad. Eventually (after it was clear she was not pregnant) Muhammad received a revelation declaring that 'A'ishah was innocent, and he determined on a showdown with his leading opponent, 'Abd-Allah ibn-Ubayy. He took no direct measures, however, but called a meeting of the Medinan clans and asked the clan heads to suspend 'clan protection' in the case of those who were slandering his family so that he might deal with them. The leaders of the two main clan-groups in Medina, the Aws and the Khazraj, vied with one another in expressing their readiness to take Muhammad's part, and it was so clear that 'Abd-Allah ibn-Ubayy had little support from the Medinans that no more is heard of his opposition to Muhammad. This showdown with 'Abd-Allah ibn-Ubayy and the failure of the Meccan siege of Medina shortly afterwards doubtless strengthened Muhammad's position; and from this time onwards his powers in the Constitution may have been largely effective.

A further strengthening of Muhammad's position was brought about by the 'pledge of good pleasure' in 628 in the course of an expedition to the outskirts of Mecca (at al-Hudaybiyah). At a critical point in the course of events the Muslims made a pledge to Muhammad. There are different accounts of the contents of the pledge; there are good inferential grounds, though no direct evidence, for thinking that it was a pledge to do whatever Muhammad decided. All the leading Muslims in Medina, native Medinans and Emigrants alike, took this pledge. If this interpretation of the 'pledge under the tree' is correct, then it placed the earlier Muslims in a position not unlike that of the later converts, for the latter, as a condition of being accepted as allies, had to promise to obey God and His Messenger.

Athough in the last year of two of Muhammad's life the body politic ruled by him was comparatively large, there were no permanent arrangements for administration—nothing that could be called a civil service. Muhammad seems to have appointed men to perform special jobs on an *ad hoc* basis. He appointed men to lead expeditions, to deal with the groups in south Arabia which had become Muslim, to collect the *zakat* (or 'legal alms') which recent allies were obliged to pay, to look after the booty or the prisoners after a battle, to receive the due proportion of the harvest from the 'protected' Jewish settlements, and so on. In his entourage at Medina there were a number of men able to write, and one or other of these was given the job of writing any document required.

On the whole the ruling institution of the Islamic state during Muhammad's lifetime was simply the Arab tribal chiefship with some slight modifications. The chief modification was the pledge to obey made by the later allies, if not by the majority of the Muslims. With the position of chief there was combined also something of the position of arbiter in disputes The religious charisma of Muhammad's prophethood would enhance his authority as an arbiter, and would also make many people more inclined to accept him as leader. Apart from this, prophethood had little effect on Muhammad's position as ruler. Revelation produced rules for the social life of the community (in marriage and inheritance, for example), encouragement in face of the enemy, and ideational weapons against the Jews. It was not used to impose solutions of political difficulties. 'Abd-Allah was dealt with in an assembly of the old tribal character. Similarly, at the beginning of 631 when three men stayed away from an important expedition without permission their punishment of being 'sent to Coventry' was ordered by Muhammad himself, but their reprieve came by revelation. (This is not to be taken as implying that Muhammad could produce revelations at will, which he almost certainly could not do; he may, however, have had some technique of 'listening' for revelations when he thought the situation appropriate for one. Thus he would not try to obtain a revelation to deal with cases where tact and statesmanship would lead to a more satisfactory solution).

(b) The early caliphate

Muhammad apparently made no arrangements for the succession, except that, when he was too ill to go to the mosque, he appointed Abu-Bakr to lead the public worship in his place. This meant very little, however, for Abu-Bakr had been his most trusted adviser and the man most closely associated with him in the running of the Islamic state. On Muhammad's death in 632 the matter was settled by an assembly mainly of the native Medinans. Many of them wanted a Medinan to be head of the state, but they were so impressed by the argument that the state would break up unless a Meccan was at its head that they agreed to the appointment of Abu-Bakr, and pledged themselves to obey him. He was given the title of 'caliph' (*khalifah*). The word occurs in the Qur'an where it is said of both Adam and David that God has made him a *khalifah* in the earth, that is, a deputy or vicegerent, whose function is to judge justly[1]. It also suggests, however, the meaning of 'successor' or 'one who comes after'.

[1] 2.30/28; 38.26/25.

The position of Abu-Bakr was very similar to that of Muhammad in his last two years except that Abu-Bakr was not a prophet and could not receive revelations. His rule was essentially that of a tribal chief, except that he had theoretically the additional powers acquired by Muhammad. Many of the nomadic allies of Muhammad, however, regarded their promises to obey as personal promises to Muhammad, and, as they found membership of the Islamic state somewhat cramping, refused to renew them to Abu-Bakr. Thus most of his short reign of two years was spent in quelling revolts against his authority. At the same time probing raids in the direction of Syria and 'Iraq were opening the way for profitable expeditions, and once these began even the most restive nomads were convinced that it was to their advantage to remain members of the Islamic state. The basis of the caliphate may thus be said to be utilitarian. When Muhammad died a considerable body of Muslims, including the most influential ones, were convinced that it was in their best interests that the Islamic state should continue in being. The conviction could be justified either on religious or on political grounds. If the Islamic state was to go on, then it must have a head, since, as an Arab writer put it, 'the people do not prosper in anarchy'[1]. It is curious that this office of caliph, though one of the distinctive marks of Islam, has no basis in Islamic ideation. The derivation of the name from the Qur'an does not imply that the actual office was in any way formed by Qur'anic ideas. Something had to be done to keep things going, and this was what suggested itself to the men on the spot.

In the two decades after Muhammad's death the Arabs conquered an empire—the rich provinces of Syria, Egypt and 'Iraq, and lands beyond them both east and west. These conquests made certain changes necessary in the ruling institution, though not such extensive changes as might have been expected. Although the territory and the income of the Islamic state had greatly increased, there had been no such increase in the number of full members of the state, that is, of the persons directly subject to the caliph. Nearly all the inhabitants of the conquered lands became 'protected groups' and were ruled only indirectly. Thus a provincial governor had only to rule directly over the Arabs in the province, who were mostly on a military footing, and from the others to collect the appropriate taxes in bulk—the collection of the tax in detail was usually a matter for the authorities of the 'protected group'.

[1] Ibn-'Abd-Rabbi-hi, *Al-'Iqd al-Farid*, Cairo (1885)/1302, i.5; quoted by C. A. Nallino, *Raccolta di Scritti*, iii.69. Cf. al-Ghazali, *Al-Iqtisad fi-'l-I'tiqad*, Cairo, n.d., who argues that an Imam is necessary to maintain the ordinances of religion.

164

The Integration of Political Life

One important change was that of the residence of the caliph. Trivial as this may seem, it must be regarded as having contributed to a considerable change in the character of the ruling institution. The first to leave Medina was the fourth caliph 'Ali (656-661), who, perhaps because of his involvement in military operations, made his chief centre at Kufah in 'Iraq. Mu'awiyah, the first Umayyad caliph (661-680), was governor of Syria when 'Ali was appointed caliph, and did not acknowledge him. After 'Ali's assassination and his own acceptance as caliph throughout the Islamic state, he continued to make Damascus his capital. The effect of the change was to make the assembly of Muslims in Medina of much less importance. Up till 656 the caliph, resident mostly in Medina, had to justify his administrative decisions before the assembly of influential Muslims there and to discuss all sorts of matters with them. This became increasingly difficult for a busy administrator who had to issue commands to armies hundreds of miles away in several different directions. The Umayyads in Damascus no doubt lived to some extent as Arab chiefs and discussed affairs of state with the most influential men in the city; but these would largely be from circles that had been associated with the Umayyads and would be less likely to argue for radically different policies. At the same time the caliph would have the provincial garrison at hand and would therefore have some of the military backing whose absence is so marked in the accounts of the events which led to the death of the third caliph 'Uthman in 656.

Another important change was the introduction of the dynastic principle. In pre-Islamic times there had been no law of primogeniture in the selection of tribal chiefs. It often happened that a man died before his eldest son was very old, and only a person of mature wisdom could effectively lead a desert tribe. It was customary, however, in most tribes to select the chiefs from a single family. This may be said to have happened in the case of the first four heads of the Islamic state, if the early Emigrants are regarded as a single family or clan. On each occasion it may be said that it was the best qualified of this group who was made caliph. Although the Shi'ites later made much of the fact that 'Ali belonged to Muhammad's clan of Hashim, this had nothing to do with his selection in 656; he was then chosen because he was the most eminent of the early Emigrants still alive. Already at the elections of the third and fourth caliphs, however, there were indications that this method of election was unsatisfactory. In certain respects the distinction between the Emigrants and the later Meccan converts was disappearing, and party interests were tending to follow the lines of the old clan rivalries. Indeed the election of 'Uthman gave a chance to his clan of

165

'Abd-Shams or Umayyah—one of the two or three most powerful clans in pre-Islamic times—to seize the supreme power, and in the person of Mu'awiyah this it proceeded to do.

As the years went by Mu'awiyah thought about who would succeed him, and realized that another election would mean intrigue and counter-intrigue and would lead to chaos. He therefore tried before his death to ensure the succession to his son Yazid by getting all the leading Muslims to swear loyalty to him. Many did, but some evaded the oath. On Mu'awiyah's death in 680 a number of the latter gathered in Mecca. Before Yazid could force them to acknowledge him, he himself had died (in 683), leaving only a sickly boy to succeed him who also died a few months later. The chaos foreseen by Mu'awiyah came about, and for a dozen years the caliphate was rent by the Second Civil War. Meanwhile the leading men of the clan of Umayyah met and agreed that they would all support one of the senior members of the clan, Marwan. They were eventually successful, and the office of caliph remained in the hands of descendants of Marwan until 750. Even after it passed to the 'Abbasids the dynastic principle was still followed. There was indeed little else that could be done. Islamic ideation provided no way of giving any man a *right* to succeed to the caliphate. The dynastic principle at least limited the right to succeed to a certain family, though in the absence of a law of primogeniture no particular person was inevitably marked out for the office. In most cases a reigning caliph seems to have designated which of his kinsmen was to succeed him, but this did not always happen.

In matters of administration there were great developments under the Umayyads. To begin with the Arabs simply took over the existing civil administration in the conquered provinces and adapted it to their own needs. This involved continuing to use the languages already in use, and it was only in the caliphate of 'Abd-al-Malik (685-705) that Arabic began to replace them. The higher administrative posts, of course, were held by Muslim Arabs. In Syria the Arabs saw something of Byzantine methods of administration and began to borrow from these in building up their secretariat. It is now realized by scholars, however, that perhaps as early as 725 the attraction of Persian methods was being felt, and the way was being prepared for the adoption of the Persian system by the 'Abbasids[1]. This was not a matter with which Islamic ideation was concerned to any extent, but changes in the form of the administration are an indication of changes in the conception of the ruling institution, and these are matters of ideational concern.

[1] Cf. EI (2), art. ' 'Abd al-Hamid b. Yahya' by H. A. R. Gibb.

The Integration of Political Life

There was in Medina a group of persons sometimes called the 'pious opposition' who accused the Umayyads of having transformed the divinely appointed caliphal rule into a *mulk*—a word which means 'kingdom' but aroused the emotions in Arabs which 'tyranny' arouses in the British. It is easy to see how they came to make this charge. They were the descendants of a considerable section of that assembly of Muslims at Medina which had had some say in the affairs of the caliphate so long as the caliph resided at Medina. What they were really protesting against was the change from the old Arab system of the chief in the assembly to the new system of the chief who, because he was very busy, had little time for assemblies and often just gave orders without justifying them. That had certainly been the form of the ruling institution during Muhammad's lifetime, but ultimately it could hardly be said to be more Islamic than the Umayyad system. The protest of the 'pious opposition' was in fact ideological; they gave the old system, in which they themselves had had more importance, a religious halo to which it had little right. The 'Abbasids, at least to begin with, were on good terms with the 'pious opposition', and the charge that the Umayyads had made the caliphate into a *mulk* was regularly repeated by 'Abbasid historians.

(c) The caliphate after 750

The 'Abbasid dynasty came to power in 750 in place of the Umayyads by effecting a new balance of forces within the Islamic state. For this new balance of forces they had a new ideational basis. In all that went to bringing about this change of dynasty there was probably much shrewd political calculation. Certain elements in the ideation may have been adopted by the leaders of the 'Abbasid movement because they believed these ideas would promote their own political aims and not because they believed that the ideas were true. This possibility may be neglected at the moment, however, since the general question of attempts by politicians to 'use' ideational systems for their own ends will be dealt with presently. In any case there must among the adherents of the 'Abbasid movement have been widespread belief in the truth of the ideas on which it was based. The three main forces whose support was gained by the 'Abbasids were the non-Arab Muslims, the groups with Shi'ite sympathies, and the groups who found a mouthpiece in the 'pious opposition' at Medina.

Something has already been said about the grievances of the non-Arab Muslims, often referred to as the 'clients' or *mawali*. In becoming Muslims they had also to become clients of Arab tribes, and that meant they had an inferior status to the Arab Muslims.

M   167

They were probably also at a disadvantage financially. The 'Abbasid movement espoused the cause of the non-Arab Muslims and was in turn well supported by them. Abu-Muslim, the general who led the 'Abbasid armies to victory, was himself a client and thought to be of Persian stock. The victory of the 'Abbasids therefore meant a redress of grievances for the non-Arab Muslims, though many of the details are not clear. It was presumably no longer necessary for the Persian or Aramaean convert to become the client of an Arab tribe. Perhaps this was because the stipend-roll passed into disuse. Certainly the social hierarchy established by the stipend-roll was replaced by another. The 'Abbasids adopted a system of administration based on the Sasanian. The ruler was absolute and unapproachable; he governed through a vizier and several secretaries of state along with an army of minor clerks or secretaries. This system meant the erection of a new social hierarchy of officials and other courtiers, and this new hierarchy was entirely the creation of the caliph. Because of the part played by Persians and Aramaeans in the rise of the 'Abbasids, and because of their capabilities, there were many of these in this hierarchy. Thus the Arab aristocracy, in part created by the stipend-roll and in part going back to pre-Islamic times, lost its position in the Islamic state (though the caliphs continued to hold receptions for the descendants of early Muslims), and instead there was a mixed aristocracy of men who had been elevated by the caliphs and who could easily be reduced in rank again. So far as the non-Arabs were concerned, this meant that they had as much political influence and social prestige as the Arabs, and were no longer in an inferior position. Indeed, the change meant that the Islamic state had become one in which all races were on an equality.

The Shi'ite movement was in essence a group of men—or a number of groups—who found significance and security in being the followers of a charismatic leader. The 'Abbasids adopted a form of Shi'ite doctrine according to which the charisma belonged to the whole 'house of the Prophet', that is, to the whole clan of Hashim. To begin with, in order to gain the support of as wide a circle as possible, the leader of the movement was not explicitly named. His emissaries and agents called on men to give allegiance to 'him of the house of the Prophet who should be chosen'. Only when victory was in sight did they announce that the man 'chosen' was a descendant of Muhammad's uncle al-'Abbas. Once in power they emphasized their charisma and their connexion with Muhammad. They used his staff, his cloak and his seal. They were known by titles which indicated divine support—al-Ma'mun (bi-'llah), ar-Rashid (bi-'llah), al-Mahdi (bi-'llah), that is, he who is given authority by God, he who is directed by God, he who is guided by God. Despite these attempts to meet the needs of the Shi'ites, however, there were still many who were dissatisfied—doubtless because the need for a charismatic leader was not their only need, but perhaps to some extent because they sensed that the 'Abbasids were making use of Shi'ite ideas for their own aggrandisement. Such malcontents turned to other forms of Shi'ite doctrine. Nevertheless at first the 'Abbasids had much support from those who found in them the charismatic leaders they were looking for. As many Shi'ites were non-Arabs, this line of policy worked in with the previous ones.

The third main force from which the 'Abbasids gained support was the movement for the establishing of a *sunnah* or 'beaten path' for the community. As has been suggested above, it is difficult to account for the development of Islamic law except on the supposition that there was a widespread demand among the Muslim Arabs for such a guide to conduct. It may not have been a conscious demand, but merely a sense that something was missing. They had been living for centuries on the basis of customary law, and they felt strange and insecure without such a basis. 'The new *sunnah*, however, must be one in keeping with the religious foundation of the Islamic community. The Kharijites, with their insistence that the community is a holy community, the 'people of Paradise', express one facet of this demand. The presence of moderate Kharijites in Basrah, along with other scholars of less extreme political views but of genuine religious interests, must have meant that this was one of the centres where during the later Umayyad period, this demand for an Islamic *sunnah* was becoming a conscious one. The main centre, however, where the demand was being consciously formulated was Medina. In that city a number of scholars—some of them descendants of noted Companions—had remained politically neutral both in the struggle between 'Ali and Mu'awiyah and in that between the latter's kinsmen and the rival caliph, Ibn-az-Zubayr, at Mecca. This group or party became increasingly critical of the Umayyads. They openly expressed their sympathy with the 'Abbasids, and when these came to power, appear to have been given a measure of recognition, at least in some informal way. Certainly the juristic scholars in Medina and 'Iraq attained a position of influence in the early decades of the 'Abbasid caliphate, such as was not achieved by the corresponding group in the independent Muslim state of Spain until at least half a century later[1].

As a result of the association of these three forces or movements—

[1] There was probably a distinct increase in the influence of the jurists after the 'battle of the suburb' in 818.

the non-Arab Muslims, some of the Shi'ites, and the 'pious opposition' and their followers—with the 'Abbasid dynasty, the Islamic state in the first half-century of 'Abbasid rule became more fully integrated on an Islamic basis. What is of interest at this point of the present study, however, is that along with this islamization of various aspects of the life of the community went the abandonment of a ruling institution developed out of the Arab tribal chiefship and its replacement by a completely different type of institution based on the Persian imperial tradition. This change had nothing to do with Islamic ideation. A ruling institution of the Umayyad type had shown itself to be unsatisfactory in practice (as is indicated by the beginnings of interest in the Persian system), and it was therefore replaced by something which promised to be more satisfactory. There was a formal connexion with what had gone before through the retention of the title of caliph and similar matters. The 'Abbasids were also, as members of the clan of Hashim, closely linked with the early history of Islam. Yet on the whole there was nothing specifically Islamic about the new ruling institution, and it was adopted for purely political reasons.

Little need be said about the subsequent history of the office of caliph. For reasons which need not here be discussed the 'Abbasid ruling institution broke down—perhaps in the circumstances of the time the empire had become too large to be ruled from one centre once the initial impetus and enthusiasm had been lost. Local governors began to demand that their office should be made hereditary, and the caliph, too weak to reject the demand, pretended that he had appointed the first governor's heir as his successor. He thus retained only a semblance of power, and eventually even the central provinces of the caliphate were ruled by self-appointed military leaders to whom the caliph gave the title of 'sultan'. The 'Abbasid caliphate of Baghdad was destroyed by the Mongols in 1258, was later restored in Egypt as an office with only formal powers, was transferred to the Ottoman sultans (or more probably assumed by them) in 1517, and finally abolished by the Turkish government in 1924. In the later stages the caliphate is not a ruling institution, but some prestige attached to the name, and various political groups try to gain advantages from this prestige.

It is not necessary for present purposes to consider the ruling institutions which replaced the caliphate, since they came into existence in spite of Islamic ideation and not because of it. Mostly they were based on military power, and controlled the subject populations by the ability to use force if necessary, since the latter were usually politically inert. There were various ways of securing cohesion within the ruling group, one of the most interesting being the extension of their slave household by the Ottoman sultans. Apart from their military prestige the actual rulers of the Islamic world no longer had any charisma that would impress a Muslim as such. Perhaps it is because there was no contemporary charismatic leader that Muslims began to emphasize and exaggerate the superhuman qualities of Muhammad.[1] Even a moderate thinker like al-Ghazali insists in opposition to Isma'ili and Fatimid propaganda that the main body of Islam has in Muhammad its 'infallible imam'.

(d) The recalcitrance of the ruling institution

There is a proper autonomy of ruling institutions. The men who rule large states must see to it that their rule provides peace and security from both internal and external enemies. Their choice of particular policies and of the very form of their institution is therefore primarily dependent on the criterion of effectiveness in practice[2]. Only where two alternatives are of approximately equal effectiveness may other considerations be taken into account. Within the Islamic world, however, this autonomy of ruling institutions ought always to have been exercised in conformity with Islamic principles, and indeed in subordination to them. Yet at many points we find that ruling institutions, pursuing the supreme end of their own power, attempt to make Islamic ideation subservient to this. The manipulation of religious ideas in order to bring about greater political uniformity was not, of course, anything new. In particular it had been a regular practice of Byzantine emperors. Such a practice is not necessarily contrary to the interests of the religion (that is, of the religious society as a whole), and may lead to its expansion; we are reminded how Paul thought the interests of Christianity were being promoted by those whose motive in preaching was to cause trouble to himself.[3] On the part of ruling institutions, however, attempts to make use of religious ideation for their own purposes must be adjudged to proceed from a certain recalcitrance, an unwillingness to submit themselves to the religious ideation, which seems to be ultimately an incomplete belief in its truth[4].

---

[1] This is one of the main conclusions of Tor Andrae in his book *Die Person Muhammeds in Lehre und Glauben seiner Gemeinde*, Stockholm, 1918.

[2] Thus the *jihad* against Constantinople was continued despite vigorous opposition because of the great wealth of the city and of the lands it dominated, whereas the *jihad* into France was soon dropped, presumably because the booty did not compensate for the trouble involved; cf. p. 159 above.

[3] *Philippians*, 1.12-18.

[4] The general question here raised is further discussed below, pp. 178ff.

The Integration of Political Life

From an early period the government of the Islamic state had to use force to repress certain sectarian tendencies. If the wars of 'the apostasy' are set aside as an anti-Islamic movement and not a sectarian movement within Islam, then the first examples are the campaign of 'Ali against the Kharijites in 657 and the campaigns of Mu'awiyah and later Umayyads against both Kharijites and Shi'ites. In these cases the government could hardly have acted otherwise than it did since sectarianism was bound up with military insurrection. It can probably never be asserted with certainty that the Umayyads took measures against sectarianism as such. There are numerous cases of their seizing and executing sectarians while these were leading peaceful lives, but in all these cases it is possible that they thought the men in question were taking part in intrigues that might eventually have led to insurrection. While theological heresy, in later periods of Islamic history, has often been linked with political disaffection and intrigue which might lead to armed revolt, it also seems clear that in many cases Islamic governments repressed heretical views where there was no political danger. One such case is the torture and execution of the mystic al-Hallaj by the 'Abbasids in 922[1]. It came to be recognized as one of the duties of the caliph to uphold the true religion against 'innovators', that is, heretics[2].

Subsequently the Seljuq sultans acted similarly. Since they came to power as opponents of the Buyid sultans, who were Shi'ites, it was convenient for them to pose as champions of Sunnite orthodoxy, and indeed the great danger their regime had to meet during the eleventh century was the growth of Isma'ili beliefs at the hands of Fatimid and other progagandists. We possess the *Treatise of Government* written for the Seljuq sultan Malik-Shah (1072-92) by his vizier Nizam-al-Mulk, and find that in it, while the repression of heresy is assumed to be one of the functions of the sultan, the main emphasis is on positive measures to strengthen true doctrine. The sultan is to make a practice of holding regular audiences with theologians and scholars so that he himself may be thoroughly familiar with the orthodox standpoint and the theological questions at issue; he is also to be careful not to appoint as officials persons known to have heretical views[3]. In other words, the sultan is to be careful to keep on good terms with the theologians so that he may enjoy their support.

[1] Louis Massignon, *La Passion d'al-Hallaj*, Paris, 1922. For the earlier treatment of *zandaqah* cf. G. Vajda, 'Les Zindiqs en pays d'Islam au début de la periode 'Abbaside', *Rivista di Studi Orientali*, xvii. 173-229.

[2] Cf. al-Mawardi (d.1058), *al-Ahkam as-Sultaniyyah*, 23; *Adab ad-Dunyah wa-'d-Din*, Cairo (1910)/1328, 110.

[3] Nizam-al-Mulk, *Siyasat-Nameh*, tr. Ch. Schefer, Paris, 1893, chs. 8, 42.

The Integration of Political Life

The most notorious example of the manipulation of religious ideas for political purposes in Islamic history is the Mihnah or Inquisition from 833 to 849, when the government tried to make all judges and similar officials accept the doctrine that the Qur'an was something created by God and not, as His Word or Speech, something that belonged eternally to His being. The usual accounts of this[1] deal solely with the ideational aspect, but a perusal of the general history of the period shows that the 'Abbasid government was trying to achieve a new balance of forces and in particular to win the support of a number of persons of moderate Shi'ite sympathies; correspondingly the abandonment of the Inquisition came about when the government realized that they were not gaining Shi'ite support to an appreciable extent and were forfeiting some of the support of the theologians and of the masses who followed them.

The Inquisition of 833-849 was a foretaste of new developments (though later there was greater subtlety). Not only the 'Abbasid caliphs but many other rulers tried to manipulate religious ideas in order to buttress their rule. This meant in effect that they had to come to some sort of understanding with the scholar-jurists or ulema (as had indeed been done in the movement which brought the 'Abbasids to power). The understanding usually seems to have been to the effect that the scholar-jurists were allowed complete control of certain spheres of life (such as, theological dogma and the legal foundations of the social structure), provided they gave the ruler a free hand elsewhere and in general supported him. While this looks like a bargain between equals, it was not in fact so. The ruler appointed men to the judgeships and other official positions which were the consummation of the career of the scholar-jurists, and thus they were almost entirely at his mercy. Their only strength was in their ability to rouse the populace, but where there were several rival groups of scholar-jurists this was not easy, since they opposed one another. Most rulers were careful to study the requirements of the main body of juristic opinion, and to comply with it to the extent of suppressing views which the jurists disliked. This is what Nizam-al-Mulk advised the Seljuq sultan Malik-Shah to do. There was a similar state of affairs in Egypt and Syria under the Mamluks[2]. In practice it tended to mean that certain jurists tried to use the 'civil arm' against others. Ibn-Taymiyyah (d. 1328) suffered from unmerited persecution of this kind in Damascus and Cairo, and was

[1] W. M. Patton, *Ahmed b. Hanbal and the Mihna*, Leiden, 1897; A. J. Wensinck art. 'Mihna' in *EI* (1).

[2] Cf. E. Strauss, 'L'Inquisition dans l'Etat Mamlouk', *Rivista di Studi Orientali*, xxv. 11-26.

several times imprisoned.[1] The same sort of thing must have been happening under the Seljuqs, for al-Ghazali (d.1111) wrote a book (entitled *Faysal at-Tafriqah*) in which he argued that the accusation of 'unbelief' was being made far too widely, since it was not properly applicable in cases of slight divergence; he himself had suffered somewhat from reckless accusations of this type.

The 'Abbasid caliphs controlled not merely the legal profession but also the historians. The control was not so close, being probably exercised mainly through patronage; yet it was singularly effective. The early history of Islam was rewritten to glorify the ancestors of the 'Abbasids and to defame those of the Umayyads. The 'Abbasid version became the standard one of many events, and other versions were suppressed—perhaps not so much by deliberate exclusion as by falling into desuetude. Historians who hoped for the caliph's favour would tend to omit passages and versions which did not redound to the glory of the 'Abbasids.

In a sense this manipulation of ideas, as we have called it, marks a new type of ruling institution, or at least a new sub-species of the Persian type. It is not a tyranny controlling solely by military force. It is not even primarily a tyranny controlling what men think through the use of potent instruments (though to a great extent it does this). For one thing it does not entirely control what men think; the great tradition of Islamic scholarship gives even time-serving scholar-jurists a certain independence, since no ruler could expect them to fly in the face of tradition. Beyond all these considerations, it remained a fact that the ordinary Muslim could look at the great Islamic society or community and feel that he belonged to it and that it was in a sense his—that it did not belong to one or more ruling groups, however great their powers might be. In other words, the Islamic state or state-system had gone a long way towards being a genuine community.

4. CONCLUSIONS

(a) The extent of political integration in Islam

Our investigations have shown one area in which Islam had great success in integrating the political life of its adherents. That was in the formation of the *ummah* or Islamic community, which, while it had a religious basis, was also a political body. The success was not merely in forming such a body, but in managing to attach to it some of the valuable attitudes which, in the case of the pre-Islamic Arabs,

[1] Laoust, *Essai*, esp. 125-143.

174

had been attached to the tribe. One such attitude, arising from the feeling of brotherhood between the members of a tribe, led to a strong feeling of brotherhood among the members of the Islamic community, and this feeling contributed to the recognition of the equality of non-Arab and Arab within the community. Another valuable attitude was respect for the *sunnah* or 'beaten path' of the tribe (that is, its mores), and this attitude, together with the expectation that a community like the Islamic would have its 'beaten path', had much to do with the establishment of Islamic law and of the whole social structure of which that law was the foundation. All this was a great achievement, and integrated the political life of the Muslims to a high degree, in that it formed a body politic in which were to be found very favourable conditions for the practice of the Islamic religion and the attainment of its end of salvation, that is, of a significance which transcended the historical process.

On the other hand, there was a failure to produce a ruling institution capable of maintaining the original political unity of the Islamic world. This failure, however, can hardly be attributed to the Islamic religion as such. One does not expect to find political blueprints in the basic ideation of a religion. As has been asserted above, there is a proper autonomy of the sphere of politics, and the finding of a ruling institution capable of unifying the Muslims is a task which belongs to this autonomous sphere. The failure is to be attributed to the politicians and members of ruling institutions, though it may be added, to excuse their failure, that in the circumstances of the time with its poor communications and the limited political experience of the great majority of the Muslims, especially the non-Arab Muslims, there probably was no way of ruling so as to maintain political unity. The masses were certainly not ready for anything resembling Western democracy.

The importance must not be overlooked, however, of what Islam actually did achieve by way of producing a ruling institution adapted to its needs. Because of the strength of community-feeling and because of the attachment of the Muslims to the 'beaten path' of their community, it was necessary for ruling institutions to respect this 'beaten path'. This respect, as has just been seen, took the form of an understanding between the rulers and the jurists, according to which the rulers did not meddle with the social structure or associated mores. There is a sense in which it does not matter who rules a community of Muslims provided he respects their social and religious observances, and provided he is not an advocate of an alternative ideational system. Even the ruler with anti-Islamic ideas can make only slow headway against an Islamic community. The

175

Shiʻite princes who ruled in Baghdad from 935 to 1055, in only nominal subjection to the caliph, achieved little towards making Shiʻism dominant in their domains; and the Islamic religion spread in India and Indonesia under the British and Dutch governments, which were in the main officially neutral, while the anti-Islamic measures of the French in North Africa have not availed to check it. In many cases, however, Islam has done better than this, and has produced a ruling institution which, while preserving its proper autonomy and acting out of a concern for its own interests, has committed itself to the maintenance of the Islamic social structure and the support of the guardians of that, the scholar-jurists.

It remains to ask how far the integration achieved in the Islamic community under the ʻAbbasids and also under other rulers was a genuine integration and how far it was a false integration, a mere superficial uniformity produced by totalitarian methods. The parallel with totalitarianism will have been obvious. It may perhaps be illustrated by a passage from Karl Mannheim on modern totalitarian regimes. After noting how changes in military technique, in methods of government and administration, and in the means of forming public opinion have led to 'a much greater concentration of power in the hands of the few', he continues :

> On top of this there is also the possibility that the whole mechanism whereby people rise and fall in the social scale is controlled. . . .
> The totalitarian state, where it exists, makes full use of this technique and apparatus to further co-ordination. And, unfortunately, to such a state co-ordination means a rigid conformity.
> Conformity is desired, firstly, because it is simpler to govern people who are identically conditioned, and secondly, because those at the top are often narrow-minded and primitive in their outlook, being frequently the products of the petty bourgeoisie, and primitivism is characterized by its intolerant treatment of deviations. [1]

In the ʻAbbasid caliphate there had been no great changes in military technique, but there had been changes in methods of administration, there was a new means of forming public opinion through the understanding with the scholar-jurists, and there was a new social hierarchy which was subject to the control of the caliph. How far did all this lead to mere conformity instead of to a genuine integration in which no important element of society was denied an appropriate function in the whole ?

An important difference between the ʻAbbasid state and those of Hitler and Mussolini is that the latter were in their infancy. Their ideational basis was still to a great extent fluid. They were not

[1] *Essays on Sociology and Social Psychology*, London, 1953, 257.

176

subject to the limitations created by a fixed tradition. Something of the difficulties of having a fixed tradition is seen in the way the Russians have to bend and twist their tradition to adapt it to the changes of policy dictated by current circumstances. For a time the necessities of politics could only be satisfied by a Stalinist interpretation of the tradition; but after the death of Stalin the fresh necessities of politics required the abandonment of Stalinism, and this abandonment had to be justified as a return to genuine Leninist interpretations of the tradition. Despite this recalcitrance of the tradition the ruling institution in Russia has, by and large, control of ideation. In the 'Abbasid state, on the other hand, there was a tradition of over a century controlling both ideation and many aspects of social life, and there was a body of intellectuals who were coming to be recognized as the exponents of this tradition. There were ways of modifying and reinterpreting the tradition, of course, but it could not be completely neglected. In particular the existence of the body of experts in the tradition meant that the ruling institution did not directly control even the modification or reinterpretation of the tradition.

Another difference is that there was among the Muslims a deep movement towards uniformity, arising from the feeling that having a 'beaten path' was an essential part of being a community—especially a holy or charismatic community. This is something the 'Abbasids did not create but found already in existence. They fostered it and used it for their own purposes. Its presence, however, meant that such uniformity as was achieved was not merely convenient for the rulers, but met a deep need of the ordinary Muslim. Thus it was not a uniformity imposed on him from without, but one which he willingly accepted because it led to a realization of significance. It is the last point at which the Muslim differs from the subjects of modern totalitarian states. All men have probably some need for uniformity, but the Muslims, especially the Arab Muslims, had been so moulded by their previous tradition that only where there was a large measure of uniformity could they find a fulfilment of the community's potentiality for significant life.

The existence of a tradition and of a body of at least partly independent experts in it, and the special place of uniformity in the political outlook of the Muslims, together suggest that in the Islamic state there was a high degree of genuine integration. There were still many dissatisfied groups, of course, but even in their dissatisfaction they often approved in general of the Islamic community, were proud to belong to it, and only found fault with it in minor respects[1].

---

[1] Cf. the concern of the Mu'tazilite writer al-Khayyat to show that this sect was part of the community.

In a delicate matter of this sort, where objectivity is not easy, one would not be justified in saying more.

(b) *The relation of the political sphere to the religious*

It has been taken for granted throughout this chapter that there is a proper autonomy of politics, and the course of the investigation has shown how in fact political decisions are usually made on the basis of purely political considerations and in neglect of religious considerations. Some further study of the relation between the political and religious fields, however, seems to be forced upon us by the discussion of the manipulation of religious ideas by ruling institutions. If a politician can use religion for his own ends, does that not show that the sphere of politics is superior to that of religion? In view of the examples given, can it still be maintained that it is religion which is using the politicians and not *vice versa*?

In order to get an answer to this question it is desirable to look at some fairly concrete situations, and in particular to consider the decisions of individuals, both as individuals and as members of societies. Now, when we look at men's decisions it appears that the religious decision is the most fundamental (where 'religious' is taken in a wide sense as referring generally to whatever has to do with the ultimate significance of life). The supreme end of human life is to attain significance. One indication that this is the supreme end is that cases occur where it overrides the highly important end of maintaining one's life. To go on living (in certain circumstances) may only be possible by acting in a way which destroys the significance of one's life; and then death is cooly and deliberately chosen. Socrates refusing to escape from prison, and the Japanese aristocrat committing hara-kiri, are examples. Another indication that the attainment of significance is the supreme end is that it is not properly speaking the object of any decision by a man, but is presupposed in his decisions. His fundamental decision is to try to attain significance by adopting some particular way of life; normally this is the course of conduct, together with its ideational basis, prescribed by some religion or quasi-religion, but there are many people whose attempts to attain significance are inconsistent and incoherent.

Even when a man has made a decision to adopt a definite way of life in this sense, that does not determine completely his decisions about the daily conduct of his life, any more than a decision to spend a fortnight in France determines how each day and hour is to be spent. The fundamental or governing decision, in both cases, only controls the subsequent decisions to the extent of setting certain limits that they must observe. In particular, the decision to follow a certain religion does not entail adopting any specific economic system. In the modern world we see societies which are predominantly Christian, Muslim, Hindu, Buddhist and Marxist, all alike busily developing an industrial civilization on the basis of modern technology. As explained above (in chapter 2) men have little choice with regard to their economic system, but are bound to choose the system that is economically most efficient. The connexion of this with the attainment of significance is that in order to attain significance according to his chosen religion a man has to keep himself alive, and in order to do this he has to have food and shelter—the primary products of any economic system. Thus the economic system is a means to the attainment of the end of significance.

Further, an economic system is merely one aspect of the life of a society, and therefore presupposes a society and its structure. A particular type of economy can work after a fashion in association with various types of social and political structures, but it appears to be the case that for each type of economy there is in general an optimum form of social and political structure. The pre-Islamic Arab tribal society would seem to have been the optimum social and political structure for a nomadic economy in Arabian conditions. Thus the political and social structure of a society are those which are needed to make its economic system work well, and, indeed, to work at all. In fine, the political aspect of its life is part of the means to its attainment of significance. If the matter is viewed in this way, then politics is subordinate to religion.

Yet this does not answer the question. Politicians undoubtedly make use of religious ideas for their own purposes. Is there not an important sense in which what is used is subordinate to the user? Let us therefore consider the further question: Whose ends are in fact best served by the transaction, the politician's or the religion's? There seem to be two distinct types of case, according to what happens to the religion. In either case, the politician, in seeking to increase his own power, is to some extent acting on the basis of a decision to try to attain significance in his life by increasing his power rather than to do so by practising the Muslim way of life. He may increase his power, and he may die while his power is at its height, so that, in so far as his decision about significance goes, he has been completely successful; but history suggests that the cult of power can have no more than a temporary success, and that no enduring civilization can be built on it. In so far as religious ideas are propagated by the politician, however, there is a chance that the religion will prosper. This is the first type of case. If this happens, the success of the religion is likely to be of much longer duration than that of the politician. In this case, then, the religion benefits more than the politician from the latter's action. A modern example is the encouragement of nationalistic ideas by Britain, France and America during the First World War in order to discomfit Austria-Hungary and Turkey; but subsequently nationalism grew and prospered, and almost overwhelmed the countries which had used it for their own ends.

In such cases religious or quasi-religious ideas focus deep movements in men's hearts and give them direction. When this happens the politician is powerless; as Bismarck said, he cannot create events, he can only steer with the tide. The second type of case occurs when, after the politician has been making use of religious ideas, the tide of the religion, instead of rising, recedes. Something of this sort seems to have occurred under the 'Abbasid dynasty. The main bearers of the ideational system, the scholar-jurists, became largely subservient to the ruling institution. At the same time they made the ideational system more rigid and less adaptable to the changing needs of the times. Gradually it ceased to be the natural expression of the religious needs of the masses. They lost confidence in the scholar-jurists and in their official religion, and turned to the cult forms of the sufi (mystical) brotherhoods which began to flourish in the twelfth century[1]. In the eleventh century al-Ghazali had attempted to reunite the scholarly stream and the mystical, but he had been only partly successful. Ibn-Taymiyyah (d.1328) tried to revivify the official religion at the expense of the sufi brotherhoods, but he had few followers (until after a long interval among the Wahhabis in Su'udi Arabia). The cleavage between the official religion and that of the common people, though never absolute, has continued to exist.

On the whole, the attempts by the 'Abbasid and other ruling institutions to use Islamic ideation for their own ends, by co-operating with the scholar-jurists and controlling them, have done little in the long run to strengthen the rulers. They have helped the Islamic religion to become more unified and probably also in some respects to become genuinely integrated; but at the same time they have introduced a serious weakness. Nevertheless the fact that misguided rulers are sometimes able to weaken a religion is no reason for denying that in general the sphere of politics is subordinate to that of religion.

[1] This is expounded more fully below in chapter 7, sect. 4.

VI

THE INTEGRATION OF THE MORES

T HE use of the term 'mores' requires no justification in sociological circles, but, since this book may be read by students of
Islam who are not familiar with the usage, it may be useful to
quote a definition.

Underlying and sustaining the more formal order of institutions and
associations there exists an intricate complex of usages or modes of
behaviour developed spontaneously or apart from specific establishment
or enactment.

In their aspect of spontaneous development and of being social
phenomena these are what W. G. Sumner called 'folkways'.

The *mores* are the folkways considered under a particular aspect, as
regulators of behaviour, not merely as ways of behaving.[1]

The mores thus include what is commonly called morality, but they
do not imply any conscious acceptance of moral principles, and they
include matters outside the sphere of morality, such as points of
etiquette and social manifestations connected with religious cults.
This conception of mores is specially suitable in dealing with Islam,
since Islam does not make the distinctions current in the West
between morality, etiquette, and cult practices.

1. RELIGION AND THE MORES

(a) The problem of particularity

If we restrict ourselves for a moment to the purely ethical sphere, we
find a problem confronting us, of which it is necessary to attempt a
solution. On general grounds it might be assumed that the ethical
sphere would show an autonomy over against religion similar to that
found in the political sphere. Such an autonomy would be in accordance with the conception of natural law and all the facts out of
which that conception grew. Actually, however, there is a certain
close connexion between religion and morality. There is a distinctive

[1] R. M. McIver, *Society, a Textbook of Sociology*, New York, 1937, 16f.

Christian morality and a distinctive Muslim morality. This may be called the problem of particularity. Why should a religion have a distinctive ethical system associated with it?

The extent of the autonomy of ethics is considerable. Many examples are to be found of societies accepting new ethical principles in place of their previous ones because the new principles were the basis of practices which were socially useful and beneficial. At the present time many parts of the Islamic world are adopting a large measure of monogamy in practice, though polygamy is part of the Islamic tradition. This change, however, may not be entirely due to an awareness of the social evils of polygamy (though such an awareness is certainly present), but may come about partly from a desire to be like the West. A clearer example of a moral change based on social welfare is that Soviet Russia, after at first adopting a lax attitude to marriage and divorce, now officially encourages permanent marriages and makes divorce difficult. The abolition of slavery by Western states in the nineteenth century is often connected with Christianity; but the connexion is tenuous, since slavery had been tolerated in Christendom for eighteen centuries, and a concern for social welfare had much to do with the adoption of the policy of abolition.

Further, while it seems to be the case that for men to attain significance they must act in accordance with the mores of their society, this requirement of action according to the mores does not specifically determine the mores themselves. That is to say, significance may be attained through the following of different mores. It is commonly held that no blame attaches to those who live according to their lights, even if some of their conduct would be blameworthy in the case of other men whose 'lights' were greater and who therefore ought to have known better. All this tends to suggest that, though there is a close connexion between religion and morality, yet morality retains a large measure of autonomy. It is therefore puzzling that there should be a specific Christian ethic and a specific Muslim ethic.

The solution of the problem appears to be this. A new religion usually arises in a situation where an extensive social change is required, but where there is not sufficient dynamic apart from religion to bring about that change. Hence religion appears as an ideational system specially linked with certain social changes. Thus, Muhammad at Mecca was trying to induce the pagan merchants to give up certain individualistic abuses of the nomadic system, while Jesus implicitly attacked the isolationism of the Pharisees of his time. The opposition which developed in both cases is a measure of the inertia to be overcome, and this inertia would not have been overcome but for the release of psychical energy through the religious idea-tion. Thus, Islam, in its conception of the judgement of men on the Last Day, provides an individualistic sanction against current abuses. In the circle of Qur'anic ideas, however, the sanction of the Last Day is linked up with assertions that certain kinds of conduct are worthy of punishment and certain others of reward. Because of the occurrence of these ethical assertions in the Qur'an, that is, in the ideational core of Islam, the points mentioned tend to be specially emphasized by Muslims and to give a distinctive colouring to Islamic ethics.

That appears to be the main reason for the connexion of a religion with a particular ethical system; but there is also another point which requires to be noted. When a new religious movement meets opposi-tion, it has to make the best use of its psychical energy. One of the functions of religious worship and other social manifestations of religion is to maintain and increase the psychical energy available. At first the new religious movement may have found the old worship sufficient (as happened with both Christianity and Islam), but it ceases to be sufficient when the movement has to meet the greater stresses caused by opposition. The movement then gradually organizes itself as a definite community, marked off from the members of the old community who have not joined the new movement, and gains in strength from the social cohesion and worship of the new movement. The organization of the new move-ment as an independent community involves the adoption of certain distinctive social and cultic usages. The cultic usages are the most obvious, since in adopting social usages regard must always be paid to the effect on the general welfare, whereas many cultic usages are neutral in respect of their effect on welfare. The distinctive character of Islam is marked by such matters as the form of its ritual worship or 'prayer', by turning towards Mecca instead to towards Jerusalem (like the Jews) or towards the east (like many Christians), and by its use of the human voice instead of a ram's horn or a bell for summon-ing the faithful to worship. There are also some distinctive usages which may in part have been adopted in order to mark its difference, at first from Arab paganism and later from Judaism and Christianity; among these usages one might reckon certain practices connected with marriage and inheritance, the forbidding of Muslim women to marry outside the community, and the forbidding of the use of wine. When usages are thus adopted, it is difficult for a community to abandon them without losing its identity, and they therefore come to be specially associated with it.

N   183

The Integration of the Mores

(b) The sociological consideration of extraneous influences

The integration of the mores may be said to occur in Islam in three forms or stages. Firstly, there is the adjustment of nomadic mores to a settled economy and the removal of the disharmony resulting from the change of economy. Secondly, after the Islamic community had come to include many non-Arabs, there was a certain measure of assimilation of the non-Arab practices of these new Muslims. Thirdly, there may be some modification of practices adopted by the community in order to make them more coherent with its fundamental ideational system. The total result of these three integrative activities, which will be dealt with separately in the three following sections, has been the attainment of a large measure of uniformity throughout the Islamic world. There is also, of course, considerable diversity; but the question whether Islam is one or many is in the main existential, that is, one where the scholar's own feelings and interests are involved and where any answer he gives is therefore liable to be tainted with ideology[1]. In the present study it is not necessary to attempt an answer to the question, but only to consider how the existing measure of uniformity has been attained and what has made its attainment possible. Even this restricted discussion, however, raises theoretical issues, about which some preliminary words will be useful.

The issues may be approached by considering Sir Hamilton Gibb's formulation of three 'laws' governing the adoption by one culture of elements from another.[2]

(1) . . . cultural influences (. . . genuinely assimilated elements) are always preceded by an already existing activity in the related fields, and . . . it is this existing activity which creates the factor of attraction without which no creative assimilation can take place.

(2) The borrowed elements conduce to the expanding vitality of the borrowing culture only in so far as they draw their nourishment from the activities which led to their borrowing in the first place.

(3) A living culture disregards or rejects all elements in other cultures which conflict with its own fundamental values, emotional attitudes, or aesthetic criteria.

These laws apply primarily to the second form of integration mentioned above, namely, the assimilation of non-Arab practices, but the consideration of the 'already existing activity' is also relevant to the other forms of integration. Indeed, the most important subject

[1] Cf. Montgomery Watt, 'Thoughts on Islamic Unity', *Islamic Quarterly*, iii. 188-195.

[2] The Influence of Islamic Culture on Medieval Europe', *Bulletin of the John Rylands Library*, xxxviii. 82-98, esp. 85-7.

of study in the present chapter will be these already existing activities which supply the dynamic for the processes of integration.

At this point a word might be interposed about the conception of syncretism. Examination of the actual use of the word suggests that there is frequently an ideological taint about it. When a writer calls a religious movement syncretistic, most often he is expressing subjective disapproval of it, and not making a scientifically objective statement. All the higher religions have assimilated extraneous elements, but they are not usually called syncretistic. In other words, not every culture with elements from different sources is regarded as syncretistic. Perhaps one might say that a movement or culture is syncretistic where the extraneous elements have been imperfectly assimilated, or where the extraneous elements are so numerous as to swamp the original elements. Even if some such definition is accepted, however, it is difficult, perhaps impossible, to make the requisite determination objectively. It therefore seems better in the present state of affairs to avoid the word 'syncretism'.

2. THE QUR'ANIC TRANSFORMATION OF NOMADIC MORES

The integrative process during Muhammad's lifetime is witnessed to chiefly by the Qur'an, since for the Western scholar there are so many uncertainties in the Traditions about Muhammad's words and deeds. It will be convenient to consider separately the mores belonging to the ethical sphere and those which the Westerner would regard as religious.

In the ethical sphere the primary task of Islam was the removal of the disharmony which had arisen as a result of the change from a nomadic to a mercantile economy. The disharmony was immediately due to the individualism of the rich merchants of Mecca who, selfishly intent on amassing wealth for themselves, disregarded the nomadic mores whereby the leading men of a clan or family provided for the poor and unfortunate in it. In the Meccan period, therefore, the Qur'an was not concerned to introduce anything novel in the ethical sphere, but simply to recall men from reliance on wealth to generosity and the acknowledgement of the duties of providing for the poor and needy. What the Qur'an does provide is a sanction for those elements of the nomadic mores to which it was recalling the Meccans. It asserted that all men come to God on the Last Day to be judged, and that according as their conduct has been good or bad they will be sent to Paradise or the Fire. This was a sanction which, if they believed the Qur'anic assertions, would have weight with the individualistically minded, especially since it was also asserted that neither wealth nor family influence would help a man in that judgement.

Even after Muhammad went to Medina, the changes in the purely ethical sphere were not extensive. Certain changes, of course, were entailed by the establishment of a community of Muslims, in that for certain purposes this religious community took the place of the community based on kinship. It ceased to be a crime to kill a fellow-clansman if he was a pagan, but instead it became a crime to kill a fellow-Muslim. This merely meant, however, that the nomadic mores, instead of being based on the kinship group, were based on the religious community. Apart from this the Muslims continued in general to live according to the former mores. Even the *jihad* or holy war was essentially a transference of the nomadic practice of the razzia so that its basis was the Islamic community. The chief changes were in respect of sexual relations and matters of inheritance. In the former case some of the old folkways were condemned—and by civilized standards they were very lax—and rules were promulgated which had the effect of bringing a measure of unity where previously there had been great diversity of practice. The rules for inheritance ensure that property is fairly distributed between the nearest kinsmen of the deceased and prevent strong individuals taking advantage of the weak in the confusion of the change from communalism to individualism.

The transformation brought about by the Qur'an was greatest in the case of the cultic mores. The effective religion of the pre-Islamic Arabs was a tribal humanism, but there were also many vestiges of an earlier animism. We do not know much about the earliest forms of Muslim worship. The Muslims are said to have frequented the Ka'bah and to have performed acts of worship there. A Qur'anic verse which speaks of a pagan 'hindering a servant (? of God) when he prays' (96.9f.) presumably implies that the Muslims had some forms of their own instead of or in addition to the usual forms; and the Muslims certainly engaged in night vigils during the Meccan period. It is clear then that they combined certain old cultic forms with various new practices, though we cannot be certain of the details until a much later period.

Tribal humanism may be said to have been modified and incorporated in the new movement by regarding the Islamic community as a tribe, and attaching to it some of the feelings formerly attached to the tribe. The stories of former prophets in the Qur'an are parallel to the poets' 'boasting' of the noble deeds of the ancestors of the tribe. More important, the implicit belief of the pre-Islamic Arabs that a man's life attained significance through membership of a noble tribe was partly replaced by a similar belief about membership of the Islamic community; eventually (and in contradiction to the earliest Qur'anic doctrine of the Last Day) it was widely held by Muslims that every Muslim, whatever his conduct, was by his membership of the Muslim community assured of Paradise in the end.

As animism had provided most of the existing cultic mores, it is more prominent in the forms of the Islamic cult. Animistic symbols and practices could easily be taken over and given an Islamic interpretation because they were already 'superstition', something left over, rather than elements in a living religion. The most important example of this is the acceptance of the Ka'bah or sanctuary of Mecca as a shrine of God, together with the retention of some of the ceremonies connected with it such as the sevenfold circumambulation. The sources speak of a number of idols in the Ka'bah, but it is tolerably certain that the original deity of the Ka'bah was the Black Stone, possibly of meteoric origin, which is built into the wall of the Ka'bah and solemnly kissed by Muslim pilgrims. After a time the Black Stone was presumably thought of as the seat of the deity and not the deity itself, but by Muhammad's time even this conception must have been almost obliterated. Certainly the Qur'an (106.3) by speaking of 'the Lord of this House' treats the Ka'bah as a shrine of God. The change here from polytheism to monotheism was probably facilitated by the form of the Arabic word for 'God'. *Allah* is the equivalent of *al-ilah*, and the latter (and so presumably also the former) can mean 'the god' in a polytheistic sense as well as 'God' in a monotheistic sense. The Greek language offers an exact parallel; *ho theos* is the regular term for 'God', but it can also be used for 'the god', for example, of Delphi, who is only one of many. Especially if, as seems likely, a 'vague monotheism' was already accepted by the more enlightened Meccans, it would be easy to claim this shrine of *Allah* for 'God' instead of 'the god'. The claim was later supported by the assertion that God had commanded Abraham to purify the spot for worship (22.26/27).

Not all animistic practices were retained, however. In accordance with the third law stated in the previous section, everything connected with idolatry was extirpated as being contrary to the very foundation of Islam. Idols were destroyed and various pagan taboos were disregarded or rather publicly flouted. The Qur'an itself, however, like the Bible, sanctions belief in supernatural beings below the rank of divinity, namely, angels, jinn and demons, and this was regarded as compatible with monotheism.

There was some difficulty to begin with over pagan shrines other than the Ka'bah. The story of the 'satanic verses' is the evidence for this[1]. Muhammad, it is reported, once received what he thought to be a genuine revelation, which ran as follows:

> Have ye considered al-Lat and al-'Uzza,
> And Manat, the third, the other ?
> These are the swans exalted,
> Whose intercession is to be hoped for.

This delighted the pagan Meccans, for they took it as an acknowledgement of the worship at their pagan shrines, and they joined Muhammad when he prostrated himself. Later, however (though it is not certain how much later), Muhammad realized that the third and fourth verses were not a genuine revelation, but had been suggested to him by Satan, and that the true continuation of the first two was:

> Have ye male (issue) and He female ?
> In that case it is a division unfair.
> They are nothing but names which ye and your
> fathers have given. . . .

This naturally annoyed the pagans who had been delighted by the previous version, and increased the opposition to Muhammad. The point to notice, however, is that Muhammad did not at first see any incompatibility. Presumably he thought that these three deities, each of which had an important shrine in the Meccan region, were something like angels. In time, however, he came to see that, as things were working out in practice, worship at these three shrines was in conflict with the monotheism he was preaching. The fact that these deities were sometimes called 'daughters of God' would not necessarily imply any of the family relations that existed among the gods and goddesses of the Greek pantheon, since the Arabs regularly used 'son' and 'daughter' to express abstract relations; but there would always be some danger of misinterpretation. The whole incident is interesting and important, however, and shows that the Muslims decided only gradually which animistic practices were compatible with montheism and which were not.

One aspect of the Arab outlook made it easy for Islam to incorporate practices which had originally be animistic. A practice could be regarded as commanded by God, and human beings did not require to ask reasons for God's command. Thus the sanctuary at Mecca was sacred because God had so decreed; the circumambulation of the Ka'bah was obligatory for Muslims because God had so decreed; and so on with many other rites which came to form part of

[1] Cf. *Muhammad at Mecca*, 101-10.

the pilgrimage. When one looks at the details of what later became established Muslim usage,[1] one finds vestiges of animism omnipresent. On the whole Islam may be said to have been successful in assimilating and integrating the animistic substratum in Arab culture. Many of the outward forms of animism were retained but they were placed in a setting of Islamic ideation. For long traces of animism might linger in the souls of the mass of Muslims, but the probability was that, provided Islam remained a living religion, these traces would eventually after some centuries be expunged or transmuted. There was always the danger, of course, with the retention of numerous animistic forms that something of the essential spirit of animism might remain alive and might once more flourish if the vitality of Islam decreased. In the heartlands of Islam, though animism has not been extirpated, it cannot be said to flourish; but in places on the periphery of the Islamic world, such as West Africa, there has been a bitter struggle between Islam and animism for domination of the souls of converts, with time usually on the side of Islam.[2]

Since it is thus easy for Islam to accept the outward forms of animism, there must have been some important reason for rejecting those animistic practices which it rejected. It is not easy to discover in every case the rational of Islam's acceptance or rejection of animistic practices, except that nothing connected with idolatry was allowed to remain.[3] Further, it is almost certain that Islam's insistence on God's uniqueness and on the nothingness of all other alleged deities grew with the growth of opposition and was to some extent determined by the precise form of the opposition. It was stated in the previous section that a religious movement, when it finds itself being opposed, takes steps to mark itself off as a separate entity from the old religious community out of which it has grown. In the case of Islam the question of one unique God or many gods became the focus of the tension between the Muslims and their opponents. We cannot say precisely why this should have been so. Presumably it was largely due to the activities of the opposition. The uniqueness of God was certainly implicit in the Judaeo-Christian tradition from

---

[1] Eg. Ibn-Abi-Zayd al-Qayrawani, *La Risala*, ed. and tr. L. Bercher, Algiers, 1949; al-Ghazali, *Bidayat al-Hidayah*, in Watt, *The Faith and Practice of al-Ghazali*.

[2] Cf. H. A. R. Gibb, *The Structure of Religious Thought in Islam*, in *Muslim World*, xxxviii. (1948). 24-28.

[3] C. *Muhammad at Medina*, 309-15. Animistic ideas were involved in some of the old marital practices which were rejected because they were contrary to the new appreciation of the dignity of the individual.

which the central conceptions of Islam were derived, but this relationship does not in itself account for the Muslim emphasis on the uniqueness of God. The emphasis must be due to the fact that this was a suitable rallying-point in the struggle between the reforming movement led by Muhammad and the anti-reform party led by the rich merchants.

These considerations bring us to the question of the 'already existing activites' which underlay the early development of Islam. Two such activities may be distinguished. Firstly, Muhammad and the early Muslims were working for a reform of Meccan society, and this reform would have its social, intellectual and religious aspects. Secondly, after opposition appeared, Muhammad and the Muslims were concerned to give their movement a distinctive form which marked it off from the rest of Meccan culture. The former of these activities was integrative in that it attempted to remove disharmonies which had appeared in Meccan society, while the latter was also integrative, since by marking off Muslims from non-Muslims it bound the Muslims closer to one another. In actual life the two activities would merge into one another. When Muhammad began to preach and to publish the revelations he had received, his aim was doubtless to reform Meccan society be getting people to accept his doctrines. A member of the audience might either accept or reject Muhammad's assertions. If he accepted them, he was expected to adopt a certain manner of life called *tazakki*. Unfortunately we do not know exactly what is meant by *tazakki*. Perhaps it meant giving away a proportion of one's wealth, or perhaps it only meant aiming at moral purity. In either case those who accepted Muhammad's message and practised *tazakki* were distinguished from those who rejected his message and did not practise *tazakki*. Thus even the first activity led to a certain marking-off of followers of Muhammad from opponents. The process of marking-off was intensified when the uniqueness of God came to be emphasized, but so long as the Muslims remained at Mecca they were not wholly separated from the other Meccans. With the move to Medina the Muslim community became much more nearly a separate entity, but even at Medina it probably had alliances with pagans in the early years. At Medina, too, it began to mark itself off not merely from pagans, but also from Jews and Christians. The reforming activity was also operative during the Medinan period, of course, and the Muslim community there was one from which the previous disharmonies had been largely removed.

3. THE ASSIMILATION OF NON-ARAB PRACTICES

One of the most interesting features of Islam is the way in which this religion of the Arabs has spread to many other peoples and has carried with it much of the mores of seventh-century Arabia. This expansion of Islam did not begin until after Muhammad's death. Up to that time the integrative activities of Islam were operating purely within Arab culture except in so far as foreign mores and ideas (notably Judaeo-Christian ideas) had already become acclimatized there. To a great extent the Muslim community at Muhammad's death still preserved the pre-Islamic mores; the only changes had been in certain matters where disharmony had appeared. On the other hand, there had been a great change in the underlying spirit. *Muruwwah* had been replaced by *din;* tribal humanism with its supreme aim of maintaining honour had been replaced by Islam. A man now belonged first and foremost to the community of Muslims and not to his tribe. Many of the old attitudes towards the tribe had indeed been transferred to the religious community; but in a new setting those old attitudes gradually became something different. At the same time the trend to individualism had been largely accepted, but a new sanction had been provided (in the doctrine of the Last Day) to encourage the observance of the pre-Islamic mores by the individualistically minded.

After the vast conquests in the two decades after Muhammad's death the situation was greatly altered. Syria, Egypt, 'Iraq and much of Persia were under the control of the Muslims. Soon Aramaeans and Persians were coming over to Islam, and these were urban peoples or peasants, with a long tradition of civilization and with very different mores from those of the nomadic Arabs. From these new Muslims a number of practices were accepted into the normal usage of Islam. Notable examples are methods of taxation, and the institutions of emphyteusis and the pious endowment (*waqf*). Some of these practices spread from the land of their origin to other Islamic lands where circumstances were favourable for their adoption[1].

The infliction of the punishment of stoning for adultery (if what is becoming the standard Western interpretation of the confused material is accepted), shows how a non-Arab custom could be

---

[1] J. Schacht in M. Khadduri and H. J. Liebesny (edd.), *Law in the Middle East*, Washington, 1955. i. 35; and in *Convegno di Scienze Morali, Storiche e Filologiche*, Accademia Nazionale dei Lincei, Rome, 1957, 204f., and 213ff.

islamized. The Qur'anic punishment for adultery is flogging[1], but some of the jurists also recognized stoning as a punishment in the case of married persons. It is reported that, when some Jews asked Muhammad about the punishment of an adulterer and an adulteress, he elicited the fact that the Torah prescribed stoning and ordered this to be carried out; another story (or a variant of this) described a Jewish rabbi trying to conceal the verse of stoning in his scripture, since it was no longer carried out by the Jews[2]. There are also references to a verse of stoning in the Qur'anic revelation, known to the caliph 'Umar but not written down because Muhammad had disliked it[3]. Out of this confusion the following account may be drawn. The normal punishment for adultery at Medina in Muhammad's lifetime was flogging, though to begin with and in certain cases it may have been house-imprisonment. When many persons from the Judaeo-Christian tradition became Muslims, they tended to retain the punishment of stoning to which they had been accustomed. Eventually stories began to be circulated showing that stoning had been sanctioned and practised by Muhammad and some of the leading Companions. Although the punishment of stoning was thus officially recognized in Islam, it is possible that it soon became rare in actual practice, since the jurists hedged it in with conditions that could seldom be fulfilled; e.g. four male witnesses must have seen the act.

The assimilation of non-Arab practices must have been going on throughout the formative period of Islamic law, which may be regarded as lasting till about 800. Matters concerning administration would tend to be adopted soon after the conquests, while matters concerning the family and the social structure were perhaps most prominent in the period from about 700 to 750. Islamic law, or the Shari'ah as we shall prefer to call it, is one of the most important and distinctive features of Islamic civilization. In one aspect it will receive fuller consideration in the following section, and in another aspect in the next chapter. Here it need only be remarked that it is primarily an ideal elaborated by somewhat academic intellectuals, and that it is not the actual law of any Islamic country except in so far as some ruling institution decrees that it is to be put into practice. Usually it

[1] 24.2; cf. 4.15/19, usually said to be abrogated. Various legal opinions are found in Abu-Ja'far an-Nahhas, *K. an-Nasikh wa-'l-Mansukh*, Cairo, 1938/ 1357, 98-102.

[2] Ibn Hisham, 393-5.

[3] Cf. *E.I.(S)*, art. 'Zina' ' (J. Schacht); al-Bukhari, *Sahih*, Hudud (86), 31f.; Ibn-Qutaybah, *Ta'wil Mukhtalif al-Hadith*, Cairo (1908)/1326, 397-404. also other references in A. J. Wensinck, *A Handbook of Early Muhammadan Tradition*, Leiden, 1927, s.v. '*Stoning*'.

is only certain parts of the Shari'ah that have legal force. Nevertheless the Shari'ah is recognized at least as an ideal throughout the Islamic world (along with the non-Arab practices which found their way into it in the formative period), and, even where it is little observed, it sets a standard which has some influence on actual practice.

Besides the assimilation of non-Arab practices in the formative period of the Shari'ah, there has been a constant process of assimilation as the Islamic religion spread further afield. This is most noticeable in some of the lands on the periphery, such as West Africa and Indonesia, where the process of assimilation is not far from its beginning. Even where there is a definite acceptance of Islam, there is often little acceptance of the social part of the Shari'ah. We find marriages being celebrated largely according to the old tribal forms, yet being regarded as Islamic marriages though they are far from fulfilling the conditions of the Shari'ah.[1] Gradually such marriages will doubtless be brought into closer conformity with the requirements of the Shari'ah, and in the course of centuries—provided the centuries are available—there would probably come to be a large measure of observance of the Shari'ah.

Unfortunately, this process on the periphery has become mingled with another process, both in the heartlands and on the periphery, namely, the adoption by Muslims of Western practices. In the social sphere the most notable aspects of this are the emancipation of women and the strong trend towards monogamy; but there are many others such as the adoption of Western clothes and forms of entertainment. Indeed, most of the outward forms of Western life are being adopted, except where they conflict with something fundamental in Islam, for example, the public consumption of alcoholic beverages. There are also other spheres where Western influence has been strong—political organization, education, even the methods of religious education and propaganda, and so forth. Because Western influence is so extensive Muslims are bound to be concerned with the question whether Islam can take so much from the West without being 'swamped' and losing its distinctive character. This danger of 'swamping' is sufficiently serious even in the purely social sphere, for much of Islam's distinctiveness comes from its social mores. The danger is rendered much greater, however, by the fact that the Islamic world is also adopting Western science, and because of that is in danger of being infected with Western agnosticism and atheism, since the Christian defence of monotheism against atheism is neglected (for reasons which will be considered later).[2]

[1] Cf. J. N. D. Anderson, *Islamic Law in Africa*, London, 1954, 154, etc.

[2] Ch. viii, §2 below.

The Integration of the Mores

Up to this point the discussion has dealt chiefly with mores in the strictly social or ethical sphere. It is also necessary, however, to mention cultic mores (which, of course, are also social usages). The history of the cultic forms of Islam is not altogether clear, but a broad outline will suffice here. It is usually held by Western scholars that the cultic forms had in the main been fixed by the time of Muhammad's death, though the details remained fluid for perhaps another half century. The cultic forms were probably one of the first parts of the Shari'ah to become definitely fixed. After this there could be no question of any assimilation of fresh cultic forms to the fixed ones. There could be no question, for example, of incorporating the posture of kneeling in the ritual worship or 'prayer'. When West Africans face the tomb of a local saint (as *qiblah*) during the ritual worship, it is natural to suppose that they must be regarded as having left the community of Islam (though such a view might be premature). Yet, while the fixed cultic forms of early Islam remain unchanged, there is scope for all kinds of additional practices. Thus in many parts of the Islamic world, such as Egypt and North Africa, there is much worship or veneration of saints, and devotions at their tombs are popular. Again, Muslims in the Middle East and elsewhere have adopted mystical practices, partly from other religions and partly in distinctive Islamic forms.

The most interesting example in this respect is the incorporation into Shi'ite Islam of the idea of the suffering saviour. This idea has a long history in the Middle East, for it can be traced back to the old myth of Tammuz and beyond. It is found in the Old Testament, and was one of the ideas actually realized in history by Jesus. It makes its way into Islam by becoming attached to the house of 'Ali and in particular to his sons, al-Hasan and al-Husayn, who are regarded as martyrs at the hands of the godless Umayyads. With the idea of the suffering saviour a whole complex of cultic forms has been introduced into Shi'ism, such as the Muharram ceremonies, when there are 'passion plays' and public manifestations of grief.[1] Such additions to the early Islamic cult tend to create a disintegrative tendency within Islam, for there is always the possibility that for those who practice them they will become the chief source of psychical energy while the ideation corresponding to them will come to guide the conduct of life. Since the cleavage between Shi'ite and Sunnite is the most serious within Islam, this question will recur in other contexts.

[1] Cf. references in *E.I.(S)*, arts. Shi'a, Muharram, Ta'ziya; also D. M. Donaldson, *The Shi'ite Religion*, London, 1933. For a description of the rites in South India, cf. G. A. Herklots, *Islam in India* (revised by W. Crooke), London, 1921. 151-75.

The Integration of the Mores

It would be desirable to include at this point a consideration of the extent to which there had been an integration of aesthetic attitudes in the Islamic world. This is a difficult subject, however, and one that has not been much studied by the general run of Islamists, though it is now receiving increasing attention. All that seems necessary, and indeed feasible, here, therefore, is to offer some preliminary considerations. The chief form of aesthetic expression among the pre-Islamic Arabs was poetry. The Qur'an is not poetry, of course, but much of it satisfies the same aesthetic feelings as were satisfied by poetry. Something of this has been communicated to Islamic literature in languages other than Arabic. A recent writer, in speaking of the unity of the various literatures within the Islamic community, attributes this among other things to 'the authoritativeness of certain principles of form and presentation';[1] and it may be presumed that those who accepted these principles had in part entered into the aesthetic experience of the Arabs. The matter is very complex, however. There is a definite continuity between the later works of Arabic literature and the pre-Islamic poetry, despite the fact that many of the later writers were not Arabs by birth. It is also clear that in many ways later Arabic literature was influenced by the Persian aesthetic experience; and even the heartlands of Islam were affected by the contacts between Muslims and the Romance people of Spain and Southern France.

While poetry was of the highest importance among the Arabs, the representative arts did not flourish. There was a strong feeling among certain sections of the population of the Middle East against the representation of natural objects and particularly of the human form. The feeling is almost certainly religious in origin. It finds expression in the Second Commandment of the Old Testament, but that need not be its only source. The strength of the feeling is shown by the Iconoclastic Controversy in Eastern Christendom in the eighth and ninth centuries, which ended in the compromise by which two-dimensional representation (pictures and icons) was permitted, but not three-dimensional. Such a feeling discouraged aesthetic expression through representational art. Nevertheless, where it was strong, Muslims who wanted to express themselves vistually, were able to devise the intricate geometrical designs which developed into a thing of great beauty, or could turn to architecture and calligraphy, where Islamic artists reached a very high level. Where the feeling against representation was not strong, Muslims practised painting,

[1] G. von Grunebaum, in *Studia Islamica*, i. 112; other factors mentioned are 'the identity of the basic existential experience', 'the identity of the fundamental intellectual interests', and 'the kindred political and social organization'.

195

and in this field Persian miniatures are justly famous. Geographical and social distance doubtless combined to prevent serious clashes over this point in the Islamic world; the iconoclastic masses would not travel to the regions where painting was held in esteem, and illiterate proletarians would have no access to valuable books in court libraries. In this sphere, then, what one finds is not integration but a compromise which lessens the chances of conflict.

Music was present in pre-Islamic Arabia as the accompaniment of poetry. To the urban dweller, however, it seems to have been primarily the accompaniment of feasting and wine-drinking; and this led to its being viewed with disfavour by the more puritanical Muslims. It had no place in the earliest cultic forms of Islam, but later, when out of mysticism had developed the dervish order, some of them gave a large place to music in their ritual. Once again this is not complete integration.

It now remains to ask about the prior activities underlying these various processes of assimilation. The two activities already mentioned as underlying the developments of the Qur'anic period—the reforming of society and the creating of a separate community with distinctive characteristics—are also operative to some extent wherever non-Arab usages are being adopted. Two other activities are also to be distinguished which may be labelled islamization and indigenization. Islamization springs from the desire of recent converts to be truly Muslim, while indigenization is the activity of adapting Islam to the local situation.

Men in Mecca and elsewhere in Arabia had been interested in social reform before Muhammad began to preach, and the reform that was necessary was the removal of the disharmonies caused by the change from a nomadic to a settled economy. With the conquests fresh disharmony was created, which it was incumbent on the authorities to try to remove. Most of the new non-Arab Muslims were either town-dwellers or peasants, while most of the Arabs in the provinces had been nomads. It was therefore more than ever urgent to adapt the nomadic mores to the conditions of settled life. Because of this urgent need various usages were adopted, such as the method of land tenure known as emphyteusis, which filled gaps in the nomadic mores. In a sense the immediate aims of the reforming activity varied from time to time according to the contemporary situation, but there is also an identity which persists throughout. Moreover, since ruling institutions are always interested in removing social disharmony and increasing uniformity, this reforming activity normally had the support of the ruling institution even when it was not inaugurated and carried out by it.

The Integration of the Mores

The activity of making Muslims a distinct community also continues, except that now it is not so much the creating of distinctive characteristics as the maintaining of those which already exist. The observance of the Islamic cultic forms marked off Muslims to a great extent, while non-Muslims were obliged to wear distinctive marks. The latter regulation is attributed to the caliph 'Umar, as part of his covenant with the Christians. At some times there was great laxity in the observance of the provisions of that covenant; at other times zealous Muslims—Ibn-Taymiyyah, for example—called for stricter observance[1]. Closely linked to this maintenance of the distinctive character of Islam was the assumption of its superiority. When the Muslims originally made themselves a separate community, they did so because they believed they were following the truth (revealed by God) while the rest of Arab society was turning away from it. That is to say, in its very inception the distinctive Islamic community regarded itself as superior to the other communities around it. It also regarded itself as superior to the Jews and Christians, alleging that these had corrupted their scriptures and had not followed in all details the revelations given to them. Thus in a sense the *raison d'être* of the Islamic community was its superiority. Moreover much of the pride formerly taken in one's tribe became attached to the religious community. This has led to an intense belief in the superiority of Islam, and in the inferiority of other (religious) communities. The Christians and Jews who had to wear different clothes from the Muslims were made to feel that that was a humiliation, and this increased the pressure on them to become Muslims.

With this we come to the third activity, namely, islamization or making oneself a proper Muslim. Because the Muslims believe so intensely in the superiority of Islam, the convert, especially when he comes from a society which is culturally inferior, feels that it is a great privilege to belong to this community. In the lands on the periphery a man often becomes a Muslim while he has still little idea of what is involved in becoming a Muslim. For years, even for generations, the attitude continues of always being ready to advance to a fuller observance of Islam. The story has already been mentioned of how Mansa Musa, the emperor of the West African state of Mali, made a pilgrimage to Mecca with great pomp in 1324, and of how he was unaware that a Muslim was restricted four wives until someone mentioned this to him in Cairo, but on hearing of the limitation at once took steps to get rid of his wives in excess of four. (It may be

[1] Laoust, *Essai*, 267, 275; A. S. Tritton, *The Caliphs and their Non-Muslim Subjects*, Oxford, 1930.

197

noted in passing that a somewhat similar activity of making oneself a proper Westerner—in all except religion—is manifesting itself in sections of the Islamic community in the present century.)

Finally, there is the activity of indigenization, which is complementary to islamization. Once a man has adopted sufficient Islamic usages to make him feel he is really a Muslim, he tends in other respects to continue in the mores of his own society or to assimilate Islamic usages to these. The minimum needed to constitute a man a real Muslim, however unchanging in theory, varies in practice from region to region and time to time, according to the stage of development. In the early stages of the conversion of a region to Islam many of its former usages are retained. Sometimes they are in exactly the form they had before; sometimes they are considerably modified in order to bring them closer to Islamic usage. Mostly, whatever seriously conflicts with the 'fundamental values, emotional attitudes or aesthetic criteria' of Islam is suppressed. Yet many usages are adopted which are at variance with the spirit, if not the letter, of Islam. It is often necessary, for example, to have feasts which correspond to the pagan feasts and take their place in the lives of the new converts. A very interesting example of this is the Palestinian Muslim feast of Nabi Musa, celebrated at an alleged tomb of Moses between Jerusalem and the Dead Sea. The curious feature of this festival is that it follows not the Islamic but the Christian calendar, and thus ensures that the Muslims have something to occupy them while the Christians have all the excitement of Holy Week and Easter. It is always a problem, of course, to know how far indigenization may go before the point of departure from the Islamic community is reached[1].

These, then, appear to be the four chief prior or underlying activities through which non-Arab practices were incorporated into Islam. The first two were already present when Islam was still restricted to Arabs, but non-Arab converts entered into these activities. The other two activities, islamization and indigenization, were chiefly the activities of non-Arabs, but in a sense they are a continuation of the first two activities. Islamization, or making oneself a proper Muslim, is an aspect of the activity of distinguishing the Islamic community from other communities; and indigenization may be regarded as a continuation of what has been called the reforming activity, since its aim is the removal of the disharmonies caused by the incorporation into Islam of men and women from an alien society. In this way the fundamental activities are reduced to two: the reforming activity which aims at removing disharmonies

[1] Cf. p. 136 above.

from contemporary society, and the activity of making Islam a distinctive community. With this conclusion in mind we turn to look at some further points through which we may come to a deeper appreciation of the results so far attained.

4. THE CREATION OF ISLAMIC MORES

Up to this point in this chapter we have been speaking of conscious changes in the mores, and it may be objected that these are not the same as the mores of primitive peoples. It has certainly to be admitted that there is a difference, but there is also some justification for speaking of the mores of high civilizations, even though some conscious thought is involved in the process through which they come into being. In the case of Islam in particular, unconscious factors make their contribution along with conscious thought. In actual life what is commonly called 'Islamic law' produces something very like the mores of a primitive people. Since it is not exactly law at all, as that is usually understood, it is referred to here as the Shari'ah. It should be noted that the word *shari'ah* properly means 'revelation' in general and is not restricted to the legal aspect of revelation. One comes across numerous instances where orientalists have translated the corresponding adjective *shar'i* by 'legal' but where 'revelational' is needed not to obscure the sense of the passage[1].

(a) The development of the Shari'ah

There have been great advances in the understanding of the development of the Shari'ah by Western scholars during the last century. A notable step forward in the critique of Islamic Tradition was made by Ignaz Goldziher towards the end of the nineteenth century, and another step, more specifically connected with the Shari'ah,has recently been made by Joseph Schacht[2]. As a result of the work of these and many other scholars, the modern Western view of the development of the Shari'ah differs considerably from the standard Muslim view. The following is a brief summary of the modern view.

[1] For *shari'ah* = revelation, cf. al-Mas'udi, *Muruj*, i. 54 ; al-Ghazali *Al-Munqidh min ad-Dalal*, Damascus, 1939/1358, 90, 92 (*shar'*), 103 (*shar'iyyah*); on p. 97 *shari'ah* seems to mean 'revelation', though I have translated it 'Divine law' (*Faith and Practice of al-Ghazali* 37).

[2] I Goldziher, *Muhammedanische Studien*, ii. Halle, 1890. J. Schacht, *The Origins of Muhammadan Jurisprudence*, Oxford, 1950; also *Esquisse d'une Histoire du Droit Musulman*, Paris, 1953; and two chapters in Khadduri and Liebesny, *Law in the Middle East*, i. 28-84.

The Integration of the Mores

For about a century after the death of Muhammad justice was administered in the Islamic state according to the customary law of the Arabs, except in so far as this had been modified by a specific Qur'anic rule or by Muhammad's own practice. On the whole, however, the exceptions were probably comparatively few, since it is chiefly for marriage and inheritance that the Qur'an gives precise rules, while Muhammad's administrative practice probably only affected a small number of points—far fewer than the mass of Tradition would suggest. In the course of time, too, the customary law of the Arabs would be modified, as judges and arbiters tried to adapt it to the fresh situations in which they found themselves. Things appear to have gone on in this way until the last thirty years of the Umayyad dynasty (720-750). Those responsible for carrying out the work of the judiciary dealt with each novel situation as seemed best to them. Beyond this there was little conscious thought about the principles underlying judicial practice. By about 720, however, there were bodies of men in 'Iraq, Medina and Syria—some with practical experience as judges, others apparently without such experience—who were beginning to discuss legal questions in a more theoretical way. These formed what Schacht calls the 'ancient schools'. One result was that the actual legal practice of each locality came to be fairly stable, though the point at which stability was reached might be far removed from the original customary law of the Arabs and might not even be very close to the Qur'anic regulations. It is in this closing period of the Umayyad dynasty, however, that the movement effectively begins which was to produce the Shari'ah and its starting-point is therefore the actual practice of this period.

In the late Umayyad period, then, there are in existence the 'ancient schools' of law with their 'living tradition'. As has been noted already in other contexts, the change of dynasty seems to have led to the increased importance of the jurists. It would be natural for each school to hold that, where there were differences, its practice was superior to those of its rivals. This would lead to arguments not merely within each school, but also between the schools. In the course of these arguments certain criteria came to be generally agreed upon. Foremost among these was the principle that those practices were to be preferred which were based on Traditions from the Prophet. As Schacht has forcibly argued, however, it was only through the work of ash-Shafi'i (d.820) that this principle was generally accepted. Previously the decisive element had been the 'living tradition' of each school. At one period jurists were content to show that what was now the 'living tradition' of their school had been upheld by its leading men in the half century before 720. Later

200

it was fashionable to claim that the present 'living tradition' was in accordance with the views of some of the leading Companions of the Prophet. The school of 'Iraq seems to have been the first to claim that its 'living tradition' was identical with the *sunnah* or 'beaten path' of the Prophet; but this claim was not founded in detail on actual Traditions of what Muhammad had said or done[1]. Ash-Shafi'i was the first to insist that the *sunnah* of the Prophet could only be determined by the content of validly attested Traditions. This criterion soon won general acceptance.

This principle led to greater uniformity in the various regional schools of law. The ruling institution also exerted some pressure to bring about uniformity.[2] Eventually there emerged a number of 'orthodox' legal schools or rather rites, all accepting ash-Shafi'i's main principle but differing about some of the other principles (such as the place of 'consensus') and about details of practice. Four of these have survived to the present time: the Hanafite, Shafi'ite, Malikite, and Hanbalite rites. The outcome of this process is the Shari'ah, and so it includes all the prescriptions of the different rites.

This account shows that the Shari'ah was not the work of the ruling or governing institution with its desire for uniformity. At most the 'Abbasid ruling institution gave some encouragemeent to those who were developing the Shari'ah by being ready to acknowledge it and by instructing their judges to apply it in certain spheres. Unfortunately there is little material about such matters in the sources, and what little there is has not yet been studied thoroughly. It is tolerably certain, however, that the 'Abbasids began by giving more support than the Umayyads had given to the jurists or religious scholars. This support encouraged the development of the Shari'ah which has just been described. Yet the 'Abbasids never gave absolute support to the views of the scholar-jurists, or even of their consensus, to the extent of decreeing that these should be universally followed. After a century or perhaps two they rather seem to have found the Shari'ah irksome.

The development of the Shari'ah, then, must be due to what may be called the 'embryonic religious institution'—a part of that area about which we have little information. There seem to have grown up groups of individuals without any official position, but interested in the forms of conduct involved in the Islamic religion, and therefore often consulted by other Muslims. These informal groups were the

---

[1] The word ' Tradition ' (with a capital) is throughout used in the technical sense of an anecdote about something Muhammad said or did.

[2] Cf. Ibn al-Muqaffa', *Risalah fi-'s-Sahabah*, 125f., quoted by Schacht, *Origins*, 95.

embryo of the 'ancient schools' of law. Because of their nature and their specific interests the basis of the Shari'ah as they developed it is ethical rather than legal in the strict sense. So much is now generally accepted. From the standpoint of the present study, however, it is necessary to ask further what was the nature of the fundamental activity in which they were engaged and out of which the development of the Shari'ah proceeded. The answer to this question should be stated as a hypothesis, though it is a hypothesis which has many facts to support it. It is that they were working for the establishment of the Islamic community as a righteous or holy community, since they believed that only when a man is a member of a righteous community is his life significant. In other words, a man will only attain to Paradise if he belongs to 'the people of Paradise'. This is very similar to the fundamental concern of the Kharijites. Now the moderate forms of Kharijite theology, and the 'orthodox' theology which did justice to the positive truth in the Kharijite views while avoiding their heresies, were developed in Basrah in the period from about 680 to 750 onwards. The main development of the Shari'ah was also in 'Iraq from about 720 onwards, though more in Kufah than in Basrah. It seems probable, then, that both the Shari'ah and the theological doctrines arose from the same fundamental activity.

If it is assumed that this hypothesis is sufficiently supported, then the appearance of the Shari'ah would imply the transfer to the Islamic community of an attitude formerly attached to the tribe. In the pre-Islamic tribe a man found significance in his life by manifesting the noble qualities of his tribe; and these noble qualities normally expressed themselves through following the *sunnah* or 'beaten path' of the tribe. In the same way the Muslim attained significance by following the *sunnah* of the Islamic community, but this *sunnah* consisted in a life of righteousness. It is doubtful whether the phrase '*sunnah* of the Islamic community' was thus used, but the idea was implicit. In the course of time the phrase '*sunnah* of Muhammad' came into use, as noted above—at first in a general way, then as the totality of the conduct described in the Traditions. This was not merely something on which the 'ancient schools' could agree; it emphasized the supernatural character of the *sunnah* of the community in that it was derived from the charismatic leader (and therefore to some extent did justice to the central idea of the Shi'ites). The name 'Shari'ah' further emphasizes this supernatural character—since it means 'revelation'. Although the Qur'an was primary and the words and deeds of Muhammad only secondary and not similarly inspired, yet the latter, that is, the *sunnah* of the Prophet, was given the same validity as the Qur'an, both because the Qur'an in various passages made obedience to Muhammad obligatory, and because what Muhammad said and did was regarded as being in accordance with specific commands of God to him[1]. Thus the Shari'ah, though largely based on Muhammad's human example, becomes a supernatural norm for the conduct of Muslims.

The importance of communal solidarity for the development of the Shari'ah is also shown by the place of 'consensus' (*ijma'*) in that development. With regard to the place of consensus in the ancient schools Schacht concludes

that the legal theory of the ancient schools of law is dominated by the idea of consensus ; that they distinguish between the consensus of all Muslims, both the scholars and the people, on essentials, and the consensus of the scholars on points of detail ; that they consider the consensus in both forms as the final argument on all problems, and not subject to error ; and that it represents the common denominator of doctrine achieved in each generation, as opposed to individual opinions (*ra'y*) which make for disagreement.[2]

Ash-Shafi'i, in Schacht's view, attempted to remove the consensus of the ancient schools and their 'living tradition' from the position of highest authority in law and to place there instead the Traditions from the Prophet. In so doing he rejected the consensus of the scholars and tolerated only the consensus of the people in general.[3] Yet, though his insistence on properly attested Traditions from the Prophet was accepted, the Muslims returned to the consensus of the scholars, and indeed to the primacy of the 'living tradition' and the consensus, except that properly attested Traditions were now included in the 'living tradition'.

As regards consensus, Snouck Hurgronje has made clear its all-important function as the ultimate mainstay of legal theory and of positive law in their final form : the consensus guarantees the authenticity and correct interpretation of the Koran, the faithful transmission of the *sunna* of the Prophet, the legitimate use of analogy and its results ; it covers, in short, every detail of the law, including the recognized differences of the several schools.[4]

The function of consensus in the development and maintenance of the Shari'ah is remarkable. On a superficial examination of the material it might have been thought that consensus was brought in either to justify usages which were not supported by a Tradition from Muhammad or to provide a principle of adaptation, since the age-old

[1] Cf. ash-Shafi'i's statements, quoted by Schacht, *Origins*, 16.
[2] Schacht, *Origins*, 82.
[3] Ib.94f.
[4] Ib.2

Arab attitude had been to regard all innovation as bad, or, in theological terms, heretical. Yet the studies whose conclusions have been quoted make it clear that neither of these suggestions is borne out by the facts. The principle of consensus had not been adopted as a convenient device in order to justify what would otherwise be difficult to justify. On the contrary, other methods of justifying the practices of the community—methods which to Westerners might appear superior—were abandoned or subordinated to the principle of consensus. The best explanation of this recurrence of consensus seems to be that it arises out of an intense belief in the community, a belief that the community is in some way supernatural, is a divinely instituted and divinely ordered community, in brief, that it is a 'charismatic community'. The saying of Muhammad, 'My community will never agree on an error', is often regarded in the West as having been invented in order to justify the principle of consensus; but the present train of thought suggests another way of looking at it. Perhaps it is an expression of this belief in the charismatic community, asserting that its charisma involves infallibility. The restriction of consensus in certain respects to that of the scholars need not be an argument against such a view, since it was the scholars who spoke of the consensus of scholars and the assertion may therefore be ideological, that is, an exaggeration of their own importance made in order to maintain or enhance their position in the community. There seems to be no gainsaying the prominence among Muslims, even if it was not always fully conscious, of an intense belief that theirs was a charismatic community, a community in and through which a man's life became significant.

This is not the place to discuss the changes that took place after the original development of the Shari'ah, such as the 'closing of the gate of *ijtihad*'. Both the original development and the subsequent changes had important repercussions on the position of the scholars and jurists in the community. The whole question of the role of the intellectuals in the Islamic community, however, though it will be adumbrated in the following chapter, is one that requires a long study devoted solely to it. Meanwhile let us consider the function of the Shari'ah in the life of the community.

(b) The function of the Shari'ah[1]

It is worth considering carefully what role the Shari'ah actually played in the life of the Islamic community. It was not, except to a

[1] Cf. Johann Fück, 'Die Rolle des Traditionalismus im Islam', *Zeitschrift der deutschen morgenländischen Gesellschaft*, xciii (1935). 1-32, esp. 11-18.

small extent, the official law of the community, that is, the law enforced by the ruling institution. Yet a great deal of time and energy was spent by some of the best brains among the Muslims precisely in the work of elaborating and systematizing the Shari'ah. It would seem, therefore, that it must be of great importance for the community. The problem is then: In what does this importance consist? In thus formulating the question it is assumed that the importance lies in something other than in providing the law to be administered in the law-courts, though in certain respects (varying from country to country) the Shari'ah does in fact do this. The importance of the Shari'ah must also lie in something other than the use of it, or of parts of it, as a political lever, though it was sometimes used in this way; for example, al-Mawardi (d.1058) in his work entitled *The Institutions of Government* is probably trying to bring about an increase of the powers of the caliph[1]. Though the Shari'ah performed such functions, they are not sufficient to account for its importance in the eyes of Muslim scholars. This must be looked for elsewhere.

The clue to the solution of the problem is provided by the hypothesis advanced above that the scholar-jurists were working for the existence of a righteous community. This might also be expressed by saying that, since the Islamic community was a divinely instituted or charismatic community, it must have a divinely given norm which it accepted and tried to follow. It is implied in this that the intellectuals who elaborated the Shari'ah were primarily interested in maintaining the charismatic character of the community, and not in raising the standard of conduct in the community. The Shari'ah might act as an ideal standard to which men were constantly trying to come closer in practice; but this was not the primary reason for their interest in the Shari'ah.

There is an interesting comparison between the Shari'ah and certain parts of the law of the Old Testament. It is the opinion of scholars that the regulations for the year of jubilee were never put into effect[1]. Why such impracticable regulations should ever have been drawn up is not clear. Perhaps they were an emphatic way of stating certain spiritual truths, such as Israel's dependence on God. In some respects the year of jubilee is an elaboration of the principle of the Sabbath, and the Sabbath is a witness to the charismatic character of the community. Thus Moses was commanded to say to the Israelites:

[1] Cf. H. A. R. Gibb, 'Al-Mawardi's Theory of the Khilafah', *Islamic Culture*, xi [1937]. 291-302; also in Khadduri and Liebesny, *Law in the Middle East*, i. 17-19.

[1] *Leviticus*, 25; cf. A. Lods, *Les Prophètes d'Israel*, Paris, 1935, 327.

205

The Integration of the Mores

Verily my sabbaths ye shall keep: for it is a sign between me and you throughout your generations; that ye may know that I am the Lord that doth sanctify you[1].

Since the sabbath was a sign of the special relationship of the community to God, that is, of its charismatic character, it is likely that part of the significance of the year of jubilee was something similar.

On the assumption that the chief interest in the Shari'ah was as a mark of the charisma of the community, we may go on to ask about some of its other functions. Doubtless among the ordinary people many were concerned that their community should be a charismatic one. For the masses, however, the Shari'ah was also important in that it provided a social framework for their lives which remained stable in the flux of political changes. To the modern Western scholar the political history of the Islamic world, and indeed of the Orient generally, presents at times a picture of great instability. It has to be remembered however, that at these times and places ruling institutions played a much smaller part in the life of society than in our modern centralized states. Despite political instability the ordinary man could feel a large measure of security provided the social order remained stable. The Shari'ah helped to establish and maintain such a social order, above all by its rules for marriage and inheritance. Moreover, even though ruling institutions could not be bound by its provisions, it was dangerous for them to flout the provisions too blatantly, and that gave a measure of protection to the individual against the ruling institution. Such protection was of great value in a world where there was a tradition for rulers to act despotically with little respect for the rights of individuals.

Something similar is true with regard to the scholar-jurists. So long as they were private individuals with no need to earn their livelihood they were in a strong position. It was doubtless because of the feeling that such independence gave strength that there was a widespread belief that to accept judicial office was to deviate from the path of virtue. In the course of time the normal career for a scholar-jurist involved the holding of various offices of a judicial character to which appointment was made by the ruling institution. There was thus considerable pressure on judges to accede to the wishes of the government, even when these were contrary to the Shari'ah and to principles of equity; if they did not so accede, they

[1] *Exodus.* 31.13 ; cf. what Lods says of various practices taken over from animism: 'Ils (sc. les Prêtres) en exigent cependant la stricte observation, *non pas à cause de leur signification* précise, qui paraît leur être indifferente, mais plutôt parce que, faisant partie de la coutume nationale, elles constituent autant de marques d'appartenance au Dieu d'Israel' (*l.c.*, 330f.)

206

The Integration of the Mores

were liable to have their career cut short. Once the Shari'ah had been firmly established, however, the scholar-jurists were in a somewhat stronger position to resist unjust demands by the ruling institution, at least in those spheres where the Shari'ah was effective. There might still be pliant self-seeking individuals who were ready to twist the rules of the Shari'ah in the interests of the rulers; but, unless this twisting was done skilfully, it would be difficult for such individuals to avoid being discredited by their fellows on the grounds that they were ignorant of the Shari'ah. It is conceivable that it was because of this situation that the scholar-jurists themselves introduced the doctrine that the 'gate of *ijtihad*' had been closed—that is, that they had no right of private judgement except in respect of the detailed application of the Shari'ah and were bound to follow the main principles of the rites to which they belonged. By thus restricting the right of judges to depart from precedent, they made it more difficult for rulers to influence their judgements improperly.

The Shari'ah, quite apart from the intentions of those who first elaborated it, has in fact promoted uniformity throughout the Islamic world, especially on the periphery. The uniformity is most noticeable in the official cultic usages, but it is also found to some extent in the structure of the family. In the heartlands of Islam there has been during the last century a movement away from the Shari'ah in such matters as commercial and criminal law (where the Shari'ah has seldom been fully effective anywhere), and even to a slight extent in matters of personal status. In the peripheral lands, on the other hand, there is usually a gradual movement towards increasing the application of the Shari'ah. Within the Shari'ah there are various distinctions: acts may be obligatory, recommended, neutral, not recommended or prohibited; within the cultic usages there is a distinction between the 'elements' (which are obligatory) and the 'usages'[1]. Such distinctions probably help to bring about uniformity in certain essentials.

So far an attempt has been made to indicate some positive functions of the Shari'ah, but it must also be asked whether it has any negative functions, that is, whether it contributes in any way to a disintegration of Islamic society. There seem to be two main points here, namely, whether the Shari'ah tends to create a gulf between the ruling institutions and those over whom they rule, and whether the relation of the Shari'ah to the idea of the charismatic community tends to widen the gulf between those to whom this idea is important (the Sunnites) and those who are more interested in a charismatic leader (the Shi'ites).

[1] Cf. E. E. Calverley, *Worship in Islam*, Madras, 1925, 19-21.

207

In dealing with the first of these questions we assume that, at least originally, the Shari'ah was an expression of what the masses of the ordinary people wanted; evidence for this would be the support given by the populace to men like Ahmad ibn-Hanbal in the struggle against the ruling institution. It seems unhealthy anywhere that there should be such a cleavage between theory and practice as there is in Islam with regard to the Shari'ah. In particular this looks like a contradiction between what ordinary men hold to be morally right and good and what the ruling institutions actually do. When one examines this question carefully, however, one finds that the cleavage is not so great as might at first sight appear. In general the ruling institutions in Islamic lands have been prepared to give effect to large parts of the Shari'ah (so far as the matter concerned them), and in particular to uphold the cultic part. This would not have been satisfactory, if the Shari'ah had been purely an ethical standard; but since the Shari'ah was first and foremost a mark of the charisma of the community, a partial acknowledgement of it was sufficient to enable it to perform its function of marking off the community as charismatic. On the other hand, this peculiar nature of the Shari'ah as the mark of charisma creates difficulties at the present time, when Islamic states try to frame modern constitutions on the basis of the Shari'ah. Since the Shari'ah was hardly a practical code even for a medieval state, it is extremely difficult to adapt it to the needs of today.

Finally, there is the question whether the Shari'ah has tended to widen the gulf between the Sunnites and the Shi'ites. The Shi'ites, of course, have their own 'law', but it does not differ from the four Sunnite rites much more than these differ from one another[1]. It accepts the principle that legal regulations are to be justified by a Tradition going back to Muhammad, but it does not accept all the Companions as reliable transmitters and often requires Traditions to be confirmed by 'Ali or one of the other imams[2]. On the whole, then, the differences between Sunnites and Shi'ites in the actual conduct, of life are small, but there is a great difference in their attitude to the Shari'ah. For the Sunnites the Shari'ah is supreme, but for the Shi'ites the imam is the guardian of their Shari'ah (which does not appear to be as extensive and elaborate as that of the Sunnites), and is therefore superior to it.[3] The imam, they consider, is the only proper

---

[1] Schacht, *Origins*, 262f.

[2] Cf. A. A. A. Fyzee, *A Shi'ite Creed*, 118ff.; id. in Khadduri and Liebesny, op. cit., 127, quoting from a Fatimid writer, 'when an imam relates a tradition from the Prophet, no authority is necessary.'

[3] 'Allama-i-Hilli, *Al-Bab al-Hadi 'Ashar* (Tr. W. McE. Miller), London, 1928, p. 66ff., §183f. For the lesser degree of elaboration cf. the absence of a

guardian of the Shari'ah, since he alone is preserved from error or infallible.

It can hardly be claimed, then, that the Shari'ah of the Sunnites has of itself widened the gap between them and the Shi'ites. What can be said, however, is that the Sunnites in their zeal for the Shari'ah neglected to make any place in their system for the charismatic leader, or at least did so only very slowly with the conception of Muhammad's infallibility and other superhuman qualities. The Shi'ites, on the other hand, did even less than the Sunnites to make a place within their own system for men with the other kind of outlook. Apart from the impact of the West, however, it might in course of time have been possible for most of the Shi'ites to be brought within the Sunnite fold.

It is perhaps worth remarking in closing that Christendom, at least in parts, seems to have been more successful than Islam in devising institutions in which there was a high degree of satisfaction both for those who wanted a charismatic leader and for those who wanted to belong to a charismatic community. The Protestants have by and large been weakest in their explicit recognition of the charismatic community, though there is nowadays great interest in the doctrine of the Church. Most sections of Christendom manifest devotion to Christ as a charismatic leader. The Roman Catholics have in addition in the Pope an actual charismatic leader, though on a lower plane than Christ. The Orthodox, especially the Russian Orthodox, appear to have the deepest sense of the charismatic community, and one that differs in some respect from that of Catholics. In the perspective of the conceptions of the charismatic leader and the charismatic community, there is thus some justification for the parallels occasionally drawn between the Shi'ites and the Protestants on the one hand and between the Sunnites and the Catholics on the other.

Shi'ite law of war and peace in M. Khadduri, *War and Peace in the Law of Islam*, Baltimore, 1955.

VII

THE INTEGRATION OF INTELLECTUAL LIFE

A T an earlier point in this study the conclusion was reached that the main function of ideation in the life of a society was to clarify and make explicit for the members of the society the ends which they were corporately pursuing, to place these ends in an order of subordination and superordination, and to state the view of the nature of reality on which this pursuit of ends was based[1]. There is therefore a sense in which all the members of the society are the bearers of the ideation, and participate in the intellectual life of the society. On the other hand, there are certain members of the society who participate more actively than the great majority in this intellectual life; they systematize the ideation, they defend it against attacks from within and without and endeavour to hand it on to succeeding generations, and they also have the main responsibility for adapting the ideation to changing circumstances. These persons may be referred to in general as the intellectuals or intelligentsia, though in most societies there are probably various groups to be distinguished among them. In Islam the most important of the intellectuals are the ulema ('*ulama*') whom we are calling scholar-jurists, though they also included theologians; many had official positions, but at times there were also some who kept themselves independent of the ruling institution. Outside the ranks of the scholar-jurists there were often writers on history, philosophy and general topics, as well as poets and belle-lettrists, who contributed to the intellectual life of their time. Sometimes members of the ruling institution had intellectual interests. From a fairly early period there were writers on mysticism, while from about the twelfth century some of these were leaders in the sufi orders or fraternities. All such groups are here regarded as constituting the class of intellectuals.

The various sections of this chapter deal with the different functions of the intellectuals. First there is a brief glance at the core of Islamic ideation in the Qur'an. Then the work of systematizing, elaborating, defending and propagating this ideational core is considered under two aspects: the intellectual side of the development of the Shari'ah, and the formulation of the standard Sunnite

[1] Cf. p. 83 above.

210

theology. A third section is concerned with the integration of Islamic ideation with the most advanced world-views of the time, while the last tries to estimate the success and failure of the intellectuals in adapting the ideation to social changes and in making it an adequate expression of the 'movement of life' in the masses.

1. THE QUR'ANIC SYNTHESIS

Once again the beginnings of Islam have to be briefly mentioned; something must be said about the degree of integration present in the ideational core found in the Qur'an, since that is the centre of all the later intellectual life of Islam.

The main conceptions in the Qur'anic message or kerygma belong to the Judaeo-Christian tradition—the conceptions of God, prophets, revelation, the Last Day with the judgement assigning eternal reward and punishment in accordance with man's conduct, and the rejection of idolatry. By the time these appear in the Qur'an, however, they have already been adapted to the categories of Arab thinking, that is, to the assumptions and preconceptions which were apparently natural to Arabs. Thus there tends to be a more complete separation of the divine and the human, leading to a more mechanical conception of revelation; while prophethood in the Qur'an comes to have some of the features of the Arab office of *hakam* or arbiter, so that latterly the prophet in the strict sense (*nabi*) is overshadowed by the 'messenger' (*rasul*). The question which interests us at the moment is the extent to which there was a genuine integration of these Judaeo-Christian conceptions with the previous thinking of the Arabs. In trying to answer this question it will be helpful to make use of the three principles invoked in the previous chapter.

The first point to notice, then, is the nature of the pre-existing activity in fields related to these Judaeo-Christian conceptions. It seems clear that this activity must have been the initial stages of the movement to bring about social reform in Mecca, and in particular to curb the rampant individualism. If this is so, the real point of contact is the conception of the Last Judgement, since this contains a sanction which is applicable within an individualistic system. It is also clear that these borrowed conceptions in Islam are nourished by the original reforming activity and contribute to its expansion. What Muhammad did could hardly be thought of except in terms of the borrowed Judaeo-Christian conceptions. That was the second principle. According to the third principle elements in the Judaeo-Christian conceptions would not be accepted into Islam if they conflicted with its 'fundamental values, emotional attitudes or aesthetic criteria'. The operation of this third principle may be seen in the Qur'anic denial of the death of Jesus on the cross. The basis of the denial is doubtless the thought that is found, for example, in the words of the Psalmist that he 'has not seen the righteous forsaken, nor his seed begging their bread';[1] but it is likely that some such thought—that the divine powers would not allow those who worshipped them faithfully to be utterly defeated by their enemies—was already present in the Arabian environment before the Qur'anic borrowings were made, even if it owed something to Old Testament influences at an earlier time[2].

The operation of the third principle is also seen in the rejection of the claims of Judaism and Christianity to be following faithfully in the tradition of Abraham. In opposition to the older religions the Qur'an sets up a conception of the religion of Abraham such that this religion has been corrupted by Jews and Christians and only restored in its purity by the Muslims. This shows that the continuity of the Qur'anic revelation with those to Jews and Christians was something of fundamental importance for the Muslims. It was so fundamental that, when the Jews denied the identity of the Qur'anic message with that of the Old Testament, it became necessary for the Muslims to reject some of the primary historical aspects of the Judaeo-Christian tradition. At the time this was probably satisfactory from the Arab point of view, since the Arabs were not historically minded and knew little of Judaeo-Christian history; but later, when Islam spread to the higher centres of Judaeo-Christian culture in Palestine, Syria and 'Iraq, it was a considerable embarrassment for Muslim scholars.

Hesitation about the extent to which Judaeo-Christian conceptions were to be accepted can be seen in some cases. One is the affair of the 'satanic verses'.[3] The fact that these were at first received by Muhammad and the other Muslims as genuine shows that they were not felt to be incompatible with monotheism, presumably because the pagan deities were regarded as a kind of angel. In other words, these early Muslims were still so much in the Arab tradition that they were prepared to accept the conception of God but not the

[1] *Psalms*, 37.25.

[2] The Qur'anic denial of the death on the cross is first and foremost a rebuttal of the Jewish claim to have triumphed over Jesus, and that presupposes that the Jews argued that he could not be the Messiah (or a messenger of God) since God had not kept him safe. Cf. *Matthew*, 4.6, and *Psalms*, 91.11f.

[3] Cf. p. 188 above.

complementary idea that the worship of idols was incompatible with this. What led the Muslims to realize the incompatibility of mono-theism and worship at the pagan shrines is unfortunately not clear. It seems likely that it was not merely greater familiarity with the Jewish tradition, but some action of Muhammad's opponents whereby they linked up their opposition to him with a defence of the pagan shrines other than the Ka'bah or criticized him on the basis of polytheistic ideas. Whatever the events leading up to the replacement of the 'satanic verses', the Qur'an came more and more to emphasize rejection of worship at the pagan shrines as one of the chief marks distinguishing Muhammad's followers from his opponents.

This is incidentally an interesting example of the way in which a social and political conflict comes to be focussed on a particular intellectual conflict. If we have been right in maintaining that the living religion of the pre-Islamic Arabs was tribal humanism and that the animism connected with the pagan shrines was a moribund survival from an earlier period, then it is somewhat fortuitous that this question of idolatry should have become a main issue between Muhammad and his opponents. That idolatry should thus have come to the forefront is probably due to a decision by the opponents that this was a point on which they could effectively challenge Muhammad and gain popular support. There are various instances in the history of Islamic theology, not to mention Christian history, where a complex struggle between two or more parties is focussed about a single intellectual point which is not the central issue between them but merely the point at which both sides decide it is most advantageous to rally their forces and join battle. This procedure may be described as a simplification of the issues, but such simpli-fication is often necessary in order to gain the support of ordinary men.

In some cases we find that, while a Judaeo-Christian conception is dominant in the Qur'an, the Arab conception has not been com-pletely displaced, and after a generation or two the latter begins to be emphasized again at the expense of the former. One example of this would be individualism. The Qur'an insists that each man has to appear before God the Judge as an isolated individual; but, as has been noticed at several points already, communalism gradually returned until the standard view came to be that what was requisite to ensure salvation was to belong to the 'people of Paradise'. Another example of this feature is the doctrine of predestination. The Qur'an emphasizes God's omnipotence in the present, but there are a few traces of the idea that every life was determined in the distant past. Later generations, however, as is evidenced by Traditions, returned to the old idea that everything had been decided in the distant past. In such matters, then, the integration effected by the Qur'an was no so great as appeared at first sight.

Despite the exceptions considered here, however, the chief Judaeo-Christian conceptions were to a great extent integrated with the previous reforming activity.

2. THE INTELLECTUALS AND SECTARIANISM

(a) The adaptation of the synthesis to changing conditions

The appearance of sects in Islam has been studied in a general way in a previous chapter. Whatever economic, social and political factors contribute to its rise, the sect in its ideational aspect is an over-emphasis or exaggeration of some facet of the original ideational synthesis. Thus the Kharijite movement arose from an exaggeration of the fact that the Islamic community was a charismatic community. The Kharijites felt that the mass of ordinary Muslims who were prepared to tolerate what in the eyes of the Kharijites was sinful were endangering the status of the community as a charismatic one. Since for them their personal salvation depended on being members of a charismatic community, they were prepared to take the most extreme measures to preserve the charismatic character of the community. They excluded sinners from it, and were even ready to murder sinners or wage war against them. Such beliefs did not merely disrupt the political unity of the community; they also tended to upset the balance of the ideational synthesis, because not all Muslims were willing to emphasize the charismatic community to this extent. There were also those Muslims who became Shi'ites; for them salvation was to be attained not through being members of a charismatic community, but through following a charismatic leader. There may also have been neutrals, but it is not clear whether they were trying to hold a balance between the charismatic leader and the charismatic community, or were emphasizing some other facet of the ideational synthesis, or were believers in the charismatic community who did not want to take part in open rebellion against their sovereign. This neutral or moderate party was the forerunner of later Sunnite 'orthodoxy'; during the Umayyad period there was strictly speaking no such 'orthodoxy'.

The theological activity of the Muslim intellectuals, who in this respect are practically identical with the scholar-jurists (except in so far as some of the revolutionary leaders developed an ideational justification of their activities), consisted in the reformulation of religious doctrines to avoid the criticisms that were made of them, and to remedy defects which had appeared in practice. The matter is best considered by looking at some examples. These will be taken from that course of development in which the extreme Kharijite movement was moderated and then replaced by the Murji'ite movement. For present purposes Kharijite theology may be regarded as consisting of four stages.

The first or active revolutionary stage of the Kharijite movement was based on the principle that the grave sinner is excluded from the community. Since he is no longer a Muslim it follows that he may properly be killed (from the Kharijite point of view). In this way their revolutionary activity was justified. In practice, however, the revolutionary activity was far from being successful. It might appeal to some of those who liked the wild life of the desert, but as time went on an increasing number of those who believed in the charismatic community and the exclusion of the grave sinner from it felt that they had no vocation to a life in the revolutionaries' camp. They had therefore to find a justification on Kharijite principles for their decision to go on living among 'grave sinners' who were destined for Hell. Their first rather lame attempts to do so are the second stage of Kharijite theology. They are little more than a denial of the doctrines of the extremists. The moderates held that it was not obligatory for a good Muslim to make the *hijrah* or 'migration' to the camp of the true believers (that is, the Kharijites), but that it was permissible for him to go on living among 'the people of war' (men who were in Kharijite eyes grave sinners, and therefore non-Muslims, against whom a Muslim might properly fight). They also described themselves as living in 'the sphere of prudent fear', that is, in circumstances in which it was not obligatory for a man to make a public declaration of his beliefs. In other words, though they thought that the governor of Basrah might justly be killed, they accepted it as a principle not to make any attempt to kill him.

This second stage was not satisfactory either practically or theoretically. Practically, it must have been difficult to go on living among people whom one ought to regard as mortal enemies. One might do it for a time, looking forward to the day when one would be strong enough to attack openly; but it could hardly be contemplated as a permanent arrangement. On the theoretical side, too, it was difficult to accept as merely temporary something that one had no intention of altering. The second stage, therefore, passes into the third stage. Less harsh judgements are passed on non-Kharijite Muslims. One man says that they are not 'idolaters' but only 'infidels,' another that they are not 'infidels' but only 'hypocrites' and so in a sense monotheists. On the latter view it becomes possible for Kharijites to admit that they are living, not in 'the sphere of prudent fear' but in 'the sphere of monotheism'. From the last point it is an easy step to go on to have with these 'monotheists' some of the personal relationships that one has with proper Muslims (that is, with one's fellow-Kharijites), such as intermarriage. By the time matters have reached this point, however, many subdivisions of the Kharijite movement have appeared, and it is becoming farcical to maintain that only the members of one's own little subdivision are true Muslims

So the fourth stage of Kharijite theology is reached, the stage of 'suspending judgement'. Some Kharijites have begun to realize that it is ridiculous to expect agreement on every point of detail. They therefore assert that it is right to suspend judgement, first on one point, then on another, so that men of different views may continue to belong to the same community. There are other Kharijites, of course, who deny the legitimacy of suspending judgement on these matters. Yet the trend towards suspension of judgement gains momentum until the fundamental principle of the Kharijite movement is questioned—the principle that the grave sinner is excluded from the community. Those who suspend judgement on the grave sinner, however, are reckoned to be no longer Kharijites but Murji'ites. The modern student is justified, however, in regarding the Murji'ites as working out one aspect of the later Kharijite ideation, since the heresiographers find it difficult to draw a hard and fast line between them and actually speak of certain groups and individuals as 'Murji'ites of the Kharijites'.

Originally, it would seem, a Murji'ite was one who suspended judgement on the question whether particular individuals belonged to 'the people of Paradise' or 'the people of Hell'. Soon, however, they developed a positive conception of what it is to be a 'believer', and most of them also found a way round this disjunction between Paradise and Hell. The positive conception was that they defined a believer (*mu'min*) as one who has some knowledge of God, though they differed about the extent of the religious knowledge required and on the question whether it had to be accompanied by public confession of faith. They were agreed, however, that a man's actions were not a part of belief, though most held that belief included belief that God had made certain actions obligatory and had forbidden others. This meant that a man who committed adultery or omitted the ritual prayer had sinned but had not ceased to be a believer. All this shows that the Murji'ites were greatly concerned with the

Islamic community just as the Kharijites had been, though they were not so concerned that it should be a righteous community. In their own way, however, they must still have regarded it as a charismatic community. Moreover this charismatic community was not merely a handful of zealots but the totality of the followers of Muhammad. Consequently the Murji'ites held that they were living, not in the Kharijite 'sphere of prudent fear', but in 'the sphere of belief'. Despite the retention of sinners within the community, however, most of the Murji'ites held that membership of it led eventually to Paradise.[1]

When these changes in Kharijite and Murji'ite doctrine are looked at closely in their contexts, it is seen that several of them have come about because the actional complement of ideation was unsatisfactory. That is to say, men became dissatisfied with the actions dictated to them by their existing ideation. In accordance with what was discovered in chapter III about the relation between action and ideation, it is difficult, if not impossible, for them to change their course of action without also changing their ideation. The previous course of action may for some time have been irksome, but it is not abandoned until ideation leading to a new course of action has been worked out and adopted. An apparent exception is found in the change from the second to the third stage of Kharijite doctrine, that is, from holding that one's 'sphere' is 'the sphere of prudent fear' to holding that it is 'the sphere of monotheism'. The exception is perhaps only apparent, however. The course of action in the second stage was to live peaceably among non-Kharijites, but, since these were still regarded as 'the people of war', the course of action must have been thought of as a temporary expedient and not as a permanent policy. The course of action corresponding to the third stage was to live peaceably among non-Kharijites as a permanent policy. Now there is no difference externally between these two courses of action (so long as one has not begun to plan an armed rising), but only a difference of internal attitude. Therefore it is possible that some men found they had in fact adopted the inner attitude proper to the third stage while holding the ideation of the second stage; the next step was then to bring their ideation into line with the inner attitude they had adopted. This exception is thus more apparent than real. It seems to be an exception because we are dealing with a course of action which can be changed without any overt act. It could even be maintained that it was not correct to speak of men adopting a new inner attitude before they had changed their ideation,

[1] Al-Ash'ari, *Maqalat*, i.149: for the Murji'ah in general the chief sources are *Maqalat*, i. 132-154; al-Baghdadi, *Farq*, 190-8; ash-Shahrastani, *Milal* i. 222-234 (London, 1850, 103-108).

217

since until they changed the ideation the new attitude could be adopted only tentatively and not definitively.

In changes of this kind the function of the intellectual is to re-fashion the existing ideation so that it supports the new course of action, or rather so that it supports some attempt to try out a possible course of action which will be superior to the past one which has been unsatisfactory. It is usually the case that men are more convinced that the existing course of action is unsatisfactory than they are that any other course of action will be more satisfactory. There is something exploratory about their procedure, and they are likely to try out the course of action which requires the least change in ideation. The changes in Kharijite doctrine described above were on secondary points, and took place within a body which was agreed about the principle that grave sinners were excluded from the community and, beyond that, on the idea that salvation came through membership of the charismatic (and righteous) community. Thus the task of the intellectuals could be described either as the devising of new courses of action which could be squared with the fundamental Kharijite ideation or as the devising of a modified ideation whose practical consequences would be satisfactory.

The change from the Kharijite to the Murji'ite position was a more fundamental one, but even still it took place within a framework of agreement—agreement on the idea that salvation is through membership of the charismatic community. This idea is now applied in a different way, however, since it is the whole Islamic community which is the charismatic community and since it is a community which includes grave sinners and (according to most Murji'ites) hopes for their salvation. What makes a man a member of the community is knowledge of what God has revealed about himself and (usually) public confession of this faith. There is thus an emphasis on religious knowledge at the expense of conduct (reminiscent of some of the Hellenistic movements of earlier centuries). Apart from this change of emphasis the Murji'ite movement may be regarded as a continuation of the Kharijite movement. The Murji'ites make explicit the position at which the Kharijites had in fact arrived. The Kharijites started from the principle of excluding the grave sinner from the community, but then so modified the consequences of this principle that they had almost abandoned it in practice. Presumably they still held that only persons of Kharijite views (or of those of some sub-division of the Kharijites) would be saved; but what in fact divided them from the great mass of law-abiding non-Kharijite Muslims was not grave sins but theoretical beliefs; thus in a sense they were already regarding the true community as constituted by knowledge or belief.

The Integration of Intellectual Life

The Murji'ites thus safeguarded by their ideation the point of most concern to the Kharijites, namely, the charismatic nature of the community, and at the same time had a satisfactory active policy. The principle of the exclusion of grave sinners had shown itself unsatisfactory in practice, and the modifications of it had landed the Kharijites in unreasonable and even inconsistent views of what excluded a man from the community. To believers in salvation through the community it must have been more satisfying to be able to identify this 'saving' community with the Islamic community. It is not necessary to suppose that many Kharijites were converted to Murji'ite views. What probably happened in the heartlands was that younger generations all followed the Murji'ites, so that there was practically no one left to carry on the Kharijite tradition. (On the periphery Kharijite doctrines were retained by groups who wanted for some economic or social or other reason to be distinct from their neighbours)[1]. It is probable, however, that some of the persons with Kharijite sympathies who did not become Murji'ites found their way into the new sect of the Mu'tazilites.

About the transition from the Murji'ite view to the standard Sunnite (Ash'arite or Maturidite) view little need be said. There was practically no change. The views of the moderate Murji'ites are really an early and undeveloped form of what later became 'orthodoxy'. Despite the attempts of some later writers to hide the fact, Abu-Hanifah, the founder of one of the four recognized legal rites of the Sunnites, was reckoned a Murji'ite by his contemporaries and immediate successors. It is only some of the less moderate expressions of Murji'ite doctrine that are heretical, such as the assertion that 'grave sins do not harm the doer'. Gradually the main body of the Muslims accepted the view that no member of the community would be eternally in Hell, that is, that the community was a charismatic one, membership of which implied ultimate salvation[2]. In this way the whole theological development which we have been examining corrected the exaggeration of the early Kharijites, yet incorporated the essential point for which they were contending in the creed of the main body of the Sunnites. This made it possible for those who looked for salvation to a charismatic community to be satisfied with Sunnite doctrines, especially when along with this theological development there was the elaboration of the Shari'ah.

[1] C. S. Coon, *Caravan*, London, 1952, 121, says of some Kharijites in N. Africa, 'heterodoxy doubtless serves to help them preserve their special-people role'.

[2] Cf. p.187 above; al-Ash'ari has almost reached this position. R.J. McCarthy, *The Theology of al-Ash'ari*, Beirut, 1953, 244f. (§§27/29, 31/28, 32).

The excessive emphasis of the Shi'ites on the idea of the charismatic leader was not so easily corrected. Correction might have been easier had some of the actual Shi'ite leaders been successful; but all failed after a comparatively short time, and none had an inspiring personality. There were mutual criticisms by the Kharijites and the Shi'ites—the Kharijites said that the leader's decisions could not be taken as infallible, but must be judged by their conformity to the Qur'an, while the Shi'ites urged that one required an inspired leader in order to apply Qur'anic principles correctly. These criticisms, however, had little effect on the party criticized, since the two groups were poles apart from one another in outlook. Nevertheless from an early period we find that the main body of Islam was tending to build up Muhammad as a charismatic leader. Evidence for this is found in the stories of miraculous events connected with Muhammad's birth and childhood recorded by Ibn-Is'haq (d.768). The Swedish scholar Tor Andrae, after an extensive study of what the Islamic community in the course of the centuries came to believe about Muhammad, considered that the Sunnites took over from the Shi'ites the various features of the imam (or charismatic leader) in so far as these could be attached to Muhammad himself.[1] An example of this being consciously done is the assertion of al-Ghazali, as a rejoinder to the Isma'ilis, that the 'infallible imam' of the Sunnites is Muhammad.[2]

The difficulty experienced by the main body in incorporating persons of Shi'ite sympathies was increased by the fact that many separatist movements adopted Shi'ite views. Various factors might lead to a policy of separatism; about the details we are for the most part badly informed, and it is not necessary to go into the matter here. It was easy, however, for a group with a tendency to separatism, especially if they were men who looked for a charismatic leader, to find some descendant of 'Ali who would be their head, either actively or passively or *in absentia*. Perhaps the greatest set-back to Islamic unity was the decision of the Safavid Shah of Persia in the early sixteenth century to make that country officially Shi'ite. This gave the Shi'ites a political focus, thereby strengthening their consciousness of themselves as a distinct body, and at the same time cut most of them off geographically from contacts with Sunnites, since, except in 'Iraq, Shi'ites tended to move from the Ottoman empire to Persia and Sunnites from Persia to the Ottoman empire. Despite this set-back and the continuance of separatist tendencies there is hope

[1] *Die Person Muhammeds in Lehre und Glauben seiner Gemeinde*, Stockholm, 1917, 302.

[2] Cf. Montgomery Watt, *The Faith and Practice of al-Ghazali*, 46.

for the restoration of unity in that the Sunnites have found a place in their system for the conception of a charismatic leader. Though the charismatic leader and the charismatic community have appeared in Islamic history as opposing conceptions, ideally they support one another, since the fact that a community has a charismatic leader helps to make it charismatic.

In this section so far, what has been described is one kind of movement or trend towards unity. The intellectuals have kept reformulating some point of doctrine (that is, some part of the ideational system) until its objectionable practical consequences are removed. There is here a struggle for existence in the ideational sphere, in the course of which only the fittest survives, that is, the formulation of the doctrine which has the most satisfactory consequences in practice. The other formulations either fail to survive altogether or do so only as the beliefs of tiny minorities. This is not the only kind of trend towards unity, however. Another kind is to be seen in the development of the views of the scholar-jurists about the 'roots of law' (*usul al-fiqh*).

In this case the differences are not so much differences in practice as in the ideational basis of practice; and the end is not the survival of the fittest (though some embryonic legal schools die without reaching maturity) but an agreement to differ. At the beginning of the 'Abbasid period, as was noticed in the previous chapter, there were 'ancient schools' of law in such places as Kufah, Basrah, Medina and Damascus, and these schools were now under some external and internal pressure to achieve greater uniformity. They differed from one another in varying degrees in the details of their practice, and also in the ways in which they justified their practice. Mostly they were content to say that such-and-such was the 'living tradition' of their own school. This was completely changed, however, by the work of ash-Shafi'i (d.820). From now onwards the main points of practice were justified, not by referring to the views of distinguished past members of the particular school, but by quoting a Tradition of something Muhammad had said or done. This method of justification was adopted also by Shi'ites and Kharijites, as well as by the main body, who from this point on may be called Sunnites. There continued to be differences of detail between the four great Sunnite rites and also differences in the view of the exact relations of the 'roots of law', namely, Qur'an, Sunnah (the example of Muhammad), individual opinion (in questions of application) and consensus. Despite all this there was a wide range of agreement, and, above all, an agreement to differ in practice, while recognizing one another to some extent.

The difference between these two kinds of trend towards unity is perhaps more apparent than real. In the second kind the ideational system is more complex and its relation to practical activities less obvious. Yet the relation is undoubtedly there, and the ideational system and the practical activities are complementary, just as in the first kind.

Before leaving this topic it is worth asking why ideational developments, such as those described, lead to unity. It would seem that the elaboration of ideation might just as easily lead to disunity; indeed, numerous cases of this could be given. It must be admitted, then, that it is not the ideation in itself which leads to unity. That is, of course, in accordance with what we found at an earlier stage in this study about the relation between ideation and social change. Without giving a full answer to the question, we might here repeat on the bases of the points just examined the suggestion made above that the chief factor making for unity is the idea of the charismatic community. This idea was behind the Kharijite and Murji'ite movements, and also behind the movement among the scholar-jurists which led to the elaboration of the Shari'ah[1] and to the acceptance of the Sunnah of Muhammad (as contained in the Traditions) as one of the 'roots of law'. The presence of this idea helps to explain the curious fact that intellectuals, primarily intent on supporting the ideational position of their own small group, yet contributed to the growth of unity. The Kharijite theologians who modified the principle of the exclusion of the grave sinner from the community were justifying the actions of a small group; but at the same time they were keeping alive the idea of a charismatic community until the time came when the main body of Muslims would be prepared to recognize the whole community as a charismatic one. All this, of course, does not mean that the labours of these theologians had no function. It was essential that an ideational system should be elaborated, since otherwise the desire of many Muslims to be members of a charismatic community could not be given practical effect.

From this discussion it is also possible to see something of the function of dogma in the life of a society. By 'dogma' here is to be understood the precise formulation of certain points in the ideational synthesis. A creed contains the formulation of a number of such points. No Islamic creed has had such wide recognition as the Apostles' and Nicene creeds of Christianity. Islamic creeds are usually the expression of the views of an individual or a school.

[1] It is to be noted that the creed is regarded as part of the Shari'ah; cf. Ibn-Abi-Zayd al-Qayrawani, *Risalah*.

Nevertheless there are a number of points on which Sunnites may be said to be agreed, and these are here spoken of as Sunnite dogmas. Their function, in a word, is to preserve some balance in the ideational synthesis on which Islamic society is based. In a large heterogeneous society, such as the Islamic one had become, there is a tendency for some groups to emphasize certain aspects of the original ideation, and for other groups to emphasize other aspects, and for the two to regard one another as 'beyond the pale'. Dogmatic formulations are a method of stating one point with sufficient definiteness to satisfy those who are interested in it but without offending those who lay emphasis on some other point. A dogma sets limits which must not be overstepped by one side or the other. In so far as a set of dogmas is accepted, it preserves the balance and comprehensiveness of an ideational system (such as the Qur'anic one) and thereby contributes to the integration of the society based on this ideational system.

Dogma has a negative side, of course, as well as a positive one. It excludes from the society, or at least from full participation in the life of the society, those who do not accept it. This is especially the case when the religious institution, which produces the dogmatic formulations, is in alliance with a political or ruling institution. The formulations may be so constructed as to exclude the opponents of those who produce them; or they may become distasteful to many people because they are associated with political pressure. This brings us back to a previous line of thought. The process of formulating dogmas does not of itself lead to unity, and may easily lead to disunity. For it to have its fullest integrative effect there must be something behind it urging men to unity.

(b) *The method of the isnad*

By way of illustration of some of the points just made it is useful to look more fully at the criteria used by Muslim scholars to determine whether a Tradition was genuine or not. In particular we must look at the way in which Muslim scholars used the *isnad* or 'chain of authorities' which was included in each Tradition. The following example of a Tradition will show how it is constructed:[1]

Abu-Musa Muhammad ibn-al-Muthanna said, Abu-'Amir 'Abd-al-Malik ibn-'Amr told us, saying, Al-Mughirah (that is, Ibn-'Abd-ar-Rahman) told us from Abu-'z-Zinad, from Musa-bn-Abi-'Uthman, from his father, from Abu-Hurayrah (may God be pleased with him), from the Prophet (God bless and preserve him), that he said, God created Adam in His image, and his height was sixty cubits.

[1] Ibn-Khuzaymah, *K. at-Taw'hid*, Cairo (1935)/1354, 28f.

According to the Islamic science of Tradition this Tradition consists of a body (*matn*), namely, the saying of Muhammad, and the chain of authorities (*isnad*). The names in the latter are those of real persons, and there are various biographical dictionaries from which something can be discovered about them. The important points are the date of death, whether they are considered reliable transmitters, and where they mostly lived. The dates are necessary to show that it was possible for each man to have heard the Tradition from his predecessor; in this case there are seven intermediaries between the Prophet and the author Ibn-Khuzaymah (who died in 923).

The Muslim Traditionists, in deciding whether a Tradition was authentic laid most emphasis on the *isnad*, and for the most part did not consider the body of the Tradition.[1] Western scholars have often criticized the use of this criterion on the ground that, while it excluded many false Traditions, it enabled many other false Traditions to be regarded as genuine. Much has been said about the imperfections of this criterion of authenticity. It would seem to be more profitable, however, to consider its function in Islamic society positively and to ask what it in fact accomplished.

The first point to notice is that a criterion of this sort is more natural in a cultural tradition based on oral material than in one based on written material. We might argue from this that, when the criterion was brought into use, the Arab element was still predominant in Islamic culture; and there is much evidence to support this view. It is normally supposed in the Traditions that each transmitter has *heard* the story from the previous one—there is no point in the chain of authorities otherwise. There are also records which show that for a time there was considerable opposition to the writing down of Traditions; but by 800 books of Traditions existed, and by 900 most of the standard collections had been made.

Keeping in mind, then, that we are dealing with a chiefly oral culture, let us try to imagine the situation in the early years of the 'Abbasid dynasty. In Basrah, Kufah, Damascus, Medina and some other centres there were the 'ancient schools' of law. These had their 'living tradition' of what constituted the proper conduct for Muslims, and they seem to have claimed that this was 'the *sunnah* of the Prophet'. They did not, however, support this claim by adducing Traditions with chains of authorities going back to Muhammad. The first to do so was ash-Shafi'i (d.820). In such a situation, when many scholars were content with statements that a certain doctrine had been held by one of the earlier leaders of their school, the point

[1] Cf. al-Hakim an-Naysaburi, *Al-Madkhal*, ed. and tr. by James Robson, London, 1953 ("An Introduction to the Science of Tradition.").

of insisting on chains of authorities was not to distinguish true Traditions from false Traditions, but to distinguish doctrines which went back to Muhammad himself (and thus could be regarded as of divine inspiration) from doctrines which had been invented by Muslims at some later date. Doctrines based on Traditions going back to Muhammad may then properly be called Shari'ah or 'revelation'. Thus the introduction of chains of authorities going back without a break to Muhammad is due in the first place to the interest in the charismatic community.

About the same time or shortly afterwards persons outside the 'ancient schools' seem to have begun to invent Traditions. It is hardly too much to say that all the wisdom of the Middle East became incorporated in Traditions, ancient Arab wisdom, sentences from the Old and New Testaments, Neoplatonic and Gnostic doctrines, and maxims from Persia and India[1]. The Tradition quoted above is doubtless based on the Old Testament[2], and on secondary Judaeo-Christian tradition. Much of this material was clearly inconsistent with Islam, and must have worried the leaders of the main body of moderate Muslims, but those who believed in one or other part of it saw that by passing it off as coming from Muhammad they justified their own belief in it. Such procedure, of course, presupposes that some more genuine Muslim doctrines were already being justified by Traditions going back to Muhammad. At least, it is more likely that the practice was begun by the moderates and continued by the eccentrics than that the moderates borrowed it from the eccentrics.

It is difficult for modern Westerners to realize how difficult it was for the nascent Islamic culture, working with different categories from ours, and based on oral materials, to deal with a situation like this. It was impossible to argue that 'Muhammad could not possibly have said that, since it contradicts what he said on such-and-such an other occasion'; the Arabs had no sufficiently clear perception of logical contradiction, or belief that people could not violently contradict themselves, for any such argument to be effective. Nor does it usually seem to have been feasible to deny a story outright on any grounds whatsoever. In an oral culture, once a story has been passed round, it is remembered if it is a good one, whether it is true or not; and attempts to deny it are regarded as due to ulterior motives. An alternative that was favoured was to reinterpret the

[1] Cf. Goldziher, *Muhammedanische Studien*, ii. 158, 392-400; id. 'Neu-platonische und gnostische Elemente im Hadit', *Zeitschrift fur Assyriologie*, xxii. 317-44.

[1] *Gen.* i. 27; etc.

saying of Muhammad in one way or another. The following example will show the ingenuity that could be brought to bear on this work of re-interpretation

The main part of the Tradition quoted above, 'God created Adam in His image', was objectionable to the central strand in Islamic theology, because it was held that God was entirely different from man and transcended everything human. Expedients had therefore to be devised to avoid the obvious interpretation in the Old Testament sense. The simplest method was to assert that it meant that God created Adam in his (that is, Adam's) image. This could be given more point by saying that God created Adam in Paradise with the form he was to have on earth. Another method was to say that in the phrase 'His image' the pronoun referred to God, but meant an image or model which was in His possession. A third expedient was to provide the saying with a context in which a man was beaten or cursed; Muhammad was then made to say, 'Do not beat (or curse) his face, for God created Adam in his image', that is, in the image of the man in question; the saying was thus given the harmless meaning that all human beings bore the image of Adam. Other theologians, again, preferred to take the Traditions which had a slightly different form of the saying, 'Adam was created in the image of the Merciful', and then to say either that the Merciful was not God, or else that 'the image of the Merciful' meant 'a manifestation of His mercy, as an object of it'.[1]

This was the world in which the Muslim scholars of the centre had to work—a world in which almost anything was possible. These scholars themselves were not entirely guiltless of some invention, especially in the construction of chains of authorities for the legal doctrines of their schools. They probably argued in some such fashion as this: 'Our school holds doctrine D, and believes that it is the true *sunnah* of the Prophet; so all the earliest members of our schools must also have held it; and (where the earliest of them was not himself a Companion of Muhammad) our founder must have got it from such-and-such a Companion with whom he was known to be friendly'. On the basis of this argument an *isnad* is constructed which goes back to Muhammad without a break. Some awareness of this state of affairs is shown in the well-known saying ascribed to a man who died in 827 to the effect that 'in nothing have we seen good men more given to lies than in Tradition'[2]. The really pressing problem, however, was the invention of Traditions by those who

[1] Ibn Qutaybah, *Ta'wil Mukhtalif al-Hadith*, Cairo (1908)/1326, 275-80. For other versions of these Traditions, see A. J. Wensinck, *Handbook* s.v. Adam.

[2] Cf. A. Guillaume, *The Traditions of Islam*, Oxford, 1924, 78.

may be called the eccentrics. What was to be done about them?

What the central body of Muslims in fact did was to develop a new science of Tradition, of which an important principle was that, if a Tradition was to be accepted as sound, all the transmitters of it must be known as sound and reliable men. In most cases one found substantially the same Tradition with different lines of transmission; and this increased its chance of acceptance where all the transmitters were reliable or at least admissible. For a long time there was hesitation in accepting singleton Traditions which came by only one line; but eventually these were mostly accepted when the transmitters were reliable. Moreover, there seems to have been something like a 'gentleman's agreement' to regard as reliable all the scholars connected with the 'ancient schools' (except a few who were known to have been inclined to some heresy or other, or who were not altogether scrupulous in their methods). There were latterly great compilations of biographical notices, which included among other things reports of views about the man's reliability. The result of all this was the exclusion, at least from the consideration of the central body of scholars, of the Traditions fathered by eccentrics, which were usually not in accordance with the Islamic outlook. At the same time the position round about the year 800 was stabilized. The contemporary practice was projected back into the lifetime of Muhammad, and thus became a norm for Muslims of all succeeding generations.

To sum up this discussion, we might say that the function of the method of the *isnad* or chain of authorities consisted primarily of two things: firstly, it gave the main body of moderate Muslims a justification for holding that the Shari'ah which they were following had a charismatic origin in the words and acts of Muhammad himself; and secondly, it made it possible for this main body to attain a large measure of agreement among themselves, while excluding the more eccentric opinions which might have endangered the stability and unity of the community. These functions, too, be it noted, will be adequately performed without a strict application of the criteria to views current within the main body. This helps one to understand how ash-Shafi'i could take an apparently lax view towards questions of authenticity:

We are not much embarrassed by the fact that well-authenticated Traditions disagree or are thought to disagree, and the specialists on Traditions are not embarrassed by Traditions that are likely to be erroneous and the like of which are not well authenticated.

[1] Schacht, *Origins*, 37.
[2] *K. at-Taw'hid*. 28.

Once the method of the *isnad* had been generally accepted, it could be used for purposes other than its primary ones. It could be used to discredit Traditions held by other groups within the main body of moderates. Thus Ibn-Khuzaymah (d.923) uses weaknesses in the *isnad* to strengthen his case against the form of the Tradition discussed above in which the phrase 'in the image of the Merciful' occurred[1]. On the whole, however, there was no thoroughgoing rejection of Traditions which were not supported by a proper chain of authorities, in so far as those were current in the main body. The primary functions of the method of the *isnad* were those mentioned above.

3. INTEGRATION WITH NON-ISLAMIC THOUGHT

The world conquered by the Muslims in the first rush of their expansion was one where there was already a highly developed intellectual tradition. It was by no means a homogeneous tradition, but an intermingling of several different traditions that had originally been separate. The chief common factor was probably the Greek philosophical and scientific tradition; but this had several branches, and some of these had been combined with Judaism and various forms of Christianity not to mention gnosticism and Manichaeanism. In 'Iraq, too, there were the Zoroastrian and Persian traditions, though in Egypt there is little trace of the old Pharaonic tradition.

The Arabs who found themselves rulers of this cultured world came to it with only a naive world-view. They were careful observers of the phenomena of nature, but they had no cosmological ideas apart from the conception of 'time' as the determinant of events and a belief in various supernatural powers, mostly of a magical character and of limited range. In the recent past there had been some infiltration of this naive world-view by Judaeo-Christian ideas. The infiltration had doubtless been going on slowly for a long period, but it had been intensified by the Qur'anic preaching. The conception of a supreme God had been introduced and had partly replaced that of 'time' as the determinant of events; and the scanty Arab historical tradition had been enlarged by some of the vistas of the Old Testament. Apart from this, however, the outlook of the Muslim Arabs was still naive. When men who had been brought up in the higher intellectual cultures became Muslims, there was an inevitable tension between their general world-view and the ideational system which was the basis of the Islamic religion. It was therefore not sufficient for the Muslim intellectuals to effect greater harmony and balance within the peculiarly Islamic ideation; they had also to bring about some integration of this ideation with the older intellectual tradition of the heartlands of the caliphate.

This is a subject on which much could be written, and doubtless will be written. At first sight it does not seem relevant to the present study; but the brief consideration to be devoted to it here will show that it provides insight into some of the basic attitudes of the Islamic world.

(a) The earlier historical traditions

The historical tradition which in respect of its content had most influence on the Islamic outlook was the Biblical or Judaeo-Christian tradition. Something of this tradition was incorporated in the Qur'an, and because of this the tradition was bound to be of great interest to Muslims. One of the chief historical ideas of the Qur'an is that of Muhammad as the latest or last of a series of prophets. The series of prophets—including Adam, Noah, Abraham, Lot, Jacob, Joseph and one or two Arab non-Biblical prophets—strikes the modern Western Christian as odd, but some such list of prophets may have been in circulation in Arabia before the revelation of the Qur'an[1]. Contacts with the Jews at Medina probably showed the Muslims how Judaeo-Christian material could be used to fill in the background of the Qur'anic references, which were often allusive and required to be supplemented. At the same time some of the Muslim leaders must have come to realize the dangers for Islam that lurked in that material. Out of this developed what may be called the bipolar attitude of Islam to the Judaeo-Christian tradition (some aspects of which will be considered in the next chapter); on the one hand the Muslims were eager to learn from that tradition about the persons mentioned in the Qur'an, and accepted much narrative material, but on the other hand they restricted direct access to the tradition as far as possible.

As Muslim scholarship developed, the historians proved themselves readiest to accept Judaeo-Christian material. By means of it the Qur'anic hints about the early history of mankind were worked up into a coherent story. This story may then be said to have become an essential part of the Islamic historical tradition. Variant forms of it are to be seen in the *Annals* of at-Tabari (d.923), the *Golden Meadows* of al-Mas'udi (d.957) and the *Complete History* of Ibn-al-Athir (d.1234). It begins with the creation of the world and of Adam, then follows the story of his descendants through Noah to Abraham roughly as it is in *Genesis*. At this point there are introduced the

[1] Cf. J. W. Sweetman, *Islam and Christian Theology*, 1/2, London, 1947, 128.

stories linking up Abraham and Ishmael with Mecca, in accordance with the allusions in the Qur'an. Then the Old Testament story is continued with a considerable emphasis on Joseph. There is a fairly full treatment of Moses, and briefer accounts of Joshua, Balaam, Samuel, David and Solomon, except that the latter's relations with Bilqis (the Islamic name for the Queen of Sheba) are fully reported. After that the outline is sketchier. There is a little about the fall of Jerusalem, Daniel, the return from exile and Ezra. From that point to the birth of John the Baptist the stage is occupied mainly by Alexander the Great. There is more of the Gospel story than in the Qur'an, but little about the teaching. Some facts about the extension of Christianity are intermingled with the account of the Roman empire.

The first noteworthy feature of this part of the Islamic historical tradition is that it is firmly controlled by the Qur'an. There is a large amount of factual material not found in the Qur'an, but this additional material does not alter the broad picture given by the Qur'an. Indeed, the material has been selected to give further information about persons mentioned in the Qur'an and to fill in something of their background. Whatever is neglected in the Qur'an (like the writing prophets of Israel) tends to be neglected in historical writing. Needless to say, what is contrary to Qur'anic teaching (like the New Testament account of the crucifixion) is omitted. Some of this selection of material may be due to pre-Islamic Jewish and Christian tradition, since for Muslim scholars access would be easiest to those materials which were prominent in the living tradition of the two older religions. On the other hand, a few Muslim scholars undoubtedly had access to the text of the Bible in a language they could understand, and could have taken over other sections of the Biblical tradition had they so desired. We must therefore assume that they were not interested (at least those of them who created and maintained the central historical tradition), and that the taking over of the Judaeo-Christian historical tradition was effectively controlled by the Qur'an.

A second noteworthy feature is the way in which the older historical tradition provides the framework for the whole of the early period. Material from the Persian tradition is introduced by at-Tabari at approximately the correct point chronologically, except in so far as he brings together a number of related events. Thus, the story of Adam and Eve is followed by Persian traditions about the early development of mankind. Again, events and people of interest to Muslims are linked with the Biblical tradition. Not merely are the genealogies of the Arab tribes joined to those of *Genesis*, but the

Berbers, for example, are said to be descended from the followers of Goliath[1].

A third feature is the comparative lack of interest in everything outside the confines of the Islamic world. This is particularly obvious in a later writer like Ibn-al-Athir. In his introduction he says that he wants to give the main outlines of universal history and to avoid the chronicling of insignificant events like the dismissal of a market official by some *dhimmi* (protected non-Muslim)[2]. But his judgement of what is significant will amaze the modern Western reader, for the story of Joseph, for example, is given more space than the whole history of the Roman empire. Most of the latter is no more than a list of the emperors with the length of their reigns and some correspondences with the Muslim caliphs—matters which are useful for the establishing of chronology. It is remarkable that the great adversary against whom the caliphate had been struggling since its very beginning should receive so little attention from a historian. One would have thought that he would have made a little more of it, if only to set off the achievements of the Muslims against it.

The treatment of the Roman empire is in marked contrast to the treatment of the Persian. On a rough estimate the latter has eight times as much space allotted to it. This cannot be simply due to the fact that these were the respective amounts of material which Ibn-al-Athir found in his sources; for he could presumably have found out much more about the Roman empire had he desired to do so. He must have felt that there was no point in writing more fully about the Roman empire. The Persian empire, on the other hand, had ruled over lands which were now part of the caliphate, and over peoples who were mostly now Muslims; and its history was therefore in a sense part of the past history of the caliphate. Moreover the traditions of the Persian ruling institution had been taken over in part by the 'Abbasids. It is related, for example, that when the caliph ar-Radi (934-40) was in a mood of despondency because of his weakness, his tutor reminded him of similar situations in the lives of the previous caliphs and *of the Persian kings*.[3] More than half of the examples, too, given by the Seljuq vizier Nizam-al-Mulk in his book of advice for rulers (written about 1090), are from Persian history. In this way an element of the former Persian culture had become incorporated in the life of the caliphate. There was nothing com-

---

[1] Al-Mas'udi, *Muruj-adh-Dhahab*, i. 105; cf. Ibn-al-Athir, *Kamil*, i. 115. Perhaps this is a confused awareness of the relation between the Philistines and the Carthaginians.

[2] *Kamil*, i. 4.

[3] Al-Mas'udi, *Muruj-adh-Dhahab*, viii. 341.

parable from Byzantine culture. At the very least it was necessary for an educated man to know something about these Persian kings, and they had therefore to be adequately treated in a universal history.

To sum up the attitude of the central Muslim historical tradition to non-Islamic history, we may say that the Muslims were interested in non-Muslim history only in so far as it made a positive contribution to an understanding of the Islamic world. They were not even interested in countries that had made a negative contribution by presenting a challenge—Hindu India, for example[1]. A man like Ibn-al-Athir seems to have regarded the Islamic world as occupying the centre of the stage of world history, and most other parts of the world as being in the darkness off-stage. Consciously or unconsciously, this idea governed the historical tradition he represented, and determined the extent to which non-Muslim history was integrated into it. Something similar, of course, is true of all cultures. Despite the great efforts of Westerners during the last two centuries to study the peoples of Asia and the rest of the world, the main historical tradition in the West is still confined to Europe, largely Western Europe, and its peoples.[2]

(b) The Greek philosophical tradition

An external intellectual influence on Islam perhaps even more important than the Judaeo-Christian historical tradition was that of Greek philosophy. In one form or another the Greek tradition was the basis of the thought of Egypt, Syria and 'Iraq, though, except where Greek philosophy itself became a religion, it was usually combined with some form of religious belief, mostly some variety of Christian doctrine. In Egypt, to judge from the comparative absence of intellectual life there in the early Islamic period, many of the bearers of the Greek tradition must have been Greek (or at least non-Egyptian) by race and must have left at the Arab conquest; the Copts were probably not very interested in philosophy, and few can have become Muslims. In Syria the case of Saint John of Damascus shows that Christian bearers of the Greek tradition remained, but again there were probably few conversions to Islam. 'Iraq was

[1] Its history had been studied, notably by Al-Biruni (d. 1048); but his studies were not incorporated in the 'universal histories'.

[2] The Western study of non-Westerners is not necessarily a mark of superiority. It is more likely that it rises from the general Western belief that knowledge of things confers powers over them—a belief that, in the social sphere, at least, is open to question.

where the Islamic tradition really came to grips with the Greek tradition, and three reasons may be given for this. The bearers of the Greek tradition here were Nestorian and Monophysite Christians, who did not flee; they still continued to have close relations with various other sections of the population; probably a larger proportion became Muslim than in Syria or Egypt.

Traces of the intellectual ferment produced by the mingling of traditions can be found in Basrah before 700. The real contact with Greek philosophy began later, however. A prominent part was played by the caliph al-Ma'mun (813-33) who arranged for the translation into Arabic of a number of Greek philosophical classics. It was about this time, and indeed with encouragement from al-Ma'mun, that the Mu'tazilites came to importance as a school of speculative or philosophical theologians[1]. They would find that some knowledge of Greek philosophy was essential in order to be able to deal with objections to Islamic doctrine raised by members of other faiths. In their pioneering attempts they were sometimes wild, and they were led to adopt doctrinal positions which were unacceptable to the main body of Muslims. Yet some integration of Islamic doctrine with Greek philosophy was essential if Islam was to maintain its place in the empire it had created. We therefore find some opponents of the Mu'tazilites trying to modify their doctrinal positions without abandoning the philosophical basis. One man (though not the only one) who was adjudged successful in this was al-Ash'ari (d.935). He began life as a Mu'tazilite, but about the age of forty left them for 'the people of the *sunnah*'. One of the main schools of later 'orthodox' theologians regards him as its founder. From his time onwards a large section of Muslim theologians base their theology on cosmological ideas derived from Greek philosophy. This may be called the first wave of Greek influence.

It was followed, however, by a second wave. Once the taste for Greek thought had been acquired, the Muslims were eager to drink ever deeper. With many it became a substitute for religion, which was not surprising since Neoplatonism and Neopythagoreanism had become religions. This meant, however, that for the second time Islamic doctrine was being threatened. The man who stepped into the breach this time was al-Ghazali (d.1111). He had the standard juristic and theological education, but at one stage in his career, largely by private study, mastered the teaching of the leading

---

[1] The Mu'tazilite school may have taken its politico-religious orientation from Wasil ibn-'Ata (d. 748) and 'Amr ibn-'Ubayd (d. 762); but the combination of theology with philosophical speculation was due to Bishr ibn-al-Mu'tamir (d. 825), Abu-'l-Hudhayl (d. 841 or 850) and an-Nazzam (d. 846).

(Neoplatonic) school of Islamic philosophy, and thereafter wrote *The Inconsistency of the Philosophers* to show that their views, as well as being contrary to Islamic dogma in certain respects, were internally inconsistent. This effectively checked the philosophical movement in the Islamic world (except in Spain), but at the same time the philosophical basis of Islamic theology was extended far beyond the meagre cosmological ideas of the earlier Ash'arites.

In the long process of assimilation here briefly summarized certain familiar features will be discerned. The original interest in Greek philosophy arises from the fact that theological discussions to which it was relevant were already taking place; indeed it was almost certainly introduced into such discussions by the opponents of the Muslims. Moreover, it went on being relevant to theology, and therefore continued to be nourished by the same sources as theological activity. It should also be noticed that there was a definite selection of what was of interest. Although the chief bearers of the Greek tradition and several of those who taught philosophy to Muslims were Christians, Greek philosophy was carefully abstracted from Christian doctrine before it was taken over by Muslims. Thus the incorporation of Greek philosophy into Islam is governed by the three laws of cultural interrelations mentioned in the last chapter.

The Greek philosophical tradition included the sciences as well as philosophy in the strict sense, and with them something similar happened. In the case of some of the sciences—medicine, for example —there was no doubt an antecedent interest. To others the Muslims may have been attracted because they were part of the Greek philosophical tradition in which they had found so much of value; that there was a general enthusiasm for things Greek is shown by the translation of Aristotle's *Poetics* into Arabic, since the complete absence of drama in Arabic literature must have made it incomprehensible. The Muslims not merely mastered Greek science, and eventually handed it on to Europe through Spain, but added to it in the process[1]. The Muslim world as a whole, however, apart from a few enthusiasts, did not take readily to Greek science. There was a long struggle before the 'foreign sciences' were admitted to be worthy subjects of study alongside the 'Qur'anic sciences' (such as exegesis of the Qur'an, Arabic grammar and philology, Tradition, the critique

---

[1] For details see Sir Thomas Arnold and A. Guillaume (edd.), *The Legacy of Islam*, Oxford, 1931, 311-55 ('Science and Medicine' by M. Meyerhof); G. Sarton, *Introduction to the History of Science*, Baltimore, 1927-9; id. 'Islamic Science' in T. Cuyler Young (ed.), *Near Eastern Culture and Society*, Princeton, 1951, 83-98.

of Traditionists, and various other subordinate studies connected with Islamic law). One way of quieting the suspicions of pious Muslims was to show, as al-Ghazali does in the section of his *Deliverance from Error* dealing with the philosophers, that particular sciences like mathematics, logic, and most of physics were theologically neutral and did not necessarily involve any heretical beliefs[1]. This cleared the way for the acceptance of most of the 'foreign sciences' by the main body of Islam, but at the same time greatly reduced interest in them. Apart from the few nominal Muslims for whom philosophy took the place of religion, the chief reason for cultivating philosophy was as a propaedeutic to theology; when it was shown that they were irrelevant to theology, there was no longer any reason for making them part of normal higher education in the Islamic world. Several of them continued to be studied, but at a lower level—medicine, for instance, because there was widespread demand for treatment. For the most part, however, they ceased to be a concern of the leading Muslim intellectuals[2].

There is one more point to be made. The Muslims had assimilated whatever of the Greek philosophical tradition could contribute to their theological activity. As time went on, however, it began to seem as if Greece had once again taken its conqueror captive. Muslim theologians became much more interested in philosophy than in theology; for example, the commentary of al-Jurjani (d.1413) on a theological work by al-Iji (d.1355) gives about three-quarters of its bulk to philosophical preliminaries and only a quarter to theology proper. Respected theologians even took over views previously held by the heretical philosophers[3]. The great dogmas of Islam, over which there had been violent discussions in earlier times, were still maintained, but the general outlook of the intellectuals was an intellectualism which the modern Western student finds barren. The leaders of Islamic thought had been wonderfully successful in integrating the Islamic and the Greek traditions; but this integration had taken place at the intellectual level, and, when one looks at the relations between the intellectuals and the masses, it seems to be rather a failure to integrate.

[1] Cf. Watt, *The Faith and Practice of al-Ghazali*, 32-43.

[2] Cf. H. A. R. Gibb and H. Bowen, *Islamic Society and the West*, i/2, London, 1957, 147; also J. Pedersen, art. 'Madrasa' in *E.I.(S)*. Gibb and Bowen make the neglect of the 'rational' sciences in the Ottoman empire begin about 1550, but are doubtful whether they were part of the normal curriculum even before that.

[3] L. Gardet and M.-M. Anawati, *Introduction à la Théologie Musulmane*, Paris, 1948, 75-78.

The Integration of Intellectual Life

There was a certain awareness among Muslims of this cleavage between the intellectuals and the masses. There was a strand of Islamic thought which would have nothing to do with philosophy. Its great representative was Ibn-Taymiyyah (d.1328). It was never an important strand, but it is still alive, having taken on a new life in the Wahhabite movement, which began in Arabia in the middle of the eighteenth century and is the official form of Islam in the Su'udite kingdom (Su'udi Arabia). The philosophers of Muslim Spain in the twelfth century were also aware of the cleavage and tried to argue that the beliefs of the philosophers and the beliefs of the masses amounted to the same thing, and that there were reasons why only naive anthropomorphic ideas were satisfactory for the masses. Such theories did not remove the cleavage, however, and in any case these Spanish philosophers had little influence on the heartlands of Islam.

This question of the relation between the intellectuals and the masses is a very important one, but it concerns more than the attitude to secular thought, and must be deferred for further consideration till the next section.

(c) The encounter with Western thought

In the Ottoman empire, which included the Arabic-speaking countries, the impact of Europe and the West may be said to have been first felt about 1800, after the invasion of Egypt by Napoleon in 1798. The Muslim intellectuals (more particularly, those of the religious institution) were not adequately prepared to meet the challenges which now came to them. They had turned in on themselves. Their historical tradition had little interest in what lay outside the Islamic world, and their main educational tradition little interest in anything outside the Qur'anic sciences and their ancillary disciplines. Science and technology were looked on with disfavour and even hostility. The Muslim intellectuals were therefore not at all interested in European learning. The ruling institutions, on the other hand, in places like Cairo, Constantinople and Teheran, were very interested in European technology and those branches of European learning subservient to it, for they realized that European technology (along with other features of European society) gave the Europeans military superiority. In their endeavour to increase their military power the ruling institutions gradually took over or adapted various features of Western culture and civilization.

In course of time they realized that they must have a completely Western educational system, and this has been—or is in process of being—established in all the Islamic countries. Western education was not grafted on to the traditional Islamic education, however, but a completely separate series of educational institutions was set up. In most countries, therefore, there are now two separate educational systems. Moreover, these produce two separate types of intellectuals —intellectuals of the traditional Islamic type, still thinking in the traditional Islamic categories, and intellectuals whose education has been Western, and whose thinking is based on ideas current in the West. In the West there are countries where there is little contact between Christian intellectuals and non-Christian intellectuals, but the separation is nowhere so absolute as in the Islamic world, for the two groups have practically no common ground.

Although these intellectuals with a Western education like to think of themselves as completely Western, their selection of the aspects of Western culture to be adopted has been partly controlled by their Islamic background. In particular they have avoided whatever was repugnant to basic Islamic attitudes. Consequently they have adopted the secular and irreligious sides of Western thought, and have neglected what Westerners had to say in defence of religion against secularism and materialism, because such defence of religion has been connected with Christianity, and Islam (as will be seen in the next chapter) has a very deep-rooted suspicion of Christianity.

The present situation shows the extremely high price that has been paid by the traditional scholar-jurists for intellectual integration. Part of the price has been retirement into isolation from the rest of the world, with the result that, when the rest of the world thrust itself upon Islam, the Muslims were badly placed to meet the challenge. In the various attempts to do so the intellectual leadership has passed from the group of traditional intellectuals to a new group. The two groups now exist side by side, and it is not clear what their ultimate relationship will be. Another part of the price was the estrangement of the traditional intellectuals from the mass of the people. In the stress of recent social and political changes the masses are perhaps tending to be more religious and to look towards the Muslim intellectuals rather more than in the past ; but these intellectuals have not yet regained the position they once had as giving expression to the feelings of the people. On the other hand, the Western-educated intellectuals have so far no close contact with the masses and can move them to action only at the demagogic level. The outlook for the future is not bright; yet one cannot say that the difficulties are too great to be overcome. What can be asserted is that in the intellectual sphere apparent success in integration has been tempered by a measure of actual failure.

4. THE INTELLECTUALS, THE RULERS AND THE MASSES

At the opening of this chapter it was noted that one of the functions of the intellectuals was to adapt the ideation of a society to changing circumstances. If such adaptation is to be wholly satisfactory, it must be acceptable to the other sections of the society. A consideration of how the intellectuals adapted Islamic ideation to the various changes that occurred in the course of the centuries will therefore in part be concerned with the relations of the intellectuals to the ruling institutions and to the mass of ordinary Muslims.

(a) The formative period

When a movement of the human spirit produces a cataclysmic change, the ideational complement of action is provided by a seer or prophet through what may be called 'charismatic insight'. Such a seer and his immediate followers are not intellectuals, as the word is commonly used; but in course of time the intellectual aspects of the ideation of this new movement may become the object of special study, and in this study a small group of men may gain an expertise which is not shared by the rest of the community. They are then the intellectuals of the community, with special knowledge of the ideation on which the community is based, and with a special obligation to give the rest of the community guidance with respect to the ideation on which it is based. This was what happened in Islam. In the second half of the first century of its existence groups of pious Muslims began to discuss religious questions of interest to them. Sometimes these discussions took a theoretical turn, and eventually there were formed groups of men in the leading cities of the caliphate who had special knowledge of various theoretical matters involved in the Islamic religion. Particularly notable were the groups in Medina and Basrah. That in Medina has been called the 'pious opposition' and was chiefly concerned with practical matters, that is, rules of conduct. At Basrah the presence of supporters of the Kharijite movement caused theological questions also to be included in the scope of the discussions.

The motive drawing these men into intellectual discussions seems to have been chiefly a desire to maintain the charismatic character of the Islamic community. This led to a consideration of the Shari'ah, or the forms of conduct appropriate to members of a divinely-grounded community. This covers the discussion of legal questions at the various centres. Another aspect of this concern for the charismatic character of the community led to the formulation of Kharijite doctrine; and it is mainly out of the discussions between the Kharijites and the 'moderates' that later Islamic theology has grown. The need to defend Islam against intellectual attacks would also be present, but it probably did not become insistent till the 'Abbasid period when many non-Arab intellectuals had become Muslims. It must be remembered, however, that the leading intellectual and ascetic of Basrah[1] during the Umayyad period, al-Hasan al-Basri (d.728) was the son of an inhabitant of 'Iraq.

In this formative stage these Muslim intellectuals were only beginning to emerge from the mass of believers, and were as yet hardly distinguished from the mass in any important way. Their formulations were essentially an expression of the inarticulate thought of the ordinary Muslim, for they were subject to the same social pressures as he was. Indeed they may be adjudged remarkably successful in performing the function of an intellectual class. They adapted the Qur'anic ideation to the new needs of the times. Nomads from the desert had become the militia of a vast empire, which was in fact a military aristocracy; merchants and agriculturalists from Arabia, accustomed to living on the fringe of a nomadic culture, found themselves the administrators of this empire. It was all very different from the little city-state of Medina where much of the Qur'an had been revealed. That Islam was able to continue to appeal to Arabs and also to become a religion for non-Arabs was largely due to the discussions of these little groups of men in the various great cities.

(b) The intellectuals under the early 'Abbasids

Many of the small groups of intellectuals in the first half of the eighth century were hostile to the Umayyad ruling institution. Among the Kharijites of Basrah there was revolutionary ardour even if it did not always reach the point of actual rebellion. The so-called 'pious opposition' of Medina was less obviously involved in political life. Yet it seems to have given at least its moral support to the movement which brought the 'Abbasids to the throne of the caliphate in 750, and in return to have received from the rulers a measure of recognition for its intellectual claims. While many of these intellectuals may have been hostile to the Umayyads out of a certain personal or family rivalry, there was a deep underlying reason for their opposition. They were interested in keeping the Islamic community a charismatic one,

[1] Cf. Ibn-Khallikan, s.v.; *E.I.*(1) s.v. Much information about the early intellectual life of Basrah is to be gained from C. Pellat, *Le Milieu Basrien.*

particularly by having a system of justice based on the set of ideas and principles revealed to Muhammad. The Umayyads did not officially and ostensibly administer justice on this basis, even if their practice was not far from Muhammad's. With the coming of the 'Abbasids the ruling institution seems officially to have accepted the view that justice must be administered in accordance with revealed truth. There is no direct evidence for this point; it is an inference from other facts. The acceptance may have come about gradually. Before long, however, most of the men in the office of judge seem to be persons who had been trained in the little groups who sat about in the mosques discussing religious questions.

The recognition of the intellectuals by the ruling institution was not without its drawbacks. The ruling institution probably believed more in the canons of Persian statecraft than in Islamic principles, and doubtless was always trying to force judges to abandon strict Islamic principles for 'reasons of state'. Since a judge owed his present appointment and all future appointments to the ruling institution, it would be difficult for him to resist the pressure. We also hear of pressure on the groups of intellectuals in the various towns to try to bring the views of the separate groups into closer agreement with one another[1]. Because of the existence of this pressure from above it is not surprising that there are many Traditions and other anecdotes in which the acceptance of a government appointment is regarded as something blameworthy. Such material must be a reflection of the feeling that a Muslim intellectual's first loyalty should be to revealed truth and to the divinely-constituted community, and that the acceptance of an appointment from the caliph (at least one with a salary attached) compromised this loyalty.

An outstanding example of the refusal to sell his independence and moral integrity was Ahmad ibn-Hanbal (d.855). He was also one of the central figures in a trial of strength between the ruling institution and the intellectuals. This was the affair known as the Mihnah or Inquisition, which lasted spasmodically from 833 to 849[2]. The Inquisition was inaugurated by a decree of the caliph al-Ma'mun requiring judges to subscribe to the theological doctrine that the Qur'an was something created (and not the eternal Word of God); at the same time provincial governors were instructed to remove from office those who refused to subscribe and to punish them. The decree was part of a policy designed to gain political support from

---

[1] Cf. Pellat, 286; Ibn-al-Muqaffa', as a hostile critic, doubtless exaggerates the differences.

[2] Cf. p.173 above; further references in H. Laoust, art. 'Ahmad b. Hanbal' in *E.I.* (2).

sympathizers with the 'Alids (that is, from moderate Shi'ites), and that was doubtless uppermost in the minds of the caliph and his advisers, even if among the advisers were men prepared to defend the doctrine on theological grounds. But the use of force was also envisaged to secure adhesion to the doctrine after argument had been tried and proved unsuccessful.

This inquisition was a blow at the proper autonomy of the intellectuals in the ideational sphere, and a manifestation of the intention of the ruling institution to dominate them. Nevertheless, such was the pressure exercised by the ruling institution that most of those invited to subscribe to the doctrine did so, even when their theological views had hitherto been opposed to the doctrine. Ahmad ibn-Hanbal was one of the few who refused. He was argued with, beaten when he remained unconvinced by the arguments, and in all imprisoned for about two years. He was compelled—or else because of threatening circumstances chose—to remain in retirement and give no public lectures during most of the period. One of the points of special note is that he had wide support from the common people of Baghdad, and he may indeed have owed his life to this support. When after the accession of al-Mutawakkil the policy of the ruling institution was finally reversed (for political and not theological reasons), Ahmad ibn-Hanbal was once again honoured but, being about seventy, he could take little further part in affairs. The exponents of the Hanbalite legal rite which he founded have often been closer to the masses than the exponents of the other rites.

Another aspect of the subservience of the intellectuals to the ruling institution is to be found in the historical writing of the 'Abbasid period[1]. It is well known that at numerous points events have been given tendentious interpretations, or the order of events changed slightly, or the materials distorted in some other way; and that all this has been done to glorify the ruling 'Abbasid dynasty at the expense of their predecessors the Umayyads. The skilful manipulation of the material has completely altered the accounts of many events. The older Umayyad historical tradition has been obliterated, and only after strenuous efforts have Western scholars recovered an outline of the pre-'Abbasid version of early Islamic history. It is easy to see how the historians could thus turn themselves into a propaganda agency for the 'Abbasids. Many doubtless believed that the existing regime was a good one and to be supported; but there was also material pressure. If a man was to write history at all, then, unless he was of independent means, he had to rely on the favour and support of the caliph or of some influential member of the court,

[1] Cf. p. 174 above.

since only these had sufficient wealth; and he was most likely to gain or retain this favour if he presented the ancestors of the caliph in a good light. The historical tradition thus created has formed later Islamic thinking at all levels, but Muslims in general are unaware of the subservience of the intellectuals to the rulers at this point, so that it cannot be said to have affected the relations between the intellectuals and the masses.

The mention of historians is a reminder of the expanding intellectual horizons of the Muslims. In the eighth century a whole cluster of 'Islamic sciences' was being developed—the study of the text of the Qur'an, Qur'anic exegesis, Arabic grammar and lexicography (to provide a basis for the exegesis), pre-Islamic Arabic poetry (to provide a basis for the grammar and lexicography). These were in addition to the juristic and theological studies already mentioned, which depended largely on the Traditions, and in time required subsidiary disciplines to deal with the biographies (and trustworthiness) of transmitters of Traditions and with the life of Muhammad and later events (as the framework of the Traditions and the biographies). Parallel to the development of these sciences there was going on a vast work of translating Greek books into Arabic; the name of the caliph al-Ma'mun is specially connected with the furthering of this work, in which philosophy and the natural sciences received most attention. Something has been said in the previous section about the way in which important segments of non-Islamic intellectual traditions were incorporated into the total non-Islamic world-view. The assimilation of such 'higher learning' from books was of course distinct from the assimiliation of the more popular lore and wisdom of the Middle East by putting it into the mouth of Muhammad in Traditions[1]. All these lines of activity meant that the class of intellectuals was becoming more numerous. The successors of the Perso-Aramaean secretary class of 'Iraq may also have grown closer in outlook to the jurists proper. The extension of the class, however, probably did not greatly affect its relation to the ruling institution. Higher education was becoming more organized, and we hear of systematic instruction in Basrah by about 825[2]. Yet the Islamic sciences, particularly the study of the Shari'ah and the Traditions, remained the core of such instruction, and advancement in the careers for which it prepared was almost entirely under the control of the caliph and his immediate advisers.

In this situation the intellectuals or, more precisely, the scholar-jurists, were not completely defenceless. Their strength lay in their

[1] Cf. p. 225 above.

[2] Cf. Watt, *Free Will and Predestination*, 62.

elaboration of the Shari'ah. It was not, of course, the 'law of the land' in the way in which our parliamentary laws are. The Shari'ah only becomes effective when a ruler orders a judge to base his decisions on it or on some part of it (according to the extent of the competency of the judge). Since it had a divine source, however, no 'commander of the faithful' could altogether disregard it. While it was fluid a ruler might urge a judge to adopt the variant that was most conducive to the ruler's interests; but the more it became fixed, the more difficult it was for rulers to exert pressure on judges to go against the standard ways of interpreting and applying it. It seems very likely that this fact may have accelerated the process by which the Shari'ah became more rigid, though the old Arab idea of the *sunnah* or 'beaten path' of a community would itself produce a tendency to rigidity. One aspect of this rigidity is what is referred to as 'the closing of the gate of *ijtihad*', that is, the ending of the right of jurisconsults to depart from precedents in major decisions. Since it is not clear how the 'gate' came to be closed, it would be worth trying to discover whether part of the motive for declaring the gate closed was the desire to reduce governmental pressure on individuals; a man is better able to resist pressure to accommodate his decisions to reasons of state, if he is able to say, 'I have no competence to vary such-and-such a decision'.

The formulation of doctrine by intellectuals is presumably intended to preserve the faith of the masses. In Islam it would not be exact to say that theological doctrine preserves the Qur'anic synthesis in its original form. As has been noticed at various points in this study, the Qur'anic ideas were modified in the course of generations; for example, the individualism of the Qur'anic conception of the Last Day was to some extent replaced by a communalism. It was always claimed, of course, that modifications of this sort did not make any breach with scriptural teaching but were the true interpretation of it; and certainly there was a large measure of continuity.

What was in fact preserved by the doctrinal formulations was the outlook and attitudes of the main body of Muslims as these had developed by about 750 or 800. By 800 the nomadic Arabs had become accustomed to life in the cities of an empire, and many of the non-Arab inhabitants of the heartlands, with millennia of civilization behind them, had become Muslims. After the sweeping changes which followed the Arab conquests a certain stability had been achieved. There were further doctrinal developments after 800, but such developments, in so far as they were widely accepted, were congruent with the position in 800 and consisted in making definite what was still vague and undecided then. In all this, the intellectuals

243

in their doctrinal formulations were the mouthpiece of the ordinary Muslim. At the same time, however, they were strengthening their own position as a class. They were already, or were in process of becoming, the accredited guardians and interpreters of theological doctrine as well as of the Shari'ah. Though it is convenient to speak of those who specialized in theology as 'theologians', they were only a section of the cadre or class of scholar-jurists, and often lectured or wrote books on other aspects of the Islamic sciences. As this class of scholar-jurists strengthened their position of privilege, there also grew in them a concern for the maintenance of their position which was detrimental to the fulfilment of their responsibility to act as a mouthpiece for the masses and to give them a lead in making adjustments to changing circumstances.

(c) The cleavage between the intellectuals and the masses

While it is clear that by about 1100 the scholar-jurists had become estranged from the masses, it is not clear for what reasons and by what stages this estrangement came about. In the absence of adequate studies all that can be done is to indicate some salient points.

The Muslim intellectuals, as already noted, had some awareness of the cleavage between themselves and the masses. Al-Ghazali (d.1111) wrote an essay to maintain the thesis that ordinary men should not be allowed to engage in or even to hear theological discussions. He considered that they would misunderstand some of the arguments they heard, and that in consequence their belief in various points of doctrine would be shaken[1]. It is possible that this is in part a result of the acceptance of so much Greek thought by the educated Muslims. The ordinary people, despite the presence of Hellenism in western Asia for about a millennium, had not been deeply influenced by Greek thought. It was thus not surprising that, when the arguments of the intellectuals were couched in Greek philosophical terms, they should be misunderstood by the common people. A Muslim intellectual who lived in Spain and North Africa in the twelfth century, Ibn-Tufayl, wrote a philosophical romance about a boy who was brought up by a gazelle on an uninhabited island and who by the use of his reason developed a philosophical and mystical religion similar to that of the philosophers in Islamic countries[2].

[1] K. Iljam al-'Awamm 'an 'Ilm al-Kalam, various editions.

[2] Ibn-Tufayl (d.1185), Hayy ibn-Yaqzan: The improvement of human reason, English tr. by S. Ockley (1708), edited by A. S. Fulton, London, 1929: also The Awakening of the Soul by P. Brönnle, London, n.d.

It is implied in the story that ordinary people are incapable of apprehending the true faith (which is a philosophical one), and that the best they can have is an inferior form of faith, crude and material. Here, then, is an intellectual claiming to live on a superior plane to the masses, and apparently resigned to the existence of an unbridgeable gulf between his own class and those on the lower plane. One wonders if this undue exaltation of the place of the intellectuals is unconscious compensation for their lack of influence in the affairs of the body politic. It may be, however, that Ibn-Tufayl was more aloof from ordinary men than the scholar-jurists of Spain in his time, for he was not exactly one of them but a secretary at the court of Granada and a practitioner of medicine.

The career of al-Ghazali (1058-1111) gives some insight into the matters now under discussion. On the one hand, there is a picture of the alienation of the scholar-jurists from the masses, and on the other hand the activity of al-Ghazali himself may be regarded as an attempt to bridge the gulf. He had the training of a scholar-jurist, and from 1091 to 1095 was the most brilliant professor in the new Nizamiyyah university at Baghdad. In 1095, however, he abandoned his career for the life of a sufi or ascetic-mystic. His account of his spiritual pilgrimage, *Deliverance from Error*, makes it clear that he was utterly disgusted with the materialistic quest for worldly position and glory that dominated the profession of scholar-jurist in his time. In his writings he frequently refers to the corruption throughout the profession, and leaves no doubt that the great majority of the scholar-jurists were incapable of guiding the masses to a faith appropriate to the needs of the age. He mentions two points as having been uppermost in his mind when he made his decision to give up his professional career; the emptiness of his quest for position and prestige contrasted with what he felt to be imminent danger of hell-fire; and the irrelevance of what he taught to a man, whether himself or another, who was striving to attain to eternal life[1].

This is important evidence for the depth of the cleavage between the scholar-jurists and the masses round about 1100. About the causes of the cleavage we can only speculate. It would seem that one of the factors was the concern of the scholar-jurists to maintain the privileges of their class after they had gained some measure of official recognition. To maintain the privileges, however, involved subservience to the ruling institution. Already at the time of the Inquisition, two hundred and fifty years earlier, there had been a strong tendency to subservience. What happened in the interval has not been adequately studied, but there were probably many vicissi-

[1] Cf. *The Faith and Practice of al-Ghazali*, 56.

tudes. In particular the Ash'arite theologians, of whom al-Ghazali was one, had recently obtained a dominant position in higher education through their connexion with the rising power of the Seljuq sultans. For over a century up to 1055 the actual rulers of 'Iraq and Persia had been the Persian dynasty of the Buyids or Buwayhids, who had Shi'ite sympathies—the caliph had retained a merely nominal suzerainty. In 1055 the Seljuq Turks, who had been building up a state for themselves in eastern Persia, obtained control of Baghdad and became effective rulers of large areas of the caliphate for about a hundred years; and to consolidate their rule the influential vizier, Nizam-al-Mulk (d.1092), founded several new universities and colleges in which Ash'arite doctrines were the official theology. It is therefore a reasonable hypothesis that this liaison with the ruling institution had increased the cleavage between the scholar-jurists and the masses, even though much further study is required before the matter can be satisfactorily explained in detail.

In giving a central position in his thought to the attaining of eternal life—something of equal concern to ordinary men and intellectuals—and by criticizing official theology because of its irrelevance to this central aim, al-Ghazali was showing how to bring about a rapprochement between the intellectuals and the masses. When he gave up his professorship to become a sufi, he did not completely abandon dogmatic theology, though it came to have a less important place in his scheme of things[1]. In this way he was able to develop a form of sufi practice which was within the framework of the main ritual prescriptions of the Shari'ah and was therefore tolerable to the scholar-jurists. The latter had hitherto been opposed to sufism because of the excesses of some ecstatic sufis who claimed a measure of divinity and abandoned the Shari'ah. Al-Ghazali may also have achieved something in the way of commending dogmatic theology to the sufis and persuading them to avoid extremist positions.

It cannot be a sheer coincidence that only sixteen years after the death of al-Ghazali the first of the great sufi orders makes its appearance. It is conceivable that this is an independent response, parallel to his own, to the same situation; but it is more likely that it was influenced by his teaching and example. In 1127 'Abd-al-Qadir al-Jili, previously a scholar-jurist of the Hanbalite rite, began to preach and attract followers. These came to constitute the Qadiriyyah order, and by the founder's death in 1166 its organization was well established.[2]

[1] Cf. Gibb, *Mohammedanism*, London, 1949, 141.

[2] Cf. A. J. Arberry, *Sufism*, London, 1950, 85ff.; Gibb, *Mohammedanism*, 147-64.

Sufism had been growing for over three centuries, and in many centres there were small groups of sufis, sometimes living a common life. The constitution of an order meant both the widespread adoption of the sufi life and also the linking of such groups in a common discipline and under a common master.

The establishment of such an order met a deep religious need of the masses, and may be said to mark the beginning of a new phase in the development of Islam. Not merely did the Qadiriyyah itself spread far and wide from Baghdad, its first centre, but many other orders made their appearance. Some branched off from the Qadiriyyah, some were independent in origin. Among the best known of the early orders were the Rifa'yyiah with its centre in Basrah, the Suhrawardiyyah of Baghdad, the Badawiyyah (or Ahmadiyyah) of Egypt, the Shadhiliyyah of North Africa, and the Mawlawiyyah (or Mevlevis) of Anatolia; the founders of these orders died in 1181, 1234, 1276, 1258 and 1273 respectively. At first the orders were mostly within the main Sunnite tradition, and the founder usually claimed to be preaching only doctrines which had come to him from Muhammad, through intermediaries whom he named. In practice, however, the orders were usually independent of the official religious institution of the scholar-jurists, and under the control of their own hierarchy of shaykhs; and thus it was easy for compromises with popular belief to be introduced into the teaching of the order. Some orders strayed a long way from general Sunnite teaching. In course of time the orders as a whole obtained a great hold on the mass of Muslims, until—it would not be too much to say—the worship that mattered for the ordinary Muslim was the special ritual of the order of which he was a member or adherent, and not the 'prayer' common to all Muslims.

Besides being a consequence of the cleavage between the scholar-jurists and the masses the formation of the sufi orders interests us here as producing in their shaykhs a new group of intellectuals who to a great extent wrested the leadership of the masses from the scholar-jurists. This was especially the case when the teaching of the order deviated from normal Sunnite teaching. Some of the orders were very successful among rural populations, where official Islam had roused little enthusiasm—doubtless because the Shari'ah, coming out of a background of Arab merchants and nomads, was often irrelevant to the life of an agricultural community or even detrimental to it. It is difficult to generalize about the orders, and too much should not be made of the difference between them and the official religious institution. In most parts of the Islamic world, notably in Egypt, there seems to have been some understanding

R   247

between the orders and the scholar-jurists[1]. The result was that the orders, on the one hand, avoided glaring heresies, while the scholar-jurists, on the other hand, tolerated the orders and sometimes even welcomed them as a means of keeping the lower classes under control.

Despite such an entente, however, there was no real intellectual harmony. The ordinary man accepted those parts of the Shari'ah which were currently in force, but apart from that his ideas were controlled by the intellectuals of his order (if we may give them that name) and not by the scholar-jurists. Yet these sufi intellectuals were far from being the equals of the scholar-jurists. They probably restricted themselves to mystical theology and its subordinate studies, sometimes with a philosophical basis, but neglected other aspects of the intellectual tradition of the Middle East now taken up into Islam, such as natural science and history. Thus their world-view was never a complete one, and they never were able to dominate Islamic higher education, even if one or two men like Muhyi-d-Din ibn-al-'Arabi (1165-1240) and Ibn-Tufayl (c.1105-1185), who may be called 'philosopher-mystics', obtained considerable influence. This renunciation of the attempt to work out an all-embracing system of ideas was a source of weakness, and may have had something to do with the decline of the orders during the last half-century or so.

While the scholar-jurists were losing ground with the masses, they were gaining in political power and worldly influence. The story is a complex one and can only be adumbrated here. There were probably many ups and downs. At certain times in the seventeenth century the scholar-jurists were the most important class politically in the Ottoman empire, though there continued to be prominent officials who were not scholar-jurists[2]. In concentrating on political power, however, the scholar-jurists lowered their intellectual standards, and thereby forfeited the respect of other sections of the community in so far as that respect was based on their intellectual attainments. This mattered little so long as they retained political power, but when they lost political power they had not much else left. It was perhaps this state of affairs which made it necessary for Mustafa Kemal to reject Islam before reforming Turkey. The situation in the provinces of the Ottoman empire was similar but not so serious, for in them the scholar-jurists had often the role of representing the interests of the people against the governor. Nevertheless there was everywhere a

---

[1] Cf. Gibb and Bowen, *Islamic Society*, i/2, 185.

[2] Cf. ibid. i/2, 81-113. My colleague J. R. Walsh is of the opinion that the materials so far studied do not permit us to say how far the state of affairs described by Gibb and Bowen held *throughout* the period.

loss of respect because of their intellectual compromises for reasons of self-interest.

(d) The present situation

Since the beginning of the nineteenth century a third group of intellectuals has appeared in the heartlands of the Islamic world to compete with the scholar-jurists and the sufi shaykhs for control of the ideas of the masses. This is the constantly increasing group of men and women who have received a Western education up to university level, and who may for short be called the 'Westernizers'. These are the people who alone make it possible for the various Middle Eastern countries to function as modern states. They include professional men, civil servants and other administrators, business men, teachers and highly skilled artisans. Because they are a new social class, they have had to struggle to gain from the rest of society an adequate recognition, both financially and politically, of their importance. Turkey decisively embarked on a westernizing policy under Mustafa Kemal, but the other countries lagged behind. In Egypt, for example, it was only with the Revolution that the westernizers wrested power from the old land-owning ruling class.

It is difficult to estimate the extent to which the westernizers control the ideas of the masses. They control the press in that they are the editors and journalists, and it is possible for them to rouse the feelings of the masses against foreign exploiters and imperialists. The nationalism that is rife in most Middle Eastern countries is the creation of the westernizers. Yet their control is clearly superficial. Nationalism has no deep roots.[1] It can unite men against the foreigner until they have obtained independence, but can do little to help with the building up of an independent state. When exposed to the heat of old group rivalries, it quickly shrivels up. Except at the superficial level there is no genuine rapport between the westernizers and the masses. After thirteen centuries of Islam the grip of Islamic ideas on the masses is not easily to be loosened. Yet in the immediate future it is the westernizers who will have most say in the policies of the Islamic countries.

With regard to the sufi orders it is difficult to generalize, since the position varies from country to country. On the whole they appear to be in decline. Taha Husayn in *An Egyptian Childhood*[2] depicts the corruption of the sufi order with which his father was connected; the shaykh and his attendants trade on the ignorance and super-

[1] Cf. H. A. R. Gibb, *Modern Trends in Islam*, Chicago, 1947, 115, 119.
[2] London, 1932: English translation by E. M. Paxton of *Al-Ayyam*, Part I.

stition of the villagers to make a comfortable living for themselves. This would appear to have been typical. Perhaps a fair general statement would be that the orders have lost the ascetic discipline and genuine mystical attainment which first gained them the following of the masses. Occasionally, because of special local circumstances, they may still stand close to the masses; but they are under intellectual attack from both the scholar-jurists and the westernizers, and can neither defend themselves intellectually nor perform a practical function sufficiently important to outweigh the intellectual criticism. It is almost certain that their influence will go on decreasing.

In the Arabic-speaking countries the scholar-jurists continue to be influential within a limited sphere. In theology they are attempting to come to terms with Western thought, but cannot be said to have achieved much so far. In social matters they are trying to bring the Shari'ah more into line with the Western outlook, not by making substantive changes, but by restricting the competence of courts to certain classes of cases; for example, the legal age of marriage is not increased, but courts are directed not to entertain suits arising out of marriages contracted below certain ages (ages which would be regarded as proper in the West)[1]. The fixity of Islamic doctrine and of the Shari'ah creates a great difficulty in the way of fundamental adaptation to the needs of today. Since Muslims tend to regard all change as heresy, a thoroughgoing measure of reform is only possible where the reformer has great personal prestige and influential support. Even a dictator has to be in a strong position before he can make drastic changes in the social code of Islam. The cleavage which has been described between the scholar-jurists and the masses means that a would-be reformer commences with a heritage of suspicion rather than trust. The method of reform by restricting the competence of courts is essentially a form of dependence on the ruling institution, and shows that the scholar-jurists are still unable to deal with contemporary social problems by the intellectual methods proper to their profession. It cannot be said that reform is impossible, but the difficulties are immense.

In this situation what happens in Turkey is of the greatest importance[2]. The revolution under Mustafa Kemal had among other effects that of destroying the influence of the scholar-jurists and giving control of all aspects of the country's life to westernizers. There can

[1] Cf. J. N. D. Anderson, 'Recent Developments in Shari'a Law', *Muslim World*, xl-xlii (and as a separate book).

[2] Cf. Wilfred Cantwell Smith, *Islam in Modern History*, Princeton, 1957, Ch. 4. This book as a whole is a sympathetic study of the religious responses of Muslim intellectuals to contemporary situations.

be no restoration of the scholar-jurists or of the Shari'ah. But what is possible is a creative religious movement among westernizing intellectuals, which may effect some kind of synthesis between the Islamic and western traditions. What the Turks have taken from the West has been what was necessary for their immediate economic, social and political needs. Some may have adopted Western spiritual values at a superficial level, but there has been no deep acceptance of these values. Sooner or later, however, the westernizers will become aware of their ultimate spiritual needs; and it may be that some of them will try to meet these needs by a new and deeper understanding of their Islamic religious heritage. If this happens, there may be a genuine Islamic revival.

That is a glimpse at the future. Up to the present, however, one is bound to say that the effort to integrate the Islamic world intellectually has only had partial success. Within the small educated section of the population there was indeed from about the tenth or eleventh century A.D. a large measure of integration; but this, by increasing the power of the intellectuals, lowered their intellectual standards and widened the gulf between them and the other classes in the community. This was the position when, about 1800, the impact of the West began to be felt in the Middle East. The old intelligentsia, headed by the scholar-jurists, were unable to deal with the new situation adequately, and so a new intellectual class, the westernizers, came into being. At the present time the two groups of intellectuals continue to exist side by side in most countries, and many of the more thoughtful Muslims have two sets of ideas in separate compartments in their minds. This state of affairs may go on for a long time but not indefinitely. Unless somehow there is fusion or synthesis between the two outlooks, the Islamic world as we have known it will cease to exist.

VIII

THE INTEGRATION OF THE PSYCHE

SOME of the questions which have to be asked about the integration of the religious community are analogous to those that are asked about the integration of the pysche of an individual. It is therefore convenient to speak about the integration of the psyche in respect of a religious community. Under this heading may be grouped various general questions about the community, but this may be done, it is here assumed, without making the ontological assertion that the religious community has a psyche.

1. THE MYSTERY OF GROWTH AND DECAY

The Old Testament gives a picture of a religious community which appears to become corrupt at its very heart. From time to time the political leaders of the Israelites and the great majority of the people adopt attitudes and policies which are in part contrary to the religious foundations of the community. The salt appears to have lost its savour. Here and there a prophet stands out against the dominant trend, supported by a small body of the faithful. His criticisms are trenchant, but not always successful in appreciably altering the dominant trend. Nevertheless from time to time, often under the pressure of calamities, there also takes place a renewal and purification of the spirit of the Israelites. This lowering and raising of the spiritual temperature cannot be predicted but it has frequently happened. It is a mystery, but a reality. The Old Testament thus gives us a warrant for thinking that in other religions also such processes of decay and renewal may be found.

This point has also been put in other ways in recent thinking. It has been said that in religious (and also in national) communities there is often to be found something analogous to neurosis in the individual. The cruder forms of neurosis are not to be found in the great world-religions, since they could not have become world-religions had they not had a large measure of balance and stability. Embryonic religions, however, like recently formed sects, often exhibit serious neurosis; because of the neurotic condition such religious forms usually decline and disappear. In the world-religions, however, subtler and less immediately fatal types of neurosis are to be found. To assert the existence of such a neurosis in a religion may seem presumptuous on the part of an outsider, since he sets himself up in judgement over the religion and judges on the basis of external phenomena. Yet so far as the bare assertion of neurosis is concerned, he has as much justification as the psychiatrist who judges that an individual is suffering from neurosis. The difference is that the psychiatrist is generally allowed to have attained mental health, or at least to have reached a certain minimum degree of freedom from neurosis, whereas the observer's religious community—he must belong to one—is not obviously freer from neurosis than the religious community he studies from without. This does not mean, however, that the observer's criticisms are invalid. It only means, for example, that the Christian critic of Islam must be prepared to acknowledge that there are in Christendom similar weaknesses of attitude to those which he finds in Islam.

Another way of speaking about the decay of the inner attitudes of a community is to be found in Arnold Toynbee's account of the 'breakdowns' of civilizations. It is to be noted that he uses 'break-down' in a special sense[1]. For him the breakdown occurs at the point where the civilization ceases to respond creatively to a new situation. The breakdown is thus prior to disintegration and the cause of it. He argues that breakdowns are not normally due to external factors, physical or human, but to false attitudes within the civilization which he labels 'failure of self-determination'. This he further subdivides under such headings as 'New Wine in Old Bottles' and 'The Nemesis of Creativity'. We shall look again at the details presently. Meanwhile the point of interest is that Toynbee attributes the breakdown of a civilization to some failure of its inner spirit. The breakdown is often nearer the beginning than the end of the history of the civilization, and between the breakdown and the final disappearance of a civiliza-tion there is a series of 'rallies' and 'routs'. Nevertheless, Toynbee holds, once the breakdown has occured death is inevitable. Toynbee, of course, is dealing with civilizations, whereas we are here concerned with religious communities. We may therefore—at least provisionally —doubt whether breakdown in a religious community is inevitably followed by death. In the religious community of Israel periods of decay were several times followed by periods of renewal, and there-fore it does not seem inevitable that every failure of the inner spirit should be followed ultimately by death.

Yet another way of speaking about decay in the inner spirit of a

[1] Cf. D. C. Somervell, *A Study of History, Abridgement of Vols.I-VI*, p.273n.

society is in terms of the concept of ideology. The most important discussion of this subject is that in Karl Mannheim's *Ideology and Utopia*, but his thought has a subtlety which makes it difficult to summarize. In his view, roughly speaking, both ideologies and utopias are 'situationally transcendent ideas'; by this he means that, while purporting to be accurate accounts of the situation in which a society or group finds itself, they are in fact false in some respects. The difference between the two is that 'ideologies are the situationally transcendent ideas which never succeed *de facto* in the realization of their projected contents', whereas utopias, though 'they too orient conduct towards elements which the situation, in so far as it is realized at the time, does not contain, . . . are not ideologies in the measure and in so far as they succeed through counter-activity in transforming the existing historical reality into one more in accord with their own conceptions'[1]. In practice the distinction seems to amount to this, that an ideology is the ideational system of a class which is content with the existing social and political system (perhaps because, like the rich merchants at Mecca, in recent economic and social changes they have done well for themselves at the expense of other classes) while a utopia is the ideational system of a class which is dissatisfied with the existing system (because it has fared relatively badly in recent changes) and which wants reform or revolution.

The Kharijite doctrines which have been discussed above might be taken as examples of utopian ideation. The idea that a little band of marauders was the true Islam was an idea ludicrously incongruous with the realities of the historical situation, but it contained in itself, in the conception of the holy community, the germ of an idea that was to transform the existing historical reality until the whole of Islam became a holy community. This success is in contrast to the failure and disappearance of the paganism of the Meccan merchants who opposed Muhammad. While Mannheim's distinction between ideologies and utopias is thus a true one, it is doubtful whether it is relevant in the context of this chapter. He himself admits that it is difficult to say of any contemporary idea whether it is ideological or utopian. The truth would appear to be that most ideational systems have both ideological and utopian elements. Certainly it is most convenient in the present chapter to neglect Mannheim's distinction, and to apply the term 'ideology' to all his 'situationally transcendent ideas'.

Mannheim pays special attention to what he calls 'the problem of false consciousness'. As he puts it, 'antiquated and inapplicable norms, modes of thought, and theories are likely to degenerate into

[1] Op. cit., London, 1952, 175f.

ideologies whose function it is to conceal the actual meaning of conduct rather than to reveal it'[1]. One of his examples is that of a landowner whose estate has been transformed into a capitalistic enterprise but who still thinks of his own function in it and of his relations to his workers in terms of the former patriarchal order. The landowner's thinking is ideological, because it does not make clear to him the realities of the existing situation but rather conceals them from him. Thus one of the features of ideology is that it is in part a failure to apprehend the world as it really is. There is another feature, however, which is even more important. It is that ideology provides a moral justification for actions which, seen in a wider context (seen from the standpoint of the observer?), are immoral. In other words, ideological thinking includes false valuations, and these false valuations lead the bearers of the ideology to perform acts which the impartial observer is bound to condemn. In the case of the landowner his ideological conception of his own function may have no serious ill-effects; on the other hand, because he thinks of himself as kind and benevolent in an old-fashioned way, he may be blinding himself to the actual needs of the work-people and may be failing to deal with grievances which he could easily remedy. Thus ideology as 'an incorrect interpretation of one's own self and one's role' has both cognitive and valuational aspects, and these jointly influence conduct for the worse.

This conception of ideology at which we have now arrived, based on Mannheim's but not identical with it, may be linked up with certain other ideas. In particular it appears that where there is an ideological way of thinking there is an inflation of the ego-consciousness. This phrase (derived from Jung's psychology, and in part from Saint Paul's *phusiosis*[2]) describes a person's exaggeration of his own importance, value or significance in some respect. The landowner exaggerates his own kindness and benevolence as qualities which give a man's life significance; he doubtless thinks of himself as superior to others because he is thus kind and benevolent. Something similar happens in the case of groups and societies of various kinds, though here one should presumably speak of an inflation of the group-consciousness. A whole society may think of itself as superior to other societies because of its moral, social, political, military or religious attainments.

The further point may be made that this inflation of consciousness, whether of the individual or of the group, is bound up with awareness of separation from others. The roots of this inflation lie deep in the

[1] Ibid. 85.
[2] 2 *Cor.* 12.20, cf. 1 *Cor.* 13.5

past. It doubtless began for individuals when they first became aware of themselves as individuals separate from their clan or family. Before that, however, there had been inflation in the way the small group thought of itself as soon as it became aware of itself as a unit distinct from the large group. This may be illustrated by the way in which each of the pre-Islamic Arab tribes found it necessary to regard itself as outstanding in the various qualities which went to make up the nomadic ideal of 'manliness'. Without self-esteem of this kind it seems to be almost impossible for a group to continue in being. In practice there is mostly an element of exaggeration in the self-esteem, but cases seem to occur where the exaggeration is slight or negligible. Inflation of the group-consciousness, however, may be a serious matter. In so far as it involves an incorrect view of the situation in which the group has to act, it may lead the group to act in ways which increase its weakness and insecurity.

This may be illustrated from Toynbee's account of the various ways in which 'failure of self-determination' comes about. The most important is perhaps what he calls 'the nemesis of creativity'. Where a society has once been very successful in meeting a challenge, it tends to 'rest on its oars'. It idolizes either the whole society at its moment of success or some special institution or technique to which the success was due. What Toynbee says about 'the mechanicalness of mimesis' also falls under this conception, since the mimesis' also falls under this conception, since the mimesis of the leaders by the majority is a technique of a sort which has proved successful in certain circumstances. At the moment of success the high valuation of the society, institution or technique is justified. Unfortunately conditions change. To continue this high valuation in the changed conditions is, as Toynbee puts it, an 'idolization of the ephemeral'. It is now inflationary and ideological, and, by blinding the society to realities of the new situation, may hinder it from making an adequate response to that. (Of Toynbee's other subdivisions of the topic of 'failure of self-determination' two appear to be regarded by him as cases of 'the nemesis of creativity' but in an active instead of a passive form, namely, 'the suicidalness of militarism' and 'the intoxication of victory'. His remaining heading, 'new wine in old bottles', includes cases of the intractability of old institutions in new settings. While these cases illustrate 'failure of self-determination', none seems to be the cause of the breakdown of a civilization. They seem, too, to belong to the level of social activity rather than that of ideation. In so far as they have an ideational aspect, it could be said that there was an ideological element which prevented the transformation of the old institution in accordance with the new social movement. In any case this section does not invalidate our contention that the breakdown of civilizations is due to ideological thinking in which there is inflation of the group-consciousness).

Ideology as thus conceived is all-pervasive in human thinking. We look at theories propounded in the past about the relative parts of the mother and father in the production of a child; there was one according to which the function of the male was the almost negligible one of stimulating the female, and there was another which regarded the child as deriving his nature completely from the father, while the mother provided merely the matter or receptacle; and we ask whether these views are not ideological, exaggerating the roles of the female or the male, and doubtless corresponding with social structures in which the female or the male had a preponderant function. The idea of progress, again, is prominent in the thoughts of modern man, or at least was until recently; but is this not an ideology, an exaggeration of the importance of our technological successes, which blinds us to our moral weaknesses? People often attach much importance to the genetic account of social and religious features, with their suggestion that, because these things have a lowly origin, they cease to be valid; but is this not an ideological depreciation of the value of social tradition—an idolization of an attitude of revolt against tradition which may in some respects be justified but which is not wholly sound? Yet again, Western scholars pride themselves on the fact that the West has studied the Orient much more thoroughly than the Orient has studied Western culture, especially in its religious aspects; but may this not be due mainly to the fact that the West has been thinking imperialistically about the Orient and believes that knowledge gives power?

These examples should be sufficient to indicate that all our thinking, even when it purports to be scientific and objective, is liable to be tainted with ideology. This does not mean that all our thinking is invalid. Fortunately the different aspects of our thinking have a measure of independence. If the aspects of our thinking on which an activity is based are sound, then the activity will be satisfactory, even though in our thinking these aspects are not separated from other ideological aspects. Nevertheless, we must be constantly on our guard trying to detect ideological distortions.

It has been necessary to discuss ideology to this extent in order to indicate the standpoint from which the rest of this chapter is written. A full discussion of ideology, of course, is far beyond the scope of this study. Our immediate concern is to try to discover whether there are any ideological trends within the religious community of Islam. Since ideology is usually found in a group's conception of itself over against other groups, we shall first examine how the Islamic community thought of itself in relation to other communities. Though its relations to both the Jews and the Christians are important, and though its relations to Zoroastrians, Manichees, Buddhists and others are not without interest, it will be sufficient for present purposes to consider the Islamic attitude to one of these communities. Christianity has been selected as most suitable, since, though the attitude to Judaism was a formative factor during Muhammad's lifetime, the attitude to Christianity was more influential during the following century when Islam was growing to maturity. This is the subject of the next section. In a third section there will be some consideration of points where there has been something ideological in the relations of groups to one another within Islam.

2. THE ATTITUDE OF ISLAM TO CHRISTIANITY

The questions with which we are here to be chiefly concerned are the following. Has there been something ideological in Islam's conception of itself in relation to Christianity? Has it exaggerated its importance in various respects in order to compensate for certain weaknesses?

(a) Historical survey

(1) *The pre-Islamic Arabs.* The attitude of the pre-Islamic Arabs to Christianity was closely bound up with their attitude to the Byzantine and Abyssinian empires. The hard-living nomad, even if he despised the lack of freedom of settled peoples, could not help being attracted by the superior wealth and power, the superior technology, and all the comforts and luxuries of civilized life. Even before Muhammad appeared, Arabs were going to settle in Syria, where life was less harsh than in most parts of Arabia; while converts to Christianity among the nomadic tribes were steadily increasing.[1]

At the same time the Arabs disliked being subject to one of these empires. In the half century before Muhammad began his mission, the city of Mecca seems to have pursued a definite policy of neutrality and, though this was primarily political, it involved a certain distrust of Christianity. Even Judaism seems in parts of Arabia, and especially the Yemen, to have gone along with a policy of dependence

[1] Cf. R. Dussaud, *La Pénétration des Arabes en Syrie avant l'Islam*, Paris, 1955.

on Persia. Thus the attitude of the pre-Islamic Arabs to Christianity and Judaism seems to have been influenced by the political implications of these religions. The Arabs wanted the culture of the empires, and they felt that this was in some way bound up with their religion; but they were not prepared to adopt these religions in so far as they involved political subordination. This was part of the attraction of Islam. It was a religion in the Judaeo-Christian tradition, but was politically independent. About the time of Muhammad's death, when the Arabs were trying to find alternatives to the Islamic state with its capital at Medina, their attempts took the form of theocratic states directed by men who claimed religious charismata (the so-called 'false prophets'); the opposition to Medina was not based either on the old religion or on Christianity or Judaism.

The pre-Islamic attitude may therefore be summarized by saying that the Arabs admired Christianity, especially for the culture associated with it, but objected to its political implications.

(2) *The lifetime of Muhammad.* Muhammad's earliest conception of his relation to the older religions was that in the Qur'an he was receiving a fresh revelation of the essential message of Judaism and Christianity (and possibly of other religions also). God had sent many prophets or messengers, all with the same basic message, though there might be particular commands for specific groups of recipients. Muhammad's message was specially intended for, first, the people of Mecca, and then for all the Arabs. At this stage, then, Islam regards itself as parallel to the two older religions. It is to be for the Arabs what these religions were for the specific peoples to whom they were addressed.

Unfortunately, when Muhammad went to Medina, he found the Jews there unwilling to recognize him as a prophet with a message comparable to that of the Old Testament. Indeed, they did more than refuse to recognize him; they criticized him for such matters as his ignorance of the Old Testament, and argued that he could not be a prophet. To defend Islam against these Jewish attacks further claims had to be made for it. In particular it was claimed that Islam was a return to the pure religion of Abraham, which had been corrupted by Jews and Christians, and that the coming of Muhammad had been foretold in the Bible. In connexion with the first of these claims it was pointed out that Abraham was neither a Jew nor a Christian (which was strictly true), and that the Jews had made additions to the revealed law, doubtless in their oral law. The claim that Muhammad was foretold in the scriptures perhaps arises out of the idea, said to have been held by some Jews and others, that he was the

Messiah whom the Jews expected. Since the Muslims were completely ignorant of the scriptures, and since the Jews naturally made no attempt to provide them with passages to support their claim, the Qur'an goes on to allege that the Jews were concealing the relevant passages, and also that they were 'corrupting' the scriptures. The later developments of this doctrine of 'corruption' (*tahrif*) will be considered presently. So far as the actual statements of the Qur'an go, it only appears to mean that they made certain kinds of play with words; for example, they seem to have made use of similarities of sound between Arabic and Hebrew (or Aramaic) roots of opposing meanings in order to make fun of the Muslims[1].

Muhammad had few close dealings with Christians until the last year or two of his life. By this time his attitude to the Jews had hardened, and his attitude to the Christians came to be largely modelled on it. The Christian doctrines of the incarnation and the trinity are regarded as corruptions of the pure Abrahamic message. Of the doctrine of the atonement there is practically no trace in the Qur'an, since it seems to have been incomprehensible to the Arabs. The denial of the crucifixion of Jesus, which occurs in the Qur'an, is intended as the denial not of anything Christian but of the Jewish claim to have killed Jesus.

Throughout Muhammad's lifetime, then, the view of a parallelism between Islam and Christianity appears to have been maintained, except that Christianity was held to have lost its original purity, and in this way was inferior to Islam. There are no passages in the Qur'an which *necessarily* imply that Islam is a universal religion. Stories implying universalism are found in the biographies of Muhammad, notably one about how he sent messengers to summon to Islam the Byzantine, Persian and Abyssinian emperors and other potentates; but such stories are rejected by Western critics on account of the contradictions they involve[2]. Muhammad himself seems to

---

[1] Cf. 'The Early Development of the Muslim Attitude to the Bible', *Transactions of the Glasgow University Oriental Society*, xvi (1957) 50-62, esp. §1; also art. 'Tahrif' by F. Buhl in *E.I.*(1). The most important general discussions are: I. Goldziher, 'Uber muhammedanische Polemik gegen Ahl al-Kitab', *ZDMG*, xxxii (1878). 341-87; E. Fritsch, *Islam und Christentum im Mittelalter*, Breslau, 1930; I. di Matteo, 'Il "tahrif" od alterazione della Bibbia secondo i musulmani', *Bessarione*, xxxviii (1922) 64-111, 223-60. J. W. Sweetman, *Islam and Christian Theology*, ii/1. 178-308 summarizes the arguments of Ibn-Hazm and al-Ghazali. A later example of such word-play is probably to be seen in the Jewish habit of calling Muhammad *pasul*, 'corrupt', instead of *rasul*, 'messenger'; cf. *Zeitschrift fur Assyriologie*, xxvi. 97n.

[2] *Muhammad at Medina*, 345-7; F. Buhl, *Das Leben Muhammeds*, Leipzig, 1930, 294-8; id., 'Fasste Muhammed seine Verkündigung als eine universelle auch für Nichtaraber bestimmte Religion auf?', *Islamica*, ii. (1926) 135-49.

have been ready to regard as Muslims those Christians who acknowledged him as prophet; he doubtless considered that they had not abandoned their Christianity but had merely purified it.

(3) *The period of Arab domination.* The two hundred years or so after the death of Muhammad may be treated as a single period in the present context. As a result of the expansion of the Islamic state to a world-empire, many Christians and some Jews came under Muslim rule. The process had begun in Muhammad's lifetime, but it was accelerated so rapidly that even by 650 there must have been more Christians than Muslims in the domains of the caliph. Despite this state of affairs there was probably little contact between Christians and Muslims at the more educated levels—perhaps a little more in Syria than in 'Iraq. To begin with few Christians became Muslims.

Correspondingly during this period the main aim of anti-Christian polemics by Muslims appears to have been to prevent the ordinary Arab from the desert from being disturbed in his faith by any talk he might hear from Christians. The former allegation of concealment of prophecies of Muhammad was given story-form. A Christian boy, who subsequently became a Muslim, found two pages sticking together in his uncle's copy of the Gospel; when he separated them, he discovered a description of the expected prophet, which was exactly fulfilled by Muhammad[1]. There were similar stories about Jews. In this way the uneducated Arabs were given an effective reply to assertions that Muhammad was not a prophet because he had not been foretold. Similarly, any arguments based on the Bible are ruled out by the view found in some of the early commentators on the Qur'an, quoted by at-Tabari (d.922), that the Bible as a whole has been corrupted.

There are a number of traditions which discourage or forbid the questioning of Jews and Christians by Muslims.[2] If Muslims hear statements from people of the Book, they are neither to believe nor disbelieve; in this way they will avoid believing what is false or disbelieving what is true, since (it is implied) one can never be certain whether the people of the Book are speaking truth or falsehood. Ibn-'Abbas is reported to have recommended that, when Muslims asked for information from the people of the Book, they should reject what was contrary to the Qur'an and accept only what was in

[1] Ibn-Sa'd, *Tabaqat*, i/2. 89. 14-25. For this and the immediately following remarks cf. 'The Early Development . . .', §2.

[2] 'The Early Development . . .', §4, based on Ibn-'Abd-al-Barr, *Jami' Bayan al-'Ilm*, Cairo, n.d., ii. 40-43 (or Cairo, 1326, 119).

accordance with it. The Qur'anic injunction (10.94), 'If thou art in doubt of what We have revealed to thee, ask those who recited the Book before thee', would seem to authorize Muhammad (and after him the Muslims) to go to Jews and Christians for information; but, even at an early date, this was interpreted to mean not any Jews and Christians, but only those who had accepted Islam[1]. Even at this early period, however, a Muslim scholar like Ibn-Is'haq (d.768), realized the importance of the information to be obtained from adherents of the older religions, though in some circles he was censured for his procedure[2].

During the period of two hundred years after Muhammad's death, then, the attitude of Islam to Christianity remained similar to what it had been during the closing years of his life. Christianity was regarded as parallel to Islam, but corrupt. To this extent Islam was superior. The outstanding achievement of the period, however, was the impressing on the masses of ordinary Muslims of the view that Christianity was corrupt and unreliable. This, together with the death penalty for apostasy kept the Muslims effectively insulated from Christian propaganda.

(4) *Later times.* The growth of Muslim scholarship generally during the first decades of the 'Abbasid caliphate (from 750 on) led to a serious study of certain aspects of Biblical history. Quotations from the Bible begin to appear in Muslim works. Ibn-Is'haq in his *Life of Muhammad*[3] has a fairly accurate rendering of *John*, xv.23—xvi. 1. The Messianic passage at the beginning of *Isaiah*, 42, may have attracted attention even earlier. It occurs in various forms, one being in Ibn-Sa'd (d.844)[4]. The multiplicity of forms and the reliance on a single quotation suggests that there was still no general knowledge of the Old Testament, but only of this particular passage; yet even this is a distinct advance on the stage when it was alleged that descriptions of Muhammad's physical appearance occurred in the scriptures.

Signs of increasing knowledge of the scriptures are to be found in the report (preserved in Christian sources) of the discussion between the caliph al-Mahdi and the Nestorian Catholicos Timothy, held about 782[5]. The caliph mentions three passages where he claims that

[1] Cf. at-Tabari, *Tafsir*, ad loc.

[2] Yaqut, *Dictionary of Learned Men*, ed. D. S. Margoliouth, vi. 401.7 (quoted by Goldziher, *Koranauslegung*, 58n.)

[3] Ibn-Hisham, ed. Wüstenfeld, 150.

[4] i/2. 88. 14-24; cf. 'The Early Development . . .' §3.

[5] Ed. by A. Mingana in *Woodbrooke Studies*, ii, Cambridge, 1928; E. Fritsch, op. cit., 2, doubts its authenticity, though without convincing reasons.

Muhammad is foretold: the promise of the Paraclete in the Fourth Gospel, the mention of 'a rider on an ass and a rider on a camel' in Isaiah (xxv.7, Septuagint), and the promise of a prophet like Moses (*Deut.* xviii. 18). The caliph's modest total of three passages is dwarfed by the tale of 130 produced by a convert from Christianity in 855.[1] While much of this scriptural material may have come in the first place from converts, a scholar like Ibn-Qutaybah (d.889), born and educated as a Muslim, was able to quote a large number of passages[2].

The attempts to show that Muhammad was foretold in the Bible led to certain modifications in the Muslim attitude to it. Obviously, if the Bible was completely corrupt, there would be no point in trying to show that there were prophecies about Muhammad in it. At-Tabari, in dealing with verses of the Qur'an which earlier commentators had interpreted to mean that the Bible was completely corrupt, tries to find other interpretations which avoid any doctrine of complete corruption. Thus, in commenting on 2.75/70, which speaks of 'a party of them (sc. the Jews) hearing the word of God and corrupting it', he rejects the view of older men that this refers to their scholars and to the corruption of the Old Testament in general; he prefers to make this refer to a specific incident in the lifetime of Moses[3]. It was also held for a time that the true texts of the scriptures were still extant, and Muslim scholars claimed to have used them[4]. Another way of dealing with the question was to hold that the text of the Bible was genuine but that the Jewish and Christian interpretations of it were corrupt. This view of the nature of the 'corruption' of the scriptures is usually given as a possibility by al-Baydawi (d.1388) in his comments on the verses which speak about corruption.

The most radical attack on the scriptures was that made by Ibn-Hazm (d.1064). Basing himself on a wide knowledge of the actual text, he claimed to show that the Bible was full of contradictions. In accordance with this position he also abandoned the attempt to prove that Muhammad had been foretold in the Bible. Perhaps he was led to make this rigorous attack by conditions in Spain, where he lived and wrote; he probably wanted to stop Muslims altogether

---

[1] 'Ali at-Tabari, *Kitab ad-Din wa-'d-Dawlah*, ed. A. Mingana, Manchester, 1923. This author is not to be confused with Muhammad ibn-Jarir at-Tabari, the author of the celebrated history and Qur'an-commentary.

[2] C. Brockelmann, *Beitrage zur Assyriologie*, iii. 48-54 and *Zeitschrift fur alttestamentliche Wissenschaft*, xv (1895) 138-42; cf. Fritsch, op. cit., 77.

[3] *Tafsir*, ad loc. (i.278).

[4] E.g. Ibn-Qutaybah, *K.Ta'wil Mukhtalif al-Hadith*, Cairo (1943)/1362, 269 —'I read in the true Gospel that . . .' (*al-injil as-sahih*).

from reading the Bible. This radical attitude to the Bible did not become universal in Islam, though its simplicity commended it to the masses. Historians in particular seem to have appreciated the historical information in the scriptures, and to have held that it was necessary to make some use of them in historical studies. It was seen, too, that there were difficulties in explaining how Jews and Christians had agreed to corrupt the text[1]. On the other hand, one serious difficulty confronted the view that 'corruption' consisted in false interpretation, namely, the clear statements in the New Testament that Christ was crucified. This is probably why men like al-Baydawi hesitated to commit themselves to such a view.

To sum up, the position in respect of 'the corruption of the scriptures' may be said to be that this has been accepted as a dogma by Islam but the precise meaning of the dogma is disputed. The lack of precision in the definition of the dogma, however, does not lessen its usefulness but rather enhances it. The purpose of the dogma is to prevent doubts arising in the minds of Muslims as a result of hearing Christian statements or reading Christian books. An imprecise dogma has the advantage that, if one way of interpreting it does not meet a particular case, one may turn to another interpretation. This dogma may be regarded as the rear line of defence against Christianity. Strenuous efforts were made to prevent the great mass of Muslims from having any close contact with Christian sources of information. There were traditions forbidding them to ask questions and discouraging the use of Christian or Jewish books[2]. Christians were even prohibited from reading their sacred books publicly, that is, where Muslims could hear them[3]. If, despite these precautions, some dangerous information trickled through to the ordinary Muslim, it was rendered harmless by the dogma of 'corruption'. On the whole Islam may be said to have been entirely successful in preventing knowledge of the Bible from weakening the faith of Muslims.

An interesting example of the strength of the dogma of 'corruption' is contained in the interpretations of the story of Abraham's sacrifice of his son. The event is mentioned in the Qur'an (37.102/ 100ff). but the son's name is not given. There is no reason for supposing that to begin with anyone supposed the son was not Isaac. In course of time, however, the question became intertwined with the

---

[1] E.g. Ibn-Qayyim-al-Jawziyah (d.1350), quoted by Goldziher in *ZDMG*, xxxii. 373. Contrast the attitude of the historians Ibn-Kathir (d.1332) and as-Sakhawi (d.1497), quoted in F. Rosenthal, *Muslim Historiography*, 417 and G. von Grunebaum, *Islam, Essays*, 46.

[2] Cf. Ibn-'Abd-al-Barr, loc. cit.

[3] Al-Mawardi, 251 (tr. 306).

rivalry between the Arabs and the Persians. Isaac came to be regarded as the ancestor of the Persians (as well as of the Jews). The Persian party probably boasted of his superiority to Ishmael, the ancestor of the Arabs, both in being the son of a free woman and in being chosen for the sacrifice. The Arabs in reply claimed that the son to be sacrificed was Ishmael. Many of the early authorities quoted by at-Tabari knew that in the Old Testament Isaac was taken for the sacrifice, and at-Tabari himself (a man of Persian origin, be it noted) prefers this view. The pro-Arab party replied that this was a place where the scriptures had been corrupted; the text (in Arabic) contained the word *bikr*, 'first-born', which must mean Ishmael, and therefore the word Isaac must have been interpolated. In the end the pro-Arab party won, and it is now universally held by Muslims that the son Abraham was about to sacrifice was Ishmael[1]. In this way a view which honoured the Arabs and which supported (and was supported by) the dogma of 'corruption' overcame the natural interpretation of the Qur'an in accordance with the Old Testament. It is not too much to say that the belief that the Bible was corrupt had so come to dominate the minds of Muslims that they no longer cared whether their interpretations of the Qur'an were in accordance with the Bible or not.

This changing treatment of the dogma of the 'corruption' of the Bible is a reflection of the fact that by about 800 the Muslims had assimilated much of the culture of the Middle East, for which, whatever its ultimate source, the main vehicle in recent centuries had been Christianity[2]. The process of assimilation had been aided by the conversion of Christians to Islam. Contacts between Christians and Muslims at an educated level were now more frequent than in the previous centuries, since the two parties had more of a common basis. The Christians (and Jews) for their part had developed a polemic against Islam. This was done mainly in self-defence. The Muslim law of apostasy being what it was, there can hardly have been any converts from Islam to Christianity, but the prestige of Islam and the social advantage of conversion produced a flow of converts to Islam.

Under these circumstances Muslims were not content with the defensive attitude of the dogma of the 'corruption' of the scriptures.

---

[1] Goldziher, *Muhammedanische Studien*, i. 144f., *Koranauslegung*, 79-81; also in *ZDMG*, xxxii. 359. To his references may be added Ibn-Qayyim-al-Jawziyah, *Zad-al-Ma'ad*, Cairo, 1950/1369, i. 15-17. There is some interesting material in al-Mas-'udi, *Muruj-adh-Dhahab*, ii. 139-47; he also reports genealogies according to which the Greeks and Romans are descended from Isaac; ib. 242, 248, 293f.

[2] Cf. C. H. Becker, *Islamstudien*, Leipzig, 1924, i. 399-404.

They required an ideational justification for preaching to Christians and Jews, and for inducing them to abandon their religion for Islam; and the converts required an ideational justification for the position they were now in. Such a justification was not provided by the original idea of the parallelism of the three religions. That could only have led Jews and Christians to get rid of accretions and falsifications; but there was in fact no community which practised the pure form of Judaism and Christianity, since none of the Jews and Christians who had acknowledged Muhammad had tried to purify his existing religion; they had simply accepted Muhammad's religion in its entirety and become indistinguishable from other Muslims. For Muslim preachers and for converts to Islam there was clearly no practical alternative to straightforward acceptance of Islam and its Shari'ah. Since this practice, however, had no adequate ideational basis in the doctrine of parallelism, it was necessary to modify that by the introduction of new ideas. In particular it was asserted that Muhammad's mission had been a universal one and that the revealed ordinances of the older religions had been abrogated by the Qur'anic revelation and the Shari'ah.

Though these ideas are contrary to the general tenor of the Qur'an and of Muhammad's conduct, it was possible to find some support for them. One verse (34.28/27) literally translated runs, 'We have not sent thee save in general to the people as an announcer and a warner', while another (3.85/79) says, 'he who desires other than Islam as a religion, it will not be accepted of him'[1]. A tradition which was possibly in circulation before 750 makes Muhammad assert that, if Moses was alive, Moses would have no option but to follow him[2]. Such ideas were of course hotly disputed by the people of the Book. They produced verses of the Qur'an which implied that Muhammad's mission was only to the Arabs. The Christians tried to explain the relation of the Mosaic revelation to the Christian without using the conception of abrogation, since it had proved an effective weapon in Muslim hands. We find Ibn-Taymiyyah (d.1328) maintaining that Islam combined the Mosaic law of justice with the Christian law of grace, that it was a middle way between the severity of Moses and the mercy of Christ, and in fine that while Moses had proclaimed God's majesty and Jesus His goodness, Muhammad proclaimed His perfection[3].

[1] Presumably ' Islam ' here was originally taken to mean Abrahamic monotheism and so to include Judaism and Christianity (in their supposedly pure forms). Cf. 3.52/45, where Christ's disciples are called Muslims.

[2] Ibn-'Abd-al-Barr, op. cit., ii. 42.17-23.

[3] Fritsch, op. cit., 130-36.

The Integration of the Psyche

What has been said is, of course, far from being a full account of Islamic polemics against Christianity. There were long and intricate discussions about the doctrines of the incarnation and the Trinity. These throw little light, however, on the fundamental Islamic attitude. Some Muslims—notably ash-Shahrastani (d.1153) in his heresiology, *Kitab al-Milal wa-'n-Nihal*—were relatively well-informed even about the differences between Melkites, Jacobites and Nestorians with regard to the doctrine of the Trinity; such persons realized that the dispute between Muslims and Christians was one about the attributes of God and that Christians did not deny that God is one[1]. The Qur'anic accusation that Christians worshipped three gods clearly did not apply to the mass of Christians. It was usually held that Christians were guilty of unbelief (*kufr*) but not of idolatry (*shirk*). Ibn-Taymiyyah, however, who seems to have felt that Islam was losing ground to Christianity in Syria in his time, took a sterner view and held that in view of the veneration of saints and images by Christians they were guilty of idolatry. This, together with his view that Muhammad's mission was universal, suggests that he was aiming at the ultimate absorption of all Christians by Islam[2].

(b) Questions of Ideology

After this brief survey of how the attitude of Islam to Christianity developed with the passage of the centuries, the question arises to what extent this attitude has been based on ideology. An attempt will be made, in answering this question, to preserve the objectivity of a sociologist; but, since matters are involved in which personal commitment is necessary, complete objectivity is perhaps unobtainable.

(1) *The parallelism of Islam with earlier monotheism.* There was great audacity in the claim of a citizen of obscure Mecca that he was founding a religion parallel to Judaism and Christianity. Nowadays, with Muslims constituting nearly a fifth of the world's population, there is good justification for the claim, but it was far from obvious when it was first made. How could a man who had only about 300 followers at the battle of Badr in 624 put himself on a level with Jesus, whose followers then numbered the millions of the Roman empire and the millions outside it in both east and west? This would seem to be an undue exaggeration of his importance.

Nevertheless a case can be made out for holding that this

[1] Cf. al-Baghdadi, *Farq*, 348.

[2] H. Laoust, *Ibn Taimiya*, 277. He and his followers, of course, also attack saint-worship in Islam.

267

conception of parallelism was not ideological. There was a need to be met and Islam met this need. It was fundamentally a religious need, but politics were involved. It has been noted above that the Arabs were suspicious of both Judaism and Christianity because of their political implications. Muhammad, it has been said, 'was the answer of the East to the challenge of Alexander'.[1] The conquests of Alexander led to the flooding of the Middle East by a wave of Greek influence. This was political, cultural and religious. The political influence had been gradually receding, though in Muhammad's youth the Levant was still under the Greek-speaking rulers of Constantinople. The struggle between Greek and oriental influences, however, had been transferred to the religious plane. Christianity, an oriental religion, had invaded Europe, but there it had become amalgamated with the Greek outlook. The disputes within Christendom about the formulation of the doctrines of the Trinity and the incarnation were in part disputes between Greek-speaking Christians and oriental Christians who, though using Greek for theological discussions, had Syriac, Armenian or Coptic for their mother-tongue. The disputes were complicated by the existence of the important body of Western or Latin-speaking Christians. The formulations which were eventually accepted as orthodox represent a compromise between the Greek-speaking and Latin-speaking Christians; but it proved impossible to find formulations which would satisfy the orientals as well, and they were therefore excluded from the Church as heretics.

It is significant that the Byzantine provinces which the Arabs conquered were those where the population consisted chiefly of heretical oriental Christians. These people, so far as we can tell, objected to the intellectual domination of Greek-speakers as well as to their political domination. Thus there is a sense in which even before the appearance of the Muslims, the Church in the Middle East had failed. It had failed to deal with the problem created by the different intellectual categories presupposed by those who spoke Greek and those who spoke the oriental languages. Though the Latin terms for the doctrine of the Trinity (one *substantia*, three *personae*) were not linguistically identical with the Greek terms (one *ousia*, three *hypostaseis*), since *substantia* and *hypostasis* are etymologically equivalent, it was agreed that the two sets of terms should be regarded as equivalent. There was no agreement, however, about equivalent formulations in Syriac, Armenian and Coptic. Thus there was no formulation of Christian doctrine, generally recognized as being within the central Christian tradition, which was expressed in

[1] Christopher Dawson, *The Making of Europe*, London, 1932, 107.

the languages and intellectual categories of the oriental Christians. In other words, while Christianity expressed the Old Testament tradition in a form which suited the spiritual needs and intellectual categories of most classes of the citizens of the Roman empire, nothing similar was done to provide an expression of the Judaeo-Christian tradition for the inhabitants of the Middle East. This, then, Islam may be said to have done. Judaism, Christianity and Islam are thus three expressions, in a sense parallel to one another, of the same tradition, which might be called the Abrahamic tradition.

If there is some truth in the view thus baldly and inadequately stated[1], then the fact that the religion first preached in Mecca has become a world-religion comparable to Christianity is not accidental. Islam was able to meet a need which Christianity had not met, the need of certain of the non-Greek-speaking peoples of the Middle East for an expression of the Abrahamic tradition in their own intellectual categories. Muhammad was not in a position to foresee all the future development of his teaching, but it could be seen in his time that the Arabs were in need of an expression of the Abrahamic tradition in their own intellectual categories and without political implications. This was the essential basis of the claim to parallelism, and perhaps the chief factor in the realization by Islam of a parallel position. Later on, indeed, Islam proved itself capable of meeting other needs, such as those of West Africans moving from animistically-based tribalism to individualism; but even this is not wholly accidental, since the West African situation had important similarities with that of pre-Islamic Arabia. In general, then, we may say that, though the claim of Islam to be parallel with the older religions was not justified by its achievements when the claim was first made, yet there was an essential (or potential) truth in it, since Islam was able to approach segments of human society with which Christianity was not well suited to deal.

(2) *Muhammad in the Bible.* At first the claim that Muhammad was foretold in the Old and New Testaments seems to the Western Christian both ridiculous and presumptuous; it seems to exaggerate the importance of the Arabs, and therefore to be ideological. This first impression, however, is in part dispelled by reflexion. There are analogies between the Christian reinterpretation of the Old Testament and the Muslim reinterpretation of the Bible. The Christian interpretation of the Old Testament prophecies differs from the Jewish in many points, for example, in the passages about the suffering servant in Isaiah. In most cases the Christian interpretations

[1] I hope at some later date to be able to expound this view more fully.

are in accordance with the spirit of the Old Testament; they accept the basic principles underlying the prophecies and give them a particular application. Occasionally, however, the Christian interpretation seems to be based on a verbal accident and to arise from a naive attitude to words which attributes to them magical properties. An example of this (on the assumption that it was not originally intended to have any Messianic reference) is the passage where Isaiah says that God's sign to Ahaz is that a young woman will have a child whom she will call Immanuel, and that before he is able to discern evil from good destruction will have come upon the kingdom[1].

Muslim reinterpretation of Biblical passages is mostly only plausible where this naive attitude to words is presupposed. A possible exception is the passage where the people of God are told that God will raise up for them one of their own number, similar to Moses, who will them give them guidance[2]. This is often taken by Christians to mean that God will raise up a prophetic order (whose supreme exemplar is Jesus) so that in times of difficulty the people of God will have a prophet to guide them. With a little stretching of the sense here and there, Muhammad might perhaps be said to be one fulfilment of this prophecy. He cannot be said to have guided the people of God as a whole, but, in so far as the Arabs were on the fringe of the Abrahamic tradition, he may be said to have given guidance to a part of the people of God.

Muslim polemical writers sometimes claim that only Muhammad properly fulfils this prophecy, but this would be vigorously denied by Christians and Jews with powerful arguments. In its extreme form the claim would be presumptuous. If it was only claimed, however, that Muhammad was one out of many fulfilments of the prophecy, that would be neither presumptuous nor an exaggeration of Muhammad's importance. He belongs to the Abrahamic tradition, and that tradition had envisaged advances through charismatic religious leaders. In so far as Muhammad was extending the range of application of the Abrahamic tradition, he was an exemplification of the general principle underlying the passage under discussion. To this extent the claim that he was foretold in the Bible is justified.

(3) *Muhammad's prophethood.* It has been argued that Muhammad is a charismatic religious leader within the Abrahamic (or Judaeo-Christian) tradition, who guided some of the people of God in a time of difficulty. He may thus be called a prophet in certain senses of the

[1] *Is* 7.14; applied to Christ in *Mt* 1.23.
[2] *Deut.* 18.15, 18.

word (though Christians and Jews will add that this admission must not be taken to imply that all he says is true). The conception of prophethood, however, that was held by Muhammad and the Muslims seems to have had ideological features, and these are still influential in the outlook of Muslims at the present time and hinder their readjustment after the impact of Western civilization.

It was apparently claimed that a prophet could have revelational knowledge of historical events. For instance, there is a verse in the Qur'an[1] which, after giving a version of the story of Noah, announced: 'this is one of the accounts of the unseen; We reveal it to thee; thou didst not know it, neither thou nor thy people before this'. It is conceivable that Muhammad understood this to refer not to the bare facts of the story, which may have been known by ordinary human means, but to the significance attributed to it. Yet, even if we give Muhammad the benefit of the doubt on this point, two other points seem almost certain. One is that he himself latterly shrank from questioning Jews and Christians about their scriptures. Perhaps experience showed him that to do so was to give the Jews opportunities of discrediting him; and he may have felt that to be dependent on Jews or Christians for knowledge of the older revelations was inconsistent with his claim to be bringing another revelation comparable to them. The other point is that the body of Muslims in Muhammad's time and later have regarded the Qur'an as conveying knowledge of historical events. Where there was any contradiction between the Qur'an and the human historical tradition (if this name may be given to the historical tradition based on the Bible), they have regarded the Qur'an as more reliable[2]. In this way the Christian tradition of the crucifixion of Jesus as a historical fact is denied by Islam. Closely associated with this attitude, too, is the dogma that the Bible has been corrupted.

From this acceptance of the Qur'an as a source of historical information (with the complementary rejection of the Bible) arises an attitude of self-sufficiency in the field of knowledge. There was a period, of course, when the Arabs were assimilating the culture of the regions they had conquered, especially the culture of the heartlands of their empire. For a time they were carried away by Greek philosophy, and theologians appeared who were more Hellenic than Islamic in their outlook. Their historians likewise, in making a picture of the world upon which Islam had burst, utilized the

[1] 11.49/51; cf. 3.44/39; 12.102/103. The question is discussed in *Muhammad at Mecca*, 159f.

[2] Ibn-al-Athir (d.1234) seems to imply that the absence of the stories of Hud and Salih from the Old Testament is a sign of its corruption (*Kamil*, i.52f.)

historical records of Rome and Greece, India and China, and did not shrink from going to Jewish and Christian sources. This receptivity for extraneous material, however, was only a phase. Once the culture of the Middle East had been assimilated—or at least as much of it as the Muslims wanted—the tendency to be self-sufficient reasserted itself. Greek philosophy was given ancillary duties in the science of theology, and apart from that neglected. The real successors of the Neoplatonic school of al-Farabi and Ibn-Sina (Avicenna) were orthodox theologians like al-Iji and Fakhr-ad-Din ar-Razi. There was little interest in the history of contemporaries like the rising European powers, little interest in anything outside Dar-al-Islam. The intellectuals of Islam came to devote themselves more and more to Islamic sciences like grammar and law and less and less to 'foreign' sciences like mathematics and medicine. In short, the Islamic world lost interest in everything except itself and had no concern for what happened beyond its borders.

This self-sufficiency was perhaps fostered by the tendency to regard things Arab and (at a later date) things Muslim as superior to what was not Arab or Muslim. If a word could be given an Arab derivation, that was preferred to an admission of borrowing. When heresies appeared, it became usual to insinuate that they were due to foreign influences; thus—without historical justification, it would seem—the origin of the Kharijites was traced to a converted Jew. Greek philosophy was one of the few foreign influences that was fully admitted. Much non-Muslim material, however, was admitted into Islam in the guise of Traditions; Muhammad is even said to have commended a prayer which closely follows the Lord's Prayer of Christians[1]. This procedure made it possible for Islam to assimilate much of the culture of the Middle East, and yet ' to counteract, and, as far as possible, extinguish the influence of the earlier universalist concept (Christianity)';[2] in this way Islam came to replace Christianity as the bearer or vehicle of culture in the Middle East. The acceptance of Traditions from Muhammad as a source of law further encouraged the tendency to neglect what was not Islamic in origin or alleged origin.

In all this there has been an ideological element, an exaggeration of the importance of Muhammad's prophethood and of the Qur'anic

[1] Cf. Goldziher, *Muhammedanische Studien*, ii. 386. On the general question cf. von Grunebaum, *Islam, Essays*, 228: ' Islam has always combined a capacity for absorption of foreign elements with a certain reluctance to admit their foreign origin'.

[2] Sir H. A. R. Gibb, ' An Interpretation of Islamic History', *Journal of World History*, i. 40 and *Muslim World*, xlv (1955) 5.

revelation, even an exaggeration of the knowledge possessed by Islam after Middle East culture had been assimilated. Because of this ideological element Islam has had difficulty in adjusting itself to the circumstances of recent centuries when it was brought into closer contact with Western culture. Muslims have been slow to admit how much they had to learn from the West, and so their response to the Western impact has been retarded compared with that, for example, of Hindus. A contributory factor to this retardation has been Islam's fear of Christianity, for this has brought it about that Muslims have read mainly the writings of Western atheists and agnostics, and have tended to avoid Christian works, even when the purpose of these was to defend monotheism against its critics. In this way these ideological features have weakened Islam in its struggle with modern secularism.

(4) *Universalism.* The original doctrine of a parallelism between Islam and the older monotheistic religions was largely replaced in course of time by a doctrine of universalism, that is, that Islam was superior to all other religions and suitable for all men. When the doctrine of universalism first appeared Islam was at its heyday, and many Christians, Jews and Zoroastrians were becoming Muslims. As the ideational aspect of a historical process through which an adjustment to a new situation was being effected, the doctrine will perhaps prove to be true in essentials, but events have not yet proceeded sufficiently far for us to be able to judge this point with complete objectivity. There are certain considerations, however, which give some objective support to the view that this claim is ideological.

While Islam seems to have been flourishing when the doctrine of universalism was originally advanced, at certain later periods Islam has shown some consciousness of weakness over against Christianity, and this suggests that the exaggeration of the importance of Islam by insisting on the doctrine of universalism is in part a compensation for this sense of inferiority. This is a matter which deserves to be studied more fully over a wide field. Of one period which has received the attention of modern scholars, the age of Ibn-Taymiyyah (d.1328), it has been said:

The threat to Islam occasioned by the confessional minorities, and more especially the Christians, is indirect. The influence of Christianity on his contemporaries always appeared to Ibn-Taymiyyah both deep and formidable. Christian ascetics have gained the sympathy of Muslim *zuhhad* and have inspired them with a taste for the cenobitic life (*khalwah, rahbaniyyah*); the defence of celibacy is likewise a Christian importation.

273

The Integration of the Psyche

Popular Islam also has not escaped the solvent action of Christianity. The Muslim masses in Egypt take part in Christian festivals, and Christian influence is at the origin of the cult of saints and of the local pilgrimages.[1]

During this period there was a strong movement of popular opinion against the Christians, especially in Egypt, and this has been attributed to dissatisfaction with the high positions in government service attained by Christians, to suspicions of them because of their association with external enemies (the European powers and the Mongols), and to the general bitterness caused by the Crusades and by the reconquest of Spain[2]. There is much that is still obscure in these matters, but there is at least a *prima facie* case for suspecting an ideological factor.

Another consideration is that the grounds for holding that Islam is superior to Christianity and Judaism vary from time to time. The Qur'anic claim that Islam was the religion of Abraham in its purity meant that Islam had no positive message of salvation to present to Jews and Christians, but could only show them how to remove undesirable accretions from their beliefs. When the doctrine of parallelism, however, is abandoned for that of universalism, a multiplicity of grounds appears for holding that Islam is superior. One important reason is the great military and political successes of Islam, which were claimed to be a divinely-given confirmation of the truth of the Islamic revelation[3]. Another claim was that Islam was more in accordance with reason;[4] another that it was more comprehensive, including both the severity of Judaism and the mercy of Christianity;[5] yet another that it was a mean between excessive this-worldliness and excessive other-worldliness[6]. This very multiplicity of grounds leads to a suspicion of ideology, though by itself it would not be conclusive, since the variations might be due to

[1] Laoust, *Ibn Taimiya*, 267.

[2] Ib. 58-64; cf. L. E. Browne, *The Eclipse of Christianity in Asia*, Cambridge, 1933, 174-78.

[3] 'Ali at-Tabari, *K. ad-Din wa-'d-Dawlah*, 50-54; cf. Browne, op. cit., 184, etc.

[4] Cf. 'Ali at-Tabari, 14—Christians self-contradictory in holding that God is creator of everything visible and that Christ is uncreated; Abu-'l-Fadl al-Maliki as-Su'udi (fl.1535), *Disputatio pro Religione Mohammedanorum adversus Christianos*, ed. F. J. van den Ham, Leiden, 1877, 4—'in no religion does revelation come contrary to what reason determines, for reason is the basis of revelation in the sense that it is a witness to the truth of the vocations of prophets and messengers', but Christians, neglecting this principle, have assigned to scriptural terms like 'father' and 'son' interpretations that are contrary to reason.

[5] Cf. Fritsch, *Islam und Christentum*, 135f.

[6] Ibid.

the different situations in which the exponents of the different views found themselves.

The most weighty consideration in favour of the view that the doctrine of Islamic universalism is ideological is that Islam as a world religion would tend to exclude a full integration of certain elements which could not be omitted without loss. It has been admitted above that there was a place for Islam as an expression of the Abrahamic tradition parallel to Judaism and Christianity, and that this was so because of a failure of Christianity to be sufficiently universal to include peoples who spoke Syriac, Coptic and Armenian and who thought in terms of the intellectual categories associated with these languages. It was further implied in this admission that Islam has produced a form of the Abrahamic tradition more suited to the intellectual categories of at least some of these oriental peoples. It is a long step from that, however, to allowing that Islam has produced a form of the Abrahamic tradition in any way suited to the intellectual categories of the peoples who constitute the great body of Christendom, Catholic, Orthodox and Protestant—the Greek-speakers, Latin-speakers and their successors. The attitude of Islam towards the Bible and towards the history of Christendom has made it almost wholly unaware of the problems involved in presenting Islam to Europeans. There is little sign in Islam of any move towards the integration of rival traditions comparable to the agreement between Greeks and Latins to regard their formulations of the doctrine of the Trinity as equivalent.

This point might be made in another way. Suppose that (perhaps as the result of another world war in which all other religions were seriously weakened) Islam became the dominant religion throughout the world and that its rivals gradually faded away, could this be regarded as a satisfactory integration of world society? The answer would seem to be that it would not be completely satisfactory, and that for two reasons. One is that such a world-religion would presumably not have fully accepted and acknowledged its dependence on the Christian and Jewish traditions in its origins and in its formative period; and such a failure to accept one's past is as unhealthy for a society as for an individual. The other reason is that under the supposed circumstances those who came into Islam from traditions whose intellectual categories were rather different from the intellectual categories of the Islamic tradition would presumably have to accept without question (at least to begin with) the formulations in terms of the intellectual categories of the existing Islamic tradition. This would seem to be a loss to world society of an element of variety and richness. In course of time this loss might in some measure be made good by a movement of diversification within Islam, but this could not be reckoned on.

Arguments about this matter cannot, of course, be entirely objective. We are concerned with two policies—or should we say 'two instinctive procedures'?—to bring about the integration of smaller heterogeneous societies into one large society. The Islamic method, for the most part, is to try to produce uniformity by demanding adherence to one set of formulations based on one system of intellectual categories and by taking measures which eventually lead to the squeezing out of formulations based on other systems of categories and the adoption by all Muslims of the first system of categories. This policy or procedure is a slow one but in the end, after many centuries, it does seem to have results. If a tradition with a distinctive set of categories is denied all expression at the higher levels of thinking for a period of centuries, there is a likelihood that it will disappear altogether, though it is also possible that after a period of 'underground' existence it may appear again (as early Italian art is sometimes said to be a second flowering of the artistic spirit of the Etruscans). This is a process that has been constantly taking place throughout history. All the main cultural traditions of today have squeezed out or swamped many minor traditions and caused them to disappear completely. Only a few minor traditions have been able to keep themselves alive by becoming distinctive strands within the main traditions. Moreover all the non-Western world is under the threat of being swamped by the Western intellectual tradition in its modern form based on natural science, and even Western Christendom itself has not solved the problem of adjusting this modern form of its tradition to the very different categories of New Testament Christianity.

While there is thus a natural tendency to uniformity which operates independently of men's deliberate intentions, it would seem that Christianity to a greater extent than Islam has tried to preserve variety even while working for integration. Islam has indeed recognized the value of diversity, as, for example, in its acknowledgement of four parallel legal rites. Its insistence on keeping the Qur'an in Arabic, however, even when it has to be recited in worship by those who know no Arabic, contrasts with the translation of the Bible into every language. Christianity may thus be said to stand for a policy of integration without an insistence on uniformity. Its ideal is more that of unity in diversity, whereas Islam tends towards an ideal of uniformity, at least in theory.

The future will presumably bring some measure of world integration, but we cannot yet tell whether this will necessitate a large measure of uniformity (with a possible reappearance at a later date of some of the sunken traditions), or whether it will be possible without destroying all variety to obtain sufficient integration to keep world society from annihilating it self. There seem to be objective grounds for thinking that the retention of variety is a good thing. In so far as Christianity is more concerned than Islam about this, it is preferable as an agent of integration. This, however, is only one aspect of the matter out of many; but it does give some reasons for thinking that Islam is ideological in its claim to be universal and to supersede Christianity.

(5) *Conclusion.* Four points have been considered in which Islam might seem to be ideological. With regard to the first two, the claim to be parallel to Judaism and Christianity and to be a continuation of the Judaeo-Christian (or Abrahamic) prophetic tradition, it proved possible to make out a case for thinking that Islam was not ideological. In the claim to have revelational knowledge of historical events, on the other hand, there is an ideological factor; and it seems likely that the same is true of the claim to be a universal religion, though this point cannot be settled at the present time.

3. ISLAM'S CONCEPTION OF ITSELF

The previous section has dealt with Islam's conception of its relation to other religions, and this is in a sense part of its conception of itself. Now, however, we turn to consider some aspects of its conception of itself as it is in itself and apart from its relation to other religious communities. The point to which special attention will be paid is the extent to which this conception has been ideologically distorted by one group or other within the Islamic community. Two aspects are selected for study: the idea of a community based on a religious revelation and the idea of Islamic orthodoxy.

(a) A community based on religious revelation

To say that the Islamic community is based on revelation might seem to be a simple statement of objective fact. Yet a little reflection will show that this is not so, or at least that it is not so obvious as it appears. The statement must be looked at in its total cultural context. Islam began among the Arabs as a movement that was both religious and political. At first the religious aspect was most prominent, but with the political successes of Muhammad's lifetime and the following half-century the political aspect must for a time have loomed largest in the eyes of most of the Arabs. In fact the Arabs found themselves ruling an empire, with themselves as a military aristocracy in it. The conquered peoples, however, had a higher cultural level, and in particular a more advanced intellectual tradition. As these people became converted to Islam and shared their cultural heritage with the Arabs, or as the Arabs, through increased contacts with non-Muslims, entered into something of the cultural heritage of the region, Islam became the heir of the earlier civilizations of the Middle East. The new Islamic culture that was thus created continued much of what had been valuable in these previous cultures. Under these circumstances, then, is it true to say the Islamic community was based on religious revelation? Or is this statement an ideological distortion?

It is clear, of course, that the Islamic community would never have existed without the Arabs. From them came the original impulse, the conquering armies and the earliest imperial administrators. From them, too, may be said to have come the continuing religious dynamic, since for centuries it was mediated by the Arabic Qur'an. To them may also be attributed much of the ethical outlook of Islam, and something of its aesthetic taste, especially in literature. On the other hand, little of the intellectual features of Islamic culture came from the Arabs. It was not that they borrowed in any crude fashion. Rather there was genuine assimilation, through the adoption of scholarly methods more than of particular results. Yet, even when the Muslims were reacting against the intellectual climate of the region, they were being moulded by it, and previous cultures have left a clear mark on Islamic culture.

In these circumstances the assertion that the Islamic community is based on revelation is true or false according as you interpret it. If you mean that the dynamic underlying the movement which produced this culture came from revelation, that is true. It is easy, however, to pass from this sense to another according to which nearly everything in Islamic culture is derived from revelation; and that is ideological. It over-emphasizes the role of the Arabs and depreciates that of the other people who became Muslims.

Something of this has already been noted in the previous chapter in the way in which the Qur'anic revelation was made a criterion of the truth of a historical tradition. The distinction was also made between the Islamic sciences (those subsidiary to the study of the Qur'an and Traditions and of the Shari'ah) and the 'foreign' sciences (like philosophy and mathematics). Interest in the latter for their own sakes gradually grew less and less, but parts of philosophy, for example, continued to be studied because they had been incorporated into theology. Perhaps to be connected with this neglect of the 'foreign' sciences is the occasionalism found in Ash'arite theology. If all the events of nature proceeded not according to fixed laws but from God's inscrutable will, there would seem to be little point in the study of nature. The most serious effect of this ideological distortion in the conception of the Islamic community is the claim that much of the traditional wisdom of the Middle East came from Muhammad (as was proved by the existence of Traditions!) and the failure to admit their dependence on their predecessors. A community where there has to be systematic pretence of this kind would seem to be far from healthy. For centuries Islam has managed 'to get away with it', but the exposure of the Islamic world to modern Western scholarship has revealed the true state of matters to many thinking Muslims, while at the same time it has placed Muslims in general (because of their natural defensive reaction) at a disadvantage in assimilating some aspects of the learning of the West.

(b) A community observing the Law

Strictly speaking, though the phrase 'orthodox Islam' is often used, there is no 'orthodoxy' in Islam, except to a slight extent in theology. When we speak of 'orthodoxy' we are referring loosely to the *sunnah*, and 'orthodox Islam' is more correctly 'the main body of Sunnite Muslims'. Orthodoxy by its derivation is 'right belief', and the criterion for distinguishing between orthodoxy and heresy is doctrinal. Similarly the opposite of the *sunnah* is *bid'ah* or 'innovation', which is not restricted to false intellectual beliefs but may include novelties in practice. Though orthodoxy in the strict sense thus plays only a minor role in Islam, yet there is something whose role in the Islamic community is analogous to that of orthodoxy in other communities.

While many good people think of orthodoxy as a noble ideal, to the sociologist it is suspect.

Orthodoxy is not simply conservatism—not a primary, direct attitude of the mind—but a form of reaction. The conservative lives in his traditions unconsciously, taking them for granted and handling them lightly because he is not afraid of losing them. The reactionary, however, is rigid because he is afraid of losing a kind of certainty that is an integral part of his life. Endless uncertainty (leads) to relativism (and these are) just two sides of the same coin, different reactions to the same disturbing process which we call the crisis in valuation.[1]

[1] K. Mannheim, *Freedom Power and Democratic Planning*, London, 1951, 308. For the function of heterodoxy as helping groups to ' preserve their special-people role', cf. C. S. Coon, *Caravan*, 121.

This criticism might seem to presuppose the strict sense of orthodoxy; but there are other certainties than intellectual certainties, and Islam in particular would seem to find its certainty in membership of the charismatic community whose special characteristic was that it followed the *sunnah* or 'beaten path' which was also the *shari'ah* or divinely-prescribed code of conduct. The sociologist might therefore look upon Islam's insistence on following the *sunnah* and avoiding innovation as arising from fear of ceasing to be the charismatic community. In this way Sunnism in Islam becomes parallel to orthodoxy in Christendom, and the orthodox Muslims are those who call themselves by some such title as Ahl-as-Sunnah, the people of the *sunnah*.

The difference between Sunnism and orthodoxy is to be traced to a difference between the Greek and Arab mentalities. Knowledge was of great importance to the Greeks, and they tended to regard sin and error as due to lack of knowledge. The nomadic Arabs, on the other hand, were more concerned with following the 'beaten path' of the tribe, that is, the code of conduct through which its nobility and honour were manifested. It was easy to transfer this conception to the Islamic community. Its 'beaten path' was the 'beaten path' of Muhammad, and its nobility, that is, its charismatic character, its character of being 'the people of Paradise', depended on following this 'beaten path'.

The Muslims, of course, did not entirely overlook intellectual standards of membership of the community. Correct belief was usually regarded as part of the Shari'ah. This goes back perhaps as far as the Murji'ites, for whom correct belief was at least an important element in the test of membership of the community. The Mu'tazilites, as students of Greek philosophy, tended to put more emphasis on belief than the main body of Muslims; and it is thus not surprising that under their influence the central government in 833 introduced a doctrinal test for judges and other officials—the Inquisition. Though this particular test was soon dropped, Muslim governments in most subsequent ages have used doctrinal tests as a basis for the punishment of undesirable persons. While this would be classed as 'intellectual innovation', the mobs in the cities could usually be roused against any sort of 'innovation'. The acceptance of doctrinal tests is possibly linked up with the growth in power of the class of scholar-jurists, since it would tend to give support to their power.

One effect of this conception of Islam as a community observing a divinely-given Law was that the adjustment of the community to changing circumstances became increasingly difficult. The idea of a society following a 'beaten path' and keeping to it comes from the desert, where the essential conditions of life seem to have hardly varied for millennia until the advent of the petrol engine. It was not satisfactory, however, for the heartlands of the Islamic empire with their cities, their commerce and their old civilization. The difficulty was not at once apparent, for the adjustment of the practices of the early Muslims in Medina to the older cultures of 'Iraq, Syria and Egypt took place to a great extent in the period up to 800 before the conception of the divinely-given Law had become dominant. After that changes were still possible, but there was resistance to them. An interesting example is provided by the argument of al-Ash'ari (d.935) in defence of *kalam* (rational arguments in theology) against those who criticized this as 'innovation'. He has various lines of thought: theological discussions were not forbidden by the Prophet, so that to forbid them is innovation; the Prophet knew the details of these questions, but did not speak of them because the questions had not arisen in his time; the critics themselves do many things which Muhammad did not do.[1] Al-Ash'ari has the better of this argument, and was able to maintain his position against the critics. In due course his school became dominant in theology. Yet the critics also continued in existence, and in some ways their point of view was becoming more widely held. Though this particular innovation was accepted by the main body of Sunnites, Islam was becoming more rigid.

This rigidity showed its serious character in the nineteenth century when Islam felt the impact of the West and extensive adjustments became necessary. These could only be made with great difficulty. In recent years the authorities in Egypt and elsewhere have tried to reform legal practice and to get rid of certain abuses. The Shari'ah being unchangeable, however, the reforms can only be achieved in roundabout ways. One of the most successful is to issue decrees limiting the competence of the courts, since it has always been recognized that the ruling institution has the right to do this[2].

Such methods are of limited application, however, and the reform of the Islamic legal system cannot be said to have gone very far. Many reformers have been reduced to despair, and have decided that it was easier to abandon Islam and build something new than to change Islam. Thus, instead of reforming the traditional Islamic educational system, a new system was established alongside it for Western learning. In order to change Turkey into a modern state

[1] *Risalah fi 'stihsan al-khawd fi 'ilm al-kalam;* text and translation will be found in R. J. McCarthy, *The Theology of al-Ash'ari*, Beirut, 1953.

[2] Cf. p. i.e. 250 above.

Mustafa Kemal cut many of its ties with Islam. Perhaps after radical action of this kind, however, in which much of Islam disappears or at least is submerged, it will emerge again after an interval in a new form. Such a metamorphosis is not impossible, since Islam has always tended to recognize the *fait accompli*. The majority of Sunnite Muslims acknowledge as one of the 'roots of law' the principle of consensus or agreement (*ijma'*), and by this a change that is generally approved by Muslims may be legitimized. This is a principle that only works slowly, however; it is not an instrument for a reformer in a hurry.

Islam, then, in thinking of itself as a community observing a divinely-given law, as well as one based on revelation, tends to think ideologically. The ideas are not in themselves ideological, but they become so through the way in which they have been understood by the majority of Muslims. Because of the ideological distortion of these ideas Muslims have been impeded in their adjustment of themselves to the impact of the West. Nevertheless the ideas have in them an aspect of essential truth (in Mannheim's terms, are in part 'utopian'), and this aspect may yet be rescued from the ideological distortion. That possibility, however, brings us to the next section.

4. THE FUTURE OF ISLAM

This is not the place in which to indulge in speculations about the future course of history. Yet the studies in this book are relevant to the present and future condition of Islam, and it is therefore not unfitting to consider what light they throw on such questions.

The fundamental point is spiritual renewal or the recovery of dynamic. Is this possible for Islam? After centuries of senescence and sclerosis can it be revived and rejuvenated? Everything suggests that we are not in a position to say this is impossible. Man certainly has not enough knowledge at the moment to make such pronouncements, and it is doubtful whether he ever will have. The movement of life in the hearts of the members of a community would seem to be essentially hidden, in the sense that it is in principle beyond the reach of human science. If this is so, no amount of effort will enable us to predict the future of Islam. What our studies show us, however, is something of the presuppositions of a renewal of Islam and of the circumstances in which it would take place—in particular, the difficulties to be overcome.

So long as Christianity has not solved the problems which led to its recession and disintegration in the Middle East, there is a place for Islam and a function for it to perform. As was said above, it is possible to maintain that Islam is the form of the Abrahamic tradition best suited to the outlook of many of the inhabitants of the region. The maintenance of such a position, however, is not sufficiently inspiring to bring about a renewal of life in Islam. For one thing Christianity may manage to solve this problem in the next half century. The deeper reason, however, is that in this world, which in a material sense has become one world, men are not likely to be attracted to any religion except one which claims to have a message for the whole world.

If we look at Islam, then, from this point of view, we see that it is not unfitted to be a religion for the whole world. It has throughout its history been a missionary and universalistic religion. In seeking to win the whole world it would be acting congruently with its past record. It could make a good case, too, for thinking that its idea of a religious community based on revelation and following a divinely-given code of conduct is the only satisfactory basis for a world society. In Islam's conception of itself and of its function in the world these are elements of truth which could be developed.

The other side of the picture, however, is very dark. The obstacles seem almost insuperable. All the distorted ideological conceptions which have been noted would require to be corrected. Islam would have to admit the facts of its origin—the historical influence of the Judaeo-Christian religious tradition and of the cultural tradition of Syria, 'Iraq and Egypt. That would lead to a revised conception of the relative importance of religious and cultural factors in the growth of Islamic civilization. It would have to be prepared to learn, even in the religious sphere, from Christians and Jews; and that would be very hard. It would have to look again at the centuries in which it thought of itself as the community in whose life the history of mankind was consummated, and realize that, whatever the future may bring, its role during some of these centuries was much humbler. It would have to distinguish, more radically than has hitherto been done, between the essential principles of its divinely-given code of conduct and the temporary applications, and work out fresh applications to novel circumstances.

Can all this and more be done? It is most unlikely. Yet neither the sociologist nor the religious man (of any religion) will say that it is impossible.

EPILOGUE

The studies in this book have been concerned first and foremost with medieval Islam. Yet out of them certain ideas and general principles have come which are relevant to the problems of the world at the present day.

The first point to be made was that economic, or, more generally, material factors are fundamental, not in the sense that they determine the whole life of a society, but in the sense that they constitute the setting or framework within which the society has to live its life. This applies to the contemporary world. Advances in science and technology have led to a physical unification of the world (through aeroplanes, wireless and other means of communication) and to an economic unification of the world (through the growth of mass-producing industry and international trade and finance). This constitutes the setting of the life of the contemporary world.

The second point was that, for any given economic system, certain social systems were more suited than others. That means that, where a change of economic or material factors occurs, society becomes maladjusted in consequence and a process of readjustment becomes necessary. In this process ideas and social movement are complementary. Without ideas social discontent may lead to certain movements; only with ideas do the movements become genuine and effective social activities. In the contemporary world the social maladjustment is manifested in the threat of murderous war, and in social discontent within most countries. There is a 'blind' and ineffective movement towards harmony between the nations and within each nation; or perhaps we should say that there is a desire for this without any clear perception of how that desire may be realized. The particular difficulties of our age are thus largely distinct from the general imperfection of mankind which has been apparent in all ages, though whether they can be dealt with separately is not clear.

The present study shows that this universal desire for harmony or integration is only likely to be satisfied when there is a marriage of social discontent with an appropriate set of ideas. Only then will there be an effective movement which will achieve some measure of integration of world society. It is perhaps not necessary that this system of ideas should be mainly religious to begin with, but it must at least contain certain ideas or images or symbols which release the

284

energies of the psyche. In the long run, however, it would seem that nothing short of a religion can integrate world society. Whether this will be one of the world-religions (no doubt somewhat modified), or a reform movement within one of the world-religions, or some completely new religion, we cannot say. Man's intellect cannot say before the event which ideas are going to appeal to men and release their energies. A professing Christian cannot conceive of this future world-religion as any other than Christianity; yet history and the Bible combine to remind him that it is possible for the Church to take a false turning.

INDEX

(The Arabic article, *al-* etc., is neglected in the alphabetical order. An asterisk indicates that the reference has bibliographical details)

Index

al-Balādhurī (historian), 39*, 125
Barthold, W., 116*
Baṣrah, 70, 95, 97, 99-101, 116, 169, 202, 215, 221, 224, 233, 238f., 242, 247
bāṭin, Bāṭiniyyah, 70
al-Bayḍāwī (Qur'ān-commentator), 263f.
Becker, C. H., 265*
Bell, Richard, 66
Berbers, 34, 110, 114, 127, 129, 131, 231
Bible, 187, 229f., 260-5, 269-71, 275
bid'ah, 279
bikr, 265
Bilāl, 92, 151
al-Bīrūnī, 232
Bismarck, 180
Black Stone, 187
Bornu, 128
Bousquet, G. H., 2*
Bovill, E. W., 126*
Britain, British, 133, 144, 160, 176, 180
Brockelmann, C., 263*
brothering, 11
Browne, E. G., 123*
Browne, L. E., 274*
Bu'āth, 14f., 17, 38
Buddhism, 30, 116, 118, 150, 258
Buhl, F., 260*
Bukhārā, 118
Buwayhids, Būyids (dynasty), 125, 172, 246
Byzantines, 5f, 13f., 24f., 53, 91, 93, 112, 145, 159, 166, 171, 232, 258, 260, 268

Caetani, L., 90, 96*
Cairo, 67, 137, 173, 197, 236
caliph ; see khalīfah
Calverley, E. E., 207*
Carthaginians, 231
Central Asia, 35, 123
Chad (lake) 126, 128
Christensen, A., 116
Christian, Christianity, Christendom, 1, 13f., 16, 24, 27, 30f., 40f, 51, 55, 86, 89-93, 105, 125, 131, 134, 138, 148-51, 158f., 171, 182f., 197, 209, 211-4, 222, 228-30, 232, 237, 253, 258-77, 280, 282f., 285
Companions (sc. of Muḥammad), 169, 192, 201, 208, 226
Confederation of the Fuḍūl, 8f., 12, 48
Constantinople, 159, 171, 236, 268
Constitution of Medina ; see Medina
Coon, C. S., 219*
Copts, Coptic, 232, 268, 275
Cragg, Kenneth, 44*

Ḍaḥḥāk, 124
Dahomey, 132
da'i, ('adopted son'), 146
dā'i ('summoner', emissary), 70
Damascus, 18, 165, 173, 221, 224
dār-al-Islām ('the house of Islam'), 101, 272
Dawson, C., 268*
Day of Judgement, 11, 44, 46f., 51, 102, 157, 183, 185, 187, 191, 211, 243
Delphi, 187
Dendi, 128.
Dennett, D. C., 96*
dhimmi, 92, 150, 231
Dhū-Qār, 24
dihqān, 115, 117f.
di Matteo, I, 260*.
din ('religion'), 191
Donaldson, D. M., 194*
Dutch, 176
dynamic image, 113

East Africa, 114, 126
Egypt, 24, 31f., 67-73, 75, 82, 95, 116, 125, 131, 144, 164, 170, 173, 191, 194, 228, 232, 236, 247, 249, 274, 281, 283
Einstein, 55
Emigrants, 17f., 19, 22, 57f., 66f., 88, 96, 147, 149f., 161, 165
Etruscans, 276
Europe, Europeans, 29, 32, 40, 127, 131, 134-7, 140, 236, 274

Fage, J. D. 126*
Fakhr-ad-Dīn ar-Rāzī, 272
al-Fārābī, 272
Fāṭimah (daughter of Muḥammad), 107.
Fāṭimids (dynasty in North Africa and Egypt), 67-73, 82, 158, 171f.
Firdawsī, 123f.
France, French, 5, 133-6, 159, 176, 180, 195
Frankfort, H., 109
Fritsch, E., 260*
Friedlaender, I., 107*
Fück, J., 204*
Fuḍūl, see Confederation of
Fulani, Fulbe, 129, 133f.
Futa Jalon, 133
Futa Toro, 128, 133, 135
Fyzee, A. A. A., 208*

Gandhi, 111
Gao, 128f.
Gardet, L., 145*, 235*
Gaudefroy-Demombynes, 71*

288

Index

Index

Index

Index

Index

Date Due